ENGLISH COMPOSITION

Charles H. Vivian, Ph.D.
Bernetta M. Jackson, M.A.

BARNES & NOBLE BOOKS
A DIVISION OF HARPER & ROW, PUBLISHERS
New York, Hagerstown, San Francisco, London

L. C. Catalogue Card Number: 61–11377

ISBN: 0-06-460102-1

The excerpts from John Galsworthy: *Five Tales* ("The Apple Tree"), page 90, and *The Man of Property*, pages 183, 186, are reprinted with permission from Charles Scribner's Sons.

Manufactured in the United States of America

79 80   12 11 10

About the Authors

Charles H. Vivian received his B.A. from Brown University and his M.A. and Ph.D. from Harvard. He has held faculty positions at both these institutions and at Southern Methodist and Tufts universities; he is teaching now at the Bentley College of Accounting and Finance. His work has been mainly in the teaching of composition and the supervision of such teaching, and also in teaching, research, and publication in English literature of the Romantic and early Victorian period.

Bernetta M. Jackson received her B.A. from McKendree College and M.A. in English from the University of Illinois. She formerly taught at Southern Methodist University in Dallas and now teaches at Washington University in Saint Louis. Mrs. Jackson has been a member of the College Section Committee of the National Council of Teachers of English, an adviser to the editorial staff of *College English,* and an English language consultant for the National Board of Medical Examiners. She is a member of the Modern Language Association of America, the Conference on College Composition and Communication, the College English Association, and the American Association of University Professors.

Acknowledgments

The authors would like to express thanks to a number of colleagues for help in the preparation of this volume. It was partly at the instance of Professor Ima H. Herron of Southern Methodist University that they undertook the project initially. For critical reading of several chapters of the manuscript, they are grateful to Professor George D. Stout of Washington University; they wish especially to acknowledge his assistance in the chapter on the research paper. For valuable suggestions on the list of reference works, they are indebted to Miss Marjorie Karlson, Chief of the Reference Library; and, for checking particular lists, to Professors William H. Connor and Arthur W. Mason, all of Washington University. Finally, innumerable pieces of information, advice, and guidance were among the contributions of Mrs. Mary F. Johnson of the Barnes & Noble editorial staff.

Table of Contents

ENGLISH COMPOSITION

1 COMPOSITION AND COMMUNICATION

The majority of colleges and universities offer instruction in English composition. The titles of the courses may vary in different schools; so may the topics included. Certain courses are not specifically in composition but in communication. The latter title implies a somewhat broader coverage, with attention given not only to reading and writing but also to speaking and listening. Even in communication courses, however, the main emphasis is usually on writing.

This chapter deals with two related subjects—related in that they both have to do with questions of purpose. The first section develops the purpose or value in studying composition: it is a means to the important end of effective communication. The second section considers the purposes served by communication itself: it conveys thought and feeling, to a particular audience.

THE STUDY OF COMPOSITION

In composition, as in any other kind of study, the student should gain perspective on the subject as a whole, as well as mastering the details. What can he hope to accomplish by this work? Of what use will it be to him?

A Means to an End. The basic reason why anyone studies composition is so that he may learn to communicate with maximum effectiveness. This is the goal; all else is subordinate to this. Now, with part of the material which the student encounters in learning composition, the means-to-an-end relationship is obvious. How to build a good paragraph, how to write a particular type of essay, and so forth are the kinds of knowledge which are clearly useful for good communication. With other material, however, this relationship seems to be not so easy to grasp.

For example, a student may fail to see any great importance in correct spelling and punctuation. Why are they important? First, they are established conventions, like table manners. We avoid misspelling and faulty punctuation, as we avoid eating with our knives: to keep the respect of our readers, as of our dinner companions. This attitude is necessary for full communication. If our readers respect us, they will pay attention to what we say. Second, correct punctuation and spelling

1

are sometimes actually essential to our saying what we mean. The following two sentences imply different circumstances.

> My brother, who is in the service, will be at home soon.
> My brother who is in the service will be at home soon.

The first sentence implies that I have only one brother; the second, that I have two or more: my brother who is in the service and at least one brother who is a civilian. Again, these sentences mean very different things.

> The drought *affected* the decline in crop yield.
> The drought *effected* the decline in crop yield.

In the first sentence, the drought was only one factor; in the second, it was the whole cause of the decline.

Another student may not grasp the real value of the definitions and rules of grammar and of sentence structure. How do they serve the basic purpose? They do so in several ways. For instance, an element that contributes to the effectiveness of composition is a pleasing style. The student will wish, then, to develop a pleasing style. How shall he go about it? One thing he can do is to work for variety in his sentence structure; he can be careful to use complex as well as simple and compound sentences. Clearly, he must know what these types of sentences are. To understand them, he must know the distinction between the two kinds of clauses, and, before that, the definition of a clause. For this he must know what subjects and predicates are, and for this in turn he must understand substantives and verbs. In other words, by learning the definitions one can understand the rules and principles; by understanding and applying these he can increase the communicative effectiveness of his writing. (See Chapters 8 and 9.)

The Practical Value of the End. The ability to communicate well is of very great practical value; lack of ability to express oneself is a serious handicap. The whole area of communication involves reading, writing, speaking, and listening; almost all human activities involve at least one of these, and in all communicative skill is an asset. Even in the single field of writing, a degree of competence is essential to every person, and a high degree is a great advantage. Although fluency in writing cannot take the place of facts and ideas, it does provide a means of expressing them.

This fluency, important in school and college, remains important in later life, for in the majority of occupations writing is required. It is a truism that the quality of a letter of application for employment may determine whether the writer is granted an interview, or even the position itself. The excellence of a business report may affect the writer's career; the merit of a piece of sales literature, reflected in the subsequent volume of orders, may have a similar effect. Writing skill may not always be measurable directly in terms of academic credit or economic advantage, but it will ever be valuable in the sense of the practical, the useful, and the constructive.

Scope and Limitations. The study of composition can be profitable for anyone; it can help him develop his ability to communicate. It cannot, however, turn everyone who undertakes it into a gifted creative writer.

Writing is both a science and an art. Certain elements of writing are scientific in the sense that they are matters of rule. If one follows the rules, he can handle these elements properly. Others are artistic in the sense—a rather special sense, since art too is subject to some rules—that they are matters of native aptitude or instinct. If one has the aptitude or instinct, he can handle these elements too; if he does not have it, he will find that trying to master them by study is difficult or virtually impossible. The distinction is not absolute; there are certain matters of style and taste that lie in a middle ground between science and art.

Writing as a Science. Insofar as writing is a science, almost *any person* can learn to write with grammatical acceptability and to organize and to present his material in a logical way. This is the minimum requirement.

With application, any person can proceed some distance beyond this point. He can improve his vocabulary and develop his feeling for appropriate words. He can train himself in the use of the various constructions which will show the precise relationships among his ideas. He can learn techniques for making sentences not only correct but also emphatic. He can develop variety in his sentence structure and, with practice, vigor in his style. This is perhaps as far as he can go, depending solely on rules and on drill in applying them. But then, this degree of ability is adequate for all ordinary purposes. One ought not to be satisfied with any lesser degree.

Writing as an Art. The poet Alexander Pope wrote that

> Some beauties yet no precepts can declare,
> For there's a happiness as well as care.

Pope was referring to the writing of poetry, but the same principle applies to prose. "Care," in the sense of careful observance of all the rules of grammar and sentence structure, can help the writer up to a certain point; beyond that point lies the realm of "happiness"; that is, of native talent. If one does have native talent or special aptitude for writing, he can still profit by study, even of writing as an art; he can learn how to exercise and control and thereby take full advantage of his talent. There are rules of writing as an art; knowledge of these, and especially constant practice in applying them, can help even the writer with the greatest natural aptitude. In general—except insofar as there is overlapping with the scientific rules—the rules of art lie outside the scope of this course of instruction.

THE PURPOSES OF COMMUNICATION

The basic purpose of communication is to convey thought and feeling, to a particular audience. It is useful to consider what things are included under the headings of thought and feeling, and what the writer should remember in addressing himself to a particular audience.

To Convey Thought and Feeling. Thought and feeling do overlap. We feel strongly about some of our beliefs; and, for better or worse, our feelings often condition our thinking. Thought and feeling include many types of things that we may wish to communicate. Among these are factual information, opinions, attitudes, points of view, aspects of persons and places, and accounts of events true and fictitious.

The Four Forms of Discourse. All systematic communication in words is classified in four main categories, conventionally called the forms of discourse: exposition, argument, description, and narrative. The basis of classification is the central purpose of the communication.

EXPOSITION. The word "exposition" comes from a Latin word which means "to set forth"; the central purpose of *exposition* is to set forth or explain something. In exposition, the material which is communicated is primarily information. This information may be factual data—about existing or historical conditions, about how something works (say, a machine), about how an operation is performed, and so on. It may be an analysis or an objective interpretation of a set of facts. It may even be the fact that someone holds a particular opinion, on certain grounds—as long as the central purpose is to impart information, and not actually to impel someone else to accept the opinion as valid. Most of the reading that we do, with the exception of fiction, is expository: we read letters and reports, newspaper and magazine articles, books about public affairs and about science. The few limitations of exposition and the special distinctions to be drawn between this and the other forms of discourse are treated briefly in the following sections and are discussed more fully in Chapter 5.

ARGUMENT. The central purpose of *argument* (sometimes called *argumentation*) is to convince, to persuade the audience to adopt a certain doctrine or attitude or even course of action. What is communicated, then, is a statement of the case for a particular position on a certain issue. Argument is perhaps best illustrated, or illustrated in its purest form, in academic debate, but we encounter it more frequently in other kinds of communication. Newspaper editorials are often essentially argumentative; political oratory and campaign literature are almost always so. Even commercial advertisements are basically arguments (although of course the techniques of advertising are far removed from those of academic debate).[1]

The distinction between exposition and argument is sometimes difficult to draw. Many compositions are designed both to inform and to convince, frequently to convince by informing. Thus, to classify a piece under one heading or the other, the basic criterion is again the central or more important purpose.

DESCRIPTION.[2] The central purpose of *description* is to evoke the impression produced by the aspect of a person, a place, a scene, or the like; or, since the aspect is always colored by the writer's interpretation (and therefore the writer is never entirely objective), he does not simply evoke but in a degree creates the impression. In one sense the details of appearance are communicated, but actually these are only the means of development; the ultimate communication is the impression itself.

Of the four forms of discourse description is the one which occurs least often in a pure form. Among the most typical examples are character sketches, like the profiles in the *New Yorker* magazine. Such accounts of particular scenes as often appear in good travel literature are relatively pure description; sometimes in biography and especially in autobiography and books of reminiscence, an author will devote an extended passage to evoking the image of a place or a person. As these

---

[1] The word *propaganda* has come to designate a particular type of argumentative communication. *Propaganda* commonly has a bad connotation, because of the kinds of context in which it has most often occurred; but, as far as the denotation of the word is concerned, there can be propaganda for good as well as for bad causes.

[2] Where used to designate a form of discourse, the word *description* has a rather strict and narrow sense. In other contexts we often use the word loosely; we say that a teacher of anatomy describes the parts of the body, or that a novelist describes what happens to his characters; in these two cases the forms of discourse would be exposition and narrative, respectively. What is in a broad and general sense description of a place may actually be exposition, if it is primarily informative; for example, an account of how a city is laid out, with the location of the principal buildings.

sources imply, description is represented most frequently by passages in a composition which as a whole fulfills the function of one of the other forms of discourse.

NARRATIVE. The central purpose of *narrative* (often called *narration*) is to recount an event or a series of related events in such a way that meaning emerges in them. As in description, the details are communicated—in this case the details of the action—but the ultimate communication is the emergent meaning. The events may be obviously significant in themselves (like the epochal acts of history), or the writer by his treatment of them may develop a significance in them. Indeed with narrative, as with description, the writer can never be completely objective, and to a certain degree the meaning will always reflect his interpretation. In fiction (known as *plotted* narrative), the writer's view of human experience is the controlling and determining factor: the actions are selected and arranged, the material of the story is deliberately designed, to dramatize this view. But in factual narrative, even in the most nearly objective historical writing, there are the events and also the significance in the events; part of the latter is contributed by the writer.

The Combination of Forms. A written work of any scope may be classified under one of the four forms of discourse, depending on the central purpose of the whole. Frequently, however, two or more forms are combined in a single work.

ONE FORM, COMPRISING OTHERS. In a composition of more than a few pages, certain passages are likely to represent a form of discourse different from that of the composition as a whole. A writer of exposition may relate an illustrative anecdote (narrative) to elucidate his explanation. The same kind of interpolation often appears in argument: most sermons are examples of argument, and we are familiar with the stories that clergymen tell to enforce their points. Any extended argument has to include exposition, in order to explain the facts on which the reasoning is based. In a character sketch, which is basically description, many times the most effective means of communicating a facet of the subject's personality is by recounting an act typical of his behavior. Any piece of plotted narrative longer than the shortest short story must give space to characterization and to setting. In older fiction this space is often rather extensive; in more recent fiction the descriptive details tend to be fewer and more carefully selected, and frequently they are conveyed by suggestion rather than in a direct manner.

ONE FORM, HAVING THE PURPOSE OF ANOTHER. Then too, writing which appears to represent one form of discourse may actually have the basic purpose of another. One good example is provided by works in the form of narrative. Certain novels and short stories are written to show particular conditions under which people live: they are essentially expository in purpose. Many times this delineation of conditions is really a protest or a plea for reform: it is actually argument. Other works of fiction, in which the main emphasis lies on setting or local color, are in effect description. Whatever their ultimate purpose may be, all works of fiction are conventionally classified as narrative. This convention is one exception to the basic rule: the criterion of the form of discourse is the central purpose of the whole.

To Communicate with a Particular Audience. There is another important consideration which determines certain characteristics of a composition: the audience for whom it is intended.

Writing in a Context. Every good composition is written in a context. When a writer begins his work, he has a subject, a purpose, and an audience. He has something which he wishes to convey—thought or feeling or both. He has a purpose which he means to accomplish by the communication—to explain, to convince, to evoke a descriptive impression, or to develop meaning in a series of events. He has in mind a particular person or group of persons to whom he addresses himself.

Business and professional writing is produced under certain definite circumstances. The writer may be an employee, preparing a report on a sales promotion campaign for his employer. He may be an advertiser, drafting a commercial announcement designed to sell a particular product to the audience of a television program. He may be a drama critic, evaluating a new play for the readers of his newspaper or magazine. He may be a free-lance reporter, writing an article on a phase of current affairs. (In this example the writer must especially consider who his readers will be. If he hopes to sell the article to a magazine like *Harper's* or the *Atlantic Monthly,* he will write it in one way; if to a syndicated Sunday supplement, in a much different way.) In almost every case the nature of the intended audience will affect the manner of writing.

In composition and communication courses, the circumstances may not be established in so clear and obvious a way. The instructor may assign a whole context (not only a subject but also an audience and a purpose) or he may assign only a theme to be written and a date when it is due. *In every case when a whole context is not assigned, the student should envision a whole context for himself, including a specific audience.* This audience may be his instructor, or his classmates as a group, or the readers of the campus magazine or newspaper or another publication. Particular compositions might take the form of letters directed, for example, to parents or friends. The choice may not be completely unlimited; with certain assigned or selected subjects only one or a few kinds of circumstances might be appropriate; within these limitations, however, the student should use his imagination, and he should clearly determine in his own mind the group of readers he is addressing.

The Levels of Usage. Why is it important for the writer to be conscious of his audience? The chief reason is that in this way he may select, for whatever he is writing, the appropriate level of usage. That is, he may use the kind of language that will seem most natural to the particular audience he has in mind. By "the kind of language" we mean primarily the diction or choice of words, and the grammar. (See Chapters 9 and 10 for discussions of these subjects.) In a broad sense, certain other things may be included—the average length of sentences and paragraphs, and even the type of over-all organization—but in the strict sense, the level of usage is a matter of the grammar and the diction.

There are three levels of usage in English: the formal level, the informal or colloquial level, and the vulgar level. (The last is virtually never used in writing except for dialogue.) Bear in mind that not *every* word belongs to one and only one of the levels of usage. Indeed, the great majority of words are appropriate on any level. It is only to relatively few that the distinctions apply; these are the ones among which the writer must choose carefully, according to the level on which he is writing. Moreover, among these relatively few, not all are definitely fixed in status. Certain words are in a middle ground between the formal and informal levels and others between the informal and vulgar; at any given time a number of words are drifting in one direction or the other. The status of all words which are not completely standard—that is, acceptable on all levels including the formal—is marked by the makers of dictionaries. But in dictionaries of different dates, and occasionally even of the same date, the record of current usage differs.

THE FORMAL LEVEL. Formal English is standard English, universally understood by English-speaking people. For practical purposes the most useful criteria are negative: the formal level excludes all contractions (*I'm, isn't, don't,* etc.) and all words which are indicated in a good current dictionary to have a status other than standard. Also, it excludes all expressions which do not conform to strict principles of grammar. Formal English is the language used by a reputable writer when he is addressing an educated audience and writing in a straightforward and serious tone, in his own person; that is, except when he is writing dialogue or writing in the assumed character of a less literate person.

Although the formal level is not the only one acceptable for writing, assignments in composition courses often call for use of it. The reason for the requirement is that most students need more practice in order to use formal English effectively than they do to use informal English.

THE INFORMAL OR COLLOQUIAL LEVEL. The word *colloquial* means *conversational,* and informal or colloquial usage is the kind of language that forms good conversation. It is found in writing whenever an informal, conversational tone is proper: in personal letters and informal essays, popular articles designed for a wide or mixed audience, newspaper feature stories, and the like. Informal usage may include established contractions and words listed in a good current dictionary as colloquial, but not those marked as slang. In certain instances the rules of grammar are applied less strictly on the informal than on the formal level. (For grammatical distinctions among the levels, see Chapter 9.)

It is important to understand that when it appears in an appropriate context, the informal level is no less correct than the formal. Indeed, under circumstances which clearly call for informal usage, strict formality would be ineffective and, therefore, in a real sense incorrect. This does not mean that formal usage is stiff; on the contrary, formal English is a flexible and versatile means of expression. It belongs in certain contexts and not in others; in these others, informal usage is entirely proper.

THE VULGAR LEVEL. The characteristics of the vulgar level include the use of words which are not recognized parts of the language and therefore not recorded in dictionaries, the use of words whose status is lower than colloquial (for example, those which are understood only in limited geographical areas or by particular groups); and the use of expressions which do not conform even to informal rules of grammar. Certain types of vulgar usage are employed occasionally in writing for special effects, such as in the development of local color, but in general the vulgar level is subliterary.

Exercises

1. Indicate which of the four forms of discourse each of the following would presumably represent.

 a. A set of operating instructions accompanying a new television set.

 b. A tract distributed by an evangelistic religious organization.

 c. An article in a series entitled "My Most Unforgettable Character."

 d. A best-selling novel.

 e. A speech printed in the *Congressional Record,* constituting part of the discussion of a tariff bill.

f. An account of a summer resort area, published by an association of real estate owners in the area.

g. A short story.

h. An informal piece entitled "My Garden."

i. A theme entitled "Class Attendance Should Be Voluntary Rather Than Compulsory."

j. A chapter entitled "England in 1685" in a history book.

2. Indicate whether each of the following statements is true or false.

——a. A writer should ordinarily try to impress his audience by using language somewhat over their heads.

——b. If a theme assignment does not include a context, the student need not envision a context for himself, but may effectively write in general terms that would be appropriate to any context.

——c. Under certain special circumstances it may occasionally be appropriate for a writer to employ the vulgar level of usage.

——d. The formal level includes established contractions.

——e. Most words are appropriate on any level of usage.

——f. Level of usage is a matter of diction exclusively.

——g. On the informal level it might be appropriate to use a word which was originally slang but which has risen to colloquial status.

——h. The level of usage of any word is definitely fixed.

——i. In determining the most appropriate level of usage for a particular piece of writing, the author should consider the audience he is addressing.

——j. The ability to write well insures good grades in all school work.

3. Indicate the highest level of usage on which each of the following expressions would be appropriate.

a. Should you care to neglect this opportunity? Certainly not!

b. Do you want to pass up this chance? Not on your life!

c. Who did you say you gave it to?

d. We're afraid that they won't arrive before Sunday.

e. All men are created equal.

f. Then we were really in a fix!

g. I wasn't hep to what was going on, but John gave me the inside dope.

h. The team doesn't seem to have the old snap any more.

i. The manager hopes that he can up production next month.

j. "What, all my pretty chickens and their dam
At one fell swoop?"   SHAKESPEARE

2 CLEAR THINKING

The purposes of communication, we have said, are to convey thought and feeling. Although these two things are closely related, and in spite of the fact that they overlap in part, there remains a valid distinction between them. There is a distinction, too—although again there are close relationships and overlappings—between the methods of treating them. In the present chapter we are concerned with certain principles that apply to handling thought, to dealing with facts and ideas. These principles will be useful especially, though not exclusively, in exposition and in argument.[1]

The material discussed in this chapter will help the student to do four things: (1) make his language represent his thought as accurately as possible, (2) be familiar with and able to use the basic types of reasoning, (3) recognize and avoid common errors in reasoning, and (4) make systematic classifications and define terms properly and concisely.

LANGUAGE AND LOGIC

Good writing depends upon clear thinking; we cannot write well unless we have something sensible to say. Conversely, clear thinking depends upon the careful use of language; we cannot think clearly unless we formulate our ideas precisely in words. Essential to logical reasoning is the ability to say accurately what we mean. Therefore, in considering the principles that apply to expressing thought, we may begin with several specifically applicable to exact expression.

Using Appropriate Constructions. In general, every sentence should be written in the way—using the particular construction—that will most appropriately represent the relationships among the facts and ideas which it embodies. For example, one fact or idea may be more important than another, or less important, or they may be of equal importance; it is these comparative degrees of importance which should be indicated by construction. The constructions which can help to make these degrees clear are of two kinds: grammatical and rhetorical.

Grammatical Constructions. One way in which the comparative relationship can be represented accurately is by means of the appropriate

[1] More details about expository themes, with reference to particular types, appear in Chapter 4; more details about argument and about descriptive and narrative themes appear in Chapter 5.

grammatical construction. The choice will ordinarily lie between co-ordination and subordination.[2] *Co-ordination* indicates that ideas are of equal importance; *subordination* indicates that one idea is more important than another.

Consider this sentence:

> I have a brother, and his name is Tom.

Here, clearly, there are two ideas: first, that the writer has a brother, and, second, that the brother's name is Tom. The construction used in this sentence is co-ordination; *and* is a *co-ordinating conjunction.* The two ideas are represented as being of equal importance. Consider another version:

> I have a brother named Tom.

The construction used in this sentence is subordination; one idea is represented as being more important than the other. The idea which is emphasized is the first one—that the writer has a brother. The second one is expressed, but it has been subordinated to the first, by being relegated to the two-word subordinate construction "named Tom." Now consider one more version:

> My brother's name is Tom.

This is another subordinate construction, indicating that one idea is the more important; notice that this time the idea which is emphasized is the second—that the brother's name is Tom. The first one is still expressed, for of course the words "My brother's" indicate that the writer has a brother; but this idea has been subordinated to the second, and thus represented as being of lesser importance.

Which of these three versions is best? In general we say that the best grammatical construction is that which most accurately represents, or is most appropriate to, the relationship of the ideas. Here, their relationship is one of relative importance. But what *is* their relative importance? It depends on such considerations as who the reader is to be and what he already knows. If he already knows that the writer has a brother, then clearly the best version is the third, "My brother's name is Tom," which subordinates what he knows already and appropriately emphasizes what is new to him. Under other circumstances the second version might be best, and under still others possibly (though less probably) the first.

[2] In the present context, our concern is with the basic logical function of these constructions; a discussion of them from the specifically grammatical point of view appears in Chapter 9.

Rhetorical Constructions. Another way in which the comparative importance of ideas can be indicated is by means of the appropriate *rhetorical construction*. In this context, rhetorical construction may be equated with *word order*.[3]

The usefulness of word order in placing emphasis on particular ideas —in indicating that certain ideas are more important than others—may be summed up in two principles: (1) An idea is emphasized by being expressed elsewhere than in its normal position in the sentence. (2) The most emphatic position in a sentence is the last, at the end of the sentence; the next most emphatic is the first, at the beginning. These principles may be applied separately, but in any given manipulation of word order for emphasis it is likely that both will be involved.

Consider this sentence:

He arose suddenly and started for the door.

This is normal word order: subject (*He*), verb (*arose*), modifier (*suddenly*); then a co-ordinating conjunction (*and*) and another verb (*started*), with its modifier (*for the door*). There has been no special treatment of word order to produce emphasis. Now suppose that, in the writer's mind, one of these ideas is more important than his normal word order indicates; suppose that this more important idea is the manner of movement, expressed by the word *suddenly*. Then the writer can take this word out of its normal order and put it in the emphatic first position.

Suddenly he arose and started for the door.

The appropriate effect has been produced: by this change the manner of movement is emphasized, or represented as being important. Take another example:

He drove alone, slowly, through the night.

The normal order of subject and verb is followed by three modifiers. Of these three only the last one, " through the night," is in an emphatic position rhetorically. The other two are partially buried, so to speak. They appear and they communicate meaning, but the word order gives them no prominence. If in the writer's mind the ideas expressed by these three modifiers actually have the relative importance indicated by this word order, then this order is best. But suppose he believes that the idea

---

[3] In a larger sense, *rhetorical construction* would include other matters too, such as the use of devices like figures of speech; for these, see Chapter 10.

For another account of emphasis by word order, specifically as one of the techniques for writing emphatic sentences, see Chapter 8.

expressed by "through the night" is relatively unimportant; suppose that in the context the idea of "slowly" is more important, and the idea of "alone" is more important still. Then he ought to write,

> Slowly he drove through the night alone.

Such differences are more subtle than the difference between co-ordination and subordination.

The careful writer will use both grammatical and rhetorical constructions functionally. He will always determine the logical relationships among his ideas and employ these means to express the connections accurately. Thus he can approach the ideal of saying precisely what he means.

Limiting Loose Constructions. We may express the gist of the preceding discussion negatively: the careful writer will avoid the excessive use of *loose constructions*. In this context loose constructions are of two kinds: (1) grammatically co-ordinate constructions, which are loose because they do not indicate any different degrees of relative importance among facts and ideas, and (2) rhetorically normal constructions, which are loose because their absolutely ordinary word order does not arrest the reader's attention. These two kinds of looseness frequently appear together.

There is nothing intrinsically wrong with constructions that are loose grammatically and/or rhetorically. They are often the most appropriate and therefore the best constructions to use. The problem is that inexperienced writers, not fully aware of the different possibilities, sometimes use loose constructions to excess. The writer should remember the various possibilities for different kinds of expression—including co-ordination and subordination, normal and inverted word order—and the kinds of purposes they serve.

We have all heard people talk this way.

I have a brother, and his name is Tom, and I came home yesterday, and he was in the back yard, and I called to him, but he didn't answer me. . . .

Such overuse of loose constructions is unsatisfactory even in informal spoken English; in writing, it is unacceptable. There are two things wrong with it: first, the repeated co-ordination and simple subject-predicate pattern is childishly monotonous; second and more important, there is no appropriate indication of the relationships among the ideas. Through the use of subordination the ideas can be expressed neatly and succinctly; also, if one or more of them deserve emphasis, that emphasis can be indicated. In the example, the most important elements might be that I called and got no answer; of these two, the second might be more important than the first.

When I came home yesterday and saw my brother Tom in the back yard, I called out to him. He did not answer.

The most important element of all has been given its own separate sentence; the next most important has been placed in the emphatic final position in the first sentence. All the other ideas in the first sentence have been made to appear less important than this one by being expressed in a subordinate clause. Furthermore, since the sentence begins with this subordinate clause, which does not in itself convey complete and independent meaning, the reader is kept waiting for the essential information at the end.

THE FACTUAL BASIS

Thus far we have been discussing the use of language to express thought clearly—the use of constructions appropriate to the relationships among facts and ideas. We will now consider the thought itself, the facts and ideas and their relationships. In this section and the next we are concerned with the means by which we make sure that thought is logical, that facts and ideas are accurate, and that the relationships among them are sound and valid.

Sources of Factual Information. Logic is concerned with the relationships among facts and ideas. Sound logical reasoning, then, is based on facts which are accurate and ideas which are valid. In a discussion of logical reasoning or clear thinking, therefore, it is appropriate to consider this question: Where do we get accurate and reliable facts?

In general, we get them from two sources: our own experience and the reported experiences of others.

Personal Experience and Observation. The best kind of witness is an eyewitness, someone who was actually *there*. Although we always have to reckon with human fallibility in observing and reporting, *personal experience*—a deed which we have done, an event which has happened to us, an action which we have perceived with our own senses—is probably our most reliable source of factual information. Ordinarily we can have reasonable assurance in using facts from this source—in using them either for their own sake, as in a factual narrative, or as a basis for reasoning.

Second-Hand Sources. Reading books or talking with people may amount to personal experience as much as, say, watching a football game or playing on one of the teams. The circumstance of reading a particular book or hearing someone make a particular statement is a fact of our own personal experience. However, the *information* that we get from the book or statement represents the experience of someone else. The original experience, then, comes to us at *second hand*.[4]

Now, clearly, we should exercise caution in using information from second-hand sources. It would be foolhardy for us to believe everything that we see in print or that we hear. The amount of caution necessary depends on the reliability of any particular source. There are books on which we can rely with complete confidence, such as good standard encyclopedias. And there are people whose statements we may safely regard as trustworthy; for instance, experts in various fields when they are talking about something within the areas of their competence.

In the evaluation of sources there is no substitute for good judgment. There are pertinent questions, however, that we may raise. If the source is a book or another kind of published material (and especially if it deals with a subject, like science or technology, in which the status of current knowledge changes rapidly) we should notice when it was issued in order to determine whether the information it contains is currently reliable.[5] Another useful question about such a source may be, where and by whom it was published. Did the article appear in a reputable journal, or was the book issued by a reputable firm? Yet another, equally or more important, concerns the author: is he an authority on the subject and what is his reputation?

We should raise these last questions also about a personal informant, when we get information by word of mouth. The crucial point is his claim to authority *on the particular subject he is discussing*. If he is a business or professional man, we may usually rely at least upon the objective facts that he gives us about his business or his profession. We should not automatically have the same degree of confidence if an expert in one field talks about something that belongs in another—if a distinguished athlete, for example, discusses politics. Also, we should be careful to discount for natural partisanship. If we want information

---

[4] Of course it may actually come to us at third, fourth, or later hand. The author may be basing his book on something *he* has read or heard, and so on. For simplicity we use only the expression *second hand*. The precautions given in this section apply with all the more force as the number of hands, through which any information has passed, increases.

[5] The most significant date is that of first publication or of the original or subsequent copyright. The date of a *reprinting* (indicated, for instance, by the words "Tenth Printing, 1961") means only that the physical process of printing was repeated then; the material itself was basically unchanged. A new date of *copyright* gives assurance that the material was actually revised at that time.

about an industrial strike, we had better balance what we hear from the company executive with what the union official tells us; if possible we should also talk with an informed but impartial observer.

Fact and Opinion. The preceding example may serve also to illustrate another important principle: the necessity for distinguishing fact from opinion. At some time during the industrial strike we might hear such statements as these:

COMPANY EXECUTIVE: "We have generously offered to go more than half way toward meeting the obviously excessive demands of the strikers, but they have obstinately refused to budge an inch."

UNION OFFICIAL: "They tried to buy us off stingily with only a fraction of what we are asking—and what in all justice we ought to get. But we are resolutely standing firm."

There are facts here, but in each of these statements the facts are encrusted with words that really convey only emotional attitude or opinion. For example, in the first statement these words are "generously," "obviously excessive," and "obstinately"; in the second, "stingily," "in all justice," and "resolutely." From an informed but impartial observer of the dispute we might hear another sort of account.

IMPARTIAL OBSERVER: "The management has proposed a six-cent-an-hour wage increase instead of the eleven cents which had been demanded; the union has rejected the proposal."

In dealing with statements like the first two, whether written or spoken, we must be careful to recognize and to discount the words that convey only opinion, when we are looking for facts.

Objective facts are not the only important kind of human knowledge and belief. There are very important things that belong to the realm of opinion; for instance, value judgments in such broad areas as beauty and morality. The point is: although it may be a fact that someone *holds* a particular opinion, the opinion itself may not represent a verifiable fact or provide a sound basis for reasoning.

TYPES OF REASONING

There are two types of reasoning: induction and deduction (or inductive reasoning and deductive reasoning). Virtually any piece of reasoned discourse involving more than one or two logical steps will ordinarily include both types. The two are interdependent, and the two are basically different. In order to deal systematically with the elementary principles of logic, we shall consider each one separately.

Induction. *Induction* is that kind of reasoning which proceeds from the particular to the general. That is, in induction we begin with a number of *particular* facts and formulate a *general* statement or principle which "covers" them or indicates what they all have in common. During the early years of our life, for example, when we are beginning to develop our knowledge, presumably there are a number of occasions when we are near a fire. In each of these individual, separate, particular experiences we have a sensation of heat. Before long, though we probably do not state our conclusion explicitly, we have come to understand the general principle that fire is hot. In this we have actually reasoned by induction.

Thus induction is commonly based directly on facts. These may be drawn from personal experience, as in the preceding example, or they may be derived from second-hand sources. We might draw an inductive conclusion, for instance, about the common traits of a group of people whom we have never met, simply by reading or by being given a number of accounts of individuals in the group. More often both kinds of facts enter into the process: our own experiences are corroborated by those of others, and the inductive conclusion is reinforced by the additional evidence.

Two special types of induction are reasoning by analogy and reasoning by cause and effect.

Reasoning by Analogy. In *reasoning by analogy* we follow the inductive method in a special way. We observe particular similarities between two things, and then we generalize: we infer that the two things are similar in other ways, too. Suppose that I am deciding whether I will go to see a new film. From the advertisements I learn that it is similar in certain ways to a film that I have seen before. It has the same leading actor and actress; it is based on a book by the same writer; the story has its setting in the same country and in approximately the same period of history. The film which I have seen before was interesting and enjoyable; I reason by analogy that I will enjoy this one too, and I decide to see it. I have presumed a further and more general similarity between the two, in addition to the likenesses which, before seeing the new film, I could actually observe.

Finally, we should remember that reasoning by analogy never constitutes genuine proof, but only indicates that the conclusion is *likely* to be true.

Reasoning by Cause and Effect. Closely related to reasoning by analogy is *reasoning by cause and effect*. For the latter is based on the assumption that like causes produce like effects, or that if we have often previously seen cause *A* followed by effect *B,* the next time we see *A* we may expect to see *B* again. Here, too, we observe particular connections between things and infer a more general relationship. The preceding example of reasoning by analogy may serve also to illustrate reasoning from *cause to effect.* We may consider that in a degree the ability and talent of the actor, the actress, and the writer were causes for the merit of the first film. The decision to see the new film, then, may be based on the reasoning that these same causes will help to produce a similar effect again.

We may reason also from *effect to cause.* The classic illustration is a doctor's diagnosis: from the symptoms (effect) the doctor infers the nature of the disease (cause). Another example is a crime investigation, whether in fiction or in actual life: the detective first encounters an effect—a crime—and then, by assembling evidence and by reasoning about it, he tries to determine the cause.

Furthermore, we may reason also from *effect to effect.* If a child is born into a family in which for two or three generations several members have been gifted musically, we should think it probable that the child may be gifted in this way too. In biological terms we do not know precisely what the cause is, but we reason that if the effect has appeared in the family frequently, the effect is likely to appear again this time.

Deduction and the Syllogism. *Deduction* is that kind of reasoning which proceeds from the *general* to the *particular.* That is, in deduction we begin with a general statement or principle and apply it to a particular case. I know it to be a valid general principle, for example, that water freezes at any temperature below 32°F. On a particular occasion I learn that the temperature outdoors is 26°F. Applying the general principle, I deduce that unless I add antifreeze to the water in my automobile radiator, the water will freeze.

Thus deduction, like induction, is based on facts; at the outset, however, it is based on particular facts only indirectly. In one legitimate sense of the word it is a fact that water freezes below 32°F. But this is not a single, particular fact of the type that was exemplified before by an individual experience of heat near a fire. Rather, it is a generalization: *all* water freezes under these circumstances. Presumably this generalization was itself arrived at previously on the basis of observed particulars; that is, the generalization was the product of induction. But the generalization itself is the starting-point for deduction.

A single specimen of deductive reasoning can be expressed in the form of a syllogism, which is a conventional device for showing clearly the relationships among the ideas included. The syllogism consists of three parts: (1) the *major premise,* stating the general principle on which the reasoning is based; (2) the *minor premise,* indicating the particular case to which the general principle is applied; and (3) the conclusion, which completes the logic of the application. In syllogistic form the preceding example would appear as follows:

MAJOR PREMISE: All water exposed to a temperature below 32°F. will freeze.
MINOR PREMISE: The water in my automobile radiator is water exposed to a temperature below 32°F.
CONCLUSION: Therefore the water in my automobile radiator will freeze.

In ordinary speaking and writing, of course, the full, formal syllogism is very seldom used. Deductive reasoning is usually expressed informally, and the logic is often abbreviated. One might say, "I have to file an income tax return for last year; in my part-time job I earned $750.00." The full syllogism would be as follows:

MAJOR PREMISE (omitted from reasoning as actually expressed): All persons whose annual income exceeds a legally fixed minimum of $600.00 are required to file tax returns.
MINOR PREMISE: I am a person whose income exceeds this minimum.
CONCLUSION: Therefore I must file a tax return.

Consider another example: "I am taking physical training this year. All freshmen take it." Here, what would be the minor premise in a full syllogism is omitted: "I am a freshman." In still another example: "It is dangerous for people with heart trouble to take strenuous exercise; I have a bad heart, you know." The conclusion—"Therefore it is dangerous for me"—is omitted, but it is clear enough by implication. Even two of the three parts of a syllogism may be omitted. An athletic coach might say, "Anyone who wants to make the team must keep himself in good physical condition." This is actually only a major premise; but each person hearing the coach speak could make the application and draw the conclusion for himself: "I want to make the team; therefore I must keep myself in good physical condition."

A good way to test a deduction is to put it in the form of a full syllogism. In this form any flaws in the reasoning are relatively easy to recognize.

RECOGNIZING AND AVOIDING COMMON FALLACIES

The bulk of all possible mistakes in reasoning actually fall under a comparatively small number of types. These types are so frequently recurrent that they have been classified and in certain cases named. By becoming acquainted with the common types of fallacies, we can recognize them when we see them and not be deceived by them, and we can avoid committing them ourselves.

Common Fallacies in Inductive Reasoning. In inductive reasoning, we begin with particulars and proceed to a generalization which goes beyond them; we must be careful, therefore, not to proceed too fast or too far, not to generalize more broadly than the evidence reasonably warrants. Failure to observe this precaution may result in three sorts of fallacy: inadequate sampling, faulty analogy, and faulty causal relationships.

Inadequate Sampling. The fallacy of *inadequate sampling* (or *hasty generalization*) may occur when we generalize on the basis of too few particulars or when we ignore other particulars which actually show our generalization to be unsound. Among the most familiar and most unfortunate examples are rash statements about certain groups of people. One may see two or three noisily-intoxicated soldiers; "All soldiers are drunkards," he comments; or he even generalizes yet more broadly, "All servicemen. . . ." The fact that the great majority of servicemen conduct themselves like good citizens is not taken into account. We may hear similar statements based on inadequate sampling about racial, religious, or national groups.

We cannot make hard-and-fast rules about how many particulars are necessary to justify an inductive generalization. For practical purposes, we often generalize on the basis of a few particulars: we read two or three books by a single author, who perhaps wrote a dozen, and then we talk in universal terms about his style, attitude, and philosophy. On the other hand, if we evolve a scientific hypothesis, which is a tentative generalization, we usually subject it to numerous carefully planned and controlled testings to determine whether the evidence bears it out in every case. Under any circumstances it is well for us to observe and consider as many particulars as we readily can and to be on the alert for any which might either clearly show our generalization to be invalid or at least render it suspect.

Faulty Analogy. The fallacy of *faulty analogy* may occur when from particular similarities between two things we infer a further or more general similarity which does not really exist. It might arise in the example of reasoning by analogy that was given in the preceding section: although a new film is similar in a number of ways to one which I have seen and enjoyed, it still may disappoint me.

How can we guard against this fallacy? What clues should make us especially careful about accepting certain analogies that we encounter?

Once again there are no formulas; but we should remember that reasoning by analogy never constitutes proof; it only indicates a *probable* conclusion. Faulty analogy is especially likely to appear when the observed similarities are superficial or when the analogy is based on just a few similarities between things which have many aspects. It would obviously be rash to think that two kinds of food are equally wholesome because they come in packages of the same size and color or that two books which deal with the same general subject and which were published in the same year must be closely similar in other respects.

Faulty Causal Relationships. The fallacy of *faulty causal relationships* may occur when the cause-and-effect relationship that is inferred does not actually exist or, more frequently, when more complex relationships are involved. For an instance of possibly fallacious reasoning from cause to effect, we may consider the two films once more. Although the talents of the actors and the writer were in a degree causes for the merit of the first film, there may have been other causes operating, too; perhaps these latter did not operate when the second film was made. Perhaps the directors were not the same; perhaps the first film was produced on a larger budget; perhaps, although both films were based on books by the same author, the first book was substantially better than the second.

The danger of fallacy in reasoning from effect to cause is illustrated by the fact that even the best physicians sometimes make wrong diagnoses. A particular effect may be produced by one of several different causes—a particular set of symptoms by one of a number of diseases—and it is possible to go astray, as the doctor may do in this case, by ascribing the effect to the wrong cause.

We may err also in reasoning from effect to effect—especially when, as in the example of a child born into a family of musicians, we do not know precisely how the effect on which we base our reasoning was produced. Something may interfere to prevent the particular effect from appearing again at this time, and the child may not be musically inclined at all.

One fallacy in reasoning by cause and effect has been given a special name: it is called *post hoc ergo propter hoc* ("after this, therefore because of this"), or sometimes just *post hoc propter hoc* ("after this, because of this"). As the name implies, this error consists of presuming that if one event happens *after* another, the second one is necessarily *caused by* the first. Superstitions often embody this fallacy: if yesterday I walked under a ladder, and today I have an accident, I may superstitiously assume that the accident was caused by yesterday's event.

What are the chief precautions for guarding against fallacies in cause-and-effect reasoning? What are the tests we should apply to such reasoning when we meet it? We should make sure that when causes are assigned, they are really adequate to produce the effects; we should determine if possible whether, in each of the causal sequences which are compared, *all* the same causes and *only* the same ones are operating; we should ask whether an observed effect might have been produced by causes other than those assigned and whether something might keep an expected effect from occurring.

Common Fallacies in Deductive Reasoning. As far as the actual logical relationships among the ideas are concerned, the dangers of error are not quite so great in deduction as in induction. But in deductive reasoning there are a number of possible fallacies. Chief among these are the use of faulty premises, the drawing of a conclusion which does not follow from the premises (called *non sequitur*), and the application of the reasoning to false or irrelevant issues.

Faulty Premises. If there is something wrong with either or both of the premises in a syllogism—or with the implied premises in an informal deduction—then the conclusion may be false even if the logic itself is airtight. This is a syllogism with a faulty major premise:

> All stout persons are cheerful.
> John is a stout person.
> Therefore John is cheerful.

Although this logic is flawless, it is not true that *all* stout persons are cheerful.[6] The fact may be that John is melancholy. Of course it may happen that John *is* cheerful; the conclusion may be true. Even so, its truth is not proved by the syllogism with a faulty major premise.

The minor premise may be faulty, as in the following:

> All stout persons should try to reduce, if they can do so without endangering their health.
> John is a stout person who could reduce without this danger.
> Therefore John should try to reduce.

We might be inclined to accept this major premise, as an ideal anyway. Suppose, however, that John is not stout in the sense that this context indicates; he is stocky and has a large frame, but he is not actually over-

---

[6] In a sense the basic error here is not in deductive reasoning but in inductive: the faulty major premise is a hasty generalization based on inadequate sampling. The error is likely to have its practical effect, however, when the generalizaton is applied, as it is here, in deduction.

weight. The ambiguity of the word *stout* is responsible for a faulty minor premise, which in turn leads to a false conclusion. Clearly, if both premises are faulty, the conclusion rests on an even weaker basis.

One test that we should apply to deductive reasoning, then, whether our own or another's, is to examine the premises on which the conclusion is based. Any implied premises should be made explicit for the purpose of this examination.

Non Sequiturs. Unlike the use of false premises, the *non sequitur* (Latin for "it does not follow") fallacy is an error in the logic itself: in the relationships among the ideas, such that the conclusion does not follow from the premises. This fallacy may occur, for example, when the major premise is not a universal generalization, and therefore it does not necessarily include the particular instance cited in the minor premise:

> Many stout persons are cheerful.
> John is a stout person.
> Therefore John is cheerful.

If we accept the major premise as valid, and if John is actually stout in the sense indicated, the conclusion may still be false. Obviously, this is because John may not be one of the "many" cheerful stout persons. If the logic in a sample of deductive reasoning is to be foolproof, then, the subject of the major premise must be modified, explicitly or implicitly, by an adjective which makes the generalization universal: by a word such as *all, every, any;* or if the premise is negative, a word or words such as *no, none of, not any.*

Another principle that is useful for recognizing and avoiding *non sequiturs* is that the *subject* of the major premise must appear in the *predicate* of the minor premise:

> All *stout persons* (subject) should try to reduce. . . .
> John is a *stout person* (predicate). . . .

Otherwise, reasoning like this may result:

> All *stout persons* (subject) *should try to reduce* (predicate). . . .
> John *is trying to reduce.* (The predicate, rather than the subject, of the major premise appears in the predicate of the minor.)
> Therefore John is a stout person. (*Non sequitur*)

When this principle is expressed schematically, a proper syllogism appears in one of the two forms shown at the top of page 25.

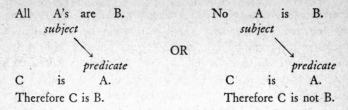

False and Irrelevant Issues. The fallacies which belong in the category of *false and irrelevant issues*—ignoring the question and begging the question—are perhaps committed more often consciously, with intent to deceive, than unconsciously; but they may occur inadvertently. Fallacies of this kind occur (1) when, although a piece of reasoning may be logically sound, it proves something else besides the point at issue or (2) when it does not really prove anything at all, but only gives a false appearance of doing so. The test we should apply, then, is to ask whether the reasoning actually proves something and if that thing is the real point at issue.

IGNORING THE QUESTION. Proving something else besides the point at issue is called *ignoring the question:* the reasoner ignores the real question and talks about something else, hoping to produce the same effect as if he were discussing the real one. A common example of this tactic is the argument *ad hominem* (or *argumentum ad hominem*); this phrase means an argument aimed or directed "at the man." Instead of trying to demonstrate a weakness in my opponent's reasoning, I assail his character. Even if the issue is completely impersonal (say, whether a new school building should be erected) I say in effect, "We cannot believe what he says, because he is a drunkard," or "because his brother-in-law is in prison." In the strict sense the argument *ad hominem* is a negative or unfavorable argument; but of course a similar fallacy may occur when I reason in favor of something. Instead of trying to show the soundness of a point of view, I simply say that it is held by a person or persons whom I characterize as admirable. If this person is really an authority on the subject, then his holding the view may be cogent. If he is only someone of whom I imply a generally or vaguely favorable impression, however, his opinion may well be irrelevant.

BEGGING THE QUESTION (ARGUING IN A CIRCLE). Giving a false appearance of proof may be the effect of begging the question or arguing in a circle. *In begging the question,* the reasoner actually assumes in his argument the truth of what he is trying to prove. I may say, "These guilty men committed the crime for which they are on trial." If they are *guilty* of the crime, then certainly they committed it;

but merely calling them guilty does not prove that they are. *Arguing in a circle* is a closely similar fallacy: the reasoner makes a statement and then justifies it by saying what amounts to the same thing in different words. For example, "Miss X ought to win the beauty contest. Why? Because she is the most beautiful girl among the contestants."

Again, I should ask myself whether the reasoning is more than just word-juggling and, if so, whether it proves the real point at issue.

CLASSIFICATION AND SHORT DEFINITION

In logical writing there are two related procedures which we have occasion to perform: (1) making systematic classifications and (2) defining terms succinctly. These operations require special care and the observance of a few rules and principles.

Classification. In *classification* we arrange items in groups or categories which are related in a systematic way; we place them, literally or figuratively, under headings which are determined according to a principle or criterion. We may classify all living things (biology) into two groups, plants (botany) and animals (zoology), and we may arrange books in the categories of fiction and nonfiction.

Basic Rules. Every systematic classification must be (1) consistent and (2) complete.

CONSISTENCY. A single act of classification must be performed according to a single principle or criterion, and the categories must never overlap; briefly, it must be *consistent*. For example, we may classify high-school or college undergraduates as freshmen, sophomores, juniors, and seniors—according to the principle of academic class. Additional classifications of undergraduates (and other groups) can be made on the basis of different criteria: the students might be classified as men and women, on the basis of sex; as dwellers on campus and off campus, on the basis of residence; or in various ways. But each case would be a separate and distinct act of classification; in no one act could more than one principle be used.

The example "All college undergraduates may be classified in four groups: freshmen, sophomores, women, and campus-dwellers" is unreasonable because presumably many freshmen and sophomores are women, certain women are campus-dwellers, and so on. If a single principle is employed, however, the categories will be *mutually exclusive;* that is, no member of any group will be a member of another also. Thus, no freshmen are sophomores, no men are women, no campus-dwellers live off campus. In this way, the rule of consistency prevents overlapping among the categories in any classification.

COMPLETENESS. Every proper classification must be *complete;* that is, the total of the groups or categories must equal the whole of the thing classified. If we classify the undergraduates on the basis of academic class, we must include all four classes. It would be false to say, "All college undergraduates may be classified as freshmen, sophomores, and juniors." By the same rule, we could not properly classify all books as either clothbound or paperbound, for there are leather and other bindings too; nor could we accurately classify all voters in the United States as Republicans or Democrats, for there are other voters (Independents and members of other, usually small, parties) who would thus not be included.

We can, of course, make statements like these: "Two classes of college undergraduates are freshmen and sophomores"; "Most current books are either clothbound or paperbound"; "The majority of voters in the United States are Democrats or Republicans." But these statements are not systematic classifications, or classifications at all in the strict sense.

In a proper classification, a word like *all* or *every* is either actually applied to the thing classified, or understood by implication. For instance: "All physical substances are solids, liquids, or gases"; "Everything in nature is animal, vegetable, or mineral." To be valid, then, the classification must be all-inclusive; the rule of completeness must be observed.

Subclassification. The same rules which apply to classification also apply to *subclassification.* A thing may be classified into groups or categories, each of which may often be subclassified, or divided further into subcategories. College freshmen might be subclassified in three groups: those who will finish their freshman work in February, those who will finish in June, and those who for one reason or another will not finish at either time. Each of the four classes might be thus grouped in three subdivisions, including the seniors with their February and June graduates and those who are not to be graduated with their class. Indeed, a classification may consist of several steps, with further and further subgroupings. A good example is the biological classification of living things, not only into the two kingdoms of plants and animals, but into a whole series of subdivisions and sub-subdivisions down through genera and species.

Short Definition. In our own writing, we often wish to make sure that our readers will understand the sense in which we are using a word. On such an occasion we may briefly define the word, give a *short definition* of it. There are longer definitions too, ranging in length from a paragraph to an extended essay or more; in a famous passage John Henry Cardinal Newman devotes over 800 words to defining *gentleman*.[7] Our concern here is with the brief form of definition, the kind usually given in a single sentence.

Definition as Classification. A short definition is an act of classification in two steps: one classification and one subclassification. Thus it consists of two parts: placing the term to be defined in a class, and then, by differentiating it from the other members of that class, placing it in a subclass by itself. The larger class is called the *genus;* the means by which the term to be defined is set off by itself is the *differentia*. In good definitions the genus is given in the form of a noun or noun phrase. The differentia may take the form of a subordinate clause, but the genus may not. (See Chapter 9.)

A freshman is a *college student* (genus) *in his first year of undergraduate study* (differentia).

A watch is a *timepiece* (genus) *designed to be worn or carried on the person* (differentia).

Wine is *fermented* (differentia) *grape juice* (genus).

Notice that the mere giving of a synonym, though it might be helpful to a reader who happened to know the synonym, does not constitute a definition; for instance, "Gaiety is merriment."

Common Errors in Definition. In order to be sure that we give good short definitions, we should be careful not to attempt to define by omitting the genus or differentia, by using an "is when" or "is where" construction, or by repeating the word to be defined.

OMISSION OF GENUS OR DIFFERENTIA. If either of the two parts of a definition is omitted, the result may be a true statement, but it will not be a definition.

GENUS OMITTED: An ammeter is used to measure electric current. (So it is, but this is not a definition.)
DEFINITION: An ammeter is an *instrument* (genus) *used to measure electric current* (differentia).

DIFFERENTIA OMITTED: A college freshman is a college student. (So he is, but so are sophomores, juniors, and seniors.)
DEFINITION: A college freshman is a *college student* (genus) *in his first year of undergraduate study* (differentia).

USE OF AN "IS WHEN" OR "IS WHERE" CLAUSE. If what purports to be a definition takes the form of an "is when" or "is where" clause, the result is neither a good definition nor usually a good sentence.

[7] *The Idea of a University,* Discourse VIII, Section 10.

INCORRECT: A foul is when you break a rule.
CORRECT: A foul is a *play or maneuver* (genus) *which involves infraction of one or more rules of the game* (differentia).

INCORRECT: A duet is where two people sing or play together.
CORRECT: A duet is a *musical composition* (genus) *designed to be sung or played by two people* (differentia).

REPETITION OF THE WORD TO BE DEFINED. In definition there is the danger of our falling into the error of repeating the word to be defined. If the definition of a word contains the word itself, or any form of the same word, the result is not likely to be useful; for if the reader does not already understand the word, he will not understand the explanation.

INCORRECT: An amateur is a player with amateur status.
CORRECT: An amateur is a player who has never played for money or its equivalent.

INCORRECT: A chiropodist is a doctor who practices chiropody.
CORRECT: A chiropodist is a doctor who treats ailments of the feet.

In like manner, if a definition contains words which for the average reader would probably be less familiar than the word to be defined, the definition will be without much value. A classic example is an excerpt from the first important English dictionary (1755), by Samuel Johnson—the definition of *network:* "Anything reticulated or decussated at equal distances with interstices between the intersections."

Exercises

1. In each of the following sentences, assume that the fact or idea which is italicized is more important than any other in the sentence. Rewrite each sentence, using a construction that will appropriately represent this importance.

a. She ran *swiftly* down the narrow path to meet them.

b. He was talking with her yesterday, and *she gave him some wonderful news.*

c. His employer told him to do the whole job, *to do it correctly,* and to get it done on time.

d. *I have been reading some stories by Poe,* and he is known as the father of the short story.

e. It may rain tomorrow, but *we will go anyway.*

2. Indicate in which of these three categories each of the following statements belongs: (1) a fact or facts on which it would be reasonably safe to

rely; (2) a purported fact or facts about which one might appropriately be skeptical, or which one would wish to verify before accepting; (3) a matter of opinion.

a. (From a commercial advertisement) This product is the most delicious dessert you can buy.

b. (From a standard encyclopedia) Shakespeare was born in 1564.

c. (From an article on public health, published in a reputable magazine in 1950) There is no known means of inoculation against infantile paralysis.

d. (From a stranger whom one overhears in a picture gallery) Now, *there* is the greatest painting of the twentieth century!

e. (From the veteran conductor of a major symphony orchestra) There is a trend in concert programing toward including more performances of contemporary music.

3. Evaluate each of the following pieces of reasoning: indicate whether it is sound or unsound; if it is unsound, name the fallacy which it involves.

a. I have tried several times, when no other fuel was available, to start a fire with green wood. In each case I have had great difficulty; and everyone I know who has made a similar attempt has had the same difficulty. I conclude that green wood simply does not burn well.

b. All college graduates earn good incomes.
  John has just been graduated from college.
  Therefore John will earn a good income.

c. I know three people in that club. Two of them are on probation, and the third one barely escaped being put on it. I can tell that all the members are pretty stupid.

d. No man can live forever.
  I am a man.
  Therefore I cannot live forever.

e. My twin brother and I took all the same courses in high school, and we always got the same or almost the same grades. He is taking chemistry now, and he got an *A* for the first semester. I am reasonably sure that I could do well in the course.

f. Relatively few women are elected to the state legislature.
  My rival for a seat in this body is a woman.
  Therefore my rival will not be elected.

g. I am sure that this college library must be just as good as the other one, because they are within a few hundred of having the same number of volumes.

h. I say we should *not* support the passing of this bill; and you will know how little you can believe my opponent's argument in favor of it when I tell you that his uncle was recently under threat of prosecution for evasion of taxes.

i. If the hurricane follows its present course and comes to this area with its present violence, there will be a great deal of property damage here.

j. John Milton wrote a tract in favor of divorce, because he was unhappy in his first marriage.

4. Classify the following, using the criteria indicated:

a. Public buildings, on the basis of their principal function or use (e.g., concert hall).

b. The months of the year, on the basis of the seasons to which they belong.

c. Table silverware, on the basis of the principal types of implement (e.g., fork). Subclassify each principal type into its subtypes (e.g., salad fork, oyster fork).

5. In your own words, without referring to a dictionary, give short definitions of the following: *automobile, chair, dictionary, overcoat, pencil*.

6. Indicate what rule or rules of classification are violated, or what errors in definition are committed, in each of the following:

a. All magazines may be classified in three groups: weekly, bi-weekly, and monthly.

b. All men in the military service of the United States are members of the Army, the Navy, or the Marine Corps.

c. A comedy is a play in which the action is comic.

d. Biology deals with living things.

e. A touchdown is when one team gets the ball across the other team's goal line.

3 THE WHOLE COMPOSITION

The present chapter develops an answer to the question: How ought the inexperienced writer proceed in writing a composition? Although the writer may correctly regard theme preparation as a single (and perhaps formidable) block of work, he should see it also as divisible, as a step-by-step process. Once he has broken it down into a series of steps, he will find it easier than he first thought. Writing a good composition remains a challenge, but by exercising care and judgment throughout, the writer can take every step successfully and can produce a good piece of work.

Before we analyze the steps in this process, we should have as clear an idea as possible of the goal—of what the end product ought to be.

QUALITIES OF A GOOD COMPOSITION

What *is* a good theme? It is only in rather general terms that this question can be answered at all, for every good composition is unique and a number of its qualities are peculiarly its own. At the same time a good theme has certain qualities in common with all good themes. In its development of a single central idea or emotional effect, the good composition is unified; in the relationships among its sentences and paragraphs, it is coherent; in the organization and disposition of its material, it is appropriately emphatic. Also, it has an element of originality, and a degree of distinction in style.

Unity. A good composition creates a clear impression of *unity*. If addressed chiefly to the reader's intellect, it presents a single central idea; if to his emotions, a single dominant effect. Every paragraph, every sentence fits organically into the pattern of the whole; that is, all parts are functional. There is no irrelevant or superfluous material, no padding, nothing which does not contribute to a purpose—the over-all purpose of the whole. A good criterion of unity is whether the central idea or dominant effect can be stated or characterized in a single sentence.

If the whole composition develops one idea or one effect, then everything in the composition contributes to that development. This is not to say that there is no room for the qualification of ideas or the shading of emotion; what the composition communicates may be an idea carefully qualified or a mixed kind of mood or feeling, with shadings care-

32

fully controlled. Ideas and emotions often *are* complex; they may contain elements which are at variance or even apparently contradictory. It is a challenge for the writer to develop an idea or effect, whether simple or relatively complex, so that every part of the theme serves the central purpose of the whole.

Coherence. The major parts in a short composition are the paragraphs.[1] *Coherence* in the composition as a whole depends upon the relationships among the paragraphs. These relationships should be close, and they should be clear to the reader.

Organic Relationships. The relationships among paragraphs will be close if they are organic; that is, if they are based on a logical coherence in the subject matter. If the topics which are developed in successive paragraphs are themselves closely related, then the paragraphs will be closely related, too. For example, in a composition designed to explain briefly the basic structure of a city government, one paragraph might be devoted to the executive branch, the next to the legislative, and the next to the judicial. Since these are the three main branches of the government, the three paragraphs in which they were discussed would reflect their homogeneity. This *organic relationship* is the most important aspect of coherence; it reflects an inner and essential coherence among the facts and ideas or feelings which the composition is intended to communicate.

Devices to Make Relationships Clear. When relationships are simple, the writer may ordinarily depend on the reader to perceive them without special help. In the composition about the city government, the writer would need only to introduce his subject, indicating that he would discuss the three branches of the government; then he could simply go ahead and discuss them, each in turn. But at times the associations among ideas or feelings, while equally close, may be somewhat more complex, and the writer may need to take special pains to make them clear.

In presenting complicated matters he may use transitional devices: words, phrases, or sometimes whole clauses or sentences, placed at or near the beginnings or ends of his paragraphs, and designed specifically to keep the reader aware of their relevance. Expressions that may serve this purpose are so numerous that there would be no point in compiling a list of them; a few examples will suffice. If the affinity is one of time sequence, successive paragraphs might begin with "First," "Soon after-

[1] In longer themes there may be parts (sections) which themselves are made up of paragraphs. In general, what is here said of the paragraphs applies also to these larger units.

ward," "A little later," "Then finally," or the like. In a series of arguments supporting a particular point of view, one might use "In the first place," "In like manner," "Moreover," and so on. If the relationship is one of opposition, "On the other hand" would sometimes be appropriate, or "If we regard the question from the other side," or simply an injected "however."

The relationships may be emphasized also by the use in successive paragraphs of synonyms of the key words, or pronouns of which the key words are antecedents. For a few further examples, in a context, consider a composition explaining a process—for instance, a photographic darkroom procedure. The connections here would be chiefly matters of simple time sequence, but there might be a few complexities which it would be important to present clearly. Certain operations might be consecutive, others simultaneous. A few of the paragraphs might be linked, then, as follows. (The words which contribute to maintaining coherence are italicized.)

. . . The preparations for printing are now complete.

The *first* step in *this process* is to place the film negative and the sensitized paper in the frame. . . . The *exposed* paper is removed, ready for *developing*.

While successive sheets are being exposed, an assistant may *develop* those which are ready. . . . This is the end of the developing procedure proper.

During all these operations, care should be taken to protect the sensitized paper from any white light except that of the printing lamp. . . .

Of course, it is ineffective to overload a composition with transitional devices. In a short theme of four or five paragraphs, it would be superfluous to link the paragraphs with expressions like "We have now completed our discussion of the first phase of the subject. Let us pass on to the second." The writer should make sure that the kinship of his ideas is clear; if it is, he should trust his reader to see it. Here as elsewhere he must exercise care and judgment.

Emphasis. The material of a good composition, a unit of thought or feeling, is arranged so as to secure appropriate *emphasis*. This emphasis may be developed by proportion, by repetition, and by placement.

Emphasis by Proportion. *Emphasis by proportion* is achieved by the allocation of proper amounts of space to the different parts of a composition. Material which is subordinate in importance, but functional and worth including, should take up a relatively small share of the total space. To the major material, clearly, should be devoted a greater amount of space. For example, in a theme defending a particular position on a controversial issue, it might be good strategy to include a brief statement of one or two arguments for an opposing position, together with an indication of how they may be met; but ordinarily the writer would use most of his space to present the arguments for his own side. On the other hand, in a theme that was intended primarily as a rebuttal of opposing arguments, this rebuttal would occupy most of the space, and only a short summary of the positive case for the writer's own position would be included.

Emphasis by Repetition. *Emphasis by repetition* is virtually self-explanatory: the judicious reiteration of an important point at various places in the composition will have the effect of emphasis. For example, in an argumentative or persuasive theme, if the main point is supported by each of a number of different arguments, this point might appropriately be restated, with varied phrasing, as each argument is set forth. The exercise of judgment is important here to avoid injudicious or unnecessary repetition, which would make the theme wordy and dull.

Emphasis by Position. The rule for *emphasis by position or placement,* in the whole composition as in the sentence (p. 13), is that the most emphatic position is at the end, and the next most emphatic is at the beginning. A good composition will begin on a strong note and end on one that is even stronger. Notice the close relationship between climax and emphasis: if the material is arranged in climactic order, then the most important point will come at the end, and thereby receive the emphasis which it deserves. For instance, in a theme about the effects of a natural disaster—a hurricane or a flood— it would be appropriate to discuss the different effects in the order of increasing gravity: first the property damage, then the incidence of disease, and then the direct loss of life. An exception to this rule is a newspaper account in which all the essential facts are given first and then followed by the subordinate details—but in general the rule holds good.

Climax and emphasis are closely related to unity. The reason is that unity is psychologically dependent on climax and emphasis. The materials that are used to develop the central idea—the topics of the successive paragraphs—may all be such as really to further that development; but if the most important material comes first, what follows may give the effect of afterthought. Thus, although the materials in themselves are logically unified, a bad arrangement may obscure this unity. On the other hand, if the materials are molded into climactic form, if the main points and especially the central idea or effect are properly emphasized, if the beginning and especially the end are strong, then the unity that is in the materials will appear clearly to the reader.

Other Qualities. Two other qualities of a good composition are originality, and distinction in style.

Originality. A good composition is *original*. The central idea of a logical theme need not be an absolutely brand-new thought, nor must the central feeling of an emotional theme be unlike any which has ever been communicated before. Such a requirement would be impossible to fulfill, for other human beings may have had similar ideas or felt similar emotions and have expressed them in writing. In each case, however, the writer's idea should be evolved from his own thought, his emotional [2] and other experience—from his own observation or his thoroughly digested knowledge of other human experience. If the idea or the feeling is his own in this sense, it is sufficiently original.

What is more important is that the way in which he *develops* the idea or the emotion be his own. In this respect his composition can be truly unique. According to the poet Alexander Pope,

> True Wit is Nature to advantage dressed,
> What oft was thought, but ne'er so well expressed.

In the compositions of inexperienced writers we may seldom find an idea developed so perfectly that it has been "ne'er so well expressed" before; but we may and ought to find it developed in such a manner that it has never before been expressed in exactly the same way. And this kind of freshness and originality may be achieved even if the main idea or feeling of the composition is common human property. It is achieved by the writer's making full use of his own thought and his own experience, wherever this material can contribute appropriately to the central development. This kind of originality is possible in virtually every composition.

Distinction in Style. The prose style of a good composition has distinction. It is more than just barely adequate to convey the writer's feelings and ideas; actually, it makes its own contribution to the total communication. The style in itself should not attract attention; rather, it should be so unobtrusive that the reader is scarcely conscious of it. The *writer,* on the other hand, should be fully conscious of it; good style is an indispensable means to the full and accurate expression of his meaning.

It may seem that excellence of style is beyond the reach of the inexperienced writer. It is doubtless true that a really distinguished style

---

[2] It is possible for a gifted writer to communicate emotion which he may have felt only by a kind of imaginative projection—as Shakespeare in *Macbeth,* for example, communicates the emotions of a murderer. But the safest course for a beginner is to deal only with feelings which he has actually had himself.

is beyond the immediate reach of many students. To develop good qualities of style—ease, flexibility, maximum appropriateness—requires considerable practice and experience; this is one reason for the require-ment, almost always made in a composition course, that the student write continually. But anyone can improve his style and almost any person with sufficient perseverance can attain a measure of distinction.

Style in the strict sense is a matter chiefly of diction and sentence structure. For specific information about these topics, see "Distinction in Diction" in Chapter 10 and "Effectiveness of Sentences" in Chapter 8.

TYPICAL PROCEDURE FOR WRITING A COMPOSITION

We should bear in mind these generalizations about the qualities of a good theme as we now follow an exposition of the principal steps—in the step-by-step process—of preparing a composition.

Choosing a Subject. The first step, logically, is *choosing a subject* for the composition. To the student the answer to the question "What shall I write about?" sometimes appears to be not a step but a jump, a jump over a high hurdle.

Optional Topics Assigned. The student may have his choice at least partly made for him. Usually the assignment of a composition includes a subject or a number of optional subjects. To be sure, even when a single topic is assigned, the student has still to exercise some choice. He may have to select a particular aspect of the subject (see "Focusing," p. 39), or he may choose among a number of possibilities which are in-cluded within the single assignment. For example, the assignment might be, "Explain the operation of a mechanical device with which you are familiar." A particular student might write about the operation of an automobile, a camera, a cash register, or a sewing machine.

The need for making a choice is most obvious when several optional topics are given. Here is a typical assignment.

> Discuss an aspect of one of the following:
> 1. The intramural athletic program
> 2. The role of young adults in a church or synagogue
> 3. Commuting to college
> 4. Current television programs
> 5. Musical activities on the campus

The student may be qualified to write on one, two, or more of the as-signed topics; if so, the basis for choice among them would be simply what subject he is best able to discuss, or what subject holds the most interest for him. If he takes part in intramural athletics, the first topic would probably be a good choice; if he is active in church or synagogue work, the second. If he commutes to college—and especially if he belongs to a club of students who live off campus, and thus has had a good opportunity to learn about the experience of other commuters too —the third; and so on.

Let us assume a particular case in which the above list of topics has been suggested to a class for a theme of about five hundred words. We will focus on one class member, John Lloyd, who is interested in music: he belongs to the band and the glee club, and another singing group; he attends concerts by the college orchestra; he has friends who are members of the orchestra and have told him about their work in this organization. Thus, he decides to take topic number five, "Musical activities on the campus." Later we shall follow John Lloyd through the steps he takes in writing a composition on this subject.

No Topics Assigned. Occasionally a theme assignment does not include suggested topics; that is, the student is to evolve a topic for himself. Sometimes the form of discourse may be indicated—the theme is to be expository, for example, or narrative—but sometimes there is no suggestion on this point either. Many writers seem to find this the most difficult kind of requirement: a theme is to be handed in, on a given date; a length may be stipulated, but no further instructions are given. In effect, then, the assignment demands that the student must have something to say.

This in turn requires simply that he be mentally awake, alive to his experience and alert to its implications. His life, though it may seem to have been routine or unspectacular, has been filled with various experiences at home, at school, at work, on vacation. He spends much of his time talking with people; reading books, magazines, and newspapers; and probably taking part in various other activities. The matter of having something to say is inseparable from the whole process of education, formal and informal; that is, from living and learning and thinking about how one has lived and what one has learned. All these things are sources of material for reflection and for writing. Thus, everyone at any given age above early childhood does have some things to say; the problem then is not the paucity of ideas, but the selection of a topic from among the number of different possibilities.

One final suggestion may be given. When optional topics are assigned, they are usually of closely comparable difficulty. When no topics are assigned, the possibilities that arise from the student's own experience and reflection may vary widely in this respect; certain ones may be easier to deal with than others. The easiest topic may not be the best choice. One which is more challenging to the writer may stimulate him to better work. And the instructor may invoke the standard questions used in evaluation: What was the author of this theme trying to do? How well has he done it? How important or worthwhile was the attempt itself? If the last question is asked of themes entitled "A Day at Summer Camp" and "The Essence of Liberal Education," the answers will probably be very different.

Focusing. The next step in preparing a theme may be called *focusing*. This includes the writer's consideration of the subject he has chosen and his decision on two points: (1) what particular aspect of the subject he will deal with, and (2) what central idea he will develop, or (in a theme addressed chiefly to the reader's emotions) what central effect he wishes to produce.

This important step is sometimes omitted by the inexperienced writer. He chooses a subject and then immediately asks himself what he will say about the whole subject. Logically included within the topic John Lloyd has selected—musical activities on campus—are the band, the orchestra, perhaps a chamber music ensemble, the glee club, and other singing groups; their history, personnel, performances, repertory, rehearsals, and so on. If the writer tries to discuss all these things in a five-hundred-word composition, he will produce only a disjointed mixture. What is the proper way for him to proceed?

Limiting the Subject. The proper procedure is for the writer to *limit his subject*: to select a single aspect, or a few closely related aspects, which he can cover adequately within the space limitations. This procedure will itself include two steps: considering what the aspects of the subject are, and then making the choice.

John Lloyd, in considering the aspects of his subject, might think of two classifications: the musical organizations on the campus and the phases of their activity. Either in his mind or in the notes which he might actually jot down at this point, he would have something like this:

ORGANIZATIONS		POINTS TO COVER
Band		History (Origin)
Orchestra	Instrumental	Personnel
Chamber ensemble		Performances
		Repertory
Glee club		Rehearsals
The "Chanticleers"	Vocal	
(another singing group)		

The bases for selection among these aspects of a single subject would be essentially the same ones that were used for selection among different topics: knowledge and interest. Suppose that John decides he ought to focus on either instrumental or vocal music, not both. He has really had more experience with and therefore knows more about the latter, so he chooses it. Even in the category of vocal music, however, there are two organizations, and it would be difficult to cover both adequately in a well-unified short theme. Thus he decides to confine his discussion to the group called the "Chanticleers." He thinks he will be able, and plans tentatively, to include all the points except "Rehearsals."

Fixing on a Central Idea or Emotional Effect. The second stage of the focusing process, for the writer of a primarily logical theme, is to *fix upon a single central idea* which his whole theme will develop; for the writer of a primarily emotional theme, to fix upon a single central effect which his whole theme will be designed to evoke.[3] The central idea or emotional effect should be capable of being expressed or characterized in a single sentence.

This sentence should not take the form "I am going to write about such-and-such." It should not begin with an expression like "I shall discuss" or "I mean to explain"; clearly, any sentence that began this way would be of little help to the writer in keeping his theme unified, for it might readily become too inclusive. John Lloyd might say, "I shall deal with the origin, the personnel, the performances, and the repertory of the Chanticleers, and"—for all the good that such a sentence might do— "with cabbages and kings." The sentence should make no mention of the writer himself, *as* writer. Rather, it should take the form normally of a simple statement about the subject. In formulating it, John Lloyd should ask himself, "What one thing do I want to say about this group? what one thing that applies to its origin and to the other closely related aspects equally?" After thinking for a while, John evolves this answer:

Everything about the Chanticleers—the origin of the group, their personnel, their performances, their repertory—illustrates one thing: these men sing because they enjoy singing.

Notice that this sentence represents a central idea, for a theme that will be largely expository. It implies an element of emotion also: the feeling

[3] In some cases the writer should fix upon both a central idea and a central emotional effect: for example, if his theme is to represent a combination of the intellectual and emotional forms of discourse. In general, however, the well-unified short theme will be confined largely to one form of discourse, and therefore will have either a central idea or a central emotional effect, rather than both.

of enjoyment. In the composition itself, then, John Lloyd should undertake primarily to explain his subject, but he should try also to communicate something of the enjoyment, the verve and enthusiasm, which this statement of his central idea suggests.

Obtaining Material. Having chosen and limited his subject and having fixed upon a central idea or emotional effect, the writer proceeds to obtain the material he will use in developing that idea or effect. This step includes gathering material and making a selection from what he has gathered.

Gathering Information. The writer may *gather material* from (1) his own experience and (2) the experience of others, which has been or may be communicated to him in speech or writing. These are respectively the primary and secondary sources of factual data (see Chapter 2); they are the sources of all other kinds of information as well. For the kind of short theme that is assigned most frequently, the writer will ordinarily draw principally on his own experience, and perhaps on the experience of others which he has learned about informally, by word of mouth.[4] Indeed, as we have seen, he will have chosen his subject partly on the basis of his own current experience and knowledge.

For example again, where will John Lloyd get the substance for his composition? Since he is himself a member of the group about which he is writing, he already has at least some of the information he will need. He knows about the occasions when the group performs, and he knows the songs they sing. On the other hand, let us presume that he is a freshman, and that the group was first organized a number of years ago. For information about its origin, therefore, and the personnel of the original group, he will depend on what he has learned from the older members. The chances are that he has heard the story often and is thoroughly familiar with it.

Selecting Content. If the writer has been conscientious in gathering material—from his own experience, or that of others, or both—he will probably have more than he can effectively use. He will need, then, to *make a selection* from the subject matter gathered by resolutely rejecting any information which cannot be made functional.

Here he can make good use of the central idea or central emotional effect which he has evolved previously; for the criterion of what is functional, as applied to any given piece of material, is this: Is it closely related to the central idea or effect? That is, will the material serve to support—to illustrate, to explain, to develop—that idea or that effect?

---

[4] For another kind of assignment, the research paper (Chapter 6), the writer will draw largely from written, published sources.

If the answer is yes, it should be retained and used. If the answer is no, then no matter how interesting an aspect of the subject may be in itself, it should be rigorously excluded.[5]

How will John Lloyd apply this criterion to his stock of facts? His central idea is that the group he is discussing came into existence and has continued to exist actively because its members enjoy singing together. His account of the founding of the group and its original recruiting will illustrate this point; so will his notes about its performances. But what about the matter of its repertory? Let us presume the principal feature of its repertory to be that, except at the very beginning, the group has sung original song arrangements exclusively—arrangements prepared by members of the group itself. This is an interesting fact; in writing about it John could include colorful details about certain songs and information about particular members who made special contributions to the activity. It is, however, related only remotely to his central idea. Since it was their enjoyment in singing together which brought the group into existence at the beginning, and since at that time they were not singing original arrangements, apparently the enjoyment was not dependent on any particular kind of repertory; they always enjoyed singing, whatever the songs might be. Perhaps the information about their later repertory could be related to the central idea, but the connection would be forced, or it would require too much space to make clear. Wisely, John decides to delete this material from his plan.

Organizing the Material. When the material has been gathered and screened for relevance to the central idea or effect, it is ready to be *organized*. In taking this step, the writer must consider the matter of proportion and also must arrange the material in the order or sequence most effective for presentation. These matters may in effect be dictated to a certain extent by the logical relationships among the groups of facts gathered. After these relationships have been considered, however, there may remain a number of different possibilities for arrangement. If so, the writer will want to choose carefully and be sure to fix upon the best.

Internal Logic. Both aspects of organization, proportion and sequence, are closely connected to the *internal logic* of the material itself—that is, to the natural relationships among its parts.

PROPORTION. As indicated in the discussion of "Emphasis by Proportion," proper *proportion* is achieved by devoting to each part of the

---

[5] If there still remains too much material for the composition, either only that which is *most* functional should be retained, or the subject itself should be further limited.

material an appropriate amount of space: a comparatively greater amount to the important parts and less to minor or less interesting parts. Of course, the matter of proportion is closely related to the length of the composition: in determining the respective amounts of space, the writer should be concerned not only with the relative importance of the parts but also with the scope of the whole. The writer should deliberately exercise common sense and judgment in handling this problem of proportion.

We have already seen how John Lloyd's consideration of proportion figured in his decision to delete a discussion of repertory from his plan. What proportional amounts of space will be appropriate for the subtopics which are still included in his plan—for his accounts of the origin, the personnel, and the performances of the Chanticleers? We may presume that the group had just one origin, and that it has had only one personnel policy; but the performances have been numerous. John has first-hand knowledge of many of the latter; from his own experience, he can develop his account of them with concrete, specific detail. Also, emphasis on the performances is appropriate to the assigned topic, for these are current musical activities on the campus. In his theme of about five hundred words, John may reasonably decide to devote at least two paragraphs to the performances and not more than one apiece to the origin and the personnel.

SEQUENCE. *Sequence,* too, will be determined at least in part by the nature of the material. For example, there may be a time relationship involved. Since John Lloyd plans to include an account of the Chanticleers' origin, he will almost certainly put this account at the beginning. It is not absolutely necessary that he do so; he might possibly begin with something else and later return to the origin by means of a flash back. Unless there should be a special reason to reverse the time sequence, however, the natural thing would be to begin with the origin. The same principle would apply in a composition about a process or method of procedure: clearly, one would begin with the first step and then proceed in chronological order.

There are so many ways in which the sequence may be dependent upon the material that it is practically impossible to generalize about them; but here are a few more examples. In describing a scene the writer might decide arbitrarily where to begin—in the foreground, perhaps, or at the left side—but then the rest of his description would naturally proceed from the starting point—from the foreground to background, or from left to right, respectively. Sometimes it is reasonable to begin with a definition: where a term, important in the composition, has a number of meanings but is to be used in one special sense.[6] In a theme entitled "Democracy on the Campus," for example, the writer might well begin by explaining what he means by *democracy*. In an argumentative theme addressed chiefly to the intellect, the order will be largely determined by the logic of the argument itself: the writer will proceed from the general to the particular or vice versa, according to whether the pattern of his reasoning is basically deductive or inductive.[7]

Other Considerations.[8] After he has given due weight to the material itself—to the relative importance and other relationships among the subtopics, and to the ways in which these relationships may partly predetermine the organization—the writer may still see a number of different possibilities for the arrangement of parts of the theme. In choosing among these he may be guided by at least two criteria: smooth transition, and climax.

SMOOTH TRANSITION. If there are two or more possibilities, otherwise equally good, for the arrangement of any group of subtopics, the writer should ask himself, "Which pattern will best allow for *smooth transition* from one subtopic to another?" For example, something which will naturally come at the end of a paragraph on one of the subtopics may lead smoothly to the next. Indeed, in answering this question he might even find one subtopic leading to another so readily that he ought properly to include both in a single paragraph. Let us say that John Lloyd, as he thinks about the origin and the personnel policy of the Chanticleers, sees that these two subtopics can be combined in this manner: the way in which the original group was recruited is the way also in which later replacements have been made. He can take up both subtopics, then, in his first paragraph.

CLIMAX. One other question that will often be useful to the writer in choosing among alternative arrangements is this: "Which of my sub-

---

[6] It is, however, a trite and therefore usually ineffective tactic to begin with a dictionary definition ("Webster defines ——— as '———' "). Ordinarily an introductory definition should be the writer's own.

[7] See Chapter 2, and the first and third sections of Chapter 7. (The organization and development of the whole theme and that of a single paragraph are closely similar; the chief general difference, aside from that of scope, is that the whole theme will more often employ a *combination* of different methods of development.)

[8] In a sense these "considerations" relate to the material itself also; clearly, no consideration regarding the organization of a particular composition can be divorced from the material to be presented. The considerations discussed in this section, however, are a little more general; they are applicable to any kinds of material.

topics is the most interesting or important?" An appropriate place for this subtopic is at the end of the composition, where it will stand as a final *climax*. The next most important might be placed at the beginning; or, if there are three or four subtopics which have different degrees of importance, the writer can arrange them in the climactic order of increasing importance. If he is careful with his opening sentences or paragraph, the beginning of his theme need not be weak, even though he deals with the least important subtopic first.

We remember that John Lloyd decided to devote two paragraphs to the performances of the Chanticleers. As he continues to think about his material and to develop his plans, the substance of these two paragraphs takes shape in his mind. In one of them he will generalize about the performances and include perhaps one specific example. The other he will devote entirely to one particular kind of performance: the group's singing for social functions at nearby women's colleges. The latter paragraph will be the more specific, and it has potentially a special kind of interest: the romantic. Moreover, John sees that by building on this romantic interest for contrast, he can lead up to a short concluding paragraph that will give final emphasis to his central idea. The two paragraphs on the performances, then, will be in this order: first the general, and then the more specific and particular.

Making Outlines. An *outline* is a convenient device for representing graphically the relationships including the relative importance among a set of facts and ideas. It gives the writer a simple method (1) of recording these relationships as he works them out in his mind and (2) of examining them critically and perhaps making changes at an early stage—before he has written out something that he may wish later to revise radically or even to eliminate. An outline enables him to see clearly the structure of his plan and helps him to make his composition follow and embody that structure. These functions make it so valuable a device that instructors in composition courses frequently require outlines to be submitted together with assigned themes, or sometimes before the themes themselves are due.

The writer should regard the outline as a valuable tool to use in whatever way or ways may be most helpful to him. There is no one particular time in the planning of a theme when an outline should be prepared. Plainly, a final outline cannot be drawn up until the organization of the material has been settled; but a tentative outline or outlines, freely revised, may be useful to the writer in working out that organization. Even for a short theme, one writer might jot down two or three tentative outlines as his plan progresses; these tentative plans will help him to make intelligent changes, which will be embodied in the final outline.[9] Another writer may not need to jot anything down until just before he is ready to write the composition itself. Although the writer should try conscientiously to have his outline in the best possible form before he does write his theme, he may justifiably change his plan, if a change appears to be appropriate, as late as during the writing process itself.

Outlines can be used most effectively if the writer knows the general principles and conventions and rules of outlining, the chief types of outlines, and the degree of detail appropriate for the usual purposes.

General Principles. Two general principles of outlining are that the outline should be functionally appropriate and that it should be made up of substantive headings.

FUNCTIONAL APPROPRIATENESS. The most important thing about a good outline is that it be *functionally appropriate;* that is, it should represent accurately the structure and relationship of ideas in the projected composition. The main headings in the outline should correspond logically to the principal sections of the composition. Any subdivisions under a particular heading should stand for what are actually subordinate parts of that section. To use the form of an outline without making its substance properly significant would be to use a tool for the sake of the tool rather than for the work it can do.

SUBSTANTIVE HEADINGS. In general, outline headings are most useful if they are *substantive;* that is, if they indicate *what the topics are* rather than only what their sequence or status is. For a simple example, consider again a theme about the basic organization of the government. Substantive outline headings for such a theme might be as follows:

1. Executive: the President with his Cabinet
2. Legislative: the two houses of the Congress
3. Judicial: the Supreme Court and other Federal courts

For an outline as short as this, it might seem that the purpose would be served almost equally well by captions like "Part I, Part II, Part III"; or, if the composition were to have a somewhat different kind of basic pattern, "Introduction, Development, Conclusion." Headings like these are of little value, however, to the writer of a theme of real complexity— or to his instructor or anyone else who might be trying to formulate an idea of the projected theme on the basis of the outline.

---

[9] An example of a revised outline, embodying the progressive changes made in the plan for John Lloyd's theme, appears on page 50.

Conventions and Rules. A few particular conventions and rules are useful guides in outlining. These include the conventional manner of numbering the headings, the rule of multiple subdivision, and the rule of parallel construction.

HEADING NUMBERS. The conventional way to *number the headings* in an outline is to use Roman numerals (I, II, etc.) for the major divisions; capital letters (A, B, etc.) for the largest subdivisions; Arabic numbers (1, 2, etc.) for the next largest; and small letters (a, b, etc.) for the next. Two further degrees of subdivision may be represented respectively by Arabic numbers in parentheses, and small letters in parentheses. This method is simply a convention, but it is well established and widely familiar; under all ordinary circumstances it is the best method for the writer to use.

MULTIPLE SUBDIVISION. The rule of *multiple subdivision* is that any section which is subdivided must have at least two subdivisions. This is logical, for nothing can be divided into only one part. In other words, any heading which is followed by a subheading must be followed by at least one more subheading of the same rank.

LOGICAL	ILLOGICAL
I.	I.
A.	A.
B. (etc., if appropriate)	
II.	II.
A.	A.
1.	1.
2. (etc.)	
B.	B.
1.	1.
a	a.
b. (etc.)	
2.	2.

PARALLEL CONSTRUCTION. The rule of *parallel construction* in outlining is that on any one level of subdivision, all the headings must have the same grammatical status. The rule applies, for instance, to the main (Roman-numeral) headings, since they are on one level: the first or top level, standing for the major divisions of the subject. If the first such heading is a noun phrase, the second (and third, and so on) must have this grammatical form also. (See Chapter 9 for definitions of grammatical terms.) The main sections of John Lloyd's theme might be represented in the first column below. The second version would be improper because it violates the rule of parallel construction.

PARALLEL	NOT PARALLEL
I. Origin and Personnel (noun phrase)	I. Origin and Personnel (noun phrase)
II. Performances (noun)	II. Give Performances (verb and noun)
III. Reason for Singing (noun phrase)	III. I state Chants' reason for singing. (sentence)

In general, it is good practice to employ the same grammatical form for *all* the headings in an outline, on all the levels, from the major divisions of the subject to the most subordinate headings. In a topic outline, however (see the following section), it is permissible to use different forms on different levels, provided that consistency is maintained within each one. The noun heading of John Lloyd's second main section might be followed by two subheadings in adjective form, as in the first column below, but not by subheadings of different status, as in the second.

PARALLEL	NOT PARALLEL
II. Performances	II. Performances
A. General: Singing on Home Campus (adjective with explanatory phrase)	A. General: Singing on Home Campus (adjective with explanatory phrase)
B. Particular: Singing at Nearby Women's Colleges (adjective with explanatory phrase)	B. Like to Sing at Women's Colleges (verb with infinitive phrase)

Types of Outlines. There are two principal types of outlines: the sentence outline and the topic outline. The basis of classification, as with the rule of parallel construction, is the grammatical nature of the headings.

SENTENCE OUTLINE. In the *sentence outline,* every heading is a complete sentence. This principle applies to all the levels of subdivision: the headings not only of the main sections but also of any subsections appear in sentence form. Chiefly for this reason, the sentence outline is used for relatively short and simple compositions more often than for long and complex ones. It is possible to use this type even for elaborate outlines, subdivided down to the small-letter level or beyond; but for such purposes the topic outline, discussed below, is likely to be more adaptable. If John Lloyd should use a sentence outline, representing only the three main divisions of his subject, his matured plan might look like this:

I. Though originally formed for just one special occasion, the Chanticleers became a permanent organization because the charter members, like all their successors, were men who greatly enjoyed singing together.

II. The group has performed in many different settings, for example, at a Men's Faculty Club stag dinner; their favorite setting is a dance at a neighboring women's college.

III. They need no other reason for singing, however, except that they like to sing.

A special kind of sentence outline is the *paragraph outline.* Its distinguishing characteristic is that every sentence in the outline is the topic sentence of a paragraph in the final composition. This special type is perhaps most appropriate for a short theme which is purely expository in purpose; when the main facts or ideas of such a theme have been clearly expressed, these expressions may properly serve as the topic sentences of successive paragraphs. For a theme like John Lloyd's, however, with its intended emotional overtone, the sentence and paragraph outlines would probably differ, because it is unlikely that a matter-of-fact expression of each idea would represent the most effective phrasing for each topic sentence. John would have to think about his tactics in a little more detail before he could be sure about his topic sentences. If he did think ahead in this manner, he might prepare a paragraph outline like the following: [10]

1. Like many another momentous event, the birth of the male singing group known as the Chanticleers was really accidental.

2. They have sung on many different occasions and for many different audiences.

3. The Chanticleers do have one favorite kind of occasion for singing: a dance at a nearby women's college.

4. But the "Chants" will sing virtually anywhere, at any time—just because they like to sing.

TOPIC OUTLINE. In a *topic outline,* every heading is a word, phrase, clause, or group of these elements in a combination which is not

---

[10] The sentences—because they correspond simply to successive paragraphs rather than to major topics or subtopics—are numbered with consecutive Arabic numerals rather than with Roman numerals, letters, and so on. Notice that in John Lloyd's paragraph outline there is one more sentence than in his regular sentence outline, because he plans to write two paragraphs on his second main topic.

a complete sentence. Whatever the grammatical status may be, we know by the rule of parallel construction that it should be the same for all the headings, at least on any one level of subdivision, and usually throughout the outline. We know also that ordinarily each heading should be substantive, actually indicating what the topic or subtopic is. Provided that this principle is observed, there is some latitude with regard to the length or elaborateness of the headings. They may be brief and very simple, perhaps just naming the topics; or they may be somewhat more extended, giving further information about them. The first main caption in John Lloyd's outline might appear in the form we have already seen

I. Origin and Personnel

or it might appear in a fuller version

I. Origin Essentially Accidental; Recruiting of Personnel Highly Informal.

The length and elaborateness of the headings in a particular outline will be determined by the purpose which the outline is to serve. If the writer is constructing it solely for his own guidance, for example, he will probably use short captions; if he is providing his instructor or some other person with a sketch of his plan, he will probably use longer ones.

With its flexibility and relative economy of form, the topic outline is ordinarily the appropriate type for a composition of considerable complexity—like a term paper, which will ordinarily be at least a thousand words long. For an extended example, the reader is referred to the Table of Contents of this volume. There each chapter is outlined, and the twelve chapter outlines together constitute an outline of the whole book.

With its typically shorter headings, the topic outline is especially useful as a working outline, to represent the writer's original tentative plan and also to show the changes he makes as his plan matures. John Lloyd might have prepared and revised an outline as follows. (The additions which he made after constructing the outline in its first tentative form are italicized.)

    I. Origin *and Personnel*
    ~~II. Personnel~~
    ~~III. Repertory~~
    II. ~~IV.~~ Performances
        A. General: Singing on Home Campus
        B. Particular: Singing at Nearby Women's Colleges
    III. *Chants' Reason for Singing*

The topic outline is the most versatile, or generally useful, type; it is applicable to compositions of all lengths, from two or three paragraphs to several thousands of words. Therefore, the writer who wishes to use one form consistently will do best to use this one.

Degree of Detail. How much *detail* should an outline include? The answer is a corollary of the fact that an outline is a tool, a means to an end: It should include as much detail as will be helpful to the writer in making and revising his plan and in writing the composition itself.

The proper degree of detail, then, is a relative matter. An experienced writer may be able to produce a well-organized essay of several thousand words from an outline consisting of only a few main headings, or even from no outline at all; but the inexperienced writer will do well to make his plans more comprehensive. Ordinarily an outline should contain enough detail, or should be subdivided far enough, so that there will be a heading or subheading in the outline for each paragraph in the composition.[11] Usually, the writer will not be helped by subdivision beyond this point. Paragraphs have a logic and internal structure of which he should be thinking as he writes; if he has recorded the topics of his paragraphs, he will not have to try to remember two or three topics (or subtopics) at once, and he will write better paragraphs and develop his ideas more fully.

The topic outline for a composition of a few thousands of words might properly be subdivided to the fourth degree (small letters) or even beyond. On the other hand, the outline for a short theme of five hundred words—probably three to five paragraphs—might not be subdivided beyond the second degree (capital letters). In each case the degree of detail or of subdivision would be appropriate to the scope and complexity of the composition.

Making Final Decisions. The writer has three more decisions to make before writing the actual text of his composition: decisions regarding the level of usage he will employ, the tone or attitude that he will adopt, and the title of his theme. These decisions might have been made at an earlier stage in the planning, but it is just as proper that they should be deferred until now. They are in a degree interdependent, especially the first two; also, these first two are closely connected not only with the subject or material of the theme but also with a consideration of its audience and purpose.

[11] Sometimes, in a longer theme, there may be more than one paragraph corresponding to a single outline heading; at other times, in a shorter theme, a single paragraph may include the material represented by more than one outline heading or subheading. Generally, however, this rule holds good.

Level of Usage. The writer should select the *level of usage* that will seem natural and specially suitable to his audience. (See Chapter 1.) He may choose the formal level if his subject is serious and his intention is to explain something soberly or to convince by careful reasoning addressed to the reader's intellect. Under different circumstances, the informal level might be preferable. The subject may be not quite so serious or, though still serious, it may be such that a discussion of it in informal terms would be fitting. If the purpose is to persuade by appealing at least partly to the emotions, then for most readers the informal level will probably be most effective. (In description and narrative there may be a combination of the levels, possibly including the vulgate in dialogue.)

John Lloyd's subject is of course not frivolous, but neither is it of such gravity that a relatively informal treatment would be improper. He is writing, in the first instance, for his instructor, but he envisions a wider audience of his classmates or fellow undergraduates. In explaining his subject he means his account to be taken with some seriousness, and he intends it also to be entertaining. He decides, then, to employ the informal level of usage.

Tone. *Tone* is the writer's attitude toward his subject, his audience, or both. It is closely related to level of usage and may even be said to overlap with it, for the level of usage is one of the means by which tone is communicated. Also, certain of the same distinctions obtain: tone, too, may be formal, or informal, serious or not so serious—all the way to humorous or whimsical. But with tone there are many *more* distinctions: it may be gay, sentimental, indignant, straightforward, ironical; the possibilities, including combinations and various shadings, are very numerous.

Perhaps the most useful consideration is the distinction between an impersonal and a relatively personal tone. In certain contexts the writing should be completely impersonal; in the exposition of a technical process, for example, or the objective account of how a machine or other device operates, it would be inappropriate for the writer to interpose his own personality or "stand between" the audience and the subject. In other contexts—a friendly letter, for instance, or a narrative sketch frankly based on personal experience—among the principal virtues may be the author's skillful injection of his own personality, his establishing an easy, informal, chatty relationship with his audience.

How is tone developed and communicated? The writer may develop a good personal tone, for example, without necessarily speaking in the first person. The very details of his expression, the idiom, the turns of thought and feeling, will reveal the attitude he has taken. It is important that he should give conscious and deliberate consideration in advance to the different possibilities of tone or attitude for his composition and make a proper choice. If he does this and if he employs the fitting level of usage, the tone he has selected will communicate itself.

We have already observed the considerations that led John Lloyd to decide upon the informal level of usage; these same considerations are relevant to his choice of tone. Also, we remember that although his theme will be chiefly expository, he intends to include an element of emotional appeal—to project something of the enjoyment that characterizes the group he is writing about. The tone of his composition may appropriately be fairly light, with a flicker of humor if he can manage it without strain. Although he is writing partly from his own experience, he decides not to use the first person, but still he will try to inject something of a personal flavor. Finally, there ought to be in the tone itself a suggestion of enthusiasm.

Title. If a good title for his composition has occurred to the writer at an earlier stage in his planning, he will have fixed upon it then; otherwise, it is reasonable for him to have waited until now to choose one. So far he has needed a subject, not a title. A *title* is a word or group of words prefixed to the composition; its relationship to the subject may be and usually is fairly close, but it need not always be direct and obvious.

For a serious, straightforward expository or serious argumentative theme, on the one hand, the title normally does bear a direct and immediately apparent relationship to the subject. The title for such a theme might well be "The Operation of a Diesel Engine," "How to Change a Tire," or " The Advantages of Club Membership." For a different kind of theme, on the other hand, such as one in which the tone is not so serious or the purpose involves at least an element of emotional appeal, the relationship might be a little more devious, less obvious but more suggestive. A phrase in the composition itself may sometimes be a good title; in this case the final choice of title comes even later in the whole process, after the text has been written or perhaps even after revision.

Let us say that John Lloyd decides tentatively on the simple title "The Chanticleers"; he may change it later if a better one occurs to him.

Preparing the Text. The writer has now arrived at the last major step in writing a composition: *preparing the text* itself. He has paved the way for the actual putting of the sentences and paragraphs on paper by exercising care and judgment in choosing a subject; focusing; gathering, selecting, and then organizing the material; making intelligent use of an outline; and deciding consciously upon the appropriate level of usage and tone.

This last major step actually consists of four sub-steps: writing at least one preliminary draft, putting it aside for a waiting period, revising it carefully, and then preparing the final manuscript. (If the final manuscript is preceded by more than one preliminary draft, as may oftentimes be necessary, then the first three of these sub-steps will be repeated.)

First Draft. With his plan in mind and his outline at hand, the writer should write the *first draft* of his theme rather quickly. Of course he should do the best writing he *can* do at this quick tempo, but he should not delay over particular expressions, or worry greatly about attaining the best possible phraseology in his first draft. If he is not sure of some details—like punctuation marks, or the spellings of a few words—he should put down what he believes to be correct, rather than stopping to check on them at this time. (A good practice is to encircle the item about which he is unsure and to put a question mark in the margin beside it to remind himself to check it later.) It is important that he write steadily, without interruption, so that his train of thought will not be broken.

For a short theme, the first draft should be written at one sitting. For a longer theme, which will require more than one sitting, the writer should decide in advance upon a section of reasonable length and write this at once; at his next sitting he should read over what he has written, decide upon the next section to be written, and proceed immediately. He should take whatever measures he can to avoid interruptions during a writing session.

The first draft of John Lloyd's composition, with revisions indicated, appears later in the section on revision.

Waiting Period. As long a *waiting period* as possible should elapse between the writing and the revising of the first draft. The reason is that the longer lapse of time enables the writer to be more objective in reading, constructively criticizing, and improving his own words than he would be immediately after having written them.

In the normal composition course there are practical limits on the application of this principle. If topics for short themes are assigned only a week in advance, there cannot be a very long waiting period. The student may begin to make his plans immediately after the assignment is given, but at least a day or two will probably elapse before the first draft is written. In fact, there is value in the writer's allowing himself a day or two for thinking about his topic and making his plans carefully, before he writes his first draft. For a short theme, then, the maximum possible waiting period between first draft and revision may be only four or five days. Topics for longer themes and especially for term papers may be assigned from a few weeks to two or three months in advance of a due date. For a longer theme, the writer should try earnestly to complete his first draft as long as possible before the final composition is due, to allow for an adequate waiting period.

Revision. After the waiting period has elapsed, the writer should go back to his first draft and subject it to close and critical scrutiny. Now is the time for him to check and, if necessary, correct the details that he marked while he was writing the first draft, and also to investigate any other details that he may now find questionable. He should check the larger features too, making sure that the over-all organization is logical and that the relationships among his ideas will be apparent to the reader; he should add any necessary transitional expressions to clarify connections that may have been blurred in the rapid first writing. He should be on the lookout, too, for expressions that he can shorten or eliminate without loss to the meaning—to improve the economy and generally tighten his composition. Every paragraph, every sentence, every phrase should be examined; in each case, the question in the writer's mind should be, "Is this the most effective expression for the purpose? If not, what is the best improvement I can make?" [12]

The importance of *revision* can hardly be overstated, especially since this process is probably the one most frequently slighted by inexperienced writers. Many, many potentially good themes are kept by inadequate revision from becoming as good as they should and readily could be. The temptation is great, once a draft has been written, for the writer simply to copy it off and hand it in. But resisting this temptation is fully, even richly, worth while. Revision *after* the theme has been handed in, graded, and returned is usually required; for this the student will have the benefit of the instructor's comments. But the revising that the student does on his own, *before* submitting the theme, is even more valuable. Incidentally, it will make more difference in his grade; more importantly, it will be the most helpful single exercise that he can perform for improving his own writing ability.

Next is given, for illustration, the first draft of John Lloyd's theme, with several revisions indicated.

[12] On at least the first several occasions when he is revising his work, an inexperienced writer (or one who has much trouble with mechanics) will find an even more systematic procedure helpful. He should give his paper a number of separate readings; in one, he should look for spelling errors; in another, errors in punctuation; in another, errors in grammar and sentence structure; and in yet another, possibilities for improvement in paragraphing and organization.

~~The Chanticleers~~

Song Is Supreme [13]

Like many another momentous event, the birth of the male
singing group known as the Chanticleers was really accidental. Five years ago this October, the Dramatic Club was
planning a Hallowe'en program. They were going to present
not a regular play but an original variety show; one of the
members had already worked up a script. ~~But a variety show~~
~~must have music; it must have singing, preferably group~~
~~singing. The regular Glee Club was too large for the pur-~~
~~pose and also too dignified to do the kind of singing that~~
~~would be appropriate for the show.~~[14] ∧ But Who would provide
the music? Another member, Larry Everts, ~~had the answer;~~
~~at least, he~~ soon found ~~it.~~ ∧ the answer. [15] Himself a ~~member of the~~
bass ~~section~~[16] in the Glee Club, he recruited a few of his
friends from that source and a few more singers of whose
ability he had learned by ∧ critical listening in the dormitory
shower room. He rehearsed his draftees on a few "Hallowe'en-ish" numbers and got them ready in time to sing for
the show. They all ∧ enjoyed the experience so much [17] ~~had such a good time~~ that they--and
their successors, recruited in the same informal fashion,
whenever vacancies occur--have kept on singing ever since.

They have sung on many different occasions, and for many
different audiences. In that first year, ∧ when [18] the group was
still really an adjunct of the Dramatic Club, [18] they ap-

---

[13] See the revision of the final sentence and footnote 26 below, page 58.
[14] Eliminated as superfluous; most of this goes without saying.
[15], [16] Revisions for economy without loss to the meaning.
[17] Changed to avoid repetition of the word *time*.
[18] Changed to improve the sentence structure by subordination.

peared in another variety show a few weeks later, and in

one regular musical play: when the Club presented The

                                      roistering

Beggar's Opera, the Chants were the chorus of ∧ highway-

men—a collective role which they acted and sang with
gusto.
∧ elan.[19] But from then on they have been making independ-

ent appearances, at dormitory parties, campus dances, and

other social functions. Just this year they received what

                                accolade [20]

was in effect a kind of special ∧ distinction, although at

first they had been a little skeptical about the idea—an

invitation to sing at a Men's Faculty Club stag dinner.

The Chants' singing is not precisely dignified, and they

wondered how it would strike a group of eminently dignified

                             here [21]

gentlemen and scholars. But ∧ it was a chance to sing;

that is all they needed, or ever need. Professor Gosner,

                                 wince [22]

who directs the regular Glee Club, was seen to ∧ be a

little startled at the lush barber-shop harmonies, but at

the end he applauded with obvious sincerity.

The Chanticleers do have one favorite kind of occasion

for singing: a dance at a nearby women's college. The

first time they appeared at such a function was in the

winter of their second year. It was rumored that the

                              have been [23]

making of this particular arrangement might ∧ be related to

the fact that the girl who was chairman of the Midwinter

Prom committee was wearing Larry Everts' class ring. But

no such ulterior circumstance was necessary for the con-

tinuing of what soon became a pleasant custom. In the

---

[19] Replacement of a foreign word by a fully naturalized one.
[20] Substitution of what John believes to be an apt metaphor.
[21] Changed to avoid ambiguity in the antecedent of *it*.
[22] Substitution of a more vivid expression.
[23] Changed to make the tense relationship more logical.

✓ ⸌Spring [24] the Chants sang at three more such dances, one

at that same college and two at another; and the next

autumn—after both Larry and the Prom committee chairman
        been [25]
had ∧ graduated—the appearances continued. Since then

there has been no year in which the Chants have not sung

for at least half a dozen of these dances.

    The fact that these <u>are</u> their favorite occasions implies

perhaps that romance, actual or potential, provides for

them the most pleasant kind of atmosphere for singing. But

the Chants will sing virtually anywhere, at any time—

simply because they like to sing. For the Chanticleers,
       women and wine are wonderful, but song is supreme.[26]
∧ ~~wine is good and women are better, but song is best of~~

~~all~~.

Final Manuscript. After careful revision the writer prepares the *final manuscript* which he will submit. In general he just makes a clean copy of his revised draft. This is a relatively simple process, but here too he should be critically alert. No matter how carefully he has revised, additional improvements in expression may still suggest themselves to him. If he is sure they are improvements, he should incorporate them.

The composition should be written in ink, or preferably typed; typescript should be double-spaced. The writing should appear on one side of the paper only, with ample margins. Detailed instructions for the form of the final manuscript—including how it should be endorsed with the student's name and other data, and sometimes what particular kind of paper should be used—vary among different institutions; the student should follow scrupulously whatever instructions he is given.

When the manuscript is finally completed, the writer should look it

[24] While writing his first draft, John thought *spring* should be capitalized, but he was not sure; he made a mark in the margin. Checking later, he found that the names of seasons are not capitalized.

[25] Inserted for preferable usage.

[26] Being eager to make his final sentence as effective as possible, John worked over it for a while. It occurred to him that by using alliteration (*w*omen—*w*ine—*w*onderful, *s*ong—*s*upreme) he could give the sentence a little extra fillip. Notice that he substituted the final alliterative phrase, "song is supreme," for the original title of his theme. The phrase does in a sense epitomize his central idea.

over carefully once more. Though he has taken care, he may have made mistakes in copying or typographical errors. If, as is sometimes permitted, someone else has typed the final copy, the writer should check it very closely, for he is himself responsible for everything in the composition.

Exercises

1. Indicate whether each of the following statements is true or false.

——a. The most important kind of coherence is based on organic relationships among the parts.

——b. The central effect of a composition addressed chiefly to the reader's emotions must be a single feeling, pure and unmixed.

——c. The most emphatic position in the whole composition is at the beginning.

——d. Good style is inconspicuous.

——e. A good choice of subject for an inexperienced writer would be the feelings of a condemned man on the eve of his execution.

——f. After receiving a theme assignment, the writer should sometimes allow himself a day or two to think about his subject, rather than beginning immediately to write his first draft.

——g. The writer of an argumentative theme addressed chiefly to the intellect should decide upon a central emotional effect rather than a central idea.

——h. As he writes his first draft, the writer should take time to check all mechanical details about which he is uncertain.

——i. Ordinarily a topic outline should be subdivided to the paragraph level.

——j. Level of usage is one of the means by which tone is developed.

2. Fill in the blanks in the following statements:

a. The principal criteria for choosing among optional topics for a short theme are the writer's ———— of and his ———— in the different topics given.

b. The two principal aspects of organization are proportion and ————.

c. The two chief types of outlines are the ———— outline and the ———— outline.

d. The criterion of functional material is that it be closely related to the ———— ———— or the ———— ———— ———— of the composition.

e. In a theme discussing one's country, one's alma mater, and one's God as proper objects of devotion, the best sequence in which to arrange these would presumably be: (1) ————, (2) ————, (3) ————.

3. Indicate whether each of the following would be appropriate as a statement of the central idea or emotional effect of a composition. For any that would not be, indicate why not.

    a. I shall discuss campus publications.

    b. The team should have a good average this year.

    c. Evening is a time of quietness and tranquillity.

    d. My theme will be about hunting, fishing, and trapping.

    e. My father has a good sense of humor.

4. Indicate whether each of the following brief topic outlines is logical. Diagnose any failure in logic by citing the pertinent rule.

    a. (Principal means of news dissemination)

        I. The Printed Word

            A. Newspapers and Magazines

        II. The Spoken Word

            A. Radio

    b. (Types of competitive sports)

        I. Primarily Team Sports

            A. Football

            B. Baseball

            C. Basketball

        II. Primarily Individual Sports

            A. Tennis

            B. Swimming

            C. Track

4 SHORT EXPOSITORY THEMES

Exposition is the orderly setting forth of facts and ideas. Its purpose is to explain; its language is clear and direct; its appeal is to the intellect rather than to the emotions of the reader. As we shall see from a number of examples, exposition answers questions like *What is science? What are the provinces of law? How should a student rehearse a speech?* The person who reads answers to questions like these becomes better informed on the subjects concerned. Thus, expository writing is informative writing.

Within the general form of exposition are special forms, each resulting from a particular method of explaining. This chapter describes and illustrates representative types of these special forms: extended definition, analysis, process (a special kind of analysis), summary, review, and report. It also mentions the essay type of examination, which is not in itself a special type of exposition but which may call for the use of one or more of the special types.

Most of the examples in the following discussion are formal essays. Actually, writers use the same methods, such as defining and analyzing, in informal (personal) essays as in formal essays. "How to Bathe a Pup," for instance, suggests a whimsical explanation of a process. The difference in the two types of essays is one of tone, level of usage, and the degree to which the author allows his personality to enter into his writing. (See Chapters 1 and 3 for discussions of level of usage and tone.)

DEFINITION

Definition is the exposition of the meanings of words. The users of any language set limits as to what the various words in that language shall signify. The clearer these limits are to both writer and reader, the clearer will be the communication of ideas from the mind of the writer to that of the reader. Definition is the more or less formal expounding of these limits for the purpose of clear communication.

Many English words are so firmly fixed in meaning that a writer can use them without danger of confusing his reader. Often, however, the writer has occasion to define an unfamiliar word or an abstract term for which usage has not established unmistakable limits in meaning.

In this he may use only a sentence definition, or he may extend his definition to a paragraph or more.

Sentence Definition. A formal sentence definition is a statement that names the thing to be defined, classifies it, and differentiates it from other things in the same class (see Chapter 2). In other words, the definition tells what the thing is in general and then what it is in particular. When we say, for instance, "a radiomicrophone is a mechanism that changes sound energy into electrical energy," we first group the radiomicrophone with other mechanisms, such as lamps and record players, and then set it apart from them by describing its special function. Or when we say "an anapest is a metrical foot consisting of two unaccented syllables followed by an accented syllable," we first classify the anapest with other metrical feet, such as iambs and trochees, and then differentiate it from them by noting the particular number and arrangement of its syllables.

Sentence definitions appear frequently in factual prose, as an examination of a few nonfictional books and magazines will reveal. Sometimes a sentence definition serves as part of an extended definition. It is this longer type of definition that is our chief concern here.

Extended Definition. An *extended definition,* which usually contains a sentence definition,[1] is a detailed explanation of the meaning of a term. The definition may be developed by comparison, illustration, restatement, etymology, or indeed by any method or combination of methods through which the reader will understand a term precisely as the writer does. At times the writer may attempt to avoid possible confusion in the reader's mind by explaining what a term does not mean as well as what it does mean.

Ordinarily a definition, even when extended in length, is only part of a larger composition and should therefore fit into the larger framework and supplement the larger purpose of the whole. This relationship is especially necessary when the definition explains at the outset how a term will be used in a particular composition, thus implying that in other contexts the same term may have other meanings. The next two excerpts illustrate this point and show a few of the methods which writers commonly use to develop definitions.

The author of a book about certain basic scientific principles devotes his opening paragraph to defining the term *science.*

---

[1] Although the sentence definition is not essential, it is a unifying device in writing a deductively extended definition (an initial sentence definition amplified by suitable particulars and details) or an inductively extended definition (relevant particulars and details leading up to a final sentence definition).

In this book the word "science" will be taken to include all the natural sciences, physical and biological, and also such parts of psychology and of the social sciences (anthropology, sociology, economics) as are concerned with an empirical subject-matter. It will exclude all philosophy which is not 'general science', all history which is concerned merely with the occurrence of particular historical events, and the disciplines of pure mathematics and symbolic logic which are not (except, perhaps, in a very peculiar sense) about empirical facts at all. This sense of the word "science" corresponds pretty closely with the most frequent modern use of the word (whose first public use was perhaps in the title of the British Association for the Advancement of Science, founded in 1831); it is synonymous with "natural science" if man is included within nature.[2]

The second illustration of the extended definition is part of an introductory chapter on dramatic art. The author uses etymology and examples to define the term *playwright*.

There are several names for the author of a dramatic work: the Greeks called him a poet; later ages have called him a dramatist or playwright. Of these terms, playwright is perhaps the most precise, though to students its orthography is as baffling as its etymology should be illuminating. In English, the suffix *-wright* means maker, as in *shipwright* or *wheelwright;* hence a playwright is not a playwriter but a playmaker, an artisan who, out of many materials and with divers tools, designs, shapes and builds the form of narrative we call a play. To understand the proper spelling of *playwright* is to have constantly in mind a unique characteristic of his art: he works not just with words but with many other tools, all of which must be considered in understanding the dramatic experience.

The poet and the novelist work with words, the musician with notes and sounds, the painter with colors. The playwright works with verbal tools, like the poet and novelist; with human tools, the actors, their bodies and faces, voices and movements; and with mechanical inorganic tools, the theater and its machinery. Thespis, as playwright, took the tools that were available to him—the threshing floor, the altar, the priest of Dyonysos and the chorus of worshippers—and stepped into the situation himself to create the kind of immediacy that constitutes dramatic action. The unknown Christian master [the playwright responsible for *Quem Quaeritis* (*Whom Seek Ye*), about A.D. 975], who may or may not have been one of the participating priests, followed the same method and the same inspiration in building or making his play.[3]

    [2] Reprinted with permission from Richard Bevan Braithwaite, *Scientific Explanation: A Study of the Function of Theory, Probability and Law in Science* (Cambridge: At the University Press, 1953), p. 1.

    [3] Reprinted with permission from Alan S. Downer, *The Art of the Play* (New York: Henry Holt & Co., Inc., 1955), pp. 11–12.

As we have seen, the extended definition is seldom written as an independent composition; it more often forms a significant part of a longer work. The types of exposition discussed in the rest of this chapter, though sometimes forming parts of longer works, are frequently written as independent compositions.

ANALYSIS

Closely related to definition is *analysis,* a kind of exposition often employed in short themes. Analysis is the orderly breaking down of a subject into its logical parts. We may speak of the logical parts or the different types of analysis; that is, we may analyze analysis itself. The basic types are the classification of plural subjects; the division (sometimes called partitioning) of singular subjects; and what is actually a special instance of the latter, but important enough to warrant separate consideration, the exposition of a process.[4]

Classification. In *classification,* we break down a plural subject; we classify its members according to a single basis common to all.[5] The single basis is necessary to prevent illogical overlapping of the parts. We can classify dogs, for example, on the basis of breed as Airedales, fox terriers, schnauzers, and so on. But a grouping of dogs as Airedales, watchdogs, and puppies would not be a logical classification because the basis shifts from breed to utility and then to age. We can classify automobiles on the basis of make as Fords, Chevrolets, Plymouths, Studebakers, and so on. But a grouping of automobiles as Fords, station wagons, convertibles, and pink Cadillacs would be illogical because the basis shifts from manufacture to body style and then to a combination of

---

[4] Analysis is sometimes analyzed on another basis; that is, the different types are determined according to a different criterion. Thus we speak of structural, functional, and chronological analysis. *Structural analysis* is based on the physical properties of the parts into which the subject is analyzed or on their status as distinguishable units in an actual structure, like the torso, head, and limbs of the human body. *Functional analysis,* as the name implies, is based on the purposes which the different parts serve, like the legislative, executive, and judicial branches of the government. In *chronological analysis* the parts are divisions of a continuous length of time, like morning, afternoon, and evening.

The criterion of considering whether analysis is classification, division, or exposition of a process is more generally useful and is therefore the one which is followed in the text. It may be noted, however, that of the three extended examples given, the account (pp. 65–66) of the different kinds of coal, illustrating classification, is also an example of structural analysis; the selection (pp. 66–67) about the law, illustrating division, also shows functional analysis; and the passage (pp. 70–71) from Franklin, illustrating the exposition of a process, is essentially chronological.

[5] For the basic rules of classification, see Chapter 2.

color and manufacture. The illogical groupings readily show how failure to keep a single basis throughout one stage of a classification soon leads to overlapping: Airedales could also be puppies; Fords could also be convertibles. In a logical classification the parts are mutually exclusive and, when added up, make the whole subject.

Complete and Partial Classifications. In practical composition the writer sometimes does not need to discuss all the items in a *complete* classification, but he should indicate at the outset what limitations he intends to set. A writer of a six-hundred-word theme could hardly accomplish a classification of *all* dogs on the basis of breed, but he could probably do a commendable analysis beginning "The dogs I have owned include a collie, a cocker spaniel, and a dachshund."

There are many ways to inform readers that restrictions in coverage are intentional, not inadvertent. Here are a few possible opening sentences for short themes intended to cover only certain parts of the intended classifications.

It is in Shakespeare's comedies—not in his tragedies or historical plays—that matchmaking flourishes among minor characters.

Although other remedies are being used to control hay fever, this paper is concerned only with the use of antihistamines in the treatment of this affliction.

Most travelers heading southward from St. Louis use the railroad, airline, or highway, but I prefer the river.

Such an introductory sentence serves to make clear to the reader what the scope of the ensuing discussion will be.

Natural and Arbitrary Classifications. Many classifications are actually made by *nature* and merely observed by man; others are *arbitrarily* made by man. When he classifies rocks as igneous, sedimentary, and metamorphic, the geologist is observing how rocks fall naturally into three groups according to the analytical principle of their mode of origin. When he classifies coals by ranks, however, he decides arbitrarily where one rank stops and another starts. The following analysis makes this point clear.

Coals are classified according to *ranks* by a combination of their fixed-carbon content and their physical properties. As there is a continuous gradation from low-rank to high-rank coals, the divisions adopted are necessarily arbitrary.

The lowest-rank coals are the *lignites,* so called because of their obviously woody appearance, or *brown coals,* in reference to their color. They are highly immature coals. When taken from the mine they may appear to be perfectly dry, but may contain as much as 30 to 40 per cent of water. On exposure they lose most of this water; they slack and crumble to pieces and are likely to take fire spontaneously.

The medium-rank coals are the *bituminous*. They do not slack on exposure and generally have a prismatic jointing perpendicular to their banding. As there is no hard and fast line between lignite and bituminous coal, the intermediate varieties are termed *subbituminous*. Their black color and nonwoody structure distinguish them from the lowest-rank lignites, and their tendency to slack distinguishes them from the high-rank bituminous coals.

The highest-rank coal is *anthracite*. It differs physically from the bituminous varieties by its conchoidal fracture and absence of cross-jointing. Water and volatile matter are extremely low, and nearly all the carbon is fixed carbon.

The increase in the rank of a coal, then, is marked by the progressive increase in the fixed-carbon content and by the diminution of the content of water.[6]

Division. Single units as well as groups of units can be analyzed. Corresponding to the classification of plural subjects is the *division,* or partitioning, of singular subjects. Books are classified (as in the card catalogue of a library[7]); the substance of one book is divided into parts, or partitioned (as in its table of contents).

Division is the analytical technique a writer employs when he examines the various aspects of an idea. The author of the next selection analyzes the domain of law, first on the basis of the purpose of the law, then on the basis of the degree of government concern with the law.

The field of social action which is the domain of Law divides itself into three great provinces: there is an administrative law that lays down the duties of subjects towards a government, and there are a criminal and a civil law, which are alike concerned with acts in which both parties are private persons, but which nevertheless differ, from a government's point of view, in the degree to which they affect governmental interests.

No government, of course, can be indifferent to administrative law; indeed, it is no exaggeration to say that this province of law is bound to have priority over any government's other concerns; for the first concern of a government is to keep itself in existence; it cannot exist if it does not effectively impose its authority on its subjects by preventing or repressing

[6] Reprinted with permission from C. R. Longwell, A. Knopf, and R. F. Flint, *Outlines of Physical Geology* (2nd ed.; New York: John Wiley & Sons, Inc., 1941), Part I, p. 321.

[7] In most large libraries, the card catalogue represents a multiple analysis; that is, it classifies books according to author, title, and subject.

all those acts of insubordination—ranging from high treason to arrears in the payment of taxes—in which a subject may show himself recalcitrant to a government's will; and the enforcement of governmental authority requires the formulation and execution of a body of administrative law. The same considerations lead governments, in so far as they have the strength, to concern themselves with the criminal law as well; for, though the criminal may not be attacking his government's authority intentionally or consciously in his assaults upon the life, limb, or property of his fellow subjects, he is in fact trespassing on the government's preserves by arrogating to himself, without official licence, a use of force which the government must jealously preserve as its own monopoly if it is to maintain its authority intact. It will be seen that, in concerning itself with the criminal as well as with the administrative law, a government is primarily actuated by the motive of self-preservation, and for this reason there is in these two provinces of law a close approach to uniformity in the practice of all governments of both the parochial and the universal type. On the other hand, as far as they concern themselves with civil law, governments are acting for Society's and the individual's benefit more directly than for their own: and accordingly we shall not be surprised to find an empirical survey here revealing wide differences in the practice of those universal states which are our subject in the present Part of this Study.[8]

Process. The exposition of a *process* is the explanation of how a thing works or how to do something. Such exposition is common in textbooks, in popular magazines, in leaflets accompanying manufactured products, and in numerous other places where methods of operation need to be made clear to certain groups of readers. Technically, however, the explanation of a process can hardly be considered a distinct type of exposition.

Relation to Other Expository Types. The exposition of a process is really a special type of analysis, and it may call for the use of definition.

The explanation of a process is an analysis in that the writer breaks down the total process into steps or stages and presents them, one at a time, in chronological order. A writer explaining how to administer artificial respiration, how to build a carport, or how to use a voting machine tells the reader what to do first, what to do next, and so on. The writer also makes clear the relationships among the steps and the relationship between each step and the whole operation.

The exposition of a process may include a definition, especially if the name of the process is unfamiliar to the intended readers or if the account concerns the operation of a mechanical device. An explanation

[8] Reprinted with permission from Arnold J. Toynbee, *A Study of History* (London: Oxford University Press, Inc., 1954), VII, 255–256.

of how to refute an argument, for instance, could open with a definition of the term *refutation*. An explanation of how to do rotary plowing could start with a definition that differentiates rotary plowing from other kinds of plowing and points out the special purpose that rotary plowing serves. Or an explanation of how an ophthalmoscope works might well begin with a statement defining the ophthalmoscope and describing its purpose. The writer should remember that his reason for including a definition is to help explain the process.

Adaptation to Readers. To explain a process accurately and clearly, the writer needs not only a thorough and preferably first-hand knowledge of the process itself but also knowledge of his reading audience. When he knows the level of understanding of his readers he is better able to use the right kind of language—language that is neither too technical to be understandable nor too simplified to be interesting to the readers—and to select appropriate illustrations and comparisons. Mentioning potentiometers and superheterodyne receivers without explaining what they are would be acceptable in an article intended for radio engineers but not in one intended for department-store salesmen.

A knowledge of his readers also enables the writer to select the proper verb forms. For an audience of observers, the writer ordinarily uses the third person, indicative mood (e.g., "Arctic explorers begin their preparations months in advance"), and sometimes the passive voice (e.g., "In the Midwest, potatoes are planted during the latter half of March"). For an audience of participants, the writer may properly employ the second person, imperative mood (e.g., "As soon as you have filled the crevice with plastic wood, scrape off the excess with a straight-edged knife or other implement"). For either kind of readers—observers or participants—or for a mixed audience, the writer may find it convenient to use the first person (e.g., "When I tool a book cover, I first assemble my materials"). Whatever forms he selects, the writer should use them consistently throughout his account.

The following explanations of processes illustrate what we have just said about the choice of verb forms. In the brief first example the author, obviously writing for observers, employs the third person, indicative mood (and chiefly the passive voice) to explain a heating process.

Heat is spread through a substance, or between two substances in contact with each other, by the flow of energy from warm to less warm adjacent molecules. This process is known as *conduction*. Thus, a spoon in a very hot liquid will become warm to the touch, even at the handle, which is not in direct contact with the liquid. In the same manner, the atmosphere in contact with the earth may be warmed by conduction. The subsoil also may be warmed by conduction from the topsoil. Most solids and liquids are better heat conductors than air, and moist air is a better conductor than dry air.[9]

The author of the next example uses the second person, imperative mood, in explaining a rehearsal procedure to speech students; that is, to an audience of potential participants. In keeping with the general tone, the style is informal; notice, for instance, the use of contractions. This example also demonstrates well the analytical nature of the exposition of a process.

Although there is no single procedure that will fit all individual needs, try the procedure below, following it meticulously for your first speeches and later changing it if necessary to fit your own requirements. The scheme is based on this psychological fact: the mind gives preference to a whole over its parts, to the stream of ideas in a sequence rather than the eddies. To use this procedure is to provide good insurance against omitting the main logical items and forgetting at joints and transitions. The procedure is designed, also, to keep your attention on *ideas,* not on language and phraseology.

Get acquainted with the general pattern of ideas.

Read through your speech outline silently, slowly, thoughtfully, from beginning to end. *Repeat.* (Caution: Don't back-track for any reason; and don't go back for details.)

Read the outline aloud, thoughtfully and deliberately; don't hurry.

Abandoning your outline, again go through your speech aloud *from beginning to end*. Don't back up for any reason, even if you know that you have forgotten a major item, and even if what is to be a 5-minute speech takes only a minute.

Reread silently your speech outline once again.

Practice aloud, again going through from start to finish without backing up.

If by this time the speech isn't running pretty well for you, continue to alternate silent study with oral practice.

Present an oral abstract of your speech. Include items in the abstract in this order: the purpose of your speech, the subject sentence, and the main heads. Your ability to whip through an abstract should mean to you that your mind has clearly grasped the chief parts of a patterned sequence.

[9] Reprinted with permission from L. E. Klimm, O. P. Starkey, and J. A. Russell, *Introductory Economic Geography* (3rd ed.; New York: Harcourt, Brace & Co., Inc., 1956), p. 82.

Polish the details.

Once you have control over your speech as a whole, you can afford to pay attention to details that you have been omitting or to parts that you have been stumbling over. If details are already in hand, you need not be concerned with the steps below.

Practice *transitions*. These are the hardest details for most speakers—even experienced ones—to manage well. Practice on them helps in keeping your attention on the relationship of one part of the speech to the next part, and hence strengthens your grasp on the path and structure of your ideas. In a conventionally arranged speech the chief transitions are signpost sentences or phrases at these points:

From statement of purpose to subject sentence.

From subject sentence and its preliminary explanation to main head I.

From main head I and its treatment to main head II, and so on.

From the final head and its treatment to the conclusion and summary.

Practice *other parts that have given you difficulty,* the conclusion, the introduction, examples and their details, comparisons, contrasts, quotations.[10]

Next, Benjamin Franklin, writing for a mixed audience, uses the first person to explain the way in which he improved his composition.

About this time I met with an odd volume of the *Spectator*. It was the third. I had never before seen any of them. I bought it, read it over and over, and was much delighted with it. I thought the writing excellent, and wished, if possible, to imitate it. With that view I took some of the papers, and, making short hints of the sentiment in each sentence, laid them by a few days, and then, without looking at the book, tried to complete the papers again by expressing each hinted sentiment at length, and as fully as it had been expressed before, in any suitable words that should come to hand. Then I compared my *Spectator* with the original, discovered some of my faults, and corrected them. But I found I wanted a stock of words, or a readiness in recollecting and using them, which I thought I should have acquired before that time if I had gone on making verses; since the continual occasion for words of the same import, but of different length to suit the measure, or of different sound for the rhyme, would have laid me under a constant necessity of searching for variety and also have tended to fix that variety in my mind and make me master of it. Therefore, I took some of the tales and turned them into verse; and, after a time, when I had pretty well forgotten the prose, turned them back again. I also sometimes jumbled my collections of hints into confusion, and after some weeks endeavored to

[10] Reprinted with permission from Donald C. Bryant and Karl R. Wallace, *Fundamentals of Public Speaking* (3rd ed.; New York: Appleton-Century-Crofts, Inc., 1960), pp. 205–206.

reduce them into the best order, before I began to form the full sentences and complete the paper. This was to teach me method in the arrangment of thoughts. By comparing my work afterwards with the original, I discovered many faults and amended them; but I sometimes had the pleasure of fancying that in certain particulars of small import I had been lucky enough to improve the method or the language, and this encouraged me to think I might possibly in time come to be a tolerable English writer, of which I was extremely ambitious.[11]

Recognizing Written Analyses. The ability to recognize *written analyses* as such enables the reader to provide himself with models for his own analytical composition. Since a written analysis is always reducible to outline form, the student will find that simple outlining of what he reads, especially in his textbooks, will help him recognize the analytical techniques in applied form.

Suppose that in one of his textbooks the student reads an account of prehistoric human culture. The essence of the account, he sees, is that human prehistory consisted of three ages, the first of which was a progression through three stages. He arranges these items chronologically in simple outline form, as follows, and realizes that what he has just read is an analysis: a partitioning of a singular subject (human prehistory) according to a single basis (the nature of the man-made objects which have been preserved from prehistoric times).

PREHISTORIC HUMAN CULTURE
I. Stone Age
　　A. Eolithic Stage
　　B. Paleolithic Stage
　　C. Neolithic Stage
II. Bronze Age
III. Age of Iron

The analysis can be represented equally well in a simple diagram.

PREHISTORIC HUMAN CULTURE

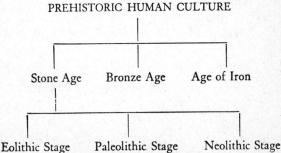

Stone Age　　　Bronze Age　　　Age of Iron

Eolithic Stage　　Paleolithic Stage　　Neolithic Stage

[11] *Autobiography* (New York: Rinehart & Company, Inc., 1948), pp. 13–14.

The student who learns to recognize and follow logical classifications and divisions in this manner will find these techniques valuable in any field of study. That is, he will be able to see similar parts in their relation to the whole thing they constitute.

Planning Analytical Themes. Topics suitable for short *analytical themes* are innumerable. The writer need only apply these questions to the things, persons, and ideas he is constantly encountering: Can I classify the members of this or that group according to a particular principle? Can I divide this or that unit on a single basis? If he finds one thing that all members of the group or all parts of the unit have in common, he is ready to answer *yes* to these questions.

A group of persons working together or assembled for a common purpose is always a potential subject for a short analytical theme. Let us suppose, for instance, that a student is a guest on an educational television program, or out of curiosity visits a local television station, and becomes interested in the crew of about ten or twelve persons he sees producing the program. If he really observes [12] what each of these persons is doing, he can gather material for an interesting analytical theme. Analyzing the crew on the basis of their duties, he may discover an organization with two categories: in the first category is one person, the producer-director, giving various orders to the other workers and controlling the buttons which transmit the images to home televiewers; in the second category are a floor manager, a technical director, a lighting director, two cameramen (one with his camera resting on the floor and one with his camera mounted on a dolly), a microphone operator, a video control operator, an audio control operator, a co-ordinator, and an announcer—each following instructions from the producer-director and each performing his own special duties. At this point in his observation the student can make a simple outline for his theme, an outline that shows the basic plan of organization of the crew. By the time he has proceeded through this basic plan with a discussion of the duties of each person, the student will have written an informative analysis of the way in which the particular television production crew he observed functions.

Notice that this proposed analysis is limited to the production crew; that is, it does not include the cast or possible guest performers. The performers would make a suitable subject for another short analytical theme.

---

[12] Observation in this case would doubtless require several visits to the studio. The writer may even find it necessary to interview certain members of the crew concerning their respective duties.

SUMMARY

A *summary* is the expression, in condensed terms, of the principal content of any piece of writing.[13] In the summarizer's own words, it sets forth briefly the central idea of the original; depending on its scope and purpose, it may also include some of the supporting material.

Approximately synonymous with summary are a few other words, bearing special connotations or usually appearing in particular contexts. A *précis*, for instance, is generally understood to be an orderly condensation that preserves the main thought, organization, and tone of the original. A *synopsis,* ordinarily used with reference to stories and plays, is a step-by-step account of the plot. An *abstract* is a very concise summary of the main points of a formal exposition or argument. The term *abstract* is often used with academic or legal reference: a Ph.D. candidate writes an abstract of his thesis; a lawyer makes abstracts of court records which may be pertinent to a case he has in hand.

A *paraphrase,* ordinarily associated with poetry, is a restatement of what is said in the original—a restatement in simpler or more literal language, reproducing the meaning of the original as precisely as possible. Unlike a précis, a synopsis, or an abstract, a paraphrase is often approximately equal to the original in length.

Steps in Summarizing. The procedure for preparing a summary of any kind consists of four steps: reading, selecting, writing, and comparing.

Reading. The first and possibly the most important step in summarizing is *reading* the original. The reading should be as careful and as frequent as is necessary in order to understand the original thoroughly. This step should include a consideration of the author's purpose in writing as well as an interpretation of his meaning.

Selecting. The second step is *selecting* from the original passage the central idea and, in the order of their importance, those supporting ideas that the purpose of the summary requires. "Selecting" as used here does not mean quoting; it means rather a mental restating of ideas in the summarizer's own words. Brief note-taking, also in the summarizer's

[13] If the passage to be summarized represents a form of discourse other than exposition, then the summary itself may appear to be otherwise than expository. For example, the summary of a persuasive sermon might have the argumentative form of the original. Virtually always, however, the basic purpose of the summary is to inform the reader what the content of the original is. (Even in the sermon summary, there is expressed or implied the idea that "the speaker exhorted his hearers to this effect"; i.e., "this is what the man said.") Therefore, the summary is properly considered to be an essentially expository genre.

own words, may be desirable if the summary is to be a long one. The notes, like the mental restatements, should reflect the relative importance of the ideas in the original.

Writing. The third step is *writing* the essential thought in brief form without referring directly to the original; if notes have been taken, as suggested in the second step, the writer should refer to them. The important thing here is to reconstruct ideas, not language, and to condense them without distorting their rank.

Comparing. The last step is *comparing* the written summary with the original passage to make sure that the essence of the original has been reproduced in distinctly different language, that the relative significance of any supporting ideas has been maintained, and that no idea which was not in the original has been introduced in the summary. This step includes whatever revising or rewriting the comparison indicates to be necessary.

Length of Summary. The summary should be shorter than the original piece of writing. How much shorter is determined by the purpose of the summary. If it is to serve as a self-aid in reviewing, the summary probably need give only a general statement of the essential thought of the original (see the summaries marked *A* in the examples which follow). If it is to serve as a note for possible use in a research paper, the summary probably should include the main supporting ideas (see the summaries marked *B*). If it is to serve as an answer to a question that calls for "details" or as an exercise in explaining the original to certain readers, the summary ought to go beyond the main supporting ideas to the lesser ones and to background information in the original (see the summaries marked *C*). Whatever its purpose, the summary never has to reflect any repetition of ideas that may appear in the original piece of writing.

In the left-hand column below is a passage written by Albert Einstein following the establishment of the League of Nations in 1919; in the right-hand column are three summaries of varying length.

PARADISE LOST

As late as the seventeenth century the savants and artists of all Europe were so closely united by the bond of a common ideal that cooperation between them was scarcely affected by political events. This unity was fur-

SUMMARY A

Problems of international scope like making the League of Nations are in the hands of politicians by default of the scholars.

SUMMARY B

In the twentieth century the politicians, not the scholars, are hand-

ther strengthened by the general use of the Latin language.

Today we look back at this state of affairs as at a lost paradise. The passions of nationalism have destroyed this community of intellect, and the Latin language which once united the whole world is dead. The men of learning have become representatives of the most extreme national traditions and lost their sense of an intellectual commonwealth.

Nowadays we are faced with the dismaying fact that the politicians, the practical men of affairs, have become the exponents of international ideas. It is they who have created the League of Nations.[14]

ling such international problems as establishing the League of Nations. Three centuries ago, it was the men of learning who fostered the ideal of an international community, and the men of affairs who were narrow nationalists. Today, unfortunately, their positions are reversed.

Summary C

Unfortunately, it is politics, not scholarship, that transcends national boundaries nowadays. The politicians, today's internationalists, have founded the League of Nations.

Up into the seventeenth century, European scholars were internationalists, all using Latin, all working in unison. Nationalism was for politicians then. But twentieth-century scholars, their Latin and their unison all but gone, are passionate nationalists who leave the realm of international ideas to the politicians.

Here are three more summaries of varying length. The document which is summarized is so well known and so readily available that it is not necessary to reprint it here; it is Abraham Lincoln's Gettysburg Address.

Summary A

The central significance of this occasion, for us who are still alive, is that we should continue to work for the accomplishment of that purpose for which our soldiers who died here gave their lives: the championing of freedom and the preservation of our truly democratic kind of government.

Summary B

In one sense it is appropriate for us to do what we have come here to do: to dedicate part of this battlefield as a cemetery. In a more fundamental sense, however, the dedication has already been made, by the battle itself.

What we say now is not important; what *is* important is what we have to do from now on. We must support the cause for which our soldiers fought here; we must make sure that those of them who were killed did not die for nothing. We must continue to promote the cause of freedom and democracy.

[14] Reprinted by permission of the Estate of Albert Einstein from *Ideas and Opinions by Albert Einstein* (New York: Crown Publishers, Inc., 1954), p. 3.

Summary C

We are fighting a civil war; its outcome will show what the prospects of permanence are for the kind of free country that was founded here eighty-seven years ago.

We have come together now, on one of the battlefields of this war, to dedicate part of the field as a cemetery for our soldiers who were killed in the battle. Our action, though proper, is really superfluous: the true dedication of this land has already been accomplished, by the brave men who fought here. Their action was important; our speechmaking is not.

But there is one kind of dedication that we genuinely can make: a dedication of ourselves to the work which they were doing. We should be impelled by their example to finish that work, so that the bloodshed will not have been a waste. We must devote ourselves to the freedom of this nation and the democracy of its government.

REVIEW

The *review,* in the specific sense in which we shall deal with it here, is an informative account of the content and qualities of a book, play, movie, concert, recording, painting, or other form of art. In a more general sense, the review may cover virtually any subject; it may be an account of something as broad as a whole system of philosophy or a whole historical era, or as narrow as a single sports event or even the work of a single player. It would hardly be going too far to say that the kind of intellectual activity which is involved in reviewing, in this general sense—digesting a subject, weighing and considering, and exercising critical judgment upon it—is the basic process of liberal education. Our present concern, however, is with only a small part of that process, or only one particular application of it. In this context the subject will almost always be a work of art, and usually in the field of literature.

Suggestions for the Reviewer. Here are several suggestions for the writer preparing his first reviews.

1. Exercise conscientious care in familiarizing yourself with the subject. If you are reviewing a book, give it a close and thoughtful reading; if a play or a film, take notes during or immediately after the performance or the showing.

2. Assume that your readers are not yet acquainted with the particular thing you are reviewing, but that they have the interest and curiosity of potential patrons. (On the basis of the information you provide in the review, they might decide whether or not to buy the book, see or perhaps read the play, or go to the film.)

3. In place of a regular title, use a heading which gives the pertinent

identifying facts. In the caption of a book review, for example, include the title, author, place of publication, publisher, date, and number of pages.

4. Classify the subject of the review in the first paragraph. In reviewing a book, for instance, inform the reader immediately of its kind. State whether the book is a novel, a biography, a song collection, or some other type of writing. The title may suggest the classification, but mention it early in the review anyway.

5. Use a central idea that will give the reader a clear, objective picture of the thing being reviewed; make every point in the review support the central idea. Observe and apply the fundamentals of composition in preparing a review as in any other theme assignment.

6. Comment on structural elements. Assume that the reader knows the general elements of a story, a concerto, or a painting, but does not know how the artist has handled them in the particular work being reviewed.

7. Keep appropriate proportion; that is, make the review reflect the relative importance of the parts that make up the whole subject. In reviewing a concert, note especially the outstanding number or the outstanding performer. In reviewing a play, dwell more on the climactic scenes than on unimportant ones, more on the protagonist than on a minor character. In reviewing fiction, avoid the lengthy, prosaic summary; rather, suggest the sequence of events and capture the spirit of the original by quoting brief, significant passages.

8. Evaluate on the basis of objective standards, not on personal taste or prejudices. Let the original be its own standard; that is, determine the intended purpose of the original (if there is a preface or introduction, it may state explicitly what the author's intention was) and then judge how well it serves that purpose.[15] Evaluate by fair standards. A raincoat that does not shed water deserves a low rating as a raincoat, although its owner considers it an attractive piece of clothing; in the same way, a biography that misrepresents the life story of its subject should not get a high rating as biography, though it may be written in an entertaining style. Just as it would be unfair to disapprove of a dress shirt because it does not shed water, so it would be unfair to deprecate a novel because it does not record historical facts.

9. Adduce specific evidence to support your critical judgment. In the review of a play, cite particular scenes; in that of a book, quote or ob-

[15] Ultimately, of course, the purpose itself is also subject to evaluation. A piece of vicious propaganda, intended to incite the reader to hatred, may serve its purpose well; but we should not place a high value upon it.

jectively summarize one or more pertinent passages to validate the opinion you are expressing.

Review by an Experienced Reviewer. As a service to their readers, many magazines and metropolitan newspapers feature book review sections. A few magazines consist almost entirely of book reviews written by experienced reviewers. The following is a review of average length quoted from such a magazine:

Helen Keller: Sketch for a Portrait, by Van Wyck Brooks (*E. P. Dutton. 166 pp., $3*), *is an appreciation by a close friend and admirer.*

Van Wyck Brooks did well by himself and his readers when he chose the word "sketch" to describe his new book "Helen Keller: Sketch for a Portrait." In a double sense, it is just that. It is a sketch because he has drawn, with firmness and perception, the lines—the structural form—on which a fuller portrait might be constructed. It is a sketch because the life of Helen Keller is manifestly impossible to report in its full detail.

Like most of my American contemporaries and hosts of people the world around, I have "always" known about Helen Keller. Yet when I finished reading the all too few pages of this book I realized that I had never known about her any of the things that mattered most; and, beyond this, I realized anew how little we know about the basic mystery of the life we take for granted in our human selves.

When Helen Keller was a child of seven she was an unruly, virtually uncontrollable fury: a bundle of latent powers, we might say, that were desperate with frustration.

When she was in her middle sixties Van Wyck Brooks could set down in his notebook the following random facts: "Helen has been out picking blueberries today. She has only to touch them to know when they are ripe. . . . Someone asked her how she knows the difference between day and night. 'Oh,' she said, 'in the day the air is lighter, and there is more motion and vibration in the atmosphere. In the evening quiet there are fewer vibrations. The air is dense and one feels less motion in things!! . . . She had witnessed the inauguration [in January 1945], standing with Jo Davidson under the magnolia trees on the snow-covered grounds of the White House . . and in the evening of what she calls 'that piled-up day' she dined with Justice Hugo Black, Thurman Arnold, and others. They discussed the various roads by which Soviet Russia and the United States might reach genuine democracy, considering their conflicting views of economic determinism. . . ."

What did the almost six decades hold that changed the unruly child into a woman who in spite of being—in the ordinary sense of these words—blind and deaf could travel from one Government hospital to another and could report, with a depth of understanding, both the nervous tensions of the patients and the miracle of cooperative surgery, medicine, and teaching organized "to help multitudes of disabled servicemen to regain their human heritage "?

What these decades held is what Van Wyck Brooks here reports. It is the story of an extraordinary intelligence and a spirit of rare beauty trapped by the inadequacies of the body—and then released by the genius of "Teacher": Anne Sullivan. It is the story of friendships—truly great friendships—Oliver Wendell Holmes, Alexander Graham Bell, Whittier, Phillips Brooks, Mark Twain—these and others, and yet others—were friends of Helen Keller not out of pity but out of wonder at her genius for living. When Caruso said to her "I have sung the best in my life for you" he spoke for a multitude of great spirits who each in his own way gave of his best.

The odd thing is that Helen Keller's triumphs over her handicaps do not so much set her apart from the rest of us as point up for all of us the amazing capacities we have to unite ourselves with our world. Her "seeing hand" becomes in effect a hand that guides our obtuse selves back toward the mysteries of the sensory universe, the human tradition of poetry and philosophy and history, and the yearning spirit within each separate individual.

This book is a sketch. Perhaps the best way for it to be filled out into a complete portrait is for each reader of it to round out in his own life the experiences that Helen Keller reminds us are within our reach.[16]

REPORT

A *report* is a factual account of pertinent, verifiable details learned through direct investigation of a specific problem. A good report is organized systematically and written in clear, unemotional language. In order to achieve the degree of objectivity desirable in a report, the writer must discipline his thinking; he must distinguish between facts and judgments based on facts. He must record what he sees and not what he wants to see, for to be of any value to its readers a report must be reliable. If the writer includes any of his own opinions or recommendations, he must label them as such.

Relation to Similar but Distinct Types. It is worth while to note the features that distinguish the report from other kinds of writing which are similar to it in some ways. The report differs from the review in the usual nature of its subject matter and in its primary emphasis on fact. The review, discussed earlier, usually deals with a work of art; the report ordinarily has a more matter-of-fact or mundane subject. Both types are expository, and both give factual information; in the review the evaluation and interpretation of this information, and the exercise of critical judgment, are characteristic features, whereas in the report personal judgments and opinions are subordinated to factual details.

[16] Reprinted with permission from Bonaro W. Overstreet, *Saturday Review*, XXXIX (March 24, 1956), 20.

The report differs from the research paper (and from the extended scholarly research paper called a dissertation or thesis) in subject matter again and especially in the typical method of investigation. The chief source of information for a research paper is written material: books, articles, etc.[17] For a report, the writer is more likely to perform on-the-spot observation—sometimes to interview persons who know about the subject, or perhaps to prepare and distribute questionnaires.

Occasions for Reports. Occasions requiring reports to be submitted to particular audiences are numerous in many areas of public and private life, wherever there is a need to communicate facts on specific problems. A salesman submits to the sales manager a report on a week's sales. A store detective provides the store's protection manager with a report on a shoplifting incident. A delegate to a national church convention presents to his home congregation a report on the convention's proceedings. A Congressman submits to a legislative committee a report on the need for flood control in his state. Whatever the circumstance, the reader of the report expects to learn facts, facts that the writer has gathered by direct investigation.

In a school context, the occasion may be "manufactured"; that is, a typical kind of problem may be assigned as an exercise in report-writing. A student might be asked to write about the organization and the duties of the campus newspaper staff or about the campus radio station if there is one. Or the assignment might take him off the campus—to investigate the municipal welfare agencies, for example, and prepare a report for a course in sociology. The possibilities for such projects are virtually without limit.

Preparation of Reports. The principal requirements for the preparation of reports are the exercise of intelligence in conducting the investigation, and the application of the principles of good composition in writing the report. The writer must go to the appropriate places and persons, observe the right things, ask the right questions, and make careful notes on his findings. (For guidance in writing the report, read Chapter 2, especially the discussion of "Fact and Opinion"; Chapter 3; and the material in Chapter 6 on handling notes.) Also, it is worth noting what the qualities of a good report are, and what general questions the writer should ask himself, whether the answers are to be explicit in the report itself, or only implicit in the way in which it is prepared.

[17] If the subject is technical or scientific, there is likely to be direct observation, perhaps in a laboratory, but this observation will be at least supplemented by reference to published writings.

Qualities of a Good Report. The qualities of a good report include accuracy, clarity, conciseness, completeness, and adherence to a firmly established point of view. The accuracy should be verifiable; that is, if someone else were to conduct a similar investigation, he should discover the same essential facts. Clarity, important in all writing, is especially so in the report as a straightforward factual account. Conciseness and completeness balance each other: the report should be as concise and economical as it can be and still cover the subject completely. In general, the point of view should be objective. Of course the writer must be selective with his material, emphasizing that which he believes to be most significant; yet this selection and emphasis must not have the effect of slanting the facts. If he has used any special criterion in determining what to include, he should say so explicitly.

Questions for the Writer to Ask Himself. There are certain questions which the writer of a report should ask himself at the outset. Indeed, he might do something like this automatically, for without answers to these questions he could hardly proceed at all. The point is that he should ask them consciously and deliberately, at the beginning of his work.

1. *What is my reason for making this report?* If the immediate reason is that he has been given the assignment in a course, he should imagine for himself an out-of-class situation in which he might be undertaking such a project. For example, he might imagine himself to be a member of a citizens' committee, making a report on a phase of civic affairs.

2. *What is the purpose of my investigation?* This question is similar to the first, but nevertheless distinct. Another way to put it would be, "What, specifically, do I want to find out?"

3. *What sources of information are available?* The writer should consider where he ought to go to make his observations, and whom he ought to approach. Although most of his information will come from direct personal investigation, perhaps there is some reading he can do about the subject or related subjects, at least for his own initial orientation.

If the report is to go beyond the purely factual—if it is to include a recommendation, or a conclusion based on an inference from the facts to be discovered—the writer should ask further questions.

4. *What method shall I use in developing my conclusions?* The initial answer to this question may necessarily be general rather than precise; the writer may realize, for example, that his basic reasoning will be inductive rather than deductive, or vice versa (see Chapter 2).

5. *Can I determine in advance what my conclusion will be?* For most

subjects, the answer to this question should very likely be *no*. Rather than starting with any preconception, the writer should first learn the facts and let his conclusion develop out of them. Only when he has completed his investigation is he in a position to draw his inferences.

6. At this point—still, presumably, before he has begun actually to write the report—he should review the facts and raise the final question, *What ought my conclusion or recommendation to be?*

A Report on a Specific Problem. Here is the type of report that a field representative might make to the president and board of directors of a company which is planning to establish a new branch. The opening paragraph states the specific problem that the writer of the report has investigated.

REPORT ON STORE SPACE AVAILABLE
IN NORTHWEST MORRISVILLE ON APRIL 15, 1960

Three stores are currently vacant and for rent in the section of Morrisville north of Tenth Street and west of Cedar Avenue, the area in which the Standard Cleaning Company plans to open a branch shop for dry cleaning and laundry service. All the stores are in brick buildings, and any one of them can be rented for less than $120.00 a month, the maximum rental that Standard pays for any of its present shops. The available stores will be referred to in this report as Store A, Store B, and Store C.

Store A, at 600 Wilson Avenue, occupies the entire ground floor of a two-story building on the corner of Wilson Avenue and Fourteenth Street. This store, which faces north, is 20 feet wide, 42 feet deep, and 11 feet high. It has a plate glass display window 12 feet wide and 5 feet high. In addition to a front entrance, Store A has a side (or east) door opening onto an area between the building and Fourteenth Street. In this space, which is reserved for use by patrons of the store, six cars can be parked. No parking is permitted on Fourteenth Street itself at this point, but parallel parking is permitted on both sides of Wilson Avenue.

The walls and ceiling of Store A are plasterboard, painted light green four years ago and now soiled in spots. The floor is wooden and has some indentations where the previous tenant, an independent grocer, had his counters. The owner of the building, Mr. R. M. Hawkins, who lives on the second floor, says that he will not redecorate the store but has no objection to the new tenant's doing so.

Mr. Hawkins says that he will lease Store A for one year at $100.00 a month and give an option for a second year at $110.00 a month. He furnishes running water for a rest room located in the rear part of the store. The tenant pays for all other utilities, including gas for a heater that was installed in the store four years ago. There is no air-cooling equipment in the store.

Store A is located in a neighborhood of two-story, two-family dwellings.

Many of the residents work in downtown department stores; others are laborers; a few are professional people. The area has been zoned for residence; but, according to Mr. Hawkins and Mayor C. L. Carter, because a business had been operating at 600 Wilson before the zoning ordinance was passed, no objection has been raised to a store at that location and no such objection is anticipated. The nearest dry cleaning and laundry establishment is in a business district four blocks away.

Store B, at 429 State Street, is one of five stores on the ground floor of an eight-story apartment hotel, the York-Hanley. Store B, which faces east, is 14 feet wide, 36 feet deep, and 10 feet high. It has a plate glass display window 7 feet wide and 5 feet high. The store has a front entrance from State Street and a side entrance from the lobby of the York-Hanley. The other businesses in the building include a drug store, a jewelry store, a beauty shop, and a restaurant. The York-Hanley has parking space in the rear for its residents and for the tenants of the stores but not for customers. There are parking meters on both sides of State Street at this point.

Store B is now being redecorated by the owner. The walls, which are plaster, are being painted yellow with a brown base; the ceiling, which is made of acoustical tile, is being painted white. A brown rubber tile floor covering has just been installed. The store will be ready for occupancy by September 1.

Mrs. Cora Grayson, the manager of the York-Hanley, says that her policy is to require the tenant to sign a two-year lease for store space. The rental for Store B is $95.00 a month, with the tenant paying for his own utilities except heat and water. Steam heat from a central heating system in the building is furnished during business hours. Running water for a lavatory in the rear part of the store is furnished; store tenants have access to rest rooms in the lobby of the building. The store has no air-cooling equipment.

Store B is centrally located in a five-block business section on State Street. In addition to the York-Hanley, which has 150 units—all occupied, according to Mrs. Grayson—there are two other sizable apartment hotels in the immediate vicinity. On the streets running off State Street are smaller apartment buildings, each housing from four to six families. The residents are chiefly professional people, many of them connected with the Morrisville Medical School, which is located three blocks to the west, or with the Morrisville Hospital Group, four blocks to the east. There are three other cleaning and laundry establishments in the business section on State Street: one across from the York-Hanley, one a block north, and the other two blocks south.

Store C, at 7842½ Perry Road, is on the ground floor rear in the new Kindler Building, a two-story building which has six stores on the ground floor and eight offices on the second floor. Five new businesses—a barber shop, a drug store, a grocery store, a shoe store, and a hardware store—have recently opened in the Kindler Building and form the main part of what is called the Perry Road Shopping Center. Store C is 20 feet square and 9 feet high. It is directly behind the barber shop and has entrances from the lobby of the building and from the rear (or south) parking lot. The Kindler Building has parking space for 150 cars: 50 cars in front of the building and 100 cars in a patrolled lot in the rear.

The walls of Store C are plaster, painted ivory. The ceiling is made of white acoustical tile. The floor is covered with black rubber tile.

Mr. J. E. Kindler, president of the Kindler Construction Company and manager of the building, says that he will rent Store C on a monthly basis for $85.00 a month. He says that he will give a one-year lease to a tenant who desires it but does not himself consider a lease necessary. The rent includes heat, air conditioning, and running water in a rest room located in the rear part of the store. The Kindler Building is centrally heated and air conditioned, but each store has its own thermostat.

Store C is in an as yet sparsely settled neighborhood where many new one-family dwellings are under construction. Most of the residents are employees of the Madison Aircraft Corporation, which is located about three miles from the Perry Road Shopping Center. There is no dry cleaning or laundry establishment between the shopping center and the aircraft plant or within a two-mile radius of the shopping center.

In the opinion of the writer of this report, Store A has the advantages of ample floor space and an adequate parking area but the disadvantages of relatively high rent and the expense of redecoration; Store B has the advantages of attractive appearance and convenient entrances (the lobby entrance is especially convenient for occupants of the building) but the disadvantage of meter parking; Store C has the advantages of air conditioning and a large parking area but the disadvantage of being located in the rear part of the building. So far as business opportunities for a shop dealing in dry cleaning and laundry service are concerned, the writer believes that their respective locations in the city cause the stores to rank as follows: Store B, first; Store A, second; and Store C, third.

EXAMINATIONS [18]

Whenever one writes an essay type of *examination,* he has an excellent opportunity to put his knowledge of exposition to practical use. The examination may call for one or all types of exposition discussed earlier in this chapter.

The best answer to each question in an examination of the essay type is in fact a short expository theme. The question itself, if turned into a statement, provides the central idea for the theme and suggests the method of development. A question may call for an extended definition of a term, an analysis of an idea, an explanation of a process, a summary of a chapter, a review of an article, a report of an experiment, or a

[18] For a full treatment of this subject, see J. N. Hook, *How to Take Examinations in College,* "College Outline Series" (New York: Barnes & Noble, Inc., 1958).

variation or combination of these. Whatever the type, the theme should be as carefully organized and developed as any other assignment in expository writing. It should do what the question requires: it should not do more, it should not do less, and it certainly should not do something other than meet this requirement precisely.

Exercises

1. Answer each of the following questions with one complete sentence.

a. What is the primary purpose of exposition?

b. What is the difference between a natural and an arbitrary classification?

c. For what kind of reading audience may the writer appropriately use the second person, imperative mood, in explaining a process?

d. What is the general rule concerning the length of the summary?

e. Is the following evaluation fair or unfair? Why? "Lytton Strachey's biography of Queen Victoria is weak in plot."

2. On what basis has each of the following classifications been made?

a. The spectators at the football game included children, adolescents, and adults.

b. The autumn leaves visible from my window are red, yellow, and brown.

c. Lakes may be designated as salt lakes, bitter lakes, alkali lakes, and borax lakes.

d. Sentences are classified in the following ways:

    (1) as declarative, interrogative, imperative, and exclamatory sentences;

    (2) as simple, compound, complex, and compound-complex sentences; and

    (3) as loose, balanced, and periodic sentences.

e. Throughout the season the concert-goers fell into three groups, at least from the conductor's point of view: those who came to chat with their companions, those who came to see the fashions in clothing, and those who came to listen to the orchestra with genuine interest and pleasure.

3. In accordance with the explanations and illustrations in this chapter, identify the types of exposition in the following passages. If a passage represents a combination of types of exposition, mention the different types and point out which one is primary.

a. In this type of presentation [the problem-solution plan], the speech is divided into four major parts: (1) the Attention Step, (2) the Problem Step, (3) the Solution Step, and (4) the Appeal Step. The first step tells the hearer that all is not right with the world—there really *is* a problem to be faced. The second step defines, explains, and diagnoses the problem precisely, looking especially to its nature and causes. The third step brings forth the solution and demonstrates that it will not only remove the causes that give rise to the problem, but will be the *best* solution possible. The final step seeks to paint the solution in the most attractive and compelling light possible, usually by associating it with the desires, wishes, and ideals of the audience.[19]

b. *Immensee* is of the type known in German as the *Rahmenerzählung* (frame story). The frame is represented by the opening and closing chapters, which present to us the old man. His revery is the story proper—a series of pictures, not closely connected and with the outlines but vaguely drawn. The author is skillful in his use of the frame phase of the story. In the first chapter he excites our interest in the old man and we wish to know the cause of his sorrow. The moonlight on the picture of Elizabeth starts the aged dreamer on his revery: the transition from the frame to the narrative resembles that of dissolving pictures. Storm [the author] then leaves the old man behind and tells the story himself. At the end he bridges the gap between narrative and frame by carrying over into the picture of the old man a most important motif—the symbolic representation of Elizabeth by a water lily.[20]

c. The 4-H Club is a rural-youth organization directed by the United States Department of Agriculture Extension Service in co-operation with the state agricultural colleges and having as its purpose to improve practices in the farm home, on the farm, and in the farm community. It is an organization with a program of activities—with separate divisions for boys and girls—on the national, state, county, and community levels. The 4–H members carry on projects varying from planting gardens and preserving food to raising livestock, experimenting with grain, and testing new machinery; they make demonstrations at their local meetings and conduct exhibits at county and state fairs. The 4–H Club's emblem is the four-leaf clover; its motto, "To make the best better." The "4 H's" are named in the membership pledge:

> I pledge my head to clearer thinking,
> my heart to greater loyalty,
> my hands to larger service,
> my health to better living.

---

[19] Bryant and Wallace, *op. cit.*, pp. 394–395.

[20] Reprinted with permission from Bayard Quincy Morgan and Elmer O. Wooley, Introduction to Theodor Storm's *Immensee* (Boston: D. C. Heath & Company, 1927), p. xv.

5 SHORT NON–EXPOSITORY THEMES

The form of discourse which we most often have occasion to use, for practical purposes anyway, is exposition. For this reason, in the typical composition course, most of the writing is likely to be expository; for this reason too, Chapter 4 was devoted entirely to expository themes. We do use the non-expository forms of discourse, however, either singly or in combination. For this reason argument, description, and narrative are discussed in the present chapter.

EMPHASIS ON EMOTIONAL APPEAL

In the non-expository forms of discourse appeal to the reader's emotions is emphasized to a greater extent than in exposition. This general rule has a few exceptions. Technical description, for instance (see p. 98), is addressed to the reader's intellect, and sometimes narrative may be intellectual in tone. The most characteristic type of argumentative composition, formal academic debate, may be almost purely intellectual. To this kind of argument, what is said in the next few pages does not apply; if this were the *only* kind, the discussion would not apply to argument at all. There is another variety, however, represented by advertising copy, by much political campaign literature, and often by newspaper editorials, which makes large use of emotional appeal. Despite the exceptions noted, most narrative and descriptive writing makes it, too.

Special Techniques of Emotional Appeal. Certain techniques are of special importance in writing which appeals to the reader's emotions. Chief among these are techniques of diction or choice of words, and of organization.

Techniques of Diction. Appropriately vivid diction is desirable in all composition, but in writing addressed to the reader's emotions it is of special importance. In this context maximum vividness of diction is achieved in part by the careful use of two types of words: those which appeal to the five senses, and those which appeal to the emotions directly. Careful use of these words includes giving them prominence, so that their full effect will be felt.

SELECTING WORDS WITH SENSORY APPEAL. In order to use words that appeal to the senses, the writer should keep consciously in mind what the five senses are, and to what stimulations they respond.

Thus, for the sense of sight, he will use words which indicate size, shape, outline, color, brightness, dimness; for hearing, words indicating pitch, intensity, and rhythm; for taste and smell, words of sweetness, bitterness, and intensity again; for touch, words of texture, roughness, smoothness, degrees of heat or cold, and so on.

Another principle is useful in this connection. The words most effective in sensory appeal are not those which merely *describe* a sensation in general terms, but rather those which name or suggest an actual stimulus that evokes the sensation; ordinarily the more specific this stimulus is, the better. For the sense of sight, words like *beautiful, ugly, gorgeous, deformed* are not very effective in themselves. Better—to cite a few examples at random—are words such as *angular, dim, flash, flower, glow, jagged, jutting, limp, meadow, peak, shining, soar, squirm, stagger, star, wriggle.* (Notice that the examples include nouns, verbs, and modifiers; and certain words which, with or without a minor change in form, can serve as more than one part of speech.) For the sense of hearing, obviously appropriate are words that sound like what they denote, such as *bang, crackle, crash, croon, murmur, pop, rattle;* also potentially effective are words such as *artillery, melody, saxophone, silence, stillness, surf, waterfall.* For taste and smell: *acid, bacon, garbage, hay, meringue, musk, sewer, swamp, syrup.* For touch (including the feeling of temperature): *canvas, ice, mud, oily, oven, silk, velvet,* and so on.

A number of these words, and many others, may appeal to more than one sense at the same time, and of course a *combination* of such words may readily produce a complex sensory effect. For instance, if we are told that a room in a castle is "pale, latticed, chill, and silent," [1] three of our senses are appealed to at once: sight, touch (temperature), and hearing.

CHOOSING WORDS WITH DIRECT EMOTIONAL APPEAL. Words that appeal to the senses are effective in emotional writing for the psychological reason that our emotions may be aroused through our senses. There are other words that may produce a more immediate emotional effect, for they appeal to the emotions directly. Again, the most useful words are not those which describe or name the emotions—*love,*

---

[1] John Keats, "The Eve of St. Agnes," stanza 13, line 5. Although our concern is with writing prose, a few of the illustrative examples in this chapter are taken from poetry. This is because poetry usually *is* writing which appeals to the senses and the emotions—the type of writing which is being discussed here—and because with its characteristic economy and concentration poetry offers many good *short* examples of the principles involved. The principles themselves apply with equal force to emotional prose.

hate, fear, tenderness, jealousy, and so on—but those which name or suggest the objects of emotion. Probably the strongest human feelings are those connected with religion and with family relationships; potentially the most powerful emotion-arousing words, therefore, are those which are associated with these contexts: *God, heaven, hell, blasphemy, sacrilege; mother, father, son, brother, home,* etc. Patriotism is likely to be a strong feeling, which gives a favorable emotional charge to words connected with or applied to one's own country and a powerfully unfavorable charge to words like *treason* and *traitor.* Naturally enough, words associated with any institution on which men place high value are potentially effective for emotional appeal.

GIVING PROMINENCE TO SENSORY AND EMOTIONAL WORDS. To achieve the full impact of the words that appeal to the senses or the emotions, the writer should make sure that they strike the reader's attention forcefully. That is, he should give them the prominence appropriate to their importance; he should take care that they are not "buried" in an inconspicuous place in a sentence. The primary means to this end are the principles of sentence structure, especially the ones pertinent to emphasis (see Chapter 8). Most useful is the principle that the most emphatic position in a sentence is at the end, and the next most emphatic is at the beginning.

There is little doubt that some of the effect of these words will be felt. Appropriate construction is necessary, however, to insure their full impact. Compare the following instances; in each case the first version is altered from the effective original.

(1) Now, pressing down upon the brow of labor this crown of thorns or crucifying mankind upon a cross of gold is the kind of thing you ought not to do.

(2) You shall not press down upon the brow of labor this crown of thorns, you shall not crucify mankind upon a cross of gold.

WILLIAM JENNINGS BRYAN

(1) It was very chilly on St. Agnes' Eve. The owl was cold, despite his heavy plumage; a rabbit walking gingerly through the frozen grass might be seen; the cold kept even the woolly sheep in their fold quiet. A man with cold hands was saying his prayers. . . .

(2) St. Agnes' Eve—Ah, bitter chill it was!
The owl, for all his feathers, was a-cold;
The hare limped trembling through the frozen grass,
And silent was the flock in woolly fold:
Numb were the Beadsman's fingers, while he told
His rosary. . . . JOHN KEATS

(1) For my own part, I should be equally well pleased if you gave me liberty or gave me death—although I don't know what course other people may want to take.

(2) I know not what course others may take; but as for me, give me liberty or give me death!   PATRICK HENRY

Techniques of Organization. In general, the same principles of organization that apply to expository themes apply to non-expository themes also (see Chapters 3 and 4). In writing addressed to the emotions, however, certain techniques are of particular importance: maintenance of mood, and progression. In a sense these are special applications of the principles of unity and of climax, respectively.

MAINTENANCE OF MOOD. In emotional writing it is important for a consistent *mood* to be maintained, a consistent quality of feeling. The details by means of which the mood is developed should be similar or mutually reinforcing in their effect; no discordant element should be admitted to break the mood. For example, consider this passage:

Spring was a revelation to him this year. In a kind of intoxication he would watch the pink-white buds of some backward beech tree sprayed up in the sunlight against the deep blue sky, or the trunks and limbs of the few Scotch firs, tawny in violent light, or again on the moor, the gale-bent larches which had such a look of life when the wind streamed in their young green, above the rusty black underboughs. Or he would lie on the banks, gazing at the clusters of dog-violets, or up in the dead bracken, fingering the pink, transparent buds of the dewberry, while the cuckoos called and yaffles laughed, or a lark, from very high, dripped its beads of song.[2]

All the details work together; nothing is inappropriate or inconsistent. Now suppose the passage were to continue, as it actually does not,

Through a break in the trees he could see a stretch of the railroad track at the foot of the hill and, across the main track, a number of sidings on which several dirty, dilapidated freight cars were standing.

The mood would be broken by this jarring incongruity.

The effect which is developed does not have to be simple or one-dimensional; it may have a degree of complexity. In the example given, the feeling is not pure and unmixed. The light is not calmly radiant but *violent*. Most of the details convey a sense of burgeoning life, but a few of the branches are rusty black, and the bracken is dead. There is a subtle suggestion of disturbance and of mortality in the otherwise

---

[2] Reprinted with permission from John Galsworthy, "The Apple Tree," *Five Tales* (New York: Charles Scribner's Sons, 1942, and London: William Heinemann, Ltd.).

idyllic beauty of the scene—a suggestion artistically in keeping with the author's over-all purpose in the story in which this passage occurs. The general effect of the passage itself is still a unified impression, as in all good descriptive writing.

PROGRESSION OR CUMULATIVE EFFECT. In emotional writing, each part of the whole should represent a *progression;* in building up the cumulative total impression, each part should be at least as effective as the preceding and if possible more effective. This principle is well illustrated by the conclusion of the speech that Winston Churchill made, early in World War II, shortly after the retreating British forces had been evacuated from Dunkirk. On the surface, this passage is a statement and a prophecy; essentially, it is a piece of argument, an impassioned exhortation.

I have, myself, full confidence that if all do their duty, if nothing is neglected, and if the best arrangements are made, as they are being made, we shall prove ourselves once again able to defend our Island home, to ride out the storm of war, and to outlive the menace of tyranny, if necessary for years, if necessary alone. At any rate, that is what we are going to try to do. That is the resolve of His Majesty's Government—every man of them. That is the will of Parliament and the nation. The British Empire and the French Republic, linked together in their cause and in their need, will defend to the death their native soil, aiding each other like good comrades to the utmost of their strength. Even though large tracts of Europe and many old and famous States have fallen or may fall into the grip of the Gestapo and all the odious apparatus of Nazi rule, we shall not flag or fail. We shall go on to the end, we shall fight in France, we shall fight on the seas and oceans, we shall fight with growing confidence and growing strength in the air, we shall defend our Island, whatever the cost may be, we shall fight on the beaches, we shall fight on the landing grounds, we shall fight in the fields and in the streets, we shall fight in the hills; we shall never surrender, and even if, which I do not for a moment believe, this Island or a large part of it were subjugated and starving, then our Empire beyond the seas, armed and guarded by the British Fleet, would carry on the struggle, until, in God's good time, the New World, with all its power and might, steps forth to the rescue and the liberation of the old.

The first sentence has a tone of relatively calm assurance, but immediately there enters a note of urgency, of the necessity for effort: "that is what we are going to try to do." The pitch begins to rise in the words and phrases charged with feeling: not only the proper nouns standing for King and country, but also words like "resolve" and expressions like "every man of them." The whole sentence beginning "The British

Empire and the French Republic" is intense with emotional rhetoric, though still couched in comparatively general terms. Now Churchill passes to the specific current situation, the extent of the Nazi power and the threat of its further extension, including perhaps even the invasion of England. Notice how the places which he enumerates as the scenes of possible fighting get closer to home. First, "we shall fight in France, . . . on the seas and oceans, . . . in the air," and then "on the beaches, . . . on the landing grounds," where invading forces might have arrived, "in the streets" of our own cities, "in the hills," to which we might have been driven. Even if we are reduced to guerrilla warfare, "we shall never surrender." Finally, facing the possibility that England might be occupied by the enemy, Churchill looks to the prospect of ultimate rescue and liberation, with the help of the British navy, of America, and of God. The emotional intensity has been built up steadily, in accordance with the principle of progression.

There are a few exceptions to this principle. In extended pieces of writing—in a long narrative, for example, like a novel—the writer may build up the emotional tension and then relax it temporarily before building it up again. Also in shorter pieces, it is scarcely possible for every successive sentence to represent a raising of the pitch, but as a rule at least every successive paragraph should do so. This is the way the cumulative emotional effect is developed.

Implication vs. Explicit Statement. One further principle has special usefulness in writing which appeals to the senses and the emotions: ordinarily *implication*—suggestion, the giving of a hint or clue—is more effective than *explicit statement*. For instance, we might make an explicit statement about a story: we might say that it is interesting, even fascinating, that its spell is irresistible. On the other hand, compare the effect of calling it "a tale which holds children from play, and old men from the chimney corner" (Sir Philip Sidney, *The Defence of Poesy*). The latter version *implies* all that the former says and makes the point much more effectively.

For another example, there is an essay in which the narrator recounts an occasion when he was telling a story to his children. His wife is dead; the children are half-orphans. At the end of the story, he says, the children disappeared, "and immediately awaking, I found myself quietly seated in my bachelor arm-chair . . ." (Charles Lamb, "Dream Children; a Reverie"). The force of the implication rests on the adjective *bachelor*. The man has no wife and no children; the whole experience was a dream. All the fatherly tenderness, all the love and understanding of children which he has demonstrated in his account are only unfulfilled potentiality; he is a lonely man. If he stated all this explicitly, he might seem a self-pitying sentimentalist. By simply implying it, however, he avoids giving this impression, and the effect is consequently much stronger.

For a final example, in a context of powerful argument or persuasion, consider the Biblical account of the woman taken in adultery (John 8:3–11). When Jesus was asked whether it was proper for the woman to be stoned to death, in accordance with traditional law, the reply was, "He that is without sin among you, let him first cast a stone at her." This simple utterance implies a number of things: all human beings are guilty; we have no right arbitrarily to condemn one particular offender, who is perhaps no worse than many others; what such a person needs is understanding and admonition to betterment ("go, and sin no more"). The simple utterance which implies all this is far superior to the explicit statement.

This greater effectiveness of implication has a sound psychological basis. For one thing, implication stimulates the reader to be mentally alive as he reads—to visualize, to feel, to use his imagination. It gives him a sense of really participating in the development of thought and feeling, of making his own contribution to it; and thus for him the meaningfulness of what he reads is heightened. Then too, implication is the process by which most of our feelings are evoked. Our experience does not ordinarily come to us tied up in neat little bundles, each bearing an explicit label to direct our reaction. Rather, it comes as a stream of sensations, which we interpret for ourselves. Therefore implication is an appropriate technique for the kind of writing that is designed to communicate experience.

ARGUMENT

Argument is that form of discourse the central purpose of which is to persuade an audience to adopt a certain doctrine or attitude or course of action. Whereas exposition is characteristically addressed to the reader's intellect and description chiefly to his emotions, argument lies in a middle ground; it appeals sometimes to the intellect, sometimes to the emotions, and often to both. When it is addressed to the intellect exclusively, what has been said of emotional appeal in the preceding section of this chapter does not apply to it; [3] otherwise the principles of emotional writing are as important for argument as for description.

---

[3] The principles that do apply to purely intellectual argument are chiefly those set forth in Chapter 2. (In a measure these principles apply to all argument, for practically all argument has at least some intellectual content.)

Representative Types of Argument. The types of argument likely to be written in the English composition course may vary in both form and content. Occasionally the form might be that of, say a speech prepared verbatim for an academic debate. The typical assignment is relatively informal: perhaps a letter to a newspaper, arguing for a particular position on a controversial issue—or a simple statement of a case directed to an audience of one's classmates. In content or subject matter, such argument may be concerned with readings in the course; for instance, a composition attacking or defending a particular point of view expressed in one or more essays that the class has read. A good topic for argument is any serious question of general interest, any substantial subject regarding which there is room for differing opinions. Two areas in which many such topics suggest themselves are public affairs, and religious and ethical issues.

Argument on Public Affairs. *Public affairs* are matters of common or public interest. These matters often have ramifications which are complex and technical: national defense involves questions of armaments and their scientific development; foreign policy involves international economic relationships; and so on. The layman is not expected to have expert or special knowledge of these subjects, but he should have informed and intelligent lay opinion regarding the pertinent issues. Such opinion is a good point of departure for the writing of argument.

Particular questions in this area are likely to be of special interest at one time, but not so at another; specific examples, therefore, can only suggest the kind of topic that might be appropriate. Good argumentative compositions might be written on the following, if the problems were being currently discussed or if measures pertaining to them had been recently proposed.

public health	federal aid to education
police protection	loyalty and security programs in
juvenile delinquency	government employment
foreign policy	conservation of natural resources

Argument on Religious and Ethical Issues. In a sense *religious and ethical issues* are not a separate category of argument, for these issues are fundamental. They are involved in most real argument, whether they are made explicit or not. To be sure, they would scarcely enter into any purely technical question like the comparative merit of different varieties of apples; as soon as a moral element is introduced, however, they have basic relevance. Among the examples given in the preceding category, religious and ethical issues would almost certainly figure in a

discussion of juvenile delinquency in a community or of loyalty and security programs; they might well figure in argument on the other
topics too.

It is perhaps in these kinds of context that one is most likely to be
dealing with ethical issues; that is, one will invoke them in the course
of discussing particular practical problems. On the other hand, there are
issues like the following, which are religious or ethical in essence.

a justification of my faith	freedom and responsibility
"mixed" marriage	conformity and nonconformity

Procedure in Argument. The first requirement for writing argument
is that the writer should be well informed on the subject he will discuss; he should have a thorough knowledge of the issue or issues involved. Regardless of the side of the question for which he will be
arguing, he should know what may be said on both sides or, if there
are more than two, on all sides.

This requirement having been met, the procedure for writing an
argumentative composition may conveniently be regarded as consisting
of four steps: formulating the thesis, analyzing the necessary demonstration, adducing and reasoning upon evidence, and anticipating and rebutting counter-arguments.

Formulating the Thesis. *Thesis* is the term ordinarily used to denote
the central idea or effect in argument.[4] Like any such idea or effect, it
should be capable of being expressed in a single sentence. *Formulating
the thesis,* then, is evolving a clear and direct statement of what is to be
proved or demonstrated.

In a formal academic debate, the thesis of the affirmative speech or
speeches is the stated subject of the debate, "Resolved: that . . ."; the
negative thesis is the reverse of this. The term *thesis* is not so commonly
applied to the central effect of an emotional argument, but in such argument this effect is analogous to the central idea of argument addressed
to the intellect. It may be made explicit—"Buy Product X," "Vote for
Candidate Y," "Throw the rascals out!"—or it may emerge by implication from the details: a feeling of approval or disapproval attached to
a person or product or idea or institution.

Argument written for a composition course is likely to be of the type
addressed chiefly to the intellect; the thesis, therefore, will ordinarily

---

[4] This sense of the word is different from the meaning it has in reference to
a scholarly dissertation (see Chapter 4). The two meanings are related, however:
the latter evolved from the circumstance that originally degree candidates were
required to defend a *thesis* or prepared position on a moot question.

be a statement of an idea. Theses might be formulated as follows for a few of the examples given on page 94:

Inoculation of children against communicable disease should be compulsory (or, should be optional).

The United States should extend financial aid only to countries whose governments are democratic.

Analyzing the Necessary Demonstration. In intellectual argument, in order to establish the thesis it is ordinarily necessary either to present a chain of reasoning or—probably more often, at least in informal argument—to cite a number of separate reasons, each of which tends independently to support the thesis. In a logical chain, each step is dependent on the preceding; but in a group of independent reasons, each one must be considered carefully with regard to its own status. Certain ones may be of such a kind that presumably the reader will accept them without proof, but others may themselves have to be validated before they will be acceptable in support of the main thesis.

For example, think of the first of the suggested theses, "Inoculation of children against communicable disease should be compulsory." The writer might wish at the outset to make a point that practically goes without saying: the decision whether or not children are to be inoculated should be made not by the children themselves, but by adults. The very fact that this does go without saying means that the writer would not have to spend time proving this point. Suppose now that the writer wishes to state as his next point that the adults who make this decision ought to be, not the parents of the children, but rather the appropriate persons of authority in the government; for example, the municipal public health officials. Here, clearly, is something in the other category, something that will have to be demonstrated.

Adducing Evidence, and Reasoning. Having determined what will presumably be accepted without question, and what will need to be proved, in order to establish his thesis, the writer proceeds accordingly. In support of the point or points that he must prove, he adduces any necessary evidence and presents his reasoning.

In argument of an informal nature, special research will probably not be required; the argument will be based on personal knowledge and observation. The process of adducing evidence, then, will not be very complex. Indeed, if the writer is addressing a discussion about an issue of local concern to other members of the community, his audience's knowledge of the subject may be so similar to his own that he will have to do little more than refer to this common knowledge.

Even in such a context, however, some particular evidence might be available and useful. In the example cited above, the argument in favor of compulsory inoculation, the writer might happen to know about one or more other communities which have had successful experience with such a system. A brief account of this experience would be pertinent evidence. He should indicate the source of his knowledge, to preclude any doubt of its reliability.

The reasoning based on the evidence suggested above, the success of compulsory inoculation in other cities, would be reasoning by analogy. Such reasoning does not amount to absolute proof, but it may nevertheless be cogent (For a treatment of the basic types of reasoning and the common fallacies to be avoided, see Chapter 2.)

The main part of the reasoning in this example might appropriately comprise analyses of the disadvantages of a purely voluntary system, and the advantages of having a requirement established by law. In the absence of such a requirement, the writer might argue, cases of disease occur which might readily have been prevented. The principal bad effect is of course the suffering of the sick children themselves, but there is also their absence from school, the danger of contagion encountered by other children who enter the community, and so on. With the requirement established, the writer might continue, these evils would be eliminated or at least minimized, and the general level of health would be improved.

Anticipating and Rebutting Counter-Arguments. Though not always essential, it is frequently a good tactic in argument to anticipate contentions that may be made on the other side and to undertake to refute them before they are advanced. To illustrate with the same example once more: one of the chief points often made against a compulsory system is that it invades the authority which parents ought properly to have in matters pertaining to their children's personal health and welfare. One way to rebut this contention would be an argument by analogy (once again, such argument is not unequivocal proof). Not so very long ago, the writer might point out, there were persons who regarded it as an invasion of parental authority for the government to require that all children go to school. Now it has been established, almost beyond the last whisper of opposition, that society has enough stake in the education of its members to warrant its exerting full authority in this area. The health of its members, the writer might assert, is just as important as their education; society has a similar stake in this area, and may therefore with similar justification also impose a requirement here.

DESCRIPTION

Description is that form of discourse which has as its central purpose to evoke the impression produced by the aspect of a place or scene, or by a person (see Chapter 1). According to some analyses, there are two kinds of descriptive writing: technical and suggestive.

Technical description is the name applied to writing which gives a straightforward, objective account of the appearance or layout or structure of a thing; for example, of the human body or of a steamship or of the system of streets in a city. It is designed chiefly to give information, is addressed to the reader's intellect, and is essentially expository.

Strictly speaking, only *suggestive description*—which evokes an impression of a place, scene, or person—constitutes a distinct form of discourse. Suggestive description is primarily emotional in tone and is characterized by what has been said about emphasis on emotional appeal. This section is concerned with descriptive writing in the strict and specific sense of suggestive description.

Representative Types of Description. Two basic types of descriptive writing are the description of a place or scene and that of a person. In the latter the interest is likely to inhere in character and personality fully as much as or more than in physical appearance; under these circumstances the description is a character sketch.

Description of a Place or Scene. In *describing a place or scene* the writer should first determine the central emotional effect or impression which he wishes to evoke. This effect may be simple, or it may be complex, with various shades of feeling. Then the writer should select the details which will most effectively develop this impression and present them as vividly as he can. He should keep his imagination alert and his "mind's eye" open; he must visualize the scene clearly himself in order to present a clear picture.

For one specific example, see the passage by John Galsworthy quoted on page 90. Here are a few subjects which might be used for good descriptive writing, with suggestions regarding the central effects that might be developed.

PLACE	POSSIBLE EMOTIONAL EFFECT
a stadium filled with spectators	excitement, enthusiasm
a street corner in a slum	squalor
a dining-room with a table laid for a banquet	opulence
the sky on a clear night	awe
a rocky seacoast in a storm	fury

In the description of any particular scene more than one kind of effect is possible. The stadium might be the scene of something very different from enthusiasm, if the details should point another way (the spectators sitting in a cold rain, the game itself dull and spiritless, and so on); the slum scene, described with emphasis on the pleasant associations of experience happy even in poverty, might be made to seem cheerful and hospitable.

Character Sketch. The *character sketch,* like the description of a place, is designed to evoke an impression, to embody an attitude, to produce an essentially emotional effect. In the character sketch the effect is likely to be somewhat more complex, because it is concerned with human personality which is in itself complex. Therefore the effect may be a little more difficult to label precisely. If the writer describes a scene, he can produce an effect of, say, excitement. If he describes a person, then the effect ought really to be one of the character and personality of the person. Clearly, this is more complex than excitement and somewhat harder to analyze.

Nevertheless, it *can* be analyzed, in a degree anyway. The writer of a character sketch normally analyzes the traits of the character and depicts them as vividly and concretely as he can. He does not merely inform the reader about them, but appeals to the reader's senses and emotions; he makes use of the techniques of emotional appeal discussed at the beginning of this chapter. Ideally, the reader should come to feel that he *knows* the person who is the subject of the sketch. If he does have this feeling, the character sketch is successful.

Good subjects for a character sketch might be:

an actual person whom the writer knows
a composite personality of two or more actual persons
a character from a work of creative literature—drama, fiction, or narrative poetry—which the writer has read
a character whom the writer himself invents

For illustration, here is a passage from the very beginning of a novel (*Northanger Abbey*) by Jane Austen. It is a sketch of the central character as a child.

No one who had ever seen Catherine Morland in her infancy would have supposed her born to be an heroine. . . . She had a thin awkward figure, a sallow skin without colour, dark lank hair, and strong features; so much for her person, and not less unpropitious for heroism seemed her mind. She was fond of all boys' play, and greatly preferred cricket, not merely to dolls, but to the more heroic enjoyments of infancy, nursing a dormouse, feeding a canary-bird, or watering a rose-bush. Indeed she had no taste for a garden, and if she gathered flowers at all, it was chiefly for the pleasure of mischief, at least so it was conjectured from her always preferring those which she was forbidden to take. Such were her propensities; her abilities were quite as extraordinary. She never could learn or understand anything before she was taught, and sometimes not even then, for she was often inattentive, and occasionally stupid. Her mother was three months in teaching her only to repeat the "Beggar's Petition," and, after all, her next sister Sally could say it better than she could. Not that Catherine was always stupid; by no means; she learnt the fable of "The Hare and many Friends," as quickly as any girl in England. Her mother wished her to learn music; and Catherine was sure she should like it, for she was very fond of tinkling the keys of the old forlorn spinnet, so at eight years old she began. She learnt a year and could not bear it; and Mrs. Morland, who did not insist on her daughters being accomplished in spite of incapacity or distaste, allowed her to leave off. The day which dismissed the music-master was one of the happiest of Catherine's life. Her taste for drawing was not superior; though whenever she could obtain the outside of a letter from her mother, or seize upon any other odd piece of paper, she did what she could in that way by drawing houses and trees, hens and chickens, all very much like one another. Writing and accounts she was taught by her father; French by her mother. Her proficiency in either was not remarkable, and she shirked her lessons in both whenever she could. What a strange unaccountable character! for with all these symptoms of profligacy at ten years old, she had neither a bad heart nor a bad temper, was seldom stubborn, scarcely ever quarrelsome, and very kind to the little ones, with few interruptions of tyranny. She was, moreover, noisy and wild, hated confinement and cleanliness, and loved nothing so well in the world as rolling down the green slope at the back of the house.

Procedure in Description. In addition to the matters that pertain generally to all writing with emotional appeal, certain considerations apply to description specifically. These include point of view, descriptive organization, and the use of concrete detail.

Point of View. The question of *point of view* arises in the planning of any description of a place or scene. Description implies an observer: from what point of view is this observer looking at the scene as he describes it? The writer of a piece of description should select one appropriate to the effect he intends to produce.

For certain descriptive compositions only one viewpoint might be feasible, but usually there are a number of possibilities. For the scene in the stadium, for example, the point of view might be that of someone sitting in the stands, perhaps in the cheering section; of a player on the field, or at ground level on the sidelines; or perhaps, if the writer has a vivid imagination, of a pilot in a low-flying plane or helicopter, towing an advertising streamer through the air.

This is not to imply that the description must be written in the first person—that the writer, imagining himself to be in one of the suggested positions, must say, "From here I see . . ."; "Looking downward to the right, I notice . . . ," etc. At times, to be sure, it is effective for the observer to emerge as a distinct personality; sometimes his identity is more important than his location. For the street corner in a slum, for instance, he might be someone who has lived in the neighborhood or a stranger visiting the scene; clearly, each of these two points of view would be appropriate to a different effect. For most purposes, however, the implied observer need not be identified; he need not even overtly appear. The description may be written in the third person and may give the impression of being objective—although of course the writer himself is interpreting the scene and controlling the emotional effect. The fact is that a clearly conceived point of view is essential to the unity of the description as a whole.

Descriptive Organization. The principles of organization for a descriptive theme are fundamentally the same as for other kinds of themes; most important are the considerations of internal logic, smooth progression, and climax (see Chapter 3). But there are particular patterns of organization which are especially likely to be appropriate in description: the spatial pattern, sometimes with an added element of the chronological, and the analytical pattern.

SPATIAL ORGANIZATION. The *spatial pattern,* as the name implies, means organization based on location in space. Plainly, it is often the best pattern for the description of a scene. The actual size of the scene may vary greatly—from one room, or one corner of one room, to half the universe (the sky on a clear night)—but always the picture will have dimensions; there will be different parts of the scene to be described, different locations in the space to be included. In what order should these be given? Here is part of the usefulness of the implied observer, of the carefully selected point of view. For, in this context, the locations are relative to the observer; they are the different parts of the scene as he is looking at it. The distinctions among their locations in space, then, are left and right, up and down, near and far, in front and behind, and so on.

The basic principle of spatial organization is simply that the writer should make systematic use of these distinctions; that is, he should follow a consciously predetermined pattern based upon them. He may begin at the left-hand side of his scene and proceed to the right, or begin at the bottom and go up, or begin in the foreground and proceed toward the background. He does not have to be absolutely inflexible; the observer's eye need not invariably move in the same direction, provided that any change is made clear to the reader; but in general the movement should be consistent.

As already suggested, an element of *time sequence* or *chronology* may enter into the organization. For example, consider the stadium again, and presume the point of view to be that of a student in the cheering section. The description might begin with the things nearest the observer: the rest of the cheering section, and the surrounding seats on the same side of the stands. Then the account might proceed down to the sidelines (with cheerleaders, etc.), out onto and across the field; then to the stands opposite—a picture similar to the first, but seen from farther away—and finally up past the flags on the opposite rim to the airplanes towing their streamers above. Then, for a detail especially appropriate if the effect is to be one of spirit and excitement, the eye might drop back down to the field, where the bands are forming at each end. The whistle blows for the end of the half; the teams leave the field; the music and the marching begin. Here is movement from foreground to background and then to mid-foreground again, and progression in time as well as in space; but the initial consistent movement in space, from near to far, is basic; the later movement back to something nearer—clearly indicated, to avoid confusion—serves a good functional purpose.

ANALYTICAL ORGANIZATION. The *analytical pattern* also involves—as indeed any principle of organization must involve—the presenting of parts in an appropriate order; the nature of these parts is different from that of various locations in space. The parts in a spatial pattern are, so to speak, already there. The writer may sometimes have to decide just where the dividing lines belong, but it is clear that there *are* divisions; no scene worth describing is entirely homogeneous. Analysis, on the other hand, is an operation performed upon something that *is* essentially homogeneous—upon a subject that does not have obvious natural divisions, but rather presents itself as an integral unity. To analyze means to break down; we cannot break anything down unless to start with it is in some sense whole. The *parts* in an analytical pattern, then, are artificially conceived; they are separated out of a larger whole by a deliberate process of abstraction.

Analytical organization is by no means peculiar to description. Actually, it occurs more frequently in other forms of discourse, especially in exposition—in the account, for example, of a process like the operation of an engine; the continuous process is analyzed or broken down into separate parts or stages for the purpose of explanation. Analytical organization is often useful in description too, although the inexperienced writer is likely to overlook its value in this form.

The analytical pattern is usually appropriate to the character sketch, the subject of which is a human personality. In describing such a subject, obviously, the writer cannot use spatial organization. Personality has no parts arranged in space; indeed, in one sense it has no parts at all; it is an integral unity, a whole. What the writer must do, therefore, is analyze this whole. If he is writing about a man named Paul, he thinks of the traits, talents, attitudes, prejudices, the kinds of impulse, of insight and of blindness, that may be considered the parts of "Paulness." They are only analytical parts, not real ones, for in Paul they are all a single entity. The writer's list of distinguishing characteristics will never be complete; a human personality is too complex for any human analysis to exhaust. Furthermore, the writer must reduce the list, incomplete though it already is, by making a selection from among the items on it. He must focus on the salient few, if he is going to develop them properly. Having made his analysis, then, he selects the three or four most characteristic traits, with perhaps a few more that are closely enough related to these to go into the same paragraphs; he arranges them in the most effective order and develops each in turn. The organization—the determination of the parts—is analytical; the development should be sensory and emotional.

Concrete Detail. The use of appropriately vivid and concrete language, desirable in all kinds of writing, is especially important in writing that is addressed to the emotions, and most especially in description. In description the effect depends upon creating an impression of the thing described; such an impression is developed not by abstractions, not by general statements, but by *concrete detail*.

This principle may best be made clear by illustration. The description of the stadium scene, it was suggested, might begin with what is nearest to the observer, the rest of the cheering section and the surrounding seats. What particular details in this area might be most vivid or most appropriate to the effect of excitement, or both? Say, a brisk breeze is blowing; a student with a turned-up fur collar bends over in his seat to tap out his corncob pipe; a small shower of orange sparks is blown along three or four seats downwind, among legs some of which are in vulnerable nylon. There is a squeal of distress—drowned immediately by a chorus of yells as everyone springs to his feet, including the squealer; she teeters on one foot as she holds the other ankle, but then drops it, oblivious to her momentary distress, so she can stand on her toes and peer down in the direction of the goal posts. A few seconds later everyone is seated again, except a bald but not-very-old graduate in the next section, who is still shouting although he has forgotten to take the cigar out of his mouth. . . . Compare the effect of a general statement like "The stadium was a scene of confused excitement." The specific details create a much more vivid impression.

NARRATIVE

Narrative writing tells a story. It is concerned, therefore, with time and with action. More specifically (as indicated in Chapter 1) narrative is that form of discourse which recounts a series of related events in such a way as to develop a central meaning. At times this meaning is little more than the obvious surface significance of the events themselves. An ordinary news story in a newspaper, for instance, may mean nothing more than that "this is what happened." Sometimes, on the other hand, the events are narrated in order to dramatize a general principle, and this is the real significance of the story, whether or not it is ever made explicit. Fables and parables illustrate this latter sort of narrative. The story of the good Samaritan, for example, is a definition of what it means to be a good neighbor.

Representative Types of Narrative. Somewhere between these two extremes are the types of narrative writing which the relatively inexperienced writer may most profitably undertake. Two such types are the straightforward true account of personal experience, and the simple plotted narrative.

Account of Personal Experience. The *account of personal experience* might appropriately be undertaken first. It is a kind of writing for which everyone does have material to use, and which even the writer with very little experience usually feels he can do. Handling it well, to be sure, will require what all good writing requires: the exercise of care and judgment.

Like any other narrative, the account of personal experience should develop a central meaning. In selecting a subject, then, the writer might fix upon an experience which has had a particular significance for him; that is, an experience from which he has learned something. This significance will be the meaning that will emerge in the story. A good account might be written on one of the following topics:

An experience that made me change my mind.
My father (mother, brother, friend) turned out to be right after all.

How I found out about feminine (masculine) psychology.
An educative mistake.
My first lesson in grass-roots politics.

Simple Plotted Narrative. The *simple plotted narrative* [5] is a more advanced type of writing. It calls for the exercise of creative imagination. This requirement does *not* place it beyond the reach of all but a talented few, for practically everyone does have such imagination. In order to use this faculty effectively in writing plotted narrative, however, the relatively inexperienced writer should be guided by a few special considerations of procedure.

More basic than any point of procedure, though, is what may properly be called a fundamental principle of writing imaginative narrative: the writer should deal with an area of experience with which he is familiar. Although what he is writing is not literally true, it should still be "true to life"; it will be, if the writer deals with a kind of life that he knows. For example, only a person who has been in military service should try to write about soldiers. In general, unless he has a kind of special background, the writer will do best to select an area of common experience, such as that of school life, home and family life, or neighborhood and community life. These afford ample material for good plotted narrative.

Procedure in Narrative. The procedure for preparing a composition which has been outlined in Chapter 3 applies to narrative as well as to other writing. A few additional principles are essential for the writer of narrative to bear in mind, and a few more for the writer of plotted narrative.

Procedure in General. The selection and the arrangement of material are among the considerations that are important in all writing but especially so in narrative. They are important because, in this context, they are likely to be overlooked or slighted. The writer of a true narrative is likely to feel, in an account of personal experience, "All I need to do is tell what happened." But in any significant human experience he cannot possibly tell *all* that happened; even when he has decided just what things he will tell, there remains the question of how he can best arrange them.

SELECTION. In planning types of writing other than true narrative, ordinarily the selection of material is preceded by the gathering of

[5] The whole category of plotted narrative includes the established forms of fiction, like the short story—a highly developed genre, with certain characteristic features, a full discussion of which would be outside the scope of this Outline; therefore the term "simple plotted narrative" is used, to exclude the full-scale short story.

material; and although it is possible to gather too much, this danger is not very great. In preparing a true narrative, however, and especially an account of recent personal experience, no gathering is necessary. The writer already has all his material in mind; he recalls vividly what happened. For this reason, he must be all the more rigorous in making his *selection*. He may be tempted to include many things merely because they did happen, and he remembers them vividly. Certain of these may be inappropriate or superfluous, and if so he ought to omit them.

In determining what should be included and what omitted, he should use what is always the basic criterion for selection: the appropriateness of each part of the material, its functional value for developing the central idea or effect. For example, consider a narrative of personal experience on the last of the topics suggested on page 105, "My first lesson in grass-roots politics." Suppose that the writer was asked, by a committee sponsoring a candidate for public office, to visit several homes in a particular area and try to enlist the residents' support. He agreed and spent two or three evenings in doing this work. The principal lesson which the experience taught him, he believes, is that most persons are concerned about their government and eager to discuss the qualifications of candidates for election. This lesson will be the central idea of the account he is going to write.

The chances are that in making these calls—especially if he was working in his own neighborhood and visiting people whom he knew—he talked about many different things besides politics: about sports, for instance, or about films or television programs. Perhaps he talked about school with a neighbor's daughter while waiting for her parents to finish their dinner. It is just possible that one or two comments made in these conversations might be pertinent to political issues or might illustrate the attitude which the writer wishes to characterize. If so, then presumably he will refer to these comments in his account. Most of this material will be irrelevant, though it was part of the whole experience on which he is basing his narrative. In selecting what to include, therefore, he will omit the bulk of this casual conversation and concentrate on the discussions which had to do directly with government.

ARRANGEMENT. Ordinarily the basic pattern of *arrangement* in a narrative is chronological. Although the basic pattern is predetermined, the writer should not just automatically begin with the earliest event, trusting simply to go straight on from there. Rather, as for any kind of composition, he should carefully plan the organization in advance. He should ask himself also whether or not any variation or departure from the strict chronological arrangement might be effective.

A factor which might sometimes make a variation appropriate, for instance, is the principle of climax or emphasis. To continue the same example used above, the account of grass-roots politics: perhaps the event which seemed to the writer to be potentially the most effective in developing his feeling about his neighbors' concern for good government occurred on the first of the two or three evenings he spent in making his calls. For maximum emphasis, he ought to save his best material for last. There is no reason why he should not depart from strict time sequence in order to secure this emphasis, provided only that he makes the modified sequence clear to the reader. A simple way to do so would be to introduce the account of this event with a statement like "What impressed me most of all, however, was the discussion I had had on the first evening, when I called on James and Helen Macallister."

For an illustration of true narrative and most of the principles here set forth, see the theme "Song Is Supreme" in Chapter 3 and the accompanying account of how it might have been planned and written.

Procedure with Fictional Narrative. The selection and arrangement of material are of course important in both fictional and true narrative, but there is not so much danger that they will be slighted in fictional narrative. In true narrative the events have actually occurred; the writer considers them, determines what central theme they embody (what feeling or idea or both), and then, as we have seen, selects from the whole experience those elements which will best develop this theme. In plotted or fictional narrative, on the other hand, the theme is the point of departure. In theory, anyway, the writer has a theme in mind from the first. His basic purpose is similar to that of the writer of true narrative: to develop this central feeling or idea. Rather than making a selection from actual experience, however, he makes up imaginary experience; that is, he invents a story. In doing so he gives attention to certain special considerations, chiefly tempo and degree of detail.

INVENTION OF STORY. Theoretically speaking, in the writing of fictional narrative, the theme comes first. This may often be the sequence actually; the theme may really be that element of the story which the writer conceives first. It may be an idea, simple or complex—anything from a homely principle like "Crime does not pay" to the philosophy of existentialism. It may be primarily an attitude or an emotion; more often it may be an idea with an emotional counterpart. Then the writer *invents a story* in which the action illustrates the operation of this idea or develops the mood of this emotion, or both.

The best kind of example here will be an actual piece of fiction—say, a novel that is widely read and familiar. Suppose the theme, which the writer has in mind, to be a feeling or idea that human life is directed by a force or forces beyond human control; that these forces are at best indifferent to human happiness, and perhaps positively malevolent; that the operation of these forces is evident in the shaping of our lives by what we call chance or coincidence. Thomas Hardy held this belief and embodied it as the theme of his novel *The Return of the Native*.[6]

On the other hand, the elements of a plotted narrative may be put together in a different sequence. What really comes first may be, not theme, but one of the other elements of fiction: plot or setting or character. A suggestion for the *plot*—that is, the action, or what happens in the narrative—may come from the writer's own life, or that of someone he knows. Examining his life reflectively, he may see in a particular episode a type of significant human experience. Whatever he perceives its significance to be, that is the theme for his story. In this case his writing of the fictional narrative will be rather similar in certain ways to the writing of true narrative. In certain ways, not in all: he will not be actually recounting the episode, but using it only as the germ of his story; he may change it a great deal, adding to as well as subtracting from it in order best to dramatize his theme.

Setting is the time and place in which the action occurs. The writer may think of a kind of setting or environment with which he is familiar. "To what type of human experience does living in this environment conduce?" he asks himself; the answer is his story. Again, he may think first of a particular *character*—a person whom he knows or a character whom he invents, perhaps by combining traits of actual persons whom he knows. Here the question out of which the narrative might emerge would be, "In what kind of human action might the essential flavor of this character be effectively illustrated?" For most relatively inexperienced writers, these latter ways of evolving a story are usually better than beginning with an abstract principle or concept of an emotion and erecting the whole superstructure of a narrative upon it.

TEMPO AND DEGREE OF DETAIL. Having invented his story, the writer knows what events will be included. In writing the story, how rapidly ought he to go through one event to the next? Or (what amounts to practically the same question) how much should he include of elements like dialogue, analysis of a character's thoughts, and so on, to flesh out and enrich certain parts of the story? What proportion of

---

[6] The preceding sentence is not a fully adequate statement of the theme of *The Return of the Native;* only the novel itself is that. In the creating of this novel we cannot be sure the theme actually came first. It *might* have come first—and that is enough for the purpose of illustration.

the total space should he devote to each element? The answer here will depend upon various considerations—including the over-all scope of the story, in actual length as well as in complexity. If the story is to be only 500 or 1000 words long or even a few hundred more, there will not be space for much detailed development; this is short compass for a plotted narrative. Under these circumstances, the action should be confined to one episode, and the whole story devoted to developing this one.

Sometimes the fictional narrative may be 2000 or 3000 or more words in length. Within these limits, the writer can and of course should invoke the general principles of proportion that apply to all writing: he should economize wherever he appropriately can and save as much space as possible for what is most important—in this case, for what will be most effective in dramatizing the theme and producing the central impression. A fictional narrative of 2000 or 3000 words is still short; therefore, the writer should usually select two or at most three episodes, including one climactic scene, for development in detail. Rather than telling a whole story in summary fashion, it is important that he treat at least some portion of the material fully.

The period of time within which the events of the story are included may vary: a few minutes, a few hours, two or three days, a week or so; usually the time covered by a short narrative will not extend much farther. Whatever the length of time, in plotted narrative it is normally a good practice to have the story itself begin relatively late in the period; for a rule of thumb, more than half way through. The story proper proceeds chronologically from there; the reader can be told about earlier happenings by various means.[7] The writer may himself briefly summarize prior events; he may give the thoughts that go through the mind of a character who is reminiscing; he may have two or more characters talk about what has occurred; he may use letters, excerpts from a diary, or similar devices. Such methods enable him to cover the antecedent action quickly and thereby to insure that what happens near the end of the period—presumably the most important and climactic action—will not be slighted.

Exercises

1. a. In the space at the left of each word below put an *S* if the word would ordinarily be relatively effective for sensory appeal, an *E* for direct emotional appeal, or an *N* for neither.

[7] This filling in of the background of previous experience is known technically as *exposition*.

_____(1) anger	_____(6) sandpaper	_____(11) pleasant
_____(2) heretic	_____(7) savior	_____(12) sister
_____(3) tinkle	_____(8) paper	_____(13) gleam
_____(4) child	_____(9) immortal	_____(14) smoke
_____(5) pretty	_____(10) molasses	_____(15) circumstance

b. Rearrange the following sentences to give appropriate prominence to the words of sensory or direct emotional appeal.

(1) Through an opening in the rocks we saw the crescent moon after we had been walking for several minutes in the cave.

(2) It was a duty enjoined upon her by her deepest faith, she realized, closing the book and staring out the window.

(3) On our side of the valley we could hear the rattle of rifle fire when we stopped talking.

(4) He reached the top of the staircase, and something cold and wet was dripping on his neck as he paused to consider.

(5) When his ship finally came back to the port after two years on the high seas or abroad, he could see his wife and children in the crowd of people who were shouting and gesticulating on the pier.

c. For each of the following, write a sentence or two which will *imply* what is said in the explicit statement.

(1) He was a loyal friend to me.

(2) She was a jealous woman.

(3) He acted like a coward.

(4) We were all afraid of him.

(5) He was a true gentleman.

2. a. Formulate a thesis for a piece of argument addressed chiefly to the intellect on each of the following issues.

(1) fraternities or sororities

(2) compulsory class attendance

(3) police protection (its adequacy in your community)

(4) Federal aid to higher education

(5) marriage between members of different religious faiths

b. For each thesis that you formulated in 2. *a*. above, state in a sentence or two an opposing argument which you might anticipate.

c. Of the following statements mark with a *D* those which would presumably have to be proved or demonstrated, with an *A* those which might reasonably be assumed, or accepted without proof.

_____(1) Many parents would be disturbed if they had reason to believe that their children were losing their religious faith in college.

_____(2) Compulsory chapel attendance provides a guarantee that the maximum number of college students will maintain their religious faith.

_____(3) The most effective single measure to be taken against juvenile delinquency is slum clearance.

_____(4) Juvenile delinquency is a social evil.

_____(5) It is desirable that all persons should subscribe to the same body of religious doctrine.

3. a. Suggest appropriate emotional effects to be developed in descriptions of the following scenes:
(1) a field of grain at sunset
(2) a college bookstore at the beginning of a term or quarter
(3) a children's swimming pool on a hot August afternoon
(4) a theater or concert hall just before a performance
(5) the site of an automobile accident on a highway
b. Suggest an appropriate point of view for each of the descriptions in *3. a.* above.

4. Indicate whether each of the following statements is true or false.

_____a. Description as a form of discourse is practically always addressed chiefly to the emotions.

_____b. Elements of contrasting emotional tone should never be admitted into a single piece of writing addressed to the emotions.

_____c. In informal argument it is not important to indicate the source of material introduced in evidence.

_____d. Analytical organization is likely to be useful for a character sketch.

_____e. Abstract or general statements are likely to be effective for evoking an emotional impression in descriptive writing.

_____f. Narrative may appeal to the intellect or the emotions or both.

_____g. The writer of an account of personal experience should recount everything that happened.

_____h. The writer of a true narrative should never deviate from a straightforward chronological sequence of events.

_____i. The first suggestion for a plotted narrative may come from a setting or a character or from actual experience as well as from an abstract idea.

_____j. In writing fictional narrative it is usually a good practice to begin the story proper more than half way through the total period of time to be included.

6 THE RESEARCH PAPER

Research is systematic investigation which brings forth the logical answer to a specific question. The *research paper* (called also the investigative paper, library paper, long paper, reference paper, or term paper) is the expository presentation of the evidence revealing that answer. Strictly speaking, the research paper contributes something new to the store of knowledge on the subject concerned.

This strict interpretation applies more rigidly to research on the graduate level than on the undergraduate level. Even the beginner, although he is not expected to make a contribution to scholarship, has a definite standard of originality to meet. His main objective is to assimilate, or bring together and make to bear upon a particular question, information that has not previously been so treated. In the process he automatically accomplishes the other objectives of the exercise.

These other objectives include (1) awareness of the importance of properly choosing and limiting a subject for research, (2) self-reliance in using a college library, (3) experience in evaluating source materials, (4) training in careful reading and purposeful note-taking, (5) discipline in the inductive method of organizing data, and (6) practice in composing and documenting a relatively long paper. These six objectives reflect the steps through which the student must proceed in fulfilling a research assignment in his composition course. Taken together, they constitute a basic learning process which is useful in any course.

This chapter explains the steps in the research process and offers suggestions to help the student become proficient in handling each step.[1] The chapter can offer no way to avoid the challenge which research presents. Research is hard work, but it is also gratifying work.

SELECTING A SUBJECT

In a way, *selecting the subject* is the most important step in the research process, for no amount of work can produce a good research paper if the subject is an inappropriate one. For the beginner, a factual topic is usually better than a judgmental or interpretive one, much better than a strongly controversial one. Working with source materials on a highly controversial topic presents special problems in recognizing the prejudices and keeping the study objective. Problems of this nature are

[1] See also "Typical Procedure for Writing a Composition" in Chapter 3.

sufficiently challenging in research on a factual topic. A good plan for the student in search of a subject is to begin with a factual question in which he is interested and on which he has an open mind.

Starting with a Question. In his classes, in his study sessions, in his recreation periods, the student encounters questions for which there are no ready answers. Perhaps he listens to a lecture on chemical progress and wonders just what developments occurred in the American chemical industry during World War II. Perhaps he studies a history lesson on Napoleon's exile and begins to speculate on which was the stronger: Napoleon's influence on the way of life on Elba, or the influence on Napoleon of events and circumstances on the island. Perhaps he hears a political speech and would like to know how well a certain United States President in the past carried out his campaign promises on a particular issue. Perhaps he sees a copy of the *Quarterly Review* and recalls having heard that the *Edinburgh Review* had an interestingly different make-up which has not been carefully analyzed in comparison with that of the *Quarterly*. Perhaps he plays a German-made violin and has wished for an opportunity to learn how violin-making in Germany relates historically to violin-making in Italy. Perhaps he reads a condensed version of Charles Dickens' *Oliver Twist* and becomes curious about how it differs from the original novel. Perhaps he is studying the architecture of windows and thinks a special knowledge of the stained glass of York Minster would be fascinating. Perhaps he reads an article on the Tonga-Kermadec Trench in the South Pacific and wonders how far the techniques of undersea exploration have been developed or how much is known of the geological, physical, and biological features of the ocean trenches. Perhaps he is particularly interested in military history and would like to know the extent to which the Allies' airborne tactics evolved during World War II. Any such question, the answering of which means drawing upon various sources of information, may be the germ of a good topic for a research paper.

When he has accumulated several promising questions, the student should select from them two or three in which he is really interested and on which he would like to be well-informed. The student's genuine interest in his subject and sincere desire for information on it will motivate him in the study and note-taking necessary for the writing of an interesting and informative final paper. Still other considerations are necessary, however, before the choice of a question is made. Important among these is the availability of material.

Considering Availability of Material. When he has narrowed his choice to two or three questions which challenge his curiosity, the student is ready to check on the materials available in his college library.[2] (Suggestions on using the library appear in a later section in this chapter.) For many subjects the materials stem from two kinds of sources: primary and secondary. Primary source material is original evidence, whereas secondary source material is, as the term implies, second-hand information on the original evidence. Although secondary sources are often helpful and should not be overlooked, first-hand sources are regularly more reliable and are therefore more frequently the main concern of the researcher.

If, for instance, the student compares a condensation of *Oliver Twist* with Dickens' original novel, he will investigate chiefly those two books, his primary sources, but he will also study the opinions of literary critics on the two versions and attempt to add something new and significant. Likewise, if he proposes to evaluate a President's record in fulfilling campaign promises, the student will scrutinize as indispensable primary sources the President's campaign speeches and the legislation of Congress during the President's term in office; in addition he will take into account as secondary sources the interpretations that historians have made of the speeches and the legislation. It is possible to write a good research paper without using primary sources (sometimes there are none), but it is unwise to ignore them.

What the student finds in the way of source materials—adequate information—in his campus library may determine for him which of his questions he should pursue. For instance, he would be unwise, no matter how interested, to choose the question "How did the make-up of the *Edinburgh Review* differ from that of the *Quarterly Review?*" unless his school library has on file copies of both of these early-nineteenth-century periodicals. (Even if an off-campus library does have such files, the student will probably find that he cannot afford the time to make frequent trips to that library.) Before he settles on any question, however, he should make as sure as he can that the question has not already been answered. If he finds a ready-made answer when he makes his preliminary investigation (or even later), he should discard the question and select another. Reviewing or summarizing one source of information does not constitute research. For this reason questions calling for biographical accounts or for explanations of processes or mechanisms do not usually make satisfactory research topics.

[2] At this point a conference with his instructor may save the student much time. If the student presents two or three questions which he thinks will yield good topics, the instructor can advise him on how to locate the best information or warn him against topics for which the evidence is uncertain or unavailable.

If he is fortunate enough to find adequate source materials (but no ready-made answers) on more than one of his proposed questions, the student can choose on the bases of interest and desire for information. But he does not yet have a limited topic or central idea for his paper.

Limiting the Subject. When he begins researching the question he has selected, the student is likely to find it too broad to be answered effectively within the limits of time and space prescribed in the assignment. For example, should the assignment call for a paper of 2500 to 3000 words within six weeks, a question like "How did the American chemical industry develop during World War II?" could be limited to the developments in rubber, paint, or another product. Or the study of the stained glass of York Minster could be focused on color, design, or another quality of the windows. Actually, the scope of the paper should remain tentative until the student has made a careful survey of the available materials and has begun to read and take notes.

As he proceeds with his examination of sources, the student should constantly keep in mind that eventually he must turn his question into a *thesis,* that is, a single declarative sentence stating the central idea of the paper. He must realize, moreover, that he can formulate this thesis only after he has critically explored sufficient source materials to see what answer to his question the facts themselves dictate. Obviously, no one can make an intelligent statement on a particular subject, such as the developments in paint during a certain period or the use of color in certain stained glass windows, until he has studied and has synthesized all the information pertinent to it. But when the question is clearly defined, when the evidence is clearly understood, the answer inevitably presents itself. The student can then formulate the answer into a thesis. This thesis, this *one* idea, when it is finally stated, should be so restricted that it can be fully developed and specifically supported within the limits set by the assignment.

INVESTIGATING THE SUBJECT

The most time-consuming and often the most challenging phase of the research process is the actual investigation of the subject. This calls for considerable work in the library and perhaps elsewhere, if some of the materials can be taken out. Before he begins *investigating the topic* for his long paper, the student has another significant task to accomplish: getting acquainted with as many of the resources of his college library as he possibly can. Doubtless his instructor will assign specific exercises in the use of library tools. In any event, the student will want to make several tours of the reference and periodical rooms, examining and learning to use effectively various reference books and indexes. If possible, he will want also to visit the stacks of circulation books.

Noting Library Organization.[3] If the library has open stacks or if he is given stack privileges for his research assignment, the student will want especially to learn the system of classification so that he can save time in locating what he needs. He will use the classification numbers when he fills out call slips in order to check out books. The two best-known systems of classification are the Dewey decimal system and the Library of Congress system.

Dewey Decimal System. In the *Dewey decimal system* all published materials are classified into ten numbered divisions, each with continuing subdivisions as needed. The following list shows only the ten main divisions and the first two steps of a continuing subdivision.

000. General Works
100. Philosophy
200. Religion
300. Sociology
400. Philology
500. Natural Science
600. Useful Arts
700. Fine Arts
800. Literature
    810. American Literature
    820. English Literature
        821. English Poetry
        822. English Drama
        823. English Fiction
        824. English Essays
        825. English Oratory
        826. English Letters
        827. English Satire
        828. English Miscellany
        829. Anglo-Saxon
    830. German Literature
    840. French Literature
    850. Italian Literature
    860. Spanish Literature

[3] Most college libraries provide their own handbooks, which students may have on request at the circulation desk, showing the floor plan, outlining the system of classification, explaining how to borrow books, and giving other useful information.

870. Latin Literature
880. Greek Literature
890. Minor Literatures
900. History

Library of Congress System. In the *Library of Congress system* all published materials are classified into twenty lettered divisions, each with continuing subdivisions as needed. The following list shows only the twenty main divisions.

A. General Works and Polygraphy
B. Philosophy and Religion
C. History and Auxiliary Sciences
D. History and Topography (except American)
E., F. American History and Topography
G. Geography and Anthropology
H. Social Sciences
J. Political Science
K. Law
L. Education

M. Music
N. Fine Arts
P. Language and Literature
Q. Science
R. Medicine
S. Agriculture, and Plant and Animal Husbandry
T. Technology
U. Military Science
V. Naval Science
Z. Bibliography and Library Science

If a book represents more than one of these twenty divisions, its classification number begins with more than one letter; the classification number of a book on medical science, for example, begins with the letters *QR*.

Making a Preliminary Bibliography. A *preliminary bibliography* is a list of books and other publications which the research worker believes will be of value to him in answering the question he has chosen to investigate. Once assembled, the preliminary bibliography (or working bibliography, as it is sometimes called) needs to be adjusted from time to time, whenever any work listed there proves useless or a helpful one comes to light. The final bibliography—that is, the bibliography which accompanies the completed paper and which lists only the works actually used—is really the preliminary bibliography in its finally adjusted form.

The necessary adjustments can be made easily if a separate 3 x 5 card is used for each entry. A card referring to a book should contain the call number; the full name of the author or the editor (followed by *ed.*), surname first; the title (underlined); the facts of publication (place, publisher, and date); and whatever note the student may see fit to write to himself about the usefulness of the book. A card referring to a magazine article should contain the full name of the author (if available), surname first; the title (in quotation marks); the name of the magazine; the volume number (if the magazine is bound); the date of issue (in parentheses); the inclusive page numbers; and whatever reminder the student may consider helpful. The following diagrams illustrate a useful system of arrangement. (The entries relate to the specimen paper at the end of this chapter.)

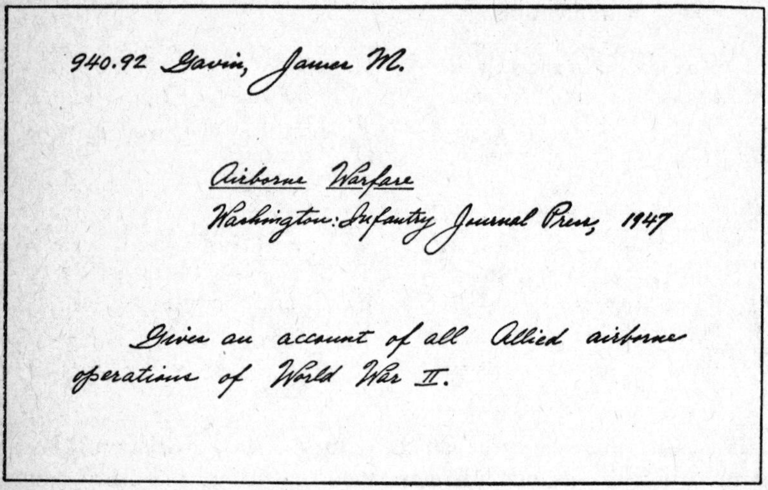

940.92 Gavin, James M.

Airborne Warfare
Washington: Infantry Journal Press, 1947

Gives an account of all Allied airborne operations of World War II.

FIG. 1.—BIBLIOGRAPHY CARD FOR A BOOK

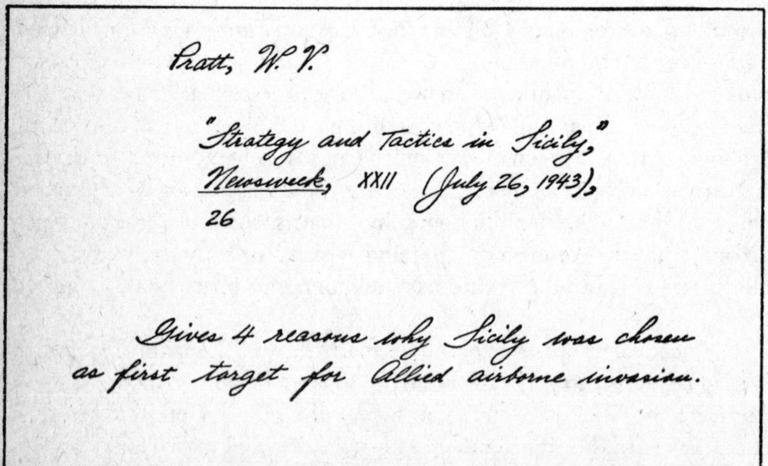

Pratt, W. V.

"Strategy and Tactics in Sicily,"
Newsweek, XXII (July 26, 1943), 26

Gives 4 reasons why Sicily was chosen as first target for Allied airborne invasion.

FIG. 2.—BIBLIOGRAPHY CARD FOR A MAGAZINE ARTICLE

Preparing a good preliminary bibliography requires much care and, usually, several work sessions in the library. The card catalogue (see below) and various other indexes, many of which are listed in the appendix of this book (pp. 405ff.), are indispensable aids for locating source materials.[4] But this stage of the research process involves more than discovering bibliographical data and transferring it to cards.

Concurrent with, and perhaps extending beyond, the compiling of the bibliography should go a preliminary survey of the subject and the formulation of a tentative outline. These steps should precede any note-taking. The survey of the subject requires careful examination of such things as tables of contents and indexes in books and scanning of relevant chapters in books and selected articles in periodicals and reference works in order to discover the logical phases of the subject. Naming these phases and arranging the names in an appropriate sequence will provide a skeleton outline—a set of headings which will serve as a filing system for the information to be gathered on the subject and will appear as brief labels (or slugs) on the note cards. This preliminary study of specific sources may also yield further bibliographical data, which often appear in footnotes or appendixes.

The historical time of the question being investigated is important at this stage of the work. For a question on recent deep sea exploration, the bibliography will include chiefly articles; for a question on the stained glass of York Minster, chiefly books. The latest editions or supplements of encyclopedias and other reference books are preferable to older ones for information and bibliographical leads on current topics; but the older editions, which in some instances are the more scholarly, often serve well for topics from the past.

Reference Works. The lists which appear in the appendix of this book (on pp. 405–417), though far from complete, include representative *reference works* available in the reference rooms of most college libraries. These lists include encyclopedias, dictionaries, wordbooks, yearbooks, biographies, reference works by subject, bibliographies by subject, and general and special indexes.

The Card Catalogue. The *card catalogue* is a card-file index of the books in the library; it is also a guide designed especially to aid the re-

---

[4] To see if a bibliography covering his subject has appeared in a book or a periodical in recent years, the student may wish to consult (or, if necessary, ask a librarian to help him consult) the *Bibliographic Index: A Cumulative Bibliography of Bibliographies* (New York: H. W. Wilson Co., 1938–). If he finds a pertinent bibliography listed, he will need to bring it up to date and possibly supplement it in other ways or select from it the works suitable for his purpose.

search worker in his quest for information. One of its important features is that each book is listed more than once in the alphabetical file; that is, each book is represented by an author (or editor, or translator) card, a title card, and possibly one or more subject cards. Hence the student can locate the book he wants if he knows only the name of its author, or its title, or the subject it treats. If he looks up the author card on a work he expects to use, he can check the cards next to it to see whether the author has written any other books on the subject. If he looks up the subject card (a good thing to do), he will find next to it the cards representing books on the same subject by other authors. And of course the cross references to subject headings given on these cards may offer further leads for extending his bibliography.

Another very helpful feature of the card catalogue is that it contains special *see also* cards to guide the student to related subject headings. After the subject cards on meteorology, for instance, will probably be cards giving cross references to "air," "atmosphere," "climate," "rain," "weather," "wind," and so on.

Examination of one catalogue card will reveal some of the typical features of the whole catalogue. The following is a reproduction of a title card issued by the Library of Congress, which supplies catalogue cards for many libraries.

378.4
M319   The Manuale scholarium; an original account of life in the mediaeval university, tr. from the Latin by Robert Francis Seybolt . . . Cambridge, Harvard university press; [etc., etc.] 1921.
      122 p., 1 1. 21^{cm}.
      Bibliography: p 119–122.

    1. Universities and colleges—Europe. 2. Education, Medieval.
    I. Seybolt, Robert Francis, 1888–   tr.

                                21-26881

    Library of Congress   LA177.M3
    ——Copy 2.
   Copyright A 624177
            [3-3]

FIG. 3.—LIBRARY OF CONGRESS CATALOGUE CARD

In the upper left-hand corner appears the call number which the library has used in classifying and shelving the book and which the student must use in checking out the book. (In this example, the call number is based on the Dewey decimal system.)

In the first two and one-half lines of print appear the complete title of the book and the information that the book was translated from the Latin by the person named. (The absence of an author's name indicates that the original manuscript was anonymous.) The three suspension periods mean that further identification of the translator appears on the title page of the book but is not reproduced on the card.

In the third and fourth lines appear the facts of publication. The use of *etc.* in brackets shows that the Harvard University Press at Cambridge is not the only publisher named on the title page of the book.

The fifth line of print explains that the book contains 122 numbered pages, that it has one unnumbered leaf following the numbered pages, and that it is 21 centimeters tall (or requires 21 centimeters of shelf height).

The sixth line indicates that the book contains a bibliography on pages 119–122.

The seventh and eighth lines show that the book is also catalogued under the two subject headings given and under the name of the translator, who was born in 1888.

The information on the rest of the card is chiefly for librarians. The number at the right, for instance, tells that the Library of Congress catalogued this book in 1921 and that this was the 26,881st book the Library of Congress catalogued in that year. Then follow the Library of Congress call number and other data with which the student need not concern himself.

Each subject card for this book is identical to the title card except that the subject under which the card is filed appears at the top of the card. Likewise, on the translator card the information *Seybolt, Francis, 1888– tr.* appears first on the card.

Now let us see what a person looking for information on the daily routine in a medieval university can learn from examining this one catalogue card. In the first place, the words "an original account of life in the mediaeval university" let him know that *The Manuale Scholarium* is about the nearest thing to a primary source that he is likely to find on his subject. In the second place, he can tell that this book contains an extensive bibliography which may lead him to other useful works. Finally, he learns that he can turn to two subject headings in the card catalogue ("Universities and colleges—Europe" and "Education, Medieval") to find cards listing other books that the library has on his subject.

As the methods outlined in the preceding pages suggest, resourcefulness is the one thing that will help the student most as he works his way through reference books, indexes, and the card catalogue in an effort to make a good preliminary bibliography. This same resourcefulness, coupled with discrimination in using the works in his bibliography, will assist him in the reading and note-taking phase of the research.

Reading and Note-Taking. *Reading* and *note-taking* are really two separate though related tasks; thoughtful reading of any source of information should precede note-taking on that source. Intelligent reading often prevents wasteful note-taking, for such reading is the writer's final means of eliminating useless items from his preliminary bibliography. The purpose of the notes is to record accurately and systematically in small units all the borrowed information the writer expects to integrate in an organic whole composition. The notes serve the further purposes of classifying the separate facts and ideas on the basis of subject matter, of identifying the sources exactly, and of making clear distinctions between the quoted and the restated materials.

Evaluation of Sources. The person who has checked carefully on the availability of material and has worked out a preliminary bibliography on his question has already done much of the necessary *evaluation of sources* when he reaches the intensive-reading and note-taking stage of his investigation. He has already distinguished between primary and secondary sources. He has already considered the relationship between the historical time of his question and the dates of his sources. And he has already noted the selectivity in the bibliographies listed in reliable reference books. Still, he should test the value of each of his sources by the following questions: (1) Is the material relevant to the question being investigated? (2) Is the author an authority on the subject? Has he had access to first-hand information on the subject? Is he free of prejudice on the subject? Is his integrity unblemished? (3) Is the style of writing forthright? The meaning clear? (4) Is the reasoning logical? Are the assumptions sound? The comparisons basic? The cause-and-effect relationships real? The generalizations qualified and supported by accurate, representative data? (5) Is the publisher a reputable one? Unless the answer to each of these questions is affirmative, there is reason to be wary of the source.

Besides evaluating the source as a whole, one should consider the relative utility of its parts. The criterion for determining when to take notes—and how many—is the usefulness of the material for the purpose at hand. The fledgling researcher often takes notes on a whole article or book (especially if he finds it interesting) instead of using only those parts that bear directly on his topic. But he can discipline his note-taking if he keeps before him as a reminder a special card on which he has written the topic he is investigating and his tentative outline. If the material he is reading does not in any way answer his question, taking notes on it would be purposeless, no matter how interesting or authoritative the source. If it does in part answer the question but does not fit under any caption in his tentative outline, his immediate problem is to decide whether the information is important enough to warrant his including a new caption to cover it.

To check on the authoritativeness of a source, the researcher can use both external and internal evidence. To evaluate by means of external evidence, he looks outside the book or article for facts and judgments concerning it or its authors. He can consult special biographical reference books (see pp. 408–409) for information on how the author's education and experience are related to the subject. He may be able to find a review of the work, or at least critical comments on it by other writers on the same subject, some of whom he has listed in his bibliography. In the introductory part of the work itself, he may find certain statements of identification concerning the author; there too he will notice the date of publication and the name of the publisher. To evaluate by means of internal evidence, he can check the author's writing for common errors in reasoning (see pp. 20–26). He can also use his own judgment and his own growing knowledge of his subject as touchstones by which to measure the reasonableness of the source.

Mechanics of Note-Taking. Notes are most usable when written on cards of uniform size, 4x6 or 5x8, one note to a card and on one side only. Careful observance of these points facilitates organization of the notes. Half-sheets or even whole sheets of paper can take the place of cards, but are not so easy to rearrange as cards. Some research workers even prefer note sheets of assorted colors and use a special color for each sub-topic, thereby organizing the notes automatically.

A good procedure in note-taking is to write on the card, in this order, (1) the source of the note, *including the page reference,* (2) the outline caption or label (slug) naming the phase of the topic with which the note deals, and (3) the note itself. A clear identification of the source of every note is necessary for accurate footnoting. If only one work by an author is being used, his last name and the page reference (for example, Gavin, p. 20) make sufficient identification on the note card, since other data for the footnote can be obtained from the corresponding bibliography card. But if more than one work by an author appears in the bibliography, the identification on the note card must include at least a short form of the title (for example, Carson, *The Sea* . . . , p. 62). An alternative method is to key the note cards to the bibliography cards with a set of symbols (for example, I, II, III, etc., or A, B, C, etc.). If the first bibliography card is marked *I,* each note card based on that source is also marked *I, along with the exact page reference.*

Substance of Notes. A note may be an isolated fact, a summary, a quotation, or any combination of these. Making notes of the first two kinds, both of which require restatement of the information in the note taker's own language, may seem unduly time-consuming, but is, in terms of the total research process, more economical than recording numerous quotations. The writer should refrain from copying long quoted passages with the idea of restating them later. A far more satisfactory method is to reduce the material at the outset to approximately the form in which it can become an integral part of the paper.

An isolated fact is ordinarily a very brief note, often less than a sentence; it is a single piece of factual information that would remain true in any context. In the note-taking process it is extracted from its context in the source and recorded for later use in another context. Just how much information makes a fact and therefore belongs on one note card depends on the writer's purpose. If he were studying the measurements of an office in order to write a report on requirements for air conditioning, he would list the three dimensions (for example, Office 109A: 18 ft. by 20 ft. by 9 ft.) as one fact on one note card. However, if his purpose were to determine requirements for painting the walls green and the ceiling white, he would make two note cards: one card with a note relating to green paint (Office 109A: 2 walls 18 ft. by 9 ft. and 2 walls 20 ft. by 9 ft.) and another card with a note relating to white paint (Office 109A: 1 ceiling, 18 ft. by 20 ft.).

A good procedure for writing a summary note is to (1) glance over the whole article or chapter, paying attention to headings, sub-headings, and other organizational devices; (2) read the whole composition for the purpose of finding the author's central idea and supporting evidence; (3) look away from the book and think through the central idea and supporting points, looking back to the book for reminders only if necessary; (4) close the book and write the information in as brief a note as possible; (5) open the book and check to see that the note preserves the meaning of the original but does not contain any of the phraseology of the original. (See Chapter 4 for more information on summarizing.)

A note should take the form of a quotation only when (1) the passage is very important indeed, (2) the passage contains evidence which the reader might question in any other form, (3) the meaning would be difficult to reproduce in any other statement, or (4) the phraseology is so apt that putting the idea into other words would detract from the effectiveness. *Anything quoted, even a phrase of two or three words, should be enclosed in quotation marks on the note card as insurance against unintentional plagiarism* [5] *later on in the paper.* Quotations chosen for any of the above reasons and skillfully incorporated in the composition usually strengthen the research paper; quotations should not be used, however, to the point of padding the paper.

The following examples illustrate the three types of notes just described. (These note cards, like the bibliography cards shown earlier, are reproductions of samples from the work of the student who wrote the research paper printed at the end of this chapter, pp. 137–160.) A special kind of note card (not illustrated here) is one recording graphic materials: tables, charts, maps, etc. If the paper would be less clear without such materials, the writer ought to provide them. If he adapts them

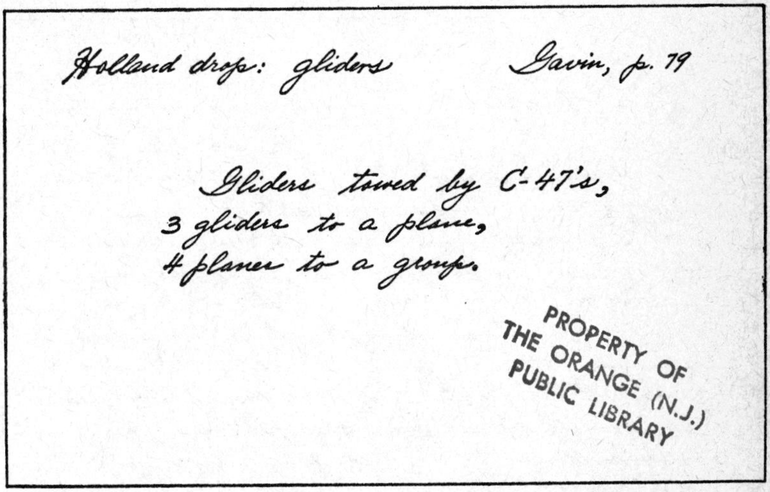

Holland drop: gliders   *Gavin, p. 79*

Gliders towed by C-47's, 3 gliders to a plane, 4 planes to a group.

Fig. 4.—Isolated Fact [6]

[5] *Plagiarism* is the use of the language or the ideas of another person without giving credit to him. Thus plagiarism is dishonest use of source materials. The ethical way to borrow the words of another is to put them into the form of a direct quotation (see rules and examples, pp. 129–131) *and* to acknowledge the source with a citatory footnote (see pp. 132–135). The ethical way to borrow ideas without quoting is to restate them in entirely new language *and* cite the source in a footnote.

[6] See footnote 7, p. 126.

from originals or bases them on information from a written source, he gives credit in the usual way with a footnote.

Why Sicily   *Pratt, p. 46*

      Pratt brings forth 4 reasons why Sicily was chosen as first Allied airborne target:

(1) It was the center of the Mediterranean theater.

(2) It was a menace to Allied sea traffic passing through the Strait of Sicily.

(3) It was the most vulnerable spot on the southern border of Axis-held territory.

(4) The sea road to Sicily from Allied-held Malta was relatively short and safe.

FIG. 5—SUMMARY [7]

The 82d   *Gellhorn "82d....,"p.47*

      This is a portion of a letter to General James M. Gavin from an unidentified paratroop lieutenant:

      "For myself, as well as all those others in the division who remember the roar of planes at night, the instant when the warning light flashes on, and the magnificence of night skies filled with swaying chutes, I want to say this: We hope with all our hearts that there will always be an 82d. If we can know that somewhere young men will dare the challenge to stand up and hook up and know the moment of pride and strength which is its reward, then a part of us will always be alive."

FIG. 6—QUOTATION [8]

---

[7] See how the researcher used these notes: turn to his footnote 38 and the text of his paper, page 157, and footnote 2 and text of his paper, page 144.

[8] The research writer decided not to use this quotation because its content and tone did not fit into his final paper.

USING THE NOTES

Meaningful notes, if they represent full coverage of the best sources of information on a research question, serve a threefold purpose. They provide the thesis, the organization, and the authority for the paper itself.

Formulating a Thesis. Steeped in his subject as he undoubtedly is by the time he nears the completion of his reading and note-taking, the research worker probably becomes increasingly aware of one evident answer to the question he started out to investigate. If not, he should analyze his notes (and take more if necessary) until he has assimilated enough evidence to answer the question honestly. The answer is not what he imagines to be true, or what he intuitively believes to be true, or even necessarily what he would like to find true; it is what the facts in his notes prove to be true. In other words, he searches out the answer to his research question by the inductive method of reasoning. The answer is an inductive conclusion which, when cast in the form of a single statement, becomes the thesis for the paper.

As an example, a person investigating how the American rubber industry developed during World War II might find that the facts in his notes point to a general conclusion like the following: The rubber industry in the United States grew to great economic importance during the 1940–1945 period, the demands of World War II merely accelerating the already inevitable expansion of the industry. If so, this is the thesis which his entire paper will need to develop and support.

Arranging an Outline. During the process of note-taking, the research worker constantly uses his tentative outline (set of captions or labels, sometimes called "slugs") to test the adequacy of his notes and vice versa. He revises his outline or supplements his notes, whichever the testing indicates. This flexibility is desirable because the information he finds may change the direction of his study. When he thinks he has completed his notes, he is ready to make a full outline—preferably a sentence outline—which will reveal any remaining gaps in his reading and note-taking and will become the framework of his paper.

Research workers usually keep assorting their note cards as they take the notes, bundling with a rubber band each group of cards bearing the same slug, or filing the groups behind appropriate guide cards. (A common mistake of inexperienced writers is to keep together the notes from a given source.) When all cards have been properly assorted according to slugs, the next step is to arrange the cards within each bundle in a logical sequence and to place the bundles in the best possible order as the basis for the full outline.

The best arrangement of the items within the outline, in accordance with the method of the whole research process, is an inductive arrangement. In other words, a coherent outline for a research paper shows specific facts, details, examples, experiments, and the like leading finally to a general conclusion. This does not mean that the thesis cannot be stated at the beginning of the outline. The thesis can and should appear at the beginning of the outline and likewise at an early point in the paper so that the reader will know what to expect the conclusion of the paper to say. The arrangement is still inductive, for it is not until the body of the outline or the paper has presented the evidence that the inquiring reader can accept the thesis as a rule instead of an hypothesis.

Making the full outline determines largely the organization of the paper; but the writer may be able to improve the arrangement of certain facts and ideas as he composes the rough draft, and therefore the outline should remain flexible through that stage of the work. (For more information on making outlines, see Chapter 3.)

Providing Authority. The notes provide the authoritative information which, when properly presented and documented, makes the content of the paper. The knowledge he gains by taking and using the notes enables the writer to think intelligently about his topic and to arrive at a valid conclusion for his paper. The note cards also provide the necessary data for the footnotes. To get the fullest benefit from them, the writer keeps the note cards as well as the outline where he can refer directly to them as he composes the rough draft of his paper.

COMPOSING AND DOCUMENTING THE PAPER

The more carefully and thoroughly the writer has completed the preceding steps in the research process, the simpler he finds the task of composing and documenting the paper. Except for giving special attention to length, notes, and documentation, he can proceed much as he would in writing any other formal expository theme.

Proportion. The research paper written as a composition exercise hardly requires a feature common in graduate research: an introduction summarizing previous research on the topic. The paper does need the traditional beginning, middle, and end; and the *proportion* should be such that the beginning and end are very brief and that the middle is relatively long.

Concise Statement of Purpose. The beginning of the paper (possibly one to three paragraphs) should be a concise statement of purpose.

The writer should say how he intends to focus the paper on a single idea—or thesis—and what that single idea is. He should make clear just what restrictions he has imposed on his investigation of the topic. The ultimate success of the paper depends on its doing what it sets out to do.

Detailed Support of Thesis. The middle of the paper (all but a few hundred words of the length prescribed by the assignment) should be a detailed and documented presentation of the evidence supporting the thesis. This evidence should appear in a logical progression (already worked out in the outline) leading into a conclusion synonymous with the thesis stated in the beginning of the paper. An earlier comment on the outline as the framework for the paper applies literally here. The writer with a good sentence outline strengthens his composition by incorporating the outline almost word for word in the text of his paper. (The beginner often errs by writing his text *around* his outline rather than including the outline.) In fact, the reader should be able to reconstruct the outline from the paper.

Concise Statement of Conclusion. The logical ending for the paper is a concise statement of conclusion on the topic. The writer carefully re-emphasizes for the reader what the investigation has brought to light.

Style. The *style* of the research paper should be direct and clear—the kind that will not interfere with the transfer of facts and ideas to the mind of an intelligent reader who wants to learn something from the paper. The reader rightfully expects precision in the paper. The writer should therefore prune any jargon or verbiage from his rough draft before he makes his final copy. He should write on the formal level. For instance, in a research paper a competent writer would never refer to Professor George Lyman Kittredge, the eminent Shakespearean scholar, as "Kitty," though in an informal character sketch he might do so.

The unobtrusive, lucid style that characterizes a good research paper is a result of other things. When a sincere writer makes an orderly investigation of a good question, assimilates significant information to answer it, and reports his findings straightforwardly to a specific reading audience, an appropriate style usually comes into being. In addition to a pervading clarity, this style has a mark of individuality born of the writer's having thought through his subject matter.

Quotations. As pointed out earlier in this chapter (in the section on "Substance of Notes"), the writer should use quotations in his research paper only for special reasons. When he does use them, however, he should observe certain conventions. The following eight rules and five examples cover most of the conventions (the asterisk in each example indicates the place where the footnote number would ordinarily appear).

1. The introduction to the quotation should tie the quotation to the text in a logical manner; the introduction and the quotation should combine to make complete sentence structure. (See any of the examples below.)

2. Any part omitted from a quotation should be indicated by three ellipsis marks (suspension periods); these spaced periods are used in addition to whatever punctuation appears in the quotation before or after the omission (See *B*.)

3. Wording must be exactly as in the original with the exception that the editor may supply extra words by placing them in brackets. (See *B*.)

4. Punctuation and capitalization must be the same as in the original with the exceptions that the first letter of the first word and the last mark of punctuation in the quotation should be adjusted to meet the needs of the sentence of which the quotation forms a part. (In *A* the first letter of the word *he* at the beginning of the quotation has been changed from a capital to a small letter. In *D* the punctuation after the word *know* at the end of the quotation has been changed from a period to a comma.)

5. A prose quotation that consists of one sentence or less than one sentence should be enclosed in quotation marks and woven directly into the text of the composition. (See *A*.)

6. A prose quotation that consists of two or more sentences and that *also* amounts to four or more lines (or whatever minimum is specified in the style sheet being used) in the manuscript should be set off from the text by single spacing and doubly wide margins: a picture-in-a-frame arrangement. The quotation should *not* be enclosed in quotation marks; only such quotation marks as may appear in the original are reproduced in the quotation. (See *B*.)

7. A single line of poetry should be enclosed in quotation marks and woven directly into the text of the composition. (See *C*.)

8. Two or more lines of poetry should be set off from the text by single spacing and should be centered between the margins so that the line-lengths of the original are retained. The lines should *not* be enclosed in quotation marks. (See *D*. The quotation marks in *D* have been reproduced because they appear in the original, where Keats uses them to show that the urn is speaking.)

A. Paragraph incorporating short prose quotation:
In his introduction to Eugene O'Neill's play *Anna Christie,* Richard A. Cordell points out that O'Neill had gathered first-hand information for the play and that "he had lived at Jimmy-the-Priest's, and old Chris he knew." * From his own experience, then, O'Neill could draw clear pictures of seaport talk.

B. Paragraph incorporating long prose quotation:

In a study of the play *Anna Christie,* the reader should remember these facts which Richard A. Cordell points out:

> The characters and the materials of the play the author [Eugene O'Neill] lifted from his own experiences and observations. . . . The materials of which *Anna Christie* is composed—sailors, booze, guns, . . . —O'Neill was acquainted with. He had lived at Jimmy-the-Priest's, and old Chris he knew.*

From his own experience, then, O'Neill could draw clear pictures of seaport talk.

C. Sentence incorporating single line of poetry:

That thought-provoking line in the poetry of Keats, "A thing of beauty is a joy forever," * is not soon forgotten.

D. Sentence incorporating two lines of poetry:

With the two lines that conclude the "Ode on a Grecian Urn,"

> "Beauty is truth, truth beauty,"—that is all
> Ye know on earth, and all ye need to know,*

the poet made an important contribution to the thought of many readers.

E. Picture-in-a-frame effect in longhand:

> With the two lines that conclude
> the "Ode on a Grecian Urn,"
>
> "Beauty is truth, truth beauty,"—that is all
> Ye know on earth, and all ye need to know;*
>
> the poet made an important contribution to the
> thought of many readers.

Documentation. Documenting the paper consists of making the necessary footnotes and the final adjustments in the bibliography. The writer inserts the footnotes, at least in tentative form, as he composes the rough draft of the paper, because at this time he can best judge which materials he ought to footnote. (He may place each footnote between a pair of horizontal lines in the text of the rough draft, thus delaying the arrangement of the footnote section at the bottom of the page until he makes his good copy.) He puts the bibliography into final form after he has finished the rough draft and knows which sources he has used.

Citatory Footnotes. Footnotes are required to cite the sources of (1) quotations, except those easily recognizable as coming from the Bible or other well-known sources; (2) summaries of borrowed ideas, opinions, or interpretations; (3) facts not commonly printed and not commonly known by fairly well-read persons; (4) borrowed charts, tables, or other graphic material; and (5) borrowed data used in graphic illustrations. The research worker himself is the best judge of whether he has relied on a source for a particular piece of information or has worked it out independently. And he is obligated to be a fair judge. There is no merit in superfluous footnoting, but there is a grave breach of ethics in failure to acknowledge real indebtedness for material used in the paper. (See p. 125 fn.) Besides giving credit to the original authors, the citatory footnotes lend authority to the paper and enable the interested reader to turn for himself to the exact sources.

There are various styles of documentation, any of which is acceptable so long as it is followed consistently within a given paper. Many publishers, periodicals, schools, sometimes even instructors, have their own style sheets which research writers are expected to follow. The student who is provided with such a style sheet should imitate the models given on it and ask his instructor about special problems not explained or illustrated on the sheet. The examples given in this chapter follow a method [9] that many instructors approve.

In any method of footnoting, the use of index numbers is necessary. An Arabic number appears in a raised position immediately after the passage concerned, and the same number appears in a raised position immediately before the corresponding footnote at the bottom of the page. The numbering of footnotes may be consecutive throughout the paper or may begin with *1* on each page that has footnotes; the former method of numbering shows a running total of the footnotes.

The footnote section at the bottom of the page should be separated from the text by a dividing line (partly or entirely across the page) at least one space below the last line of the text and two spaces above the first line of the footnotes. The first line only of each footnote should be indented, the space of indentation being the same as that for the first

[9] The method is much like that in the University of Chicago *Manual of Style* and in Kate L. Turabian's *A Manual For Writers of Term Papers, Theses, and Dissertations* (rev. ed.; Chicago, 1955). Another widely accepted manual of style for undergraduate as well as for graduate research writing is that of the Modern Language Association of America: William Riley Parker, comp., *The MLA Style Sheet* (rev. ed.; New York, 1951).

line of a paragraph. Footnotes requiring more than one line are single spaced, and double spacing is used between footnotes.

FOR BOOKS. The following examples are first references to books; these examples contain the facts of publication other than the name of the publisher. There is a growing tendency to omit all facts of publication from first citations to books when a bibliography accompanies the paper. These examples cover only common conditions in book references.

BOOK WITH ONE AUTHOR:
   [1] Donald Smalley, *Browning's Essay on Chatterton* (Cambridge, Mass., 1948), p. 78.

BOOK WITH TWO AUTHORS:
   [2] William Flint Thrall and Addison Hibbard, *A Handbook to Literature* (New York, 1936), p. 175.

BOOK WITH THREE OR MORE AUTHORS:
   [3] John Wilson Bowyer and Others, *Better College English* (New York, 1950), pp. 375–422.

BOOK WITH EDITOR:
   [4] Earl Leslie Griggs, ed., *The Best of Coleridge* (New York, 1934), pp. 107–111.

SELECTION FROM ANTHOLOGY (more than one volume and edition):
   [5] Jonathan Swift, "A Modest Proposal," *The Literature of England,* eds. George B. Woods and Others (3rd ed.; Chicago, 1947), I, 961–966.

When no bibliography accompanies the paper, the first citation should contain all facts of publication, including the name of the publisher.

   [1] Donald Smalley, *Browning's Essay on Chatterton* (Cambridge, Mass.: Harvard University Press, 1948), p. 78.

FOR PERIODICALS. The following examples are first citations of articles in periodicals. It should be noted that the abbreviations *vol.* (volume) and *p.* (page) are not used; when both kinds of numerals appear, the Roman numeral automatically stands for the volume, and the Arabic for the page reference.

SIGNED ARTICLE IN PERIODICAL:
   [6] Reginald L. Cook, "Frost on Analytical Criticism," *College English,* XVII (May, 1956), 434.

UNSIGNED ARTICLE IN PERIODICAL:
   [7] "Century of Chemistry," *Scientific American,* CLXXII (May, 1945), 265.

FOR ENCYCLOPEDIAS. The following examples are first references to articles in encyclopedias.

ARTICLE IN ENCYCLOPEDIA WITH SPECIAL PAGE NUMBERING:

⁸ "Deflection Control of Electron Streams," *Encyclopaedia Britannica,* 14th ed., 1953, VIII, 340a–340q.

ARTICLE IN ENCYCLOPEDIA WITH ORDINARY PAGE NUMBERING:

⁹ "Commune of Paris," *New International Encyclopaedia,* 2nd ed., 1926, V, 674.

FOR NEWSPAPERS. The following examples are first citations to articles in newspapers.

SIGNED ARTICLE IN NEWSPAPER OR ARTICLE WITH BY-LINE:

¹⁰ John W. Allen, "It Happened in Southern Illinois," O'Fallon [Illinois] *Progress,* March 3, 1960, p. 7, cols. 1–4.

UNSIGNED ARTICLE IN NEWSPAPER:

¹¹ "Weather a Factor in Grain Upturn," St. Louis *Post-Dispatch,* March 13, 1960, sec. C., p. 7, col. 6.

First citations should appear in shortened form whenever any of the documentary data is mentioned in the text matter. For instance, if the author's name is given in the text, the footnote begins with the title.

For citations after the first one to a particular source, short forms should be used to fit the circumstances. The abbreviation *ibid.* means that the source is the same as the one named in the immediately preceding footnote; a new page reference may be added to *ibid.* if necessary. The abbreviation *op. cit.* following the last name of an author means that the source is the same as the one by that author cited at some point earlier than the immediately preceding footnote. (See these short forms in use in the footnotes of the specimen research paper, pp. 137ff.)

Here is a list of abbreviations commonly used for the sake of brevity in documentation.

c., circa or "about," "approximately"
chap., chapter (plural, chaps.)
col., column (plural, cols.)
comp., compiler
ed., edition or editor (plural, eds.)
et al., and elsewhere; and others
f., and the following line or page (plural, ff.)
fig., figure (plural, figs.)
ibid., ibidem or "the same"
intro., introduction
l., line (plural, ll.)

n.d., no date
n.p., no place of publication
op. cit., opere citato or "in the work cited"
p., page (plural, pp.)
passim, not an abbreviation but a Latin word meaning "here and there"
  or "at various places"
sec., section (plural, secs.)
sic, not an abbreviation but a Latin word meaning "thus" and used in
brackets to indicate that the apparent error which precedes has been quoted
as it is in the original
tr., translator
vol., volume (plural, vols.)

Explanatory Footnotes. Sometimes the writer has relevant information which would aid the meaning but would disrupt the unity of his
text if he included it there. Such information he can place in an *explanatory footnote.* (The second, third, fifth, and eighth footnotes in this
chapter are explanatory footnotes.) Writers sometimes find the explanatory footnote a convenient place for the definition of a term used in the
text. (The fourth and the fourteenth footnotes in the specimen research
paper at the end of this chapter are examples of this particular kind of
explanatory footnote.) Sometimes, too, it is convenient for a writer to
add an explanatory note to a citation, thus combining these two kinds
of footnotes. The particular audience he is addressing regularly affects
the writer's judgment on the use of explanatory footnotes. For instance,
in addressing readers of *The Saturday Evening Post,* a writer would
explain technical terms that he would not explain for readers of *Scientific American.*

Final Bibliography. If he has adjusted his bibliography from time to
time throughout the research process, that is, if he has discarded the
cards listing sources that have proved useless and has added new cards
listing additional sources that have proved helpful, the writer will now
find that his *final bibliography* is almost ready. In his final bibliography
he should list all works to which he has actually referred in his paper
and perhaps a few others that have helped him in a general way to become well-informed on his subject. He should write or type the final
bibliography according to the method required by his instructor.

ARRANGEMENT. There are three common methods of arranging
entries in the bibliography: (1) in one alphabetical list under the last
names of authors and under the first important words in titles where
the authors are unknown; (2) in separate alphabetical lists for books,
magazines, newspapers, and so on; (3) in separate alphabetical lists

for works of primary importance and works of secondary importance. Whatever method is used, each entry should appear with all lines indented except the first. The purpose of this indentation is to make the alphabetical listing more apparent along the left-hand margin.

FORM. The form of each entry in the bibliography is like that of the corresponding footnote except for the following significant differences: (1) In the bibliography but not in the footnote, the author's last name appears first. (2) In the bibliography but usually not in the footnote, all facts of publication are included. (3) In the bibliography inclusive page numbers are used for articles, but no page numbers are used for books dealing entirely with the topic; whereas in the footnote a specific page reference is used. (4) In the bibliography periods are used to separate the name of the author of a book or an article from the title, and to separate the title of a book from the facts of publication; whereas in the footnote a comma is used to separate the name of the author from the title, and parentheses are ordinarily used to enclose the facts of publication of a book if included. (See the bibliography of the specimen paper p. 160. The blank line used in this bibliography means that the author is the one named in the preceding entry.)

Revision: Final Checking. In *revising* the rough draft of his research paper, the writer should use the same techniques he has found helpful in revising other types of composition. In addition, he should check his documentation to make sure that he has been accurate in all his references, that he has not omitted any necessary footnotes or bibliographical entries, and that he has followed an acceptable style consistently. It should not be necessary for him to return to the sources in the library to do his checking. If his note cards and bibliography cards are accurate, as they should be, he can verify all the quotations and other borrowings he has included in his paper, as well as the footnotes and the bibliography, by comparing them with the information on his cards. Finally, he should read the completed paper several times, each time looking for errors of one kind, such as spelling, punctuation, or grammatical errors. He should not mix the purposes of his readings.

His checking done, the researcher is ready to do the mechanical work of making good copies (often called "fair copies") of the outline, the paper, and the bibliography. These good copies he should place, in the order just named, under a properly endorsed cover sheet or title page and, if he has been so directed, inside a folder. Also, if he has been asked to submit his cards, he should check to see that he has arranged his note cards to correspond with his outline and his bibliography cards to correspond with his final bibliography.

SICILY AND HOLLAND: A STUDY OF AIRBORNE TACTICS
IN WORLD WAR II[10]

Research Paper

by

Russell J. Linsin

English Composition 11-102, Section 2

Instructor: Mr. Gottfried

Washington University

May 7, 1956

[10] Printed by permission of the author, Russell J. Linsin.

SICILY AND HOLLAND: A STUDY OF AIRBORNE TACTICS
IN WORLD WAR II

Thesis: From an experimental beginning in the July,
1943, invasion of Sicily, American airborne
tactics developed into a decisive factor in
the success of the September, 1944, invasion of Holland.

I. The 82d Airborne Division's assault on Sicily in
July, 1943, was the birth of American airborne
operations.

    A. The invasion plan was conceived at the head-
quarters of the North African Theater of
Operations and the United States Seventh
Army.

        1. The mission of the 82d Division was to
land on and capture the area around
Gela, disrupt enemy communications and
movement of troops, and assist the First
Infantry Division in capturing the landing field at Ponte Olivo.

        2. The airborne planners were faced with
several problems.

            a. Should the planes fly in formation
or bomberstream?

            b. Should the parachute drop precede
or follow the amphibious landing?

            c. Should the operation take place in
daylight or darkness?

B. Preparations were being made for the airborne invasion before the actual plan was
conceived.

1. The United States War Department set up
the Airborne Training School at Fort
Benning, Georgia.

2. The 82d Division trained for three
months in North Africa.

a. The paratroopers used photographs
to learn the topography of the land
and the location of military installations.

b. The paratroopers made fifteen practice jumps in terrain similar to
that of the Gela area.

C. The drop took place as scheduled on July 9,
1943, but not without many difficulties.

1. Bad weather caused many planes to become lost in the darkness.

a. The navigators missed their checkpoints: the island of Malta and
some points on Sicily.

b. High winds scattered many of the
troops.

2. The planes encountered heavy flak along
the mainland.

3. Friendly naval and coastal gunners fired
on the 504th Regiment by mistake.

4. Inexperience caused confusion when the
units first landed.

iii

          a.   The men used caution at the expense
              of speed in assembling and reor-
              ganizing.

          b.   The parachute artillery proved in-
              effective because of its delay in
              firing as a unit.

   D.   Despite the obstacles that had to be over-
       come, all phases of the Sicilian mission
       were eventually accomplished.

II.   The First Allied Airborne Army's invasion of
      Holland in September, 1944, one of the last air-
      borne assaults on the Western Front, was a
      highly successful operation based on experience
      from the previous landings.

   A.   The plan for this invasion was conceived at
       the headquarters of the First Allied Air-
       borne Army at Sunnyhill Park, England, the
       purpose of the invasion being to open a
       sixty-mile-long corridor to the north in
       eastern Holland.

      1.   The mission of the 82d Division was to
          seize and defend the Groesbeek Heights
          and seize the bridges over the Maas
          River at Grave and the Waal River at
          Nijmegen.

      2.   The airborne planners encountered de-
          fense measures in use by the enemy.

          a.   The Germans had an effective anti-
              airborne device called Rommel's
              Asparagus.

    b. The Germans had flooded most of the
      lowlands of Holland.

  3. The plans included the use of gliders
    and called for drop zones with suffi-
    cient clearings for glider landings;
    the zones selected were all in the
    vicinity of the Groesbeek Heights.

  4. The Royal Air Force and the United
    States Air Force got ready to fly cover
    for the airborne army.

  5. The unit commanders were briefed five
    days before the take-off and again on
    the morning of the invasion.

B. The drop took place as scheduled on September 17, 1944, and succeeded with little
  difficulty.

  1. The 82d Division required the use of
    482 C-47's and fifty gliders to carry
    7,477 parachute and glider troops.

  2. The flight occurred in daylight under
    ideal weather conditions.

  3. Enemy opposition was very light; the
    Allied air support cut down on enemy
    fighter resistance and anti-aircraft
    defenses.

  4. The troops landed in the proposed zones
    between noon and 2:00 p.m.

    a. Assembly and reorganization were
      swift; the 376th Parachute Artil-
      lery was firing as a unit just one
      hour after landing.

b. Each regiment of the 82d Division accomplished its assigned mission.

    (1)   The 504th captured the Nijmegen Bridge, the Grave Bridge, and the bridge over the Maas-Waal Canal.

    (2)   The 505th secured and defended the Groesbeek Heights.

    (3)   The 508th held the high ground from Wyler to Nijmegen, and assisted in capturing the Nijmegen Bridge and the bridges at Hater and Honinghutie.

C. The full-fledged airborne action of the Holland campaign made tactical history.

SICILY AND HOLLAND: A STUDY OF AIRBORNE TACTICS
IN WORLD WAR II

At the beginning of World War II both Russia
and Germany had many thousands of highly trained
parachute troops, and Germany had done a great deal
of experimenting with gliders. Germany had used
airborne troops in her successful 1940 invasion of
Holland and later in Crete. Not long after Pearl
Harbor, the United States War Department became aware
of the value of airborne troops and took steps to
develop American parachute units by establishing the
Army Airborne School at Fort Benning, Georgia.[1]

The 82d Airborne Division's surprise assault on
Sicily in July, 1943, was the birth of American airborne tactics. It was the first large-scale assault
by parachute attempted by the United States in World
War II. Although the Sicilian assault was considered
a success, some costly mistakes had been made; but
as the war progressed and more airborne assaults were
launched, these mistakes were remedied. One of the
last airborne assaults launched by the 82d Airborne
Division on the Western Front was that on Holland in
September, 1944. Planning based on the experience
gained in Sicily and the two succeeding landings—
Salerno, Italy, and Normandy, France—resulted in
a success never before thought possible.

----

[1]William C. Lee, "Introduction" to James M.
Gavin, <u>Airborne Warfare</u>, p. viii.

1

2

The campaigns in Sicily and Holland are significant in a study of American airborne tactics in
World War II, for these two campaigns show the development and perfection of the techniques used by
the 82d Airborne Division in the short span of just
fourteen months and four airborne assaults.

Early in 1943 the Sicilian invasion plan was
conceived at the headquarters of the North African
Theater of Operations and the United States Seventh
Army. Sicily was chosen as the target for the first
strike for four reasons: (1) it was the center of
the Mediterranean theater; (2) it was a menace to
Allied sea traffic passing through the Strait of
Sicily; (3) it was the most vulnerable spot on the
southern border of Axis-held territory; and (4) the
sea road to Sicily from the British island of Malta,
which the Allies held, was relatively short and
safe.[2]

The mission of the 82d Airborne Division in this
campaign was threefold: first, it was to land on
Sicily in the area north and east of Gela, and secure
ground in the area; second, it was to disrupt enemy
communications and prevent movement of enemy reserves; and third, it was to attach to and assist
the First Infantry Division (which would land by sea)
in capturing and securing the landing field at Ponte
Olivo.[3]

----

[2]W. V. Pratt, "Strategy and Tactics in Sicily,"
Newsweek, XXII (July 26, 1943), 26.

[3]Martha Gellhorn, "82d Airborne Division, Master
of the Hotspots," Saturday Evening Post, CCXVIII
(February 23, 1946), 22.

3

Since the airborne attack on Sicily was the
first operation of its kind ever attempted by American forces, there were several problems confronting
the planners: Should the transports fly in formation
or bomberstream,[4] as the British did? Should the
drop take place before or after the amphibious landing? Should it be a daylight drop, or one made under
the cover of darkness? Formation flying would permit
a quicker delivery of troops and would require a
smaller number of skilled navigators and pilots, but
it would prove more costly than bomberstream flying
in case of fighter interception or heavy ground flak.
Headquarters finally decided to fly formations consisting of nine ships each. Headquarters also
decided that in order for the paratroopers to have
sufficient time to assemble and reorganize, the drop
would be made three hours and fifteen minutes before
the beachhead landing of the First Infantry Division. The possibility of enemy fighters eliminated
plans for a daylight drop; the drop was to be made
at night (July 9, 1943), in the light of an almost
full moon to simplify the assembly and reorganization
of the units.[5]

The drop zones for the landings were selected
between Caltagirone and the proposed beachhead of
the First Infantry Division (as shown on map 1).[6]

_____

[4]A straight-line pattern.

[5]James M. Gavin, <u>Airborne</u> <u>Warfare</u>, pp. 2-4.

[6]<u>Ibid</u>., pp. 2-3.

4

The 505th Regimental Combat Team was to make the
initial assault; and on the following day, July 10,
the 504th Regimental Combat Team was to fly in, using
the same drop zones, and support the 505th.[7]

Some months before the actual plan of invasion
was conceived, preparations were being made for a
large—scale airborne assault. It had become evident
that the nucleus of an airborne unit is the individual parachutist; by March, 1942, the Airborne
School at Fort Benning, Georgia, was busily engaged
in training volunteers to become paratroopers.[8] To
qualify as parachutists, the volunteers were required
to pass a rigid physical examination and then survive
the three—week airborne course. All students, officers and enlisted men alike, went through the program
as equals; they ate, slept, and trained together.

The first week of training required the mastery
of four jump techniques. The first task was learning
to follow the jump commands given by the jumpmaster
inside the plane; the second, learning to exit properly from the plane; the third, learning to land un-
injured; and the fourth, learning to control and
collapse the parachute upon landing.

The second week of training was known as the
physical build—up since emphasis was on physical
training to build up the strong leg and back muscles
required for jumping. By the beginning of this
second week the men were making jumps with a practice

[7]Ibid., p. 2.

[8]Lee, op. cit., p. ix.

5

parachute harness, suspended from a thirty-four-foot
tower, and by the end of the same week they were
dropping with regulation parachutes from a two-
hundred-fifty-foot tower.

In the third week of training the men made five
live jumps from transports, each jump under different
conditions. The last jump was made at an altitude
of six hundred feet.

Classes of paratroopers were graduated from
Fort Benning at a steady rate, and by the spring of
1943 the 82d Airborne Division was at full combat
strength. The division moved to the port of embar-
kation in April, 1943, and arrived in North Africa
in early May.[9]

From the time of their arrival in North Africa
until the week of the assault in July, the men of the
82d Airborne Division trained constantly for the
coming invasion of Sicily. They used aerial photographs to become familiar with the terrain around
Gela. They memorized the topography of the land and
the location of military installations, for they
would take no marked maps into combat. They made
practice jumps in terrain similar to that of the
Gela area.[10]

On June 10 the 82d Division commander, General
Matthew B. Ridgway, accompanied by the battalion com-

---

[9]82d Airborne Division Yearbook, 1952, p. 11.

[10]Robert Devore, "Paratroops Behind Nazi Lines,"
Collier's, CXII (September 18, 1943), 18-19.

6

manders of the 82d and three officers from the 52d
Troop Carrier Command, made a night reconnaissance
over Sicily. The conditions were precisely as they
were expected to be on the actual drop one month
later; all checkpoints and terrain showed up clearly.
This was the final rehearsal before the take-off.[11]

On July 4 the 505th Regimental Combat Team, consisting of one infantry regiment; the 3d Battalion
of the 504th Regimental Combat Team; the 456th Parachute Field Artillery, Company B; the 307th Airborne
Engineer Battalion; and signal, medical, and supporting detachments were bivouacked at ten airfields
dispersed around the three Tunisian towns of Sousse,
Kairouan, and Enfidaville (as shown on map 1). The
airfields were in range of Axis bombers and had to
be scattered to make a less effective target.[12]
Final briefings were held. The last order issued
stated that all personnel and equipment would be
dropped on Sicily; no one would be returned under
any conditions. If the drop zones were missed, the
jumpmasters were to jump the men anyway and they were
to fight as best they could. These orders were fully
carried out.[13]

The planes took off on schedule on the night of
July 9, carrying 2,781 paratroopers and 891 para-
packs.[14] The flight required the use of 226 C-47

---

[11]Gavin, op. cit., p. 5.
[12]Devore, op. cit., p. 22.
[13]Gavin, op. cit., pp. 5-6.
[14]Bundles containing equipment.

7

transport planes.[15] The planes flew in a formation
such that the troops would land in proper military
order: infantry first, then artillery, and finally
the supporting units.[16]

The planned flight time was three hours and two
minutes. The planes were to fly east from Tunisia
to Malta, the first checkpoint. The flight was then
to turn left and continue north to a point near the
coast of Sicily, then move northwest along the coast
(out of range of coastal defenses) to Gela, then turn
right and proceed directly inland over Gela (as illustrated on map 1). This route was three hundred
miles long and was to be flown in tight formation
two hundred feet above the water; this altitude was
to be held in case of fighter opposition.[17] However,
a gale of thirty-five miles per hour, encountered
almost upon take-off, blew the planes off course.
There were no interplane communications, and many
planes with inexperienced navigators and pilots became lost.[18] The remaining formation was badly disrupted by flak once it reached Sicily; few planes
were actually hit, but the attack, along with the
fact that the last checkpoints had been obscured by
the preinvasion bombings, increased the pilots' confusion. All the airborne troops did land on Sicily,

---

[15]W. F. Craven and J. L. Cate, eds., _The Army
Air Forces in World War II_, II, 449.

[16]Devore, _op. cit._, p. 19.

[17]_Ibid_.

[18]Gellhorn, _op. cit._, p. 23.

8

but only one-eighth of them landed in or near the proposed drop zones (shown on map 1).[19]

On July 10 the 504th Regimental Combat Team flew in to support the 505th. Flying in good weather, the planes were mistaken for enemy aircraft by friendly naval and coastal gunners, who disrupted the formation and caused the loss of twenty-three planes. The remaining troops landed near Gela (as shown on map 1) and joined the 505th.[20]

Once on the ground, the paratroopers were much too cautious in assembling and reorganizing. Lacking combat experience, they were reluctant to sacrifice security for speed, with the result that they used few visual aids to identify the units.[21] The 456th Parachute Artillery proved to be ineffective because of the wide scattering of its members and equipment; several hours passed before it was organized and firing as a unit.[22]

Although the high winds and the confusion diminished the effectiveness of the 82d Airborne Division in its first mission, every phase of the mission was eventually accomplished. The 3d Battalion of the 504th Regimental Combat Team destroyed enemy communications and held the road from Niscemi to Biscari. The 2d Battalion of the 505th captured S. Croce

---

[19]Gavin, op. cit., p. 15.

[20]Gellhorn, op. cit., p. 23.

[21]Gavin, op. cit., p. 4.

[22]Ibid., p. 103.

9

Camerina and cleared the area for the advancing 45th
Division. The 3d Battalion of the 505th landed directly on the proposed drop zone and established
radio and patrol contact with the forces landing on
the beaches. The 3d Battalion further assisted the
landing by setting a large fire to guide the incoming
troops.[23]

Mistakes were costly in Sicily, but the invasion
proved that vertical envelopment was feasible and
almost impossible to stop. It was not difficult for
the airborne planners to envision other landings,
including that in Holland, in the near future.

After the successful invasion of Normandy in
June, 1944, which was spearheaded by the landings of
the 82d, hopes were high for an early victory in
Europe, despite the serious situation of the Allied
armies. The German army had been badly beaten, but
it still held all the major seaports in the Netherlands and in the lowlands of Belgium and France.
This circumstance was serious for the Allies, for
their seaports were so far to the rear of the advancing columns that the supply lines were becoming
badly strained and subject to constant counter-
attacks by German forces.[24] It was clear that unless
the German forces in Holland completely collapsed
there would have to be a considerable pause in the
Allied offensive of late 1944. On the other hand,
if the German forces in Holland did collapse, it

---

[23]Ibid., pp. 14–15.

[24]Ibid., p. 70.

10

would be possible for the Allies to continue the
advance into Germany with very light supply columns,
possibly reinforced by air.[25]

Out of this situation emerged the Holland plan,
its purpose being to open a sixty-mile-long corridor
in eastern Holland straight north in advance of the
British Second Army.[26] The first conference on the
plan was held September 10, 1944, at the First Allied
Airborne Army Headquarters at Sunnyhill Park, England. Present were the troop carrier commanders; the
commander of the First Allied Airborne Corps, Lieutenant General Lewis Brereton; and the commander of
the British Airborne Corps, Lieutenant General
F. A. M. Browning.[27]

The First Allied Airborne Army consisted of not
only the 82d but also the United States' 101st and
the British 1st Airborne Divisions, along with the
Polish 1st Parachute Brigade. The mission of the
First Allied Airborne Army was to capture and hold
the crossings over the canals and rivers from Eind-
hoven to Arnhem, for use by the advancing British Second Army. The particular mission of the 82d was to
seize and defend the Groesbeek Heights, a stretch of

_____

[25]Cyril Falls, "Greatest of Airborne Operations," Illustrated London News, CCV (September 23,
1944), 344; and "Arnhem--A Stage in Airborne Tactics," Illustrated London News, CCVII (October 27,
1945), 458.

[26]W. B. Courtney, "Army in the Sky," Collier's,
CXIV (November 11, 1944), 18.

[27]Gavin, op. cit., p. 72.

11

high ground surrounding the town of Groesbeek, and to
seize the bridges over the Maas River at Graves and
over the Waal River at Nijmegen (shown on map 2).[28]

The Allied airborne planners were confronted
with the problem of anti-airborne measures in use by
the enemy. The most common anti-airborne device used
by the Germans--a device known as Rommel's Aspara-
gus--consisted of poles approximately eight to ten
feet long sunk about two feet in the ground at intervals of seventy-five to one hundred feet. The poles
were connected by wires stretched in every direction,
and attached to the wires were land and personnel
mines. The whole device made a hazardous landing
area for an unsuspecting parachutist.[29] As another
anti-airborne measure the Germans had flooded most of
the lowlands of Holland.

It was evident that the drop zones of the Allies
would have to be on high ground. Also, the landing
area would have to be close to the objectives, clear
of flak and ground defenses, and in the vicinity of
the proposed flight route. The parachutists could
land in fairly rough terrain, the worst natural obstacles being tall timber and marshy areas. But
fifty gliders were also to be used, and they required
carefully selected clearings for landing zones.[30]

Since gliders had played an important role in
the successful invasions of Salerno and Normandy, it

---

[28]Ibid., pp. 73-75.

[29]Ibid., p. 47.

[30]Ibid., p. 81.

12

became evident that they would be essential in future
airborne invasions. The main advantage of gliders
is that, upon landing, the troops are an organized
combat unit carrying with them such light weapons as
mortars and howitzers. Parachutists are often scattered, as they were in Sicily, and can carry only
small arms.[31]

There were enough gliders available for the
Holland invasion, but a severe shortage of glider
pilots necessitated the hasty establishment of a
glider-pilot training program here in the States.

Volunteer enlisted men were taken from the ranks
and sent to a pre-glider school set up at Goodland,
Kansas. Here the men, in addition to following a
schedule of physical training and classwork, spent
thirty-two hours in ground school and thirty hours
in the air. They learned how to handle light-powered
planes and how to land after turning the engines off
at heights ranging from five hundred to five thousand
feet. In addition, they received instruction in
gliding, sideslipping, and approaching a landing.
Finally, they received practice in landing at night.
Those qualifying went on from pre-glider school to
glider school.

The United States Army Glider School, located at
Twenty-nine Palms, California, gave the pilots an
additional four-week course. In the first phase of
this training, the gliders were launched by automobiles at speeds up to sixty miles per hour. As the

----

[31]Keith Ayling, They Fly to Fight, p. 120.

13

pilots became more experienced, they learned the
airplane tow--first with the plane towing just one
glider, then two, and finally three gliders. After
graduation the pilots continued training until they
were able to land from any altitude into an area
fifty feet square. The qualified pilots were then
sent to England in preparation for the Holland invasion.[32] They were there by the time the planning
began to take definite shape.

The 82d Division staff conferred at the IXth
Troop Carrier Command Headquarters in Eastcote, England, near London, on September 11, 1944, the day
following the planning session at the First Allied
Airborne Army Headquarters. The Eastcote conference
emphasized the study of enemy flak, enemy gun positions, and the terrain most suitable for the parachute and glider landings. Photo coverage of the
flight route had been flown daily by the British Airborne Division and provided the necessary information
for selecting the drop zones (shown on map 2).[33]
In Sicily most of the drop zones had been obscured;
because of this experience, the strategists decided
to use pathfinder teams in the Holland invasion.
Thirty-six men were to fly in thirty minutes before
the scheduled drop and send up colored smoke to mark
the landing areas as the main body of planes approached.[34]

----

[32]Ibid., pp. 134-138.

[33]Gavin, op. cit., pp. 86-88.

[34]Ibid., p. 88.

14

Upon landing, the division would be isolated
from all artillery and armor support; therefore heavy
air support would be necessary. This support was to
come from the Royal Air Force and the United States'
Eighth and Ninth Air Forces. They were to knock out
enemy interceptors, bomb airfields within range, and
fly cover for the air column. After the landings
they were to give close support during the ground
fighting. All this meant that 1113 bombers and 1240
fighters would fly in support of the First Allied
Airborne Army.[35]

The first conference of unit commanders was held
on September 11 at Leicester; missions, drop and
landing zones, and take-off airfields were assigned
to the separate units of the division. Before moving
to their assigned airfields, the units received their
supplies, checked their equipment, and studied their
individual plans. Early on the morning of September 17 there was a final briefing of all unit commanders to prevent error and confusion in the event
that some units failed to land in their proposed
areas. Each unit commander was responsible for the
mission assigned to a certain area; each had to know
not only his own but also every other mission within
the division. This precaution proved to be of great
value in the final drop.[36]

The planes took off from England on the morning
of September 17 with the newly appointed division

---

[35]Ibid., p. 84.

[36]Ibid., pp. 88-89.

15

commander, Brigadier General James M. Gavin, in the lead ship.[37] The planes flew in groups of forty-five, with four minutes between groups. The gliders used much more space; they were towed three to a plane by C–47's with four transports to a group, and seven minutes between groups.[38]

The 82d Division consisted of the 504th, 505th, and 508th Regimental Combat Teams and the 376th Parachute Field Artillery Battalion; it required the use of 482 C–47's and fifty gliders carrying 7,477 parachute and glider troops.[39]

Enemy opposition was very light. The air support given by the British and American forces cut down on fighter resistance and anti–aircraft defenses.[40] Flak batteries were destroyed by small parachute units jumping directly upon them.[41]

The troops of the division landed on Holland soil between noon and two p.m. The weather was perfect, and every unit landed exactly where planned (as shown on map 2). Since each unit landed on its proposed drop zone, assembly and reorganization were swift. The 376th Artillery was firing as a unit just one hour after landing; it was particularly effective in this operation because the first enemy troops sent against the airborne invaders consisted of home

----

[37]Gellhorn, op. cit., p. 40.

[38]Gavin, op. cit., p. 79.

[39]Ibid., p. 98.

[40]"Vertical Envelopment," New Republic, CXI (October 2, 1944), 411.

[41]Gavin, op. cit., p. 102.

16

guards, local police, and other small, disorganized
units. These were rapidly demoralized by the con-
centrated artillery fire.[42]

The 505th landed directly on the Groesbeek
Heights and set up a defense.[43] The 504th, after
landing near the Waal River, crossed the river to the
west of the Nijmegen Bridge in collapsible boats
provided by the British and secured the north end of
the bridge intact.[44] The 1st Battalion of the 504th
then captured the bridge over the Maas–Waal Canal,

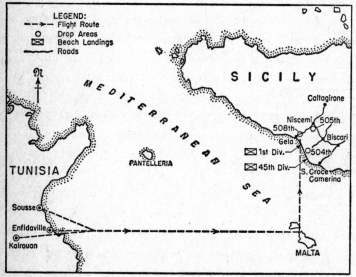

Map 1. Adapted from Gavin, op. cit., pp. 2, 3, and
12.

---

[42]Ibid., p. 103.
[43]Ibid., p. 104.
[44]Gellhorn, op. cit., p. 70.

17

and the 2d Battalion captured the Grave Bridge.[45]
The 508th landed on and held the high ground from
Wyler to Nijmegen and set up road blocks throughout
the area; it assisted other groups in capturing
the northern bridges at Hater and Honinghutie,
and the 504th in capturing the Nijmegen Bridge.[46]

American airborne tactics, born somewhat il-
literate over Sicily, had evolved to sky-writing
sophisticate over Holland. The 82d Airborne Division
had written tactical history in the sky; the message
said clearly that airborne units, suitably assigned
and properly supported, were coming into their own.

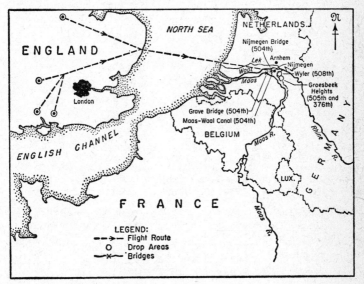

Map 2. Adapted from Gavin, op. cit., pp. 77, 78,
80, 86, and 97.

[45]Gavin, op. cit., p. 102.

[46]Ibid., p. 104.

19

BIBLIOGRAPHY

Ayling, Keith. _They Fly to Fight_. New York: D. Appleton—Century Co., 1944.

Courtney, W. B. "Army in the Sky," _Collier's_, CXIV (November 11, 1944), 18–19, 77–78.

Craven, W. F., and Cate, J. L., eds. _The Army Air Forces in World War II_. Vols. II and III. Chicago: University of Chicago Press, 1949 and 1951.

Devore, Robert. "Paratroops Behind Nazi Lines," _Collier's_, CXII (September 18, 1943), 18–19, 54–55.

82d Airborne Division Yearbook, 1952.

Falls, Cyril. "Arnhem—A Stage in Airborne Tactics," _Illustrated London News_, CCVII (October 27, 1945), 458.

———. "Greatest of Airborne Operations," _Illustrated London News_, CCV (September 23, 1944), 343–344.

Gavin, James M. _Airborne Warfare_. Washington: Infantry Journal Press, 1947.

Gellhorn, Martha. "82d Airborne Division, Master of the Hotspots," _Saturday Evening Post_, CCXVIII (February 23, 1946), 22–23, 39–40, 42, 44, 47.

———. "Rough and Tumble 82d Airborne Division," _Collier's_, CXIV (December 2, 1944), 12, 70.

Lee, William C. "Introduction" to Gavin, James M., _Airborne Warfare_. Washington: Infantry Journal Press, 1947.

Pratt, W. V. "Strategy and Tactics in Sicily," _Newsweek_, XXII (July 26, 1943), 26.

"Vertical Envelopment," _New Republic_, CXI (October 2, 1944), 411.

Exercises

1. a. What is the relation between the question the researcher sets out to investigate and the thesis he uses in his outline and his paper?

b. How does the information on the note cards relate to the question and to the thesis?

2. a. Why is it important for a student to keep his choice of topic tentative until he has checked availability of material in his campus library?

b. On what significant criteria could the student base his choice of topic if he finds that equally adequate materials are available on two tentative topics, both of which have been approved by his instructor?

3. a. What is the difference between primary sources and secondary sources? If both kinds are available, which should the writer use? Why?

b. Point out which of these sources on the Louisiana Purchase are primary and which are secondary: (1) the treaty by which the United States made the purchase from France in 1803, (2) chapters covering the subject in American history books, (3) letters and other papers written by Thomas Jefferson on the subject, (4) a recent dissertation on the subject.

4. Suppose a person beginning to investigate a certain subject has located in the card catalogue an author card representing a good book on the subject. What are the possibilities of his working from this card to extend his preliminary bibliography?

5. a. What points of information are essential on a bibliography card for a book? On a bibliography card for a magazine article? What kind of optional notation on a bibliography card is sometimes useful?

b. What is the difference between a preliminary bibliography and a final bibliography?

c. Why is it logical that an author's last name is placed first in the bibliography but not in a footnote?

6. a. What are the three basic kinds of notes that research workers use to record information from their sources? Describe each kind briefly.

b. In addition to the note itself, what points of information should be written on a note card? Why?

7. a. What is the difference between citatory footnotes and explanatory footnotes?

b. What are the purposes for which citatory footnotes are required?

8. Make each of the following lists of data into a footnote that can serve as a first citation.

a. The reference is to an unsigned article entitled "Industry's New Frontier." The article appeared in the October 4, 1948, issue of *Life* magazine. That issue is now bound in the 25th volume of a file in the library. The article appears on pages 92–96, but the reference is to a point on page 93.

b. The reference is to Ernest Hemingway's short story "The Killers" as it appears on pages 199–208 in a collection of short stories entitled *Studies in the Short Story* and edited by Adrian H. Jaffe and Virgil Scott. The collection was published in New York in 1952.

c. The reference is to page 114 of Elswyth Thane's novel *Dawn's Early Light*, which was published in New York in 1943.

d. The reference is to page 302 and page 303 of a book called *College Book of English Literature*. The book was edited by James Edward Tobin, Victor M. Hamm, and William H. Hines. It was published in New York in 1949.

e. The reference is to an article written by W. Trelease and entitled "Description of the Missouri Botanical Garden." The article appeared on pages 193–221 of *Popular Science* in January of 1903. The issue is now bound in Volume 62 of a file in the library. The reference is to a point on the last page of the article.

9. Explain the meanings and proper uses of the following: *sic, ibid., op. cit.,* p. and pp., col. and cols., ed. and eds., suspension periods, brackets in a quotation.

10. How many of these did Russell Linsin, the author of the specimen research paper (see pp. 137–160), use in organizing his materials: chronological order; spatial order; cause-and-effect relationships; inductive order; climactic order; the traditional beginning, middle, and end? Explain your answer briefly with specific references to the content of the paper.

7 PARAGRAPH DEVELOPMENT

A *paragraph* is a unit of thought or feeling, a unit ordinarily composed of several smaller units (sentences) and serving as part of a larger unit (the whole composition). The paragraph is therefore an intermediate unit in written expression. In good composition the sentences that constitute this intermediate unit are closely related in meaning. Each sentence contributes to the meaning of the group. In an expository paragraph, the kind with which we are chiefly concerned, the sentences are held together by a topic idea, either expressed in a topic sentence or implied. The paragraphs in an effective whole composition are likewise closely related. They present the successive stages of thought or feeling that make the organic whole composition. Thus the paragraph is the structural unit with which the whole composition is built.

The paragraph is also a physical unit on the page, a unit made apparent by the conventions of indenting the first line (about an inch in longhand or five spaces in typescript) and leaving blank any unneeded part of the last line. Although incidentally useful in relieving the eye, these conventions are primarily valuable as signs of the divisions of thought or feeling within the whole composition. They indicate forward movement from one phase of the subject to the next. Hence a writer who misuses the signs, who makes a physical unit of a sentence or a group of sentences not really constituting a unit of thought or feeling, inevitably misleads and confuses the reader.

A study of the paragraph is highly important for the inexperienced writer, especially if he has difficulty in organizing and developing his ideas. Once he learns how to construct good paragraphs, he is well on the way to being able to write a good whole theme. To provide the basis for such a study, the first two sections of this chapter explain the qualities of an effective paragraph and examine typical patterns of reasoning in relation to topic ideas. The third section, comparatively long because of its numerous illustrations, analyzes common methods of development. The short final section points out special purposes that paragraphs sometimes serve.

EFFECTIVENESS OF PARAGRAPHS

Once he has stated his topic idea the writer should ask himself questions like these: Why is my topic idea true? How do I know it is true? What evidence will be necessary to convince my readers that it is true? How can I best present the evidence so that it will make the truth of my topic idea clear to my readers? The answers to such questions will usually provide the details for an effective paragraph.

Generally speaking, a paragraph is effective to the degree that its internal structure is sound; its substance, concrete; and its length, appropriate. These qualities all contribute to the common purpose of transmitting a specific unit of thought or feeling from the writer to the reader. It must be remembered, however, that no conclusive test can be made of a paragraph in isolation, for its ultimate effectiveness is determined by how well it serves its purpose in the whole composition (see Chapter 3).

Internal Structure. An effective paragraph has sound internal structure. The qualities that indicate sound internal structure are unity, coherence, and emphasis. As the development of a single topic idea or emotional effect, the good paragraph is unified; as a cluster of logically related sentences, it is coherent; and as an appropriately focused group of main and supporting points, it is emphatic.

Unity. A paragraph has the quality of *unity,* or oneness, when all its parts function together in the whole development of its topic idea or emotional effect. A paragraph has unity when each sentence contributes an organic part of the whole idea or impression and when no organic part is missing. Paragraph unity therefore rests on the principles of inclusion and exclusion: inclusion of relevant materials and exclusion of irrelevant materials. An excellent way of achieving unity is by means of the topic sentence; properly used the topic sentence forces the writer to adhere to and to sustain the point he is trying to establish.

TOPIC SENTENCE. A *topic* (or *core*) *sentence* is an emphatically placed, explicit statement of the central idea in a paragraph. Frequently the topic sentence is a generalization at or near the beginning, preparing the reader for specific material within the paragraph. Sometimes it is a summarizing statement which comes late in the paragraph and effects a climax. Occasionally it occupies a position in the middle, where it draws a conclusion from preceding material and suggests that more will follow. Always the topic sentence is the most general statement in the paragraph: it must be sufficiently broad in scope to include the substance of all the other statements in the unit.

In each of the following examples the topic sentence (in italics) does much to achieve unity. First, see how an author uses an introductory topic sentence to generalize about the initiation of knights in King Arthur's time and then fills in the generalization with a detailed account of the ceremonies. A less skillful writer might have failed to use the topic sentence, leaving the reader to wonder what special idea, if any, the details were intended to convey; or, having used the general statement, he might have neglected to provide enough specific information to bear it out. Either course would have precluded unity.

The ceremonies of initiation were peculiarly solemn. After undergoing a severe fast, and spending whole nights in prayer, the candidate confessed, and received the sacrament. He then clothed himself in snow-white garments, and repaired to the church, or the hall, where the ceremony was to take place, bearing a knightly sword suspended from his neck, which the officiating priest took and blessed, and then returned to him. The candidate then, with folded arms, knelt before the presiding knight, who, after some questions about his motives and purposes in requesting admission, administered to him the oaths, and granted his request. Some of the knights present, sometimes even ladies and damsels, handed to him in succession the spurs, the coat of mail, the hauberk, the armlet and gauntlet, and lastly he girded on the sword. He then knelt again before the president, who, rising from his seat, gave him the "accolade," which consisted of three strokes, with the flat of a sword, on the shoulder or neck of the candidate, accompanied by the words: "In the name of God, of St. Michael, and St. George, I make thee a knight; be valiant, courteous, and loyal!" Then he received his helmet, his shield, and spear; and thus the investiture ended.[1]

Next, see how an author employs a concluding topic sentence to show the pertinence of an earlier anecdote and attending comments. Here, too, a less competent writer might have omitted the core sentence, depending on the reader to figure out the implications of the anecdote, or might have merely stated his conclusion without leading the reader to it through the appropriately colorful tale. Again, either course would have meant a sacrifice of unity.

Sir Walter Scott thought to flatter an old Scotswoman from whose singing he had taken down a number of ballads by showing her the printed texts of the pieces she had sung to him. But the old woman was more annoyed than amused. He had spoiled them altogether, she complained. "They were made for singing and no for reading, but ye hae broken the charm now and they'll never be sung mair. And the warst thing o' a', they're nouther

---

[1] Reprinted with permission from Thomas Bulfinch, "The Age of Chivalry" in *Bulfinch's Mythology* (New York: Random House, n.d.), pp. 305–306.

right spell'd, nor right setten down." This last phrase may have been a slash at Scott's tactful doctoring of his ballads. But would old Mrs. Hogg have been any happier even if the texts had been exactly reproduced? Probably not. There are people who hate to see wild flowers in a vase or animals in cages, and ballads in static print may well seem equally unnatural. Most of us, however, would remain blissfully ignorant of the folk ballads if to hear them meant a field trip for song-catching in the Appalachians. And the folk ballads of the olden times that got sporadically recorded in manuscripts and old ballad books would have been utterly lost if those who preserved them had felt the way Mrs. Hogg did. Nonetheless, the testy old woman's scruples bring to the fore a key fact about balladry—simply this: *ballads are songs or performances, not poems.* They are not literature, but illiterature.[2]

Occasionally a writer does not express his topic idea in a special sentence but implies it. In doing this he may still achieve unity, but he complicates his task somewhat. Without the aid of the explicit reminder, the topic sentence, he must still integrate his materials so that the completed paragraph will have at its core a single idea or effect which the reader can recognize and, if he chooses, express in a sentence. The inexperienced writer need not fear that he will overwork the topic sentence as a unifying device. Experienced writers use it frequently, if not automatically. The beginner should use it consistently.

INCLUSION AND EXCLUSION. A requirement of unity is that all information essential to the development of the topic be included. If essential information is omitted, the paragraph remains less than a unit and hence lacks oneness. Consider, for instance, a paragraph on the topic idea of the inviolability of the person of the president of the United States which omitted the fact that the president cannot be arrested. Without this essential point of information, the paragraph would be less than a unit—less than a *whole* development of the topic idea.

Again, to achieve unity all information not essential to the development of the topic must be rigorously excluded. If extraneous or superfluous material is included, the paragraph becomes more than a unit and hence lacks oneness. The paragraph on the president's inviolability must not include a statement on his salary. Such information, no matter how interesting, would not be an organic part of the developed topic idea and would therefore disrupt the unity.

Here are two examples which contain interesting material but lack unity, because the writers did not observe the principles of *inclusion and exclusion*. Each paragraph in the following passage from a student

[2] Reprinted with permission from Introduction to *The Viking Book of Folk Ballads of the English-Speaking World,* ed. Albert Barron Friedman (New York: The Viking Press, Inc., 1956), p. ix.

theme is less than a unit: the first contains the topic sentence (in italics) and part of a supporting example; the second contains the rest of the example. The two should have been combined.

People sometimes base their conclusions on irrelevant facts in an attempt to justify believing what they want to believe. I overheard an instance of this kind of fallacy at a basketball game last winter. Two spectators from the opposing schools were predicting victory for their respective teams. One based his argument on the quality of his school's gymnasium, the finest in the conference according to him.

The other argued that his team would win because his school had just spent six hundred dollars for new uniforms and equipment. Superior architecture has little to do with winning a ball game, and the assumption that new uniforms will bring victory is just as fallacious. Both spectators were using irrelevant facts to support wishful thinking.

The following paragraph from another student theme lacks unity because the last two sentences digress from the idea in the topic sentence. To provide unity, the scope of the topic sentence could have been broadened or, preferably, the passage should have been divided and further details added to develop a new topic idea (the idea that the same handicraft class brought the writer much pleasure) in a separate paragraph.

The handicraft class I directed when I was a playground leader in a park last summer gave me many reasons to fret. In the first place, I was allotted only four saws, one hammer, one drill, one screw driver, a box of nails, a box of screws, a package of sandpaper, six paint brushes, and two cans of paint for forty-five boys to use. Although I divided the boys into shifts, there were still many squabbles over how often and how long each one could use a tool. To complicate matters, some of the boys were not very adept. They kept me busy thinking up simple things for them to do, like cutting flat patterns out of wood and sanding and painting them. Worst of all, there were several boys who were bent on being destructive. I had to stop them from decorating the park benches and sawing the softball bat in half. I must say though that a good many of the boys were co-operative and talented, and I really had fun working with them. Four of them showed so much talent that I called them my "artisans" and assigned them large-scale projects like building a wishing well and setting up a miniature trading post.

Coherence. A paragraph has the quality of *coherence* when all parts cling together in a systematic arrangement. Just as this quality in the whole composition is a matter of relationships among the paragraphs, so in the paragraph it is a matter of relationships among the sentences.

The paragraph is coherent when close relationships exist among the ideas and when the sentences make these relationships immediately clear to the reader. The first major requirement in writing a coherent paragraph, then, is the inclusion of material containing essential, or organic, relationships.

RECOGNIZING ORGANIC RELATIONSHIPS. Choosing material in which *organic relationships* exist is an exercise in clear thinking, in recognizing the facts and ideas (or events if the writing is to be narrative) that can be combined in a logical way to make a unit of thought or feeling. In planning the paragraph on the president's inviolability, for example, a writer who understands the topic idea will recognize organic relationships among the following facts: the president cannot be arrested, cannot be subjected to the jurisdiction of a court, cannot be removed from office except by impeachment, cannot be deprived of executive power while impeachment proceedings are in progress; only if the president is removed from office does he become amenable to judicial process. A clear-thinking writer will see that these facts relate to the main idea of immunity and to each other as parts of a continuous set of immunities, and that consequently they *belong* in a paragraph.

Using properly related material is a vital measure but will not in itself produce coherence. The second major requirement remains: making the relationships clear to a reader who has not yet seen them. This is a matter of providing continuity in the writing. It involves smoothly leading the reader through the ideas of the sentences to an understanding of the meaning of the whole paragraph.

MAKING RELATIONSHIPS CLEAR. The more carefully he thinks through his material and plans his composition beforehand, the abler the writer will be in *making relationships among his ideas clear* to the reader. If possible, the planning should include an outline (see pp. 45–51) or at least organized notations on cards (a separate card for each paragraph) or on sections of a sheet of paper (for example, four sections marked off on a page when four paragraphs are being planned). Once he has made the necessary preparation, almost any writer will achieve more coherence if he composes the whole paragraph rather swiftly (better still the whole composition, as suggested in Chapter 3) instead of stopping to work out individual sentences.[8] By keep-

---

[8] There is often a temptation for the writer to compose in one-sentence installments; that is, to set down a fact or idea in an isolated sentence, relax awhile, then concentrate on another sentence. But this procedure, as many a composition student has ruefully learned, produces an assortment of sentence-units, not a coherent paragraph.

ing his attention on the larger unit, he will be more likely to write an integrated discussion. He will more automatically do these four things: (1) keep his ideas moving in a systematic order, (2) insert transitional expressions needed to make the order recognizable, (3) repeat important words judiciously, and (4) construct sentences from a consistent point of view. Later, as he revises, he should read each paragraph at least once for the particular purpose of testing its coherence. If the connection between ideas is not clear at any place, he will probably find that further use of one or more of the above four steps will correct the problem. Should the incoherence persist, he will need to re-examine his subject matter to see whether he is trying to force a relationship where none exists organically. If so, he must revise the content of the paragraph. When he is finally certain that he has achieved coherence, he should check for and eliminate unnecessary repetition and transitional devices.

To clarify the four steps mentioned in the preceding paragraph, we shall now examine them in more detail and see examples of coherent and incoherent writing.

Systematic Arrangement. The surest way to make relationships among ideas clear to the reader is by means of *systematic arrangement.* The writer has many arrangements from which to choose in presenting his ideas in a paragraph. But first he should examine his subject matter to see whether its inherent qualities call for a certain order, such as a temporal or a spatial order (see pp. 101–107 and examples on pp. 183–184 and 186–188). Next he should decide whether an all-over inductive pattern, deductive pattern, or combination of these would best serve his purpose (see pp. 18–20 and 180–182). Thereafter he might consider arrangements suggested by common methods of paragraph development, such as development by comparison, cause and effect, multiple reasons, enumeration, or definition (pp. 189–196). Furthermore the writer should keep always in mind that a climactic order stimulates the reader's interest (pp. 44–45).

Whatever the over-all pattern for the paragraph, the sentences having the closest interrelationships should appear in immediate succession. The paragraph on presidential immunities, for instance, may reasonably contain, along with other sentences, one sentence explaining that the president cannot be arrested and two explaining that he cannot be removed from office except by impeachment. If the sentence on arrest appears *between* the two sentences on removal from office, however, the paragraph will lack coherence; the reader's chain of thought will be interrupted, and he may not link together the two points on impeachment. Such a breach of coherence will not occur if the writer thinks and writes continuously, making each sentence idea issue from the preceding one and bear upon the following one, until he completes the unit.

The opening paragraph of Lincoln's "Second Inaugural Address" illustrates coherence gained through a time pattern in the arrangement of ideas. The first sentence tells the reader (or listener) of the present situation but through a comparison takes him back to conditions four years in the past; the second keeps him thinking of that time; the next two lead him through events from then to the present; and the last makes him think of the future.

At this second appearing to take the oath of the presidential office, there is less occasion for an extended address than there was at first. Then a statement, somewhat in detail, of a course to be pursued, seemed fitting and proper. Now, at the expiration of four years, during which public declarations have been constantly called forth on every point and phase of the great contest which still absorbs the attention and engrosses the energies of the nation, little that is new could be presented. The progress of our arms, upon which all else chiefly depends, is as well known to the public as to myself; and it is, I trust, reasonably satisfactory and encouraging to all. With high hope for the future, no prediction in regard to it is ventured.

ABRAHAM LINCOLN

Transitional Expressions. To clarify for the reader certain unapparent but real relationships in logically arranged subject matter, the writer may need to interweave his sentences with special *transitional devices.* Words like *first, later,* and *thereafter* show time relationships. (Notice Lincoln's use of *then* and *now* in the second and third sentences of the passage quoted above.) Expressions such as *in the foreground, overhead,* and *to the left* point out spatial kinship. Words like *but, however,* and *nonetheless* suggest qualifications. (See how these words function in the passage on balladry, p. 165f.) Words such as *accordingly, consequently,* and *thus* indicate causal relationships. Hundreds of other expressions point out various other kinds of relationships. These special devices are convenient writing tools but should be used only to show relationships that would not be clear otherwise. If used excessively, they tend to distract the reader. Most transitional expressions call less attention to themselves and serve their purpose better when placed in an unemphatic position within the sentence instead of at the beginning or the end.

Repetition. Another way to clarify related thoughts and achieve coherence in the paragraph is to repeat important words and phrases or to use synonyms for them. The same care is necessary with *repetition* as with transitional devices. In excess, repetition also tends to annoy the reader; but it is a very helpful technique if used judiciously. In the paragraph on the president's inviolability, for example, the word *president* would be an important verbal link and could appear as the subject in two or three sentences and also as the subject complement or direct object or still another element in other sentences. To avoid excessive repetition, the term *chief executive* could be substituted, and the pronoun *he* (including its other forms: *him, his, himself*) would almost certainly be needed several times. So long as its antecedent (*president*) remained clear and its person and number (third person, singular) remained consistent, the pronoun could appear in different forms—perhaps functioning as the subject in one sentence and the object of a preposition in another—and would still promote coherence in the paragraph. (See Lincoln's repetition of the word *right* and his use of the first person, plural pronoun in different forms—*we, us, ourselves*—in the passage on p. 172.)

Consistency in Grammatical Structure. The repetition that produces consistency in the grammatical structure of sentences in a paragraph is more fundamental to coherence than the repetition of key words and is more difficult to accomplish. This kind of repetition is more fundamental because it prevents disconcerting shifts in the sentences and lets the reader concentrate on the meaning of the paragraph. It is more difficult because it involves various grammatical elements and their functions. Fortunately, though, a certain degree of consistency is likely to occur automatically when, as suggested earlier, the writer thinks of the paragraph as a unit and writes without delays between sentences. An additional degree usually results from his revising later to eliminate any unnecessary shifts.

When he composes a group of sentences having *consistent grammatical structure*, the writer does several things in particular. He keeps the same subject (not necessarily the same word, since he may use synonyms or pronouns) through several sentences. He presents his material from the same point of view and in the same tone. He avoids shifts in the number and person of pronouns and keeps the same tense, voice, and mood of verbs as far as is practicable. When he has equally valuable ideas to relate, he places them in the same kind of sentence element; that is, he uses parallel structure. In all these things the writer is doing the reader the service of clarification; hence he is achieving coherence. (For a full explanation of sentence structure and grammar, see Chapters 8 and 9.)

The examples which follow illustrate many of the points mentioned in the preceding paragraph. The Lincoln passage, which is the last paragraph of his "Second Inaugural Address," shows a high degree of consistency in grammatical structure. The two versions of the student paragraph on library experience illustrate several inconsistencies and other causes of incoherence and also demonstrate ways of revising to achieve coherence.

In the one-sentence paragraph quoted below, Lincoln employed obvious repetition in structure to clarify the relationships among his ideas. Notice especially the parallelism in the first three prepositional phrases (as well as the contrast between the first two), in the succession of infinitive phrases, in the phrases that reflect the man-woman-child sequence, and in the final two prepositional phrases. Lincoln also used a subtler kind of repetition to make this paragraph coherent. It is repetition, with interesting variations, in the rhythm and tempo of the phrases. The effect is poetic and, being so, makes the passage memorable.

With malice towards none, with charity for all, with firmness in the right, as God gives us to see the right, let us strive on to finish the work we are in,—to bind up the nation's wounds,—to care for him who shall have borne the battle, and for his widow, and his orphan—to do all which may achieve and cherish a just and lasting peace among ourselves, and with all nations.

ABRAHAM LINCOLN

In writing a theme on his experience with libraries, a second-semester college student decided, reasonably enough, to include a paragraph on what he had done in libraries before entering college, another on what had happened during his first semester in using the college library, and a third on what he was currently learning as he worked on his first research paper. In its original form the first of these paragraphs, shown here with italics added, contained many interesting details but had little coherence.

ORIGINAL FORM: INCOHERENT	CAUSES OF INCOHERENCE
Before I entered college my acquaintance with libraries was meager. My first library experience was with the Bookmobile, which came to the grade school I attended *twice a month.* I entered the Bookmobile on many of its visits. I always borrowed or returned the same book, a big blue one on jungle animals. In high school most of my study periods	Part of topic idea (other part at end of paragraph). Misplaced modifier. Transition needed between ideas. Shift to passive voice.

ORIGINAL FORM:
INCOHERENT (CONT.)

CAUSES OF
INCOHERENCE (CONT.)

were spent in the library, but I did not use much of that time to familiarize myself with it. *Some of my tenth grade teachers insisted* on book reports, and then *the librarian always received* a request for a book on Indians. When I was in the eleventh grade, *someone gave* me a book entitled *The Long Valley*, by John Steinbeck. I became a Steinbeck fan and checked out four other books by Steinbeck. *In the twelfth grade I elected speech instead of English.* I missed the experience of looking up material for a term paper and used the library only to read articles on baseball, the topic on which I made most of my speeches. *I joined the Navy and was gone four years. Take my word*, when *you are* in the Navy *you have* a chance to mature and learn the value of books. I became interested in science from my best friend aboard ship. *He had been* to college and majored in chemistry. I read all the scientific books and magazines in the ship's library and even wished I had more. *The only other time I recall using a library before I came to college was back in junior high school, when I checked out a few books on photography, my hobby at the time.* I can see now that *my reading interests were pretty sporadic before I came to college.*	Shift in point of view and in subject of main clause.
	Shift in point of view and in subject of main clause.
	Shift in point of view and in subject of main clause.
	Relevance of idea not clear immediately.
	Relevance not clear immediately.
	Shift in mood and tone. Shift to second person and present tense.
	Shift in point of view and subject.
	Idea out of natural time sequence used in rest of paragraph.
	Part of topic idea (should be included in first sentence).

In the revised form of the paragraph the interrelationships among the interesting details have been made clear.

REVISED FORM: COHERENT

AIDS TO COHERENCE

Before I entered college, my acquaintance with libraries was meager, largely because my reading interests were sporadic. My first library experience was with the Bookmobile, which came *twice a month* to the grade school I attended. I entered the Bookmobile on many of its visits *but* always to borrow or return the same book, a big blue one on jungle animals. *My next library experience, in junior high school, was not much more extensive: I checked out a few books on photography, my hobby at the time. The same pattern continued through high school.* Although I *spent* my study periods in the library, I did not familiarize myself with it.	A unifying topic sentence (including the whole topic idea).
	Modifier correctly placed (no longer misleading).
	Transitional word.
	Transitional statement. Now in natural time sequence.
	Transitional statement. Active voice (consistent with voice

Revised Form: Coherent (cont.)

Whenever one of my tenth-grade teachers insisted on a book report, *I* simply *asked* the librarian for a book on Indians. In the eleventh grade, when I became a Steinbeck fan through a gift of *The Long Valley, I checked out* four other books by Steinbeck. In the twelfth grade, by *electing speech instead of English* I missed the experience of looking up material for a term paper, and I used the library only to read articles on baseball, the topic I used for most of my speeches. *Then, during a four-year enlistment in the Navy, I began to mature and to realize the value of books.* From my best friend aboard ship, *a chemistry major,* I gained an interest in science. I read all the scientific books and magazines in the ship's library and, *for the first time in my life, looked forward to using a well-stocked library.*

Aids to Coherence

of other action verbs). Consistent point of view: consistent use of first person as subject of main clause. Relevance of idea immediately clear. Transitional word. Shift in mood and tone avoided. Person and tense now consistent. Appositive to eliminate shift in viewpoint. Transitional idea preparing reader for next paragraph on writer's experience in library.

Emphasis. A paragraph has the quality of *emphasis* when each of its parts occupies the amount of space and the position best suited to communicating to the reader its total thought or feeling. In other words, the emphatic paragraph is constructed to show what is important and what is subordinate in its content. Emphasis is secured by repetition, by proportion, and by position.

EMPHASIS BY REPETITION. Repetition of key words or phrases is perhaps the simplest way of securing emphasis in the paragraph. Seeing the same expression several times keeps the reader thinking of a particular idea. But *emphasis by repetition* should not be overdone: using a key word or phrase three or four times in a paragraph is usually more effective than using it a dozen times. Synonyms or pronouns referring to a specific antecedent are often helpful in creating appropriate repetition. Parallelism, or repetition in sentence structure, which we have noticed as a means to coherence, may also produce emphasis.

In the following paragraph the author emphasizes the satirical effect of his description of a dinner party by starting all the main clauses in the same way (*There was* or *There were*), by using such similar words as *vast* and *vaster,* and especially by repeating the phrase *cooing ladies.*

There was vast music, vaster food; there were uncomfortable scientists explaining to golden cooing ladies, in a few words, just what they were up to and what in the next twenty years they hoped to be up to; there were the cooing ladies themselves, observing in tones of pretty rebuke, "But I'm afraid you haven't yet made it as clear as you might." There were the cooing ladies' husbands—college graduates, manipulators of oil stocks or of corporation law—who sat ready to give to anybody who desired it their opinion that while antitoxins might be racy, what we really needed was a good substitute for rubber.[4]

EMPHASIS BY PROPORTION. Closely related to emphasis by repetition is *emphasis by proportion.* Appropriate emphasis results when the amounts of space allotted to ideas vary according to the relative importance of the ideas. The writer automatically gives more space to a certain idea when he repeats a key word or uses synonyms, but he may apportion the space more directly. In a paragraph that includes three examples, he may secure emphasis by presenting the least important example in one sentence, a more important example in two sentences, and the most important example in three or four sentences. By proportionate fullness of detail he will call the reader's attention to the chief illustration.

In the first sentence of the following excerpt, the writer presents four points. He then emphasizes the fourth point by devoting exclusively to it the remaining two sentences of the paragraph. His arrangement of the points shows also the writer's awareness of an inherent temporal order: understanding the question naturally comes first, selecting the correct materials for answering it comes next, and so on.

The ideal answer to a subjective examination will reveal that (a) you understand the question, what it implies and what it does not imply; (b) you know the necessary facts and how to relate them, separating relevant from irrelevant material; (c) you can present material in an orderly manner; (d) you can make clear whatever you have to say. It is upon the final ability that a completely successful answer depends. For it is an ever-true adage that knowing a thing without being able to communicate it effectively is only half-knowing it.[5]

EMPHASIS BY POSITION. The reader's attention dwells naturally on the most prominent parts of any unit of writing. A good way, then, to emphasize the important ideas is to place them where the reader is likely to notice them. In the paragraph, as in the sentence (p. 221) and in the whole composition (p. 35), the most conspicuous position is at the end, and the next most conspicuous position is at the beginning. Thus a

---

[4] Reprinted with permission from Sinclair Lewis, *Arrowsmith* (New York: Harcourt, Brace and Co., Inc., 1925, and London: Jonathan Cape Ltd.).

[5] J. N. Hook, *How To Take Examinations in College,* "College Outline Series" (New York: Barnes & Noble, Inc., 1958), p. 94.

paragraph gains *emphasis by position* when it begins with a strong point, presents a lesser point next, and then proceeds in climactic order to its strongest point. Many emphatic paragraphs start with a topic sentence and follow it with supporting statements in strictly climactic order.

The example quoted above has emphasis by position as well as by proportion because the author not only allots more space to his fourth point than to any other but also discusses it last. The following example has emphasis by position because an ascending arithmetical order is apparent in its last three sentences, which make an analysis of the general first statement.

At an educated guess, we as a nation are now using around 275 billion gallons of water a day. Less than 10 per cent of the total is for domestic purposes, either through municipal water systems or from rural wells. More than a third, around 100 billion gallons a day, is necessary for irrigation. The rest, well over half, goes for the needs of industry.[6]

If we were to examine further the paragraphs given here to illustrate emphasis, we would find that they have unity and coherence also; and in reviewing those that illustrate coherence, we would find them unified and emphatic. Indeed any good paragraph has all three of these qualities.[7]

Concrete Details. An effective paragraph contains vivid, *concrete details*. The principles governing the rhetoric of the paragraph—including the rules of unity, coherence, and emphasis (just discussed), the methods of logical reasoning (explained in Chapter 2 and reviewed in the next section of this chapter), and the various methods of paragraph development (explained later in this chapter)—have one thing in com-

---

[6] John Robbins, "Water: How Fast Can We Waste It?" *Atlantic Monthly,* July, 1957, p. 31.

[7] See pp. 187–188 for notes on unity, coherence, and emphasis in the analysis of another paragraph. See pp. 214–224 and pp. 32–35 for information on these qualities in the sentence and the whole theme.

Many persons can increase their understanding of unity, coherence, and emphasis by relating them to concrete objects: (1) A handful of dry sand has unity but no coherence; a handful of wet sand has unity and coherence. A quantity of wet sand molded in the form of a cone has unity, coherence, and emphasis. (2) A cupful of grapes has unity but no coherence; a cupful of grape jam has unity and coherence. A bunch of grapes has unity, coherence, and emphasis. (3) The pieces of a mosaic thrown together in a heap have unity but no coherence. A mosaic with all its pieces inlaid according to a basic design has unity, coherence, and emphasis.

mon: they all suggest patterns which the writer can fill in with concrete details to transmit his thoughts and feelings to the reader. The examples throughout this chapter show how this filling in is done. We have already seen, for instance, that the paragraph on initiation into knighthood, which illustrated unity, contains a series of details—from the knight's "severe fast" before the ceremony to the bestowing of "his helmet, his shield, and spear" at its completion. Later in the chapter we shall see a model of description that mentions such details as "domelike forehead," "steady eyes," "immense white moustache," and "strong jaw" to create the image of an old man. And we shall read, among others, a paragraph of enumeration that mentions "wood pulp and ink," "clean and shiny" books, and "dog-eared and dilapidated" books to differentiate among the kinds of book owners. Attentive reading of the best works soon reveals that the best writers consistently use concrete details.

A comparison of two paragraphs from themes written by college freshmen to fulfill the same assignment will further illustrate the value of specific details. Each student described his first airplane ride to develop the point that he had feared the unfamiliar and found experience instrumental in overcoming his fear. The first student wrote an introduction announcing his central idea and then presented four relevant examples (one of which was his first flight) in four separate paragraphs. His plan was sound, but his theme lacked conviction because he described each experience in broad generalizations instead of using concrete details. Here is his paragraph on the flight experience.

Another example of how I dreaded something unfamiliar was my first plane ride. I was nervous for days beforehand. When the time came I really did not want to go, but decided I should. Getting on the plane and waiting was bad enough, but the take-off was worse. That really scared me. Somehow I lived through it, and after awhile I began to look around. Everything seemed to be going all right, and before long the butterflies that had been bothering me were gone. The landing hardly bothered me at all. Since then I have taken several more plane trips and have decided that flying is the best way to travel a long distance.

The paragraph does not give the reader the specific information he needs in order to *see* and *feel* what the writer had seen and felt. How old was the writer at the time of the flight and what was the occasion for it? Why did he decide he "should" go? What did he think, say, or do when he was "really scared"? Exactly what did he notice to make him conclude that "everything seemed to be going all right"? These and other questions need to be answered with specific details for the paragraph to be effective.

The second student used his first flight as a sustained example in the five paragraphs of his theme. His plan was not necessarily better than the first student's, but his theme was more informative and convincing because he included comparatively few general statements and many specific details. Like the first student, he introduced his topic in his first paragraph. In the second, he described his childhood fear of height, which had been reflected in two recurring dreams, one of them involving aircraft. Next he related how, when he was twelve, his pleasure in anticipating a summer at boys' camp became secondary to secret fear after his parents decided to send him part of the way to camp by air, and how the mental turbulence shifted to physical pain and fever the day before the flight. In the fourth paragraph, he described his imaginings as he left his parents in the terminal and approached and climbed the stairs to the four-engine Constellation. Here is his last paragraph.

As soon as I was inside the plane, I hurried into a seat and fastened the safety belt as tightly as I could. I checked the window and found that I could look over the left wing and see propellers. Before I could collect my jumbled thoughts, I heard a cough and a sputter and saw the propellers begin to turn. They turned increasingly faster as the accompanying roar grew louder. I felt my stomach approach my mouth when two men in coveralls rolled the steps away, then felt it recede a little as we taxied to the end of the runway. Although I knew what he would do next, I stiffened when the pilot stopped and gave the plane full throttle in a neutral position to give it the necessary thrust for the take-off. I could see tall grass at the side of the runway bend under the tremendous wind from the propellers. There was a jerk as the pilot released the brakes, and then the plane was speeding down the runway. I closed my eyes and gripped the armrests of my seat. I could feel the safety belt cutting into my stomach and perspiration trickling into my eyebrows; but I dared not release my grip. When I opened my eyes, I was amazed to find that we were at least a thousand feet above the ground. The take-off had been so smooth that I had not realized when it occurred. I was immediately absorbed in what I now saw from the window. The view of suburban Saint Louis, intermittently concealed by drifting clouds, reminded me of the make-believe place I had built with miniature trees, houses, and cars around a toy train. I felt as if I were in a different world looking down on a fairyland. I took a deep breath, unloosed my aching hands, and looked around inside the plane. A woman in front of me was reading a book. In front of her a young man and a girl were laughing. A pretty stewardess was coming down the aisle with a tray. On the other side two boys not much older than I were talking and glancing out the window as if they were riding in a bus. The man directly across from me was asleep. The stewardess handed me a cup of hot chocolate and asked, grinning, "Your first flight?" I answered confidently, "Yes ma'am, thank you." The chocolate tasted better than anything I had had for a week. I rested my forehead against the window and gazed down at a new fairy-land: patches of trees and fields and a river. I was no longer afraid.[8]

This paragraph recreates for the reader rather precisely what the writer had experienced. The reason is that the writer not only included details but also selected them for a particular purpose: to show his fear reach its peak and be replaced by a feeling of security. The greater length, though not in itself a reason for making the paragraph more effective than the previous example, results from the inclusion of details.[9]

Length. Although paragraph *length* is not dictated by precise rules, it is governed by the requirements of appropriateness. The length of an effective paragraph is appropriate to the purpose of the paragraph and the method of development. In a given composition, the paragraphs that evolve minor topics should be relatively short; those which evolve major topics, relatively long.[10] But a major topic developed by one method, illustrative instances for example, may require more space than a major topic developed by another method.

Appropriateness in length also implies moderation: extremes in para-graph length should be avoided. Paragraphs of one or two sentences should not be used except for such special purposes as introducing a topic, making a transition, recording dialogue, or summarizing a dis-cussion. It is also wise not to write extremely long paragraphs. If a topic idea cannot be developed adequately in six or eight sentences, it may need to be partitioned logically and the parts or phases evolved in separate paragraphs. Moreover, it is especially important to avoid groups of very short or very long paragraphs, for such groups would tell the reader little about the relative importance of the writer's ideas.

[8] From "Afraid? Not Me!" Theme No. 3 (unpublished) written by David Hanks in English Composition 101, Section 35, at Washington University, Saint Louis, Missouri, October 13, 1958.

[9] For information on the choice of words to produce vividness and concrete-ness, see Chapter 10.

[10] The last example above is exceptionally long for a paragraph in a student composition. Its length (approximately 400 words) is at least partly justified by its climactic function; except for an introduction of fewer than 100 words, the other paragraphs in this same 1000-word composition range from 150 to 250 words.

For examples of paragraphs appropriate in length for their respective purposes in a whole composition, see John Lloyd's "Song Is Supreme" in Chapter 3.

LOGICAL REASONING IN THE PARAGRAPH

There are three basic patterns of logical reasoning in paragraph development: inductive, inductive-deductive, and deductive patterns. The inductive pattern implies that the writer's thinking has proceeded from the specific to the general; the inductive-deductive pattern, from the specific to the general and back to the specific; the deductive pattern, from the general to the specific. (For a full explanation of induction and deduction, see Chapter 2.)

Inductive Pattern. In developing a paragraph by means of the *inductive pattern* the writer presents particular instances of a like kind and leads from them into a valid generalization which serves as his topic sentence. (Thus, in this inductive pattern, the topic sentence is likely to appear late in the paragraph, often at the very end.) The result may be referred to as a periodic paragraph, which, like a periodic sentence, cannot be considered structurally complete at any point before the end. (See pp. 211–212 for information on periodic, balanced, and loose sentences.) Here is an illustration of the inductive pattern of development.

As an early-morning pastime Susie, my tortoise-colored kitten, would frequent the utility room, swing open the small metal door on the gas heater, and peer at the mechanism inside. During the daytime her favorite toy was not the usual ball of yarn or sprig of catnip but a small musical top that she learned to spin with admirable dexterity. And late at night, when there was sometimes a gentle tapping in the study next to my bedroom, the cause always proved the same: in the darkness a soft little paw was playing feline rhythms on the keys of my typewriter. *For a kitten, Susie had an unusual interest in mechanical things.*

Notice that three recurring examples of the kitten's interest precede the general conclusion or topic sentence (in italics). This type of reasoning —from representative examples to a general conclusion—is inductive.

Inductive-Deductive Pattern. In developing a paragraph by means of the *inductive-deductive pattern* the writer first presents particular instances and a resulting generalization, then applies the generalization to a new instance. In the last part of such a paragraph the reasoning— from a general rule to specific application of that rule—is deductive. As given below, the material on the kitten has been adapted to the inductive-deductive pattern of development.

Soon after we had adopted Susie, a tortoise-colored kitten, I noticed that as an early-morning pastime she would frequent the utility room, swing open the small metal door on the gas heater, and peer at the mechanism inside. Before long I found that during the daytime her favorite toy was not the usual ball of yarn or sprig of catnip but a small musical top that she learned to spin with admirable dexterity. *In fact, I soon concluded that, for a kitten, Susie had an unusual interest in mechanical things.* So it was that the first time I was awakened late at night by a gentle tapping in the study next to my bedroom, I was not alarmed, for I realized immediately that in the darkness a soft little paw was playing feline rhythms on the keys of my typewriter.

Here two recurring examples precede the general observation or topic sentence. The generalization is then applied to the third, or last, example. The result is a semi-periodic paragraph, which, like a balanced sentence, can be considered structurally complete but not fully developed in meaning at a point before the end. In other words, the paragraph could end before the final example is introduced but would then be less rich in meaning.

Deductive Pattern. In developing a paragraph by means of the *deductive pattern* the writer begins with a generalization (the topic sentence) and proceeds with specific elaboration or application of the general idea. This type of paragraph may end with a restatement of the topic idea (that is, with a "clincher" sentence), but the basic pattern is still deductive. Inexperienced writers usually find that placing the topic sentence first helps them to stick to the topic, to unify the paragraph. The following adaptation of the material on the kitten illustrates the deductive pattern of development.

I already knew that Susie, my tortoise-colored kitten, had an unusual interest in mechanical things. I was sure, therefore, one morning when I saw her go into the utility room and swing open the small metal door on the gas heater, that she would sit and peer at the mechanism inside. That is just what she did. When I offered her a ball of yarn and a small musical top, I expected her to prefer the latter as a toy. She did, and learned to spin it with admirable dexterity. And when I was awakened late one night by a gentle tapping in the study next to my bedroom, I knew immediately that in the darkness a soft little paw was playing feline rhythms on the keys of my typewriter.

Here the generalization is acknowledged first and is then applied to three specific instances. The result is a loose paragraph, which, like a loose sentence, can be considered structurally complete but not fully developed in meaning at one or more points before the end.

Within these three basic patterns (inductive, inductive-deductive, and deductive patterns), writers employ various methods of paragraph development, sometimes singly, sometimes in combination. The most common of these methods are explained and illustrated in the following section.

METHODS OF PARAGRAPH DEVELOPMENT

As we have already noted, good writing is specific writing. Whatever their purpose—to describe, entertain, explain, or persuade—good writers respect the fact that detailed evidence is necessary to clarify a generalization and convince the reader of its truth. Accordingly, they use various methods of paragraph development, sometimes unconsciously, to give specific content to their general ideas and feelings. Paragraph development commonly involves one or more of the following means of specification: pictorial details, chronological incidents, illustrative instances, definition, enumeration, multiple reasons, cause and effect, and comparison.

Although the experienced writer may be able to develop effective paragraphs without particular awareness of how he does so, the beginner usually benefits from conscious use of proven methods. Analyzing different kinds of paragraphs, such as the examples on the following pages, is also good practice. Remember, however, that a paragraph out of context loses some of its significance. For this reason, read carefully the comments accompanying each excerpt as well as the excerpt itself. Then, as practice time allows or composition assignments arise, try out the groups of suggestions listed at the ends of these discussions. In each case, consider the whole group of suggestions while gathering and selecting material and planning the paragraph. Get the material and the total procedure well in mind first; then write the paragraph rather swiftly as a unit. For, after all, the importance of studying methods of development lies in learning to organize material into paragraphs that are real structural units in a whole composition.

Pictorial Details. Paragraphs of description are frequently used to supplement other forms of discourse, especially narrative. A writer who wants his readers to form a certain mental picture of a person or a place selects the details he thinks will best create that picture and presents them in an orderly manner within a paragraph.[11] For the writer of description, as for the artist who paints a portrait or a scene, this matter of selection is vastly important; unlike the photographer, the writer or the painter cannot possibly include all details and therefore must depend upon his selection to create the image he desires. Further-

[11] See Chapter 5 for information on spatial and analytical organization of description.

more, the selected details must characterize the person or place in a way suitable to the composition of which the paragraph is a part.

The following passages of description are from novels. The author of the first excerpt is describing a fictitious person, the elderly host at a family gathering, and ascribing to him a little less selfishness, a little more fortitude, a little less greed, a little more wholesomeness than he ascribes to several of the old man's relatives elsewhere in the same chapter.

In the centre of the room, under the chandelier, as became a host, stood the head of the family, old Jolyon himself. Eighty years of age, with his fine, white hair, his dome-like forehead, his little, dark grey eyes, and an immense white moustache, which drooped and spread below the level of his strong jaw, he had a patriarchal look, and in spite of lean cheeks and hollows at his temples, seemed master of perennial youth. He held himself extremely upright, and his shrewd, steady eyes had lost none of their clear shining. Thus he gave an impression of superiority to the doubts and dislikes of smaller men. Having had his own way for innumerable years, he had earned a prescriptive right to it. It would never have occurred to old Jolyon that it was necessary to wear a look of doubt or of defiance.[12]

Here are details that suggest old age—self-righteous old age—but, more to the point, items that establish a certain degree of sturdiness and dignity and strength of character in old age. The details, most of which describe the head, facial features, and figure of the character, appear in the order in which they would probably strike an actual observer. (Hair, forehead, eyes, moustache, and jaw, for instance, are mentioned in the order an observer would notice them in a glance that started at the top of the subject's head and moved downward; the eyes are mentioned a second time, indicating the way an observer is naturally impelled to look again at impressive eyes.) The last three sentences contain interpretive commentary by the author. These last sentences and the elliptical clause *as became a host* in the first sentence illustrate how a writer can clarify his reason for using a particular selection of *pictorial details*.

In the next example another novelist is describing a trip of two characters riding mules through a snowstorm and the impression which the storm makes, particularly on the main character, the Bishop.

At four o'clock [in the morning] they were on the road, Jacinto riding the mule that carried the blankets. He knew the trails through his own mountains well enough to follow them in the dark. Toward noon the Bishop

[12] Reprinted with permission from John Galsworthy, *The Man of Property* (New York: Charles Scribner's Sons, 1949, and London: William Heinemann Ltd.).

suggested a halt to rest the mules, but his guide looked at the sky and shook his head. The sun was nowhere to be seen, the air was thick and gray and smelled of snow. Very soon the snow began to fall—lightly at first, but all the while becoming heavier. The vista of pine trees ahead of them grew shorter and shorter through the vast powdering of descending flakes. A little after midday a burst of wind sent the snow whirling in coils about the two travelers, and a great storm broke. The wind was like a hurricane at sea, and the air became blind with snow. The Bishop could scarcely see his guide —saw only parts of him, now a head, now a shoulder, now only the black rump of his mule. Pine trees by the way stood out for a moment, then disappeared absolutely in the whirlpool of snow. Trail and landmarks, the mountain itself, were obliterated.[13]

Although the description is presented from the omniscient-author point of view, sentences like the one beginning "The Bishop could scarcely see his guide . . ." help the reader to experience the storm in the way the Bishop does. The details appear in climactic order; that is, they describe the storm as it evolves from a threatening sky to a snowfall that obliterates the mountain. The details also appear in chronological order as they naturally would in the development of an actual storm. Such care in keeping description true to laws of nature is a mark of good writing.

In the following excerpt the author is describing an interior scene from the point of view of a guest who has just arrived at the threshold of a comfortable room on a sweltering Virginia afternoon, feeling "as though he himself were steaming." The details convey the impression of coolness, a contrast to what the guest has just experienced.

The drawing-room, on the shady side of the house, had blue-green walls and woodwork, and the fabrics were the color of old gold. It gleamed with polished mahogany and brass, and the many-paned windows stood open on the garden. Sprague was resplendent in white linen with fine Mechlin lace at his throat and wrists, and his Aunt Anabel floated in a pale blue tiffany gown with a white gauze cap and fichu. It made one cooler just to look at them.[14]

Here the order of presentation—from details describing the room to those describing its occupants—is from the less to the more important and prepares for the final sentence, which relates how the appearance of the host and hostess affects the guest. At the same time the final

[13] Reprinted with permission from Willa Cather, *Death Comes for the Archbishop* (New York: Alfred A. Knopf, Inc., 1947), pp. 125–126.

[14] Reprinted with permission from Elswyth Thane, *Dawn's Early Light* (New York: Duell, Sloan & Pearce, Inc., 1943), p. 44.

sentence prevents the reader from misinterpreting the earlier details. A competent writer takes such precautions.

When writing a descriptive paragraph, carefully consider and follow these instructions.

1. Limit the topic (one person, not all the members of a family; one field, not a whole farm) to permit use of carefully chosen details.

2. Select details for a single purpose or impression (the impishness of a child or the lushness of a field, not all the facets of childhood or all the attributes of a field).

3. Present the details in an appropriate order (spatial, analytical, climactic) and from a definite point of view so that the reader can adopt an observer's position.

4. Use specific words that will create clear, accurate images for the reader (*one-footed robin* creates a more distinct image than *poor bird*).

5. Include facts and interpretations if necessary to clarify for the reader what the images signify.

6. Make the paragraph support the over-all purpose or central idea of the whole composition.

Chronological Incidents. In narrative writing the author frequently presents incidents in chronological order to block out the units or stages of action in his story. Sometimes small incidents combine into a larger incident to form a paragraph; at other times one incident stands alone. A change in time or place, a new movement or speech by a character, or an explanation of antecedent action might occasion the beginning of a new paragraph. Division into units is somewhat more flexible in narration than in other forms of writing; consequently, narrative paragraphs are interestingly varied in length.

The variety in length of the six consecutive paragraphs which follow is quite appropriate. The first is transitional; its one sentence prepares the reader for a kind of flash back in which the main character is to recall an episode from a time preceding that of the present story. The second is a typical narrative paragraph developed by *chronological incidents* and relevant details. These incidents and details combine to give the main character's first reaction to the girl he later marries; since the condition of this marriage is important in the present story, the paragraph is justifiably an extensive one. The third, fourth, and fifth paragraphs record conversation and are short because the speeches and accompanying explanations are short. The sixth, again a series of chronological incidents and relevant details, relates another significant phase of the courtship: the young woman's unresponsiveness and the man's scheme to acquire her as one might go about acquiring a valuable piece of property. Since this paragraph comes very near to expressing the theme of the present story, the relative length is again appropriate. The entire excerpt is taken from a point in the story where the wife has reminded the husband of his premarital promise to free her if the marriage failed, and he is stubbornly trying to continue to "own" her.

And memories crowded on him [Soames Forsyte] with the fresh, sweet savour of the spring wind—memories of his courtship.

In the spring of the year 1881 he was visiting his old school-fellow and client, George Liversedge, of Branksome, who, with the view of developing his pine-woods in the neighbourhood of Bournemouth, had placed the formation of the company necessary to the scheme in Soames's hands. Mrs. Liversedge, with a sense of the fitness of things, had given a musical tea in his honour. Later in the course of this function, which Soames, no musician, had regarded as an unmitigated bore, his eye had been caught by the face of a girl dressed in mourning, standing by herself. The lines of her tall, as yet rather thin figure, showed through the wispy, clinging stuff of her black dress, her black-gloved hands were crossed in front of her, her lips slightly parted, and her large, dark eyes wandered from face to face. Her hair, done low on her neck, seemed to gleam above her black collar like coils of shining metal. And as Soames stood looking at her, the sensation that most men have felt at one time or another went stealing through him—a peculiar satisfaction of the senses, a peculiar certainty, which novelists and old ladies call love at first sight. Still stealthily watching her, he at once made his way to his hostess, and stood doggedly waiting for the music to cease.

"Who is that girl with yellow hair and dark eyes?" he asked.

"That—oh! Irene Heron. Her father, Professor Heron, died this year. She lives with her stepmother. She's a nice girl, a pretty girl, but no money!"

"Introduce me, please," said Soames.

It was very little that he found to say, nor did he find her responsive to that little. But he went away with the resolution to see her again. He effected his object by chance, meeting her on the pier with her stepmother, who had the habit of walking there from twelve to one of a forenoon. Soames made this lady's acquaintance with alacrity, nor was it long before he perceived in her the ally he was looking for. His keen scent for the commercial side of family life soon told him that Irene cost her stepmother more than the fifty pounds a year she brought her; it also told him that Mrs. Heron, a woman yet in the prime of life, desired to be married again. The strange ripening beauty of her stepdaughter stood in the way of this desirable consummation. And Soames, in his stealthy tenacity, laid his plans.[15]

The six paragraphs taken together show the continuity in time and the consistency in tone and viewpoint that are qualities of good narrative

[15] Galsworthy, *The Man of Property,* pp. 105–106.

writing. Also, each of the two long paragraphs moves toward its own climax, and the six together have a single, larger climactic order. This matter of climax is especially important when the writer's chief purpose is to entertain, as it usually is in narration.

Here are practical suggestions on writing the narrative paragraph.[16]

1. Include the events that constitute one stage of action, one fairly short and simple unit of a longer, more complex action. Begin a new paragraph when the action calls for a lapse of time; a shift of scene; or a change in point of view, as from one speaker to another in conversation.

2. Use specific details, making them so vivid that the reader can arrive at his own interpretive generalization. (Rarely use an explicit topic sentence in a narrative paragraph.)

3. Arrange the events in chronological sequence (or use a variation if desirable for emphasis, but make the natural time-order clear to the reader).

4. Pay special attention to verbs as a means of advancing the narrative. Choose specific verbs. (*Little Tommy scampered* . . . or *Martha begged* . . . tells more of what is happening than *Little Tommy left* . . . or *Martha said.* . . .) Use the active voice as much as possible (*Mike read the letter and tossed it into the fire* is more forceful than *The letter was read and tossed into the fire by Mike.*)

5. Use adverbial elements (*early, that same day, after she had reconsidered*) to clarify the time sequence for the reader, but use them discriminately.

6. Since the paragraph presents one of several stages in a whole narration, make it function within a climactic as well as a chronological sequence.

Illustrative Instances. Supporting a general topic with *illustrative instances* is one of the most useful methods of developing an expository paragraph. Inexperienced writers often have the tendency to generalize too readily. Thus, the beginning writer should guard against this pitfall by remembering to use a sufficient number of pertinent illustrations to substantiate his topic idea. The author of the following paragraph uses almost a dozen illustrations to support his opening statement concerning the exhibits at the World's Fair of 1958 in Brusseis.

In most respects the national characteristics ran true to form at Brussels. The Dutch pavilion, devoted to the obsessive national problem of water control, was a masterpiece of invention. A model farm, a giant wave-making

---

[16] See Chapter 5 for information on short narrative themes.

machine, an actual section of dike, the bridge of a ship, tulip fields, and road signs all provided a brilliant re-creation of the energetic mode of life of the Netherlands. The British scored heavily—particularly with the royalistic Belgian visitor—by an entrance hall emblazoned with the rich ceremonial trappings of monarchy. The Swiss pavilion was impeccable in all the minutiae of presentation, and its food was the best; West Germany, a model of orderly, precise exhibition technique. Many of the Latin countries, with a fine disregard for deadlines, opened late, especially Italy, Spain, and Brazil. Theory won out over practice with the French, whose startling cantilevered pavilion ran afoul of a treacherous terrain in construction, and its completion was delayed interminably by compound misfortunes. The Japanese garden was a placid Oriental retreat, and the Moroccan and Tunisian pavilions combined to produce a strident, bustling bazaar.[17]

To a certain extent the author follows a geographical pattern in arranging his examples: he starts with countries of Europe and proceeds to those of other continents. From another viewpoint, since his topic idea concerns nationalism, his grouping of certain countries regardless of location is logical; for instance, Italy, Spain, and Brazil belong together as Latin countries even though two are in Europe and the third in South America. An element of comparison is also evident in the organization: France, the last country to get its pavilion finished, is mentioned just after the Latin countries, who were also late; Switzerland and West Germany, whose displays were both notably precise, are discussed in the same sentence; and the final sentence of the paragraph shows a vivid contrast between Asian and African exhibits. These factors of organization are worth noticing because in the well-written paragraph of illustrative instances, each instance not only earns *a place* but also earns *its particular place*.

The following reminders will help the inexperienced writer to use illustrations effectively in paragraph development.

1. Limit the topic idea to a single phase of the central idea to be developed in the whole composition.

2. Write a clear, concise topic sentence, preferably a simple sentence. (A sentence like *This paragraph will be about economic gain and migrations* would be unsatisfactory because it does not actually state a topic idea. *The desire for economic gain has prompted large-scale migrations* would be a satisfactory topic sentence.)

3. Select, on the bases of cogency and interest, enough of the best illustrations to substantiate the idea in the topic sentence. Assume that

---

[17] Reprinted with permission from James S. Plaut, "The Arts and the People at Brussels," *Atlantic Monthly,* July, 1959, p. 66.

the reader is not already familiar with that idea or at least is not already convinced that it is valid.

4. Decide on the pattern of logical reasoning best suited to the purpose of the paragraph, and remember to place the topic sentence accordingly. (See the preceding section in this chapter.)

5. Within a suitable pattern of logical reasoning, arrange the illustrations systematically; for instance, use a chronological, climactic, or semi-climactic order (second-best example first, then the others in ascending order of importance).

6. If necessary for clarity or appropriate for emphasis, include a freshly worded restatement of the topic idea.

Definition. A paragraph of *definition* is often included as a part of an expository or argumentative composition in order to clarify the meaning the writer intends when he uses a certain term. The topic sentence he writes for this kind of paragraph is a sentence definition in which he classifies the term in question and differentiates it from other members of the same class (see pp. 27–28). He is then able to extend his meaning by such methods as citing examples, comparing the term with a more familiar one, or even pointing out what the term does not signify.

The author of the following passage begins with two sentence definitions of the ballad, but it is really the second of these that serves as the topic sentence.

A ballad is a song that tells a story, or—to take the other point of view—a story told in song. More formally, it may be defined as a short narrative poem, adapted for singing, simple in plot and metrical structure, divided into stanzas, and characterized by complete impersonality so far as the author or singer is concerned. This last trait is of the very first consequence in determining the quality or qualities which give the ballad its peculiar place in literature. A ballad has no author. At all events, it appears to have none. The teller of the story for the time being is as much the author as the unknown (and for our purposes unimportant) person who first put it into shape. In most forms of artistic literature the personality of the writer is a matter of deep concern to the reader. The style, we say, is the man. The individuality of one poet distinguishes his works, however they may vary among themselves, from the works of all other poets. Chaucer, for instance, has his way, or his ways, of telling a tale that are not the way, or the ways, of William Morris. If a would-be literary artist has no individuality that we can detect, we set him down as conventional, and that is an end of him and of his works. In the ballad it is not so. There the author is of no account. He is not even present. We do not feel sure that he ever existed. At most, we merely infer his existence, at some indefinite time in the past, from the fact of his product: a poem, we think, implies a poet; therefore somebody must have composed this ballad. Until we begin to reason, we have no thought of the author of any ballad, because, so far as we can see, he had no thought of himself.[18]

The author elaborates on one particular point of his sentence definition: the impersonality or apparent anonymity that differentiates the ballad from other short narrative poems. The resulting emphasis indicates how important he considers this feature of the ballad.

Here are suggestions on extending a definition to the length of a paragraph. In parentheses are sample statements which, if placed together in succession, would make a paragraph defining the term *slick ice*.

1. Write an original sentence definition of the term to be explained. (*Slick ice* is a colloquial expression used in the Midwest to designate ice formed by freezing rain or sleet.)

2. Clarify by restating the definition, possibly from a negative point of view, and using illustrations. (*Slick ice* is not used in references to ice made by nature in other ways, such as that formed in lakes and rivers by sub-freezing temperatures when there is no rain or sleet. Nor is the term used to name the machine-made kind available at any season in the modern refrigerator or freezer.)

3. Elaborate on the difference between the thing being defined and others in its class. (When a Midwesterner says to his neighbor, "We're in for a slick-ice storm," he is expecting a thin coating of ice, a glaze, to cover the streets and all other exposed surfaces, including the small twigs of trees and stems of shrubs.)

4. If possible, include enlightening comments on its origin or derivation. (The origin of the term is uncertain, but apparently there is a relation between it and the colloquial meaning *deceptive, tricky,* or *smooth* commonly attached to the word *slick,* as in *slick trick.* Whether he calls it *slick ice* or not, anyone who has tried to walk or drive on a layer of frozen rain and sleet knows that it is smooth in both the literal and sub-literal senses.)

Enumeration. A paragraph of *enumeration* usually begins with a topic sentence stating precisely how many points will be covered. The points then appear in numerical order with accompanying clarification, or, if they call for lengthy, separate explanations, the paragraph of

---

[18] Reprinted with permission from George Lyman Kittredge's Introduction to *English and Scottish Popular Ballads,* edited from the ballad collection of Francis James Child by Helen Child Sargent and George Lyman Kittredge (Boston: Houghton Mifflin Co., 1904), p. xi.

enumeration may serve merely as an introduction. In either case, the numerical arrangement makes good organization almost automatic.

Notice how the author of this excerpt introduces his topic and then explains as he enumerates.

There are three kinds of book owners. The first has all the standard sets and best-sellers—unread, untouched. (This deluded individual owns wood pulp and ink, not books.) The second has a great many books—a few of them read through, most of them dipped into, but all of them as clean and shiny as the day they were bought. (This person would probably like to make books his own, but is restrained by a false respect for their physical appearance.) The third has a few books or many—every one of them dog-eared and dilapidated, shaken and loosened by continual use, marked and scribbled in from front to back. (This man owns books.) [19]

The thought is especially easy for the reader to follow here because the author provides appropriate coherence and emphasis by describing the three kinds of book owners in ascending order of their sincerity.

Writing a good paragraph of enumeration requires systematic thinking. Try to put these recommendations in practice.

1. Write a topic sentence that specifies the number of parts in the topic idea. (Say *The mayor used three arguments in explaining to the voters the need for a new tax,* not *The mayor communicated with the voters about the need for a new tax.*) Because the special function of this kind of topic sentence is to forecast, place it first in the paragraph.

2. Develop the parts of the topic idea in a logical sequence (with the strongest or most important point last if possible) and in detail proportionate to their relative importance.

3. Show the relationship of each part to the whole topic idea and, as far as is necessary for clarity, the interrelationships among the parts.

Multiple Reasons. In developing a paragraph by *multiple reasons,* the writer cites many reasons to prove the soundness of his topic idea. Ordinarily he starts with a topic sentence and then presents his grounds for believing in it. This selection shows that good reasons often acquire their authenticity from factual details.

Women in our society complain of the lack of stimulation, of the loneliness, of the dullness of staying at home. Little babies are poor conversationalists, husbands come home tired and sit reading the paper, and women who

[19] Reprinted with permission from Mortimer J. Adler, "How to Mark a Book," *Saturday Review,* XXII (July 6, 1940). 11.

used to pride themselves on their ability to talk find on the rare evening they can go out that their words clot on their tongues. As the children go to school, the mother is left to the companionship of the Frigidaire and the washing machine. Yet she can't go out because the delivery man might come, or a child might be sent home sick from school. The boredom of long hours of solitary one-sided communication with things, no matter how shining and streamlined and new, descends upon her. Moreover, the conditions of modern life, apartment living and especially the enormous amount of moving about during the war, all serve to rob women of neighborhood ties. The better her electric equipment, the better she organizes her ordering, the less reason she has to run out for a bit of gossipy shopping at the corner store. The department stores and the moving-picture houses cater to women —alone—on their few hours out. Meanwhile efficient mending services and cheap ready-made clothes have taken most sensible busy work out of women's hands and left women—still at home—listening to the radio, watching television.[20]

Each reason cited tells *why* modern women complain of boredom in the home. In other words, the author presents a number of reasons serving a common purpose.

In developing a paragraph with multiple reasons, remember the suggestions below and carefully test the material for authenticity.

1. Write a topic sentence announcing clearly the fact, belief, or course of action to be supported.

2. Use several reasons to show why the topic idea should be accepted, and be sure they are all authentic. Reasons will be authentic if they are based on one or more of the following: factual details, conclusive experimentation, the word of an authority on the topic being discussed, a universally accepted generalization. (Do not expect the reader to accept personal opinions as evidence.)

3. Arrange the reasons with particular attention to coherence. (Notice how in the preceding example each reason for the complaint on loneliness prepares the reader for the next reason.)

Cause and Effect. A paragraph developed by *cause and effect* also involves reasons, for the writer's main purpose is to clarify the relationships between certain events or situations and their consequences. The discussion may move from cause to effect, or from effect to cause. In the passage below, the author begins with a reason for a certain situation and then shows each succeeding situation as a result of the previous one.

[20] Reprinted with permission from Margaret Mead, "What Women Want," *Fortune,* XXXIV (December, 1946), 174.

One of the reasons for calling some people immature is that they are incapable of confronting defeat, tragedy, or unpleasantness of any kind. Such persons usually cannot endure an "unhappy ending" *even in a set of symbolic experiences.* Hence the widespread passion for happy endings in popular literature, so that even stories about unhappy events have to be made, in the end, to "come out all right." The immature constantly need to be reassured that everything will always come out all right.[21]

The content of this paragraph may be analyzed as a chain of reasoning: Certain people are labeled immature *because* they cannot face adversity. *Because* they cannot face adversity, these people cannot stand unhappy endings in literature. *Because* these people object to unhappy endings and clamor for happy ones, writers of popular literature supply happy but unrealistic endings to their stories of tragic events. *Because* the endings are happy, these popular stories satisfy the immature readers' ever-present need for reassurance.

In the preceding example and analysis the causes and effects appear one by one. Another way of showing cause-and-effect relationships is to trace a set of causes through to a set of results:

For many years Christians from western Europe had made pilgrimages to the Holy Land for the purpose of worshiping at the tomb of Jesus, which was known as the Holy Sepulcher. This worship had been permitted by the Mohammedan Arabs who were in control of Palestine; but after the conquest of the Holy Land by the Seljuk Turks, who were more aggressive Mohammedans, worshiping at the holy places became more difficult and dangerous. The Pope appealed to the feudal lords and knights to cease fighting their Christian neighbors and combine against the infidel Turks, in a holy war for the purpose of rescuing the Holy Sepulcher. At a meeting in 1095, Pope Urban II preached a holy war against the Turks. As a result, several religious military expeditions were organized, which continued for almost two hundred years. These expeditions are known as the Crusades. As military expeditions, they failed, for while Jerusalem was taken and held for a time by the Christians, it was recaptured by the Turks. In spite of the military failure of the Crusades, they had many important social, intellectual, and commercial effects, because the people from western Europe were brought into contact with the East. Intellectual curiosity and study were stimulated. The East had many products, such as spices, perfumes, silks, precious stones, and other articles which the West wanted. The Crusades therefore stimulated trade.[22]

[21] Reprinted with permission from S. I. Hayakawa, *Language in Thought and Action* (New York: Harcourt, Brace & Co., Inc., 1949), p. 134.
[22] Reprinted with permission from Fremont P. Wirth, *The Development of America* (New York: American Book Company, 1956), p. 13.

The author allots approximately half of his paragraph to a description of events which functioned as causes and the other half to an explanation of the results. He leads the reader from cause to effect with the transitional phrase "As a result" at the middle of the discussion.

Writing a paragraph of the kind illustrated here requires careful judgment beforehand, as these suggestions indicate.

1. Make sure that the cause-and-effect relationship is real and that knowledge of it is necessary for the reader to understand the composition as a whole. (See pp. 22–23 for an explanation of faulty causal relationships.)

2. Determine, on the basis of the amount of material needed to clarify the relationship, whether a single cause and its result(s) or a set of causes and results should be explained in a paragraph.

3. Determine, on the basis of the emphasis desired, whether the discussion should move from cause to effect, or vice versa. (Since the end of any unit of composition is more conspicuous than the beginning, movement from cause to effect emphasizes the effect, and movement from effect to cause emphasizes the cause.)

4. Follow the predetermined arrangement closely, including adequate detail and, if necessary, a few transitional devices.

Comparison. In developing a paragraph by *comparison* the writer cites similarities and differences (or perhaps concentrates on one or the other) between two or more things in the same general class. He shows, for instance, how two places, two persons, two ideas, or two situations resemble or differ from each other. The comparison is literal, not figurative.

The following paragraph, written early in the nineteenth century, compares the needs for government in the United States and Europe, the point being that the different situations warrant different kinds of government.

With respect to aristocracy, we should further consider, that before the establishment of the American States, nothing was known to history but the man of the old world, crowded within limits either small or overcharged, and steeped in the vices which that situation generates. A government adapted to such men would be one thing; but a very different one, that for the man of these States. Here every one may have land to labor for himself, if he chooses; or, preferring the exercise of any other industry, may exact for it such compensation as not only to afford a comfortable subsistence, but wherewith to provide for a cessation from labor in old age. Every one, by his property, or by his satisfactory situation, is interested in the support of law and order. And such men may safely and advantageously reserve to themselves a wholesome control over their public affairs, and a degree of freedom, which, in the hands of the *canaille* of the cities of Europe, would be instantly perverted to the demolition and destruction of everything public and private. The history of the last twenty-five years of France, and of the last forty years in America, nay of its last two hundred years, proves the truth of both parts of this observation.[23]

A point mentioned earlier in this chapter is particularly applicable to this example: a paragraph out of context cannot signify quite the same thing it does in context. In a paragraph following the one quoted here, Jefferson tempers his contrast of Europe and America by describing a noticeable change in the climate of thought in Europe at the time, a change in favor of talents and virtue instead of established wealth and aristocratic birth. This kind of enlightenment, he thinks, will in time make more Europeans increasingly capable of self-government. Thus Jefferson does not intend his contrast to be so pronounced as it seems in the isolated paragraph.

Here are four guides for writing a paragraph of comparison.

1. Select as subjects for comparison two or more members of the same general class. If the purpose is to explain something unfamiliar, compare it to a well-known thing of its kind. (For an American reader, compare the Swiss Parliament to the United States Congress.)

2. Select for specific comparison the main features which the subjects have in common (such as the number of houses, the membership, and the duties of the Swiss and American legislatures). As far as possible, integrate the discussion by comparing the features one by one (preferably do not describe the Swiss Parliament as one topic and then turn to the United States Congress as another topic).

3. Point out any significant characteristics that are unique in one or the other of the subjects being compared.

4. Select the arrangement that will provide the highest degree of coherence and the most appropriate emphasis. Common alternatives are: grouping together the features that have the greatest similarities, then those that have the greatest differences; reversing the first alternative; discussing the features in climactic order regardless of the amounts of resemblance or difference.

Sustained Analogy. An *analogy* is a figurative comparison; in other words, the things being compared are not from the same general class. For instance, a person is compared, not with another person but with a

[23] Thomas Jefferson, in a letter to John Adams (October 28, 1813), as printed in Frederick C. Prescott's *Alexander Hamilton and Thomas Jefferson* (New York: American Book Company, 1934), pp. 378–379.

tree; or a storm is compared, not with another storm but with war. The analogy is *sustained* when the comparison is kept alive throughout a paragraph or possibly even longer. We might say that a *sustained analogy* is an extended metaphor or simile (see pp. 307–308). This method is useful when a writer finds he can best clarify something abstract and unfamiliar by likening it to something concrete and familiar.

In this excerpt the author, who pretends to be looking back in time from the year 2000, shows how an economic situation is analogous to a stagecoach.

By way of attempting to give the reader some general impression of the way people lived together in those days [in 1887], and especially of the relations of the rich and poor to one another, perhaps I cannot do better than to compare society as it then was to a prodigious coach which the masses of humanity were harnessed to and dragged toilsomely along a very hilly and sandy road. The driver was hunger, and permitted no lagging, though the pace was necessarily slow. Despite the difficulty of drawing the coach at all along so hard a road, the top was covered with passengers who never got down, even at the steepest ascents. These seats on top were very breezy and comfortable. Well up out of the dust, their occupants could enjoy the scenery at their leisure, or critically discuss the merits of the straining team. Naturally such places were in great demand and the competition was keen, every one seeking as the first end in life to secure a seat on the coach for himself and to leave it to his child after him. By the rule of the coach a man could leave his seat to whom he wished, but on the other hand there were many accidents by which it might at any time be wholly lost. For all that they were so easy, the seats were very insecure, and at every sudden jolt of the coach persons were slipping out of them and falling to the ground, where they were instantly compelled to take hold of the rope and help to drag the coach on which they had before ridden so pleasantly. It was naturally regarded as a terrible misfortune to lose one's seat, and the apprehension that this might happen to them or their friends was a constant cloud upon the happiness of those who rode.[24]

The preceding is one of several paragraphs of sustained analogy on the same topic. By a succession of points of comparison between the unfamiliar and the familiar, the author illuminates for the reader a complex economic situation. In using the same method, less experienced writers should be careful not to force comparisons where basic differences exist. A superficial or false analogy (see pp. 21–22) is as unconvincing as a logically developed one is convincing.

[24] Reprinted with permission from Edward Bellamy, *Looking Backward* (Boston: Houghton Mifflin Co., 1931), pp. 10–11.

Next are a few reminders for writing a sustained analogy.

1. Since the purpose of a sustained analogy is almost always to clarify a difficult, unfamiliar subject, select from a different general class a second subject already familiar to the reader and having enough real similarities to make a logical analogy possible.

2. Explain one by one the strange or complex features of the unfamiliar subject by stating or clearly implying how they resemble the corresponding but well known or simple features of the familiar subject.

3. Arrange the points in the sequence that is best suited to the subject matter. (Notice that in drawing the analogy between the economic system and the stagecoach the author moves from driver to team to passengers and then back and forth several times between passengers and team, a logical arrangement since the driver, hunger, was permanently situated but the passengers and the team, the rich and the poor, were not.)

Combined Methods. The examples on the foregoing pages have been selected to illustrate separately the common methods of paragraph development which good writers use. As suggested earlier, however, experienced writers frequently *combine* two or more methods in clarifying a topic idea. The result is a complex kind of structure that cannot be readily classified. In the next excerpt (shown with italics added), the author employs enumeration, cause and effect, illustrative instances, and comparison to develop the idea that when inhabitants reach a certain typical point in their demand for public service their community is likely to be incorporated as a village. The marginal notes indicate where the author uses these methods and how he achieves unity, coherence, and emphasis.

PARAGRAPH DEVELOPED BY COMBINED METHODS

When a portion of a New England town, or of a Western township, or of a county that does not have township government, becomes more thickly settled than the rest and begins to take on a semi-urban aspect, its inhabitants are quite certain to demand more public services, *such as* fire protection, street paving and lighting, water supply, and sewerage facilities, than the town, township, or county authorities will be willing to provide. *Sooner or later such communities are likely to be incorporated as villages or boroughs.* State law often requires that a community seeking incor-

ANALYSIS

Enumeration forecasting range of examples of topic idea.

Cause and effect.
Transitional phrase.
Examples within supporting idea. Continuation of cause, effect.
Transition. Topic idea.
Words (*incorporated, villages*) to be repeated

PARAGRAPH DEVELOPED BY COMBINED METHODS | ANALYSIS (CONT.)

poration shall meet certain standards of area and population, and that the question of incorporation be submitted to a popular vote. In Illinois, *for example,* any area of not more than two square miles, with at least 100 inhabitants, if not already within a village or city, may become a village by a vote of the people at a special election. It *then* remains a village until it has 1000 inhabitants, when it may (but is not obliged to) change to a city government. *On the other hand,* there are villages in Vermont, Maine, and Connecticut with only a few score inhabitants. Incorporation gives a village power to undertake community services of *the kinds referred to above,* to levy taxes and borrow money to support them, and to have its own village government, *distinct from the governments of township and county.* There are more than 10,000 *such* incorporated villages in the United States, and they are found *in all parts of the country,* including New England and the southern and western states—although by far the greater number are in the north-central section, where Illinois alone has some 800.[25]

ANALYSIS (CONT.)
for coherence, emphasis.
General statement on process. Transition.
Specific instance, emphasized by relative length and concrete details.

Transitional phrase. Contrasting instances. Resumption of chain of cause, effects (enumerated). Linking phrase. Unifying phrase, supplementing part of first sentence. Linking word. Summarizing statement. Unifying phrase, returning to first idea. Repeated examples. Specific example, in emphatic position.

As a single reading of this passage shows, complex paragraph structure does not confuse the reader. Normally it makes the meaning clearer to him.

Here are two final suggestions for paragraph development.

1. Do not hesitate to combine methods of development whenever the subject matter suggests more than one logical way of clarifying or supporting the topic idea.

2. Blend the methods of development so that they will not call attention to themselves as methods but will unobtrusively aid the reader in understanding the meaning of the paragraph.

PARAGRAPHS WITH SPECIAL PURPOSES

Although their usual function is to develop an idea or impression, paragraphs may serve the special purposes of introducing a topic,

[25] Reprinted with permission from William H. Young, *Ogg and Ray's Introduction to American Government* (11th ed.; New York: Appleton-Century-Crofts, Inc., 1956), p. 905

making a transition, recording dialogue, and concluding or summarizing a discussion. We have mentioned earlier that such units are often justifiably short. We shall now examine illustrations in which the special purposes and characteristic brevity are easily seen.

Introductory Paragraphs. A paragraph may serve the special purpose of *introducing a topic*. A good introduction arouses the reader's interest and facilitates his reading of the rest of the composition. Here is a one-sentence introductory paragraph of an essay in which the other paragraphs are relatively long.

There are people who have but one idea: at least, if they have more, they keep it a secret, for they never talk but of one subject.[26]

As the reader is likely to expect, the rest of the essay describes in detail various egocentric persons each of whom harps on his favorite topic instead of exchanging ideas in conversation.

Transitional Paragraphs. A paragraph may serve the special purpose of pointing out a *transition in thought,* of marking the end of one phase of a discussion and announcing a new phase. It is sometimes necessary to use a *transitional paragraph* (but only between sections of a long and complicated essay) [27] to sum up for the reader what has been accomplished so far; to let him know what will be discussed next; to call his attention to a special method of explanation, such as a series of examples, which is to be used; or to do a combination of these things. In any case, the purpose is solely to guide the reader, as it is in this illustration.

So much, then, by way of proof that the method of establishing laws in science is exactly the same as that pursued in common life. Let us now turn to another matter (though really it is but another phase of the same question), and that is, the method by which, from the relations of certain phenomena, we prove that some stand in the position of causes towards the others.[28]

[26] William Hazlitt, "On People With One Idea," *The Complete Works of William Hazlitt,* ed. P. P. Howe (London: J. M. Dent and Sons, Ltd., 1931), VIII, 59.

[27] In the typical short theme of five or six hundred words, a transitional sentence at the end of a paragraph or, more commonly, at or near the beginning of a new one is usually the largest element needed to point out how the thought is advancing. For the most part, clear transitions between paragraphs can be made in the same ways that relationships among sentences are clarified (pp. 216–221).

[28] Reprinted with permission from Thomas Henry Huxley, *Darwiniana* (New York: D. Appleton and Company, 1897), p. 368.

Even though the passage is out of context, its transitional nature is easily recognizable.

Paragraphs of Dialogue. Paragraphs may serve the special purpose of *recording dialogue*. The conventional method is to use a separate paragraph for each speech or for the speech and accompanying narration, as in the next excerpt.

"Tell me, sweet child," I said, "for I cannot realize it yet; was it really you that saved the serpent's life when I would have killed it—did you stand by me in the wood with the serpent lying at your feet?"

"Yes, señor," came her gentle answer.

"And it was you I saw in the wood one day, lying on the ground playing with a small bird?"

"Yes, señor."

"And it was you that followed me so often among the trees, calling to me, yet always hiding so that I could never see you?"

"Yes, señor." [29]

As the example shows, this method of division enables the reader to follow each speaker's point of view throughout a conversation.

Concluding Paragraphs. A paragraph may serve the special purpose of *concluding* or *summarizing a discussion*. The inexperienced writer sometimes mars the effectiveness of his composition by introducing a new topic too late and leaving it undeveloped. A good plan for the beginner is to study in context the final paragraphs of essays by experienced writers. Here is the conclusion of a carefully written magazine article.

Barometric pressures turn out to be not the cause of the weather, but simply a result, a rather unimportant secondary symptom of it. What weather actually is the Norwegians have made clear. It is the wave action of the air ocean. [30]

The paragraph restates briefly what the body of the article has explained at length.

Exercises

1. Test the internal structure of the paragraph below; comment specifically on the qualities of unity, coherence, and emphasis.

[29] Reprinted with permission from W. H. Hudson, *Green Mansions* (New York: Alfred A. Knopf, Inc., 1959, and London: The Royal Society for the Protection of Birds, and The Society of Authors).

[30] Reprinted with permission from Wolfgang Langewiesche, "What Makes the Weather," *Harper's Magazine,* CLXXXV (October, 1942), 488.

Man exists to do creatively, as craftsmanlike as may be, all things that must be done: great things like government or mothering or the healing of minds and bodies; small things like making beds or hoeing corn or driving a truck; things in the public eye like making speeches or unleashing atomic energy or making peace; obscure things like selling groceries or running a bus or teaching school. He finds inner peace who works at whatever is in front of him not for the pay he gets or for what he can buy with that pay, not for applause or gratitude, but for sheer joy of creativity. There is a vast number of tasks to be performed, most of them not romantic. They may be done in one of two ways: just to get them over with as quickly and as painlessly as possible, in which case they become a monotonous burden hard to bear; or each as beautifully as possible, in which case life is good to the taste.[31]

2. Identify and explain briefly the pattern of logical reasoning in each of these paragraphs.

a. Shortly after a new highway was opened, an automobile failed to complete a curve in the road and crashed into an abutment. The driver and two passengers were killed. A special warning sign, erected in addition to the regular ones, did not solve the problem. Within two years five similar accidents occurred at the same point, and twelve more persons died as a result. Only one driver and three passengers involved in these accidents survived. Officials then decided that a section of highway including the curve, which had come to be known as Suicide Curve, was too hazardous for public safety. They closed the section, and engineers planned reconstruction to remove the hazard.

b. A certain large city has a one-per-cent earnings tax which it collects on the income of all its residents who earn money regardless of where they earn it, and on all income earned within the city limits regardless of where the workers live. The city is surrounded by small municipalities which have no earnings tax. A lives and works in the city. B lives in the city but works in an adjoining municipality. C lives and works in this same municipality. D lives in another municipality but works in the city. E is a commuter who lives in a rural area but works in the city. A, B, D, and E pay one per cent of their earnings to the city, but C does not pay an earnings tax.

3. Name the method of paragraph development to which each of these ideas would logically lend itself.

a. I have several reasons for wanting a college education.

b. The meanings of words are constantly changing.

c. A classic is like an old friend.

d. The Charter of the United Nations establishes six main instruments of action.

e. I went through an ordeal as I prepared to tell Father about the dented fender.

f. A romanticist is a person whose thinking deals with, as Aristotle would say, the wonderful rather than the probable.

[31] Reprinted with permission from Bernard Iddings Bell, "Persistent Adolescence," *Crisis in Education* (New York: McGraw-Hill Book Co., 1949), pp. 22–23.

g. The scene from the hilltop was Elysian.

h. One of my classes in high school was much like a college class.

i. The instructor gave the impression that orderliness was the law by which he lived.

j. The spectators at a college football game are of various types.

4. Study the following paragraphs, noting the organization and the use of concrete details. For each paragraph answer these questions: Is the topic idea stated in a topic sentence or implied? If the topic idea is stated, which sentence is the topic sentence? If the topic idea is implied, state it in a sentence. What method of development is discernible in the paragraph?

a. A *promissory note* is a written promise to pay a specified sum of money on or before a specified date and is usually given as evidence of indebtedness. Such a note may be made payable only to a specified individual or payee, or "to the order" of the payee. In the latter case the payee may endorse the note and transfer its value to another person; such a note is said to be negotiable since the face of the note is payable to any bearer. In the former case, the note is non-negotiable. Practically all notes bear interest; if no rate is specified the legal rate for the state is to be understood.[32]

b. A very trivial circumstance will serve to exemplify this [principle of induction]. Suppose you go into a fruiterer's shop, wanting an apple,—you take up one, and, on biting it, you find it is sour; you look at it, and see that it is hard and green. You take up another one, and that too is hard, green, and sour. The shopman offers you a third; but, before biting it, you examine it, and find that it is hard and green, and you immediately say that you will not have it, as it must be sour, like those that you have already tried.[33]

c. Night is a dead monotonous period under a roof; but in the open world it passes lightly, with its stars and dews and perfumes, and the hours are marked by changes in the face of Nature. What seems a temporal death to people choked between walls and curtains, is only a light and living slumber to the man who sleeps afield. All night long he can hear Nature breathing deeply and freely; even as she takes her rest she turns and smiles; and there is one stirring hour unknown to those who dwell in houses, when a wakeful influence goes abroad over the sleeping hemisphere, and all the outdoor world are on their feet. It is then that the cock first crows, not this time to announce the dawn, but like a cheerful watchman speeding the course of night. Cattle awake on the meadows; sheep break their fast on dewy hillsides, and change to a new lair among the ferns; and houseless men, who have lain down with the fowls, open their dim eyes and behold the beauty of the night.[34]

d. "Good-bye, then," he said, shaking his fist in a rage, and slamming the door by which he retreated. And this time he really gave his order for march: and mounted in the courtyard. Mrs O'Dowd heard the clattering hoofs of the horses

[32] Reprinted with permission from C. H. Forsyth, *Introduction to the Mathematical Theory of Finance* (New York: John Wiley & Sons, Inc., 1928), p. 6.

[33] Huxley, *Darwiniana,* p. 365.

[34] Robert Louis Stevenson, "A Night Among the Pines," *Travels With a Donkey* (New York: Charles Scribner's Sons, 1923), pp. 112–113.

as they issued from the gate; and looking on, made many scornful remarks on poor Joseph as he rode down the street with Isidor after him in the laced cap. The horses, which had not been exercised for some days, were lively, and sprang about the street. Jos, a clumsy and timid horseman, did not look to advantage in the saddle. "Look at him, Amelia dear, driving in the parlour window. Such a bull in a china-shop I never saw." And presently the pair of riders disappeared at a canter down the street leading in the direction of Ghent road, Mrs O'Dowd pursuing them with a fire of sarcasm so long as they were in sight.[35]

e. In an age all too familiar with war the yearly cycle of the weather is well imagined in terms of combat. It is a war in which a stronghold or citadel sometimes beats off assault after assault. More often the battle-line shifts quickly back and forth across thousands of miles—a war of sudden raids and swift counter-attacks, of stern pitched battles, of deep forays and confused struggles high in the air. In the Northern Hemisphere the opponents are the Arctic and the Tropics, North against South. Uncertain ally to the South—now bringing, now withdrawing aid—the sun shifts among the signs of the zodiac. And the chief battle-line is known as the Polar Front.[36]

f. Reviews are desirable at three different times: (1) during your study of the day's assignment, (2) at the end of a week or the end of a unit of work, (3) before an examination. Here, we shall be concerned with the first two types of review, which will facilitate the pre-examination review. (The latter will be discussed in the next chapter.) [37]

g. Because of the longer hours for leisure [in the early part of the twentieth century], considerable interest was aroused in recreational activities. Athletic sports attracted large numbers of people, both as active participants and as spectators. More attention was given to reading, and millions of books on art, poetry, literature, history, and biography came off the press, while thousands of libraries were established throughout the country. Our government extended its recreational facilities through its national parks and forests. The coming of the automobile enabled people to travel more widely, and thus to enjoy more of the natural scenery of the North American continent.[38]

h. The regular rank of the cards in contract bridge is affected by the existence of a trump suit. One of the four suits may be named as trumps. In that case, any card of the trump suit will win over any card, even a higher ranking card, of one of the other three suits. The ace of spades is no good when pitted against the two of hearts, if hearts are trumps. The only thing that will beat a trump card is some higher ranking card of the trump suit.[39]

i. Pantheism and panentheism have significant similarities and differences. Pantheism is the doctrine in which God and the universe are identical. They are one and inseparable. God is immanent but not transcendent. Panentheism asserts

[35] William Makepeace Thackeray, *Vanity Fair* (New York: Rinehart & Company, Inc., 1955), p. 335.

[36] Reprinted with permission from George R. Stewart, *Storm* (New York: Random House, 1947), p. 48.

[37] Hook, *How To Take Examinations,* p. 82.

[38] Wirth, *The Development of America,* p. 652.

[39] Reprinted with permission from Josephine Culbertson, *Contract Bridge for Beginners* (Philadelphia: The John C. Winston Co., 1943), p. 12.

that God is present everywhere by His continuous energy and that He also transcends. The world is a part, but not the whole, of God's Being. Pantheism does not give personality to God; panentheism does.

j. The life of a human being is like a walk from one edge to the other of a strange village. Along a new suburban parkway a child, led by a stronger and older hand than his own, takes time to gaze about in wonder. A brilliant morning-glory, a gilded mailbox, a young pine tree near the curb, the curb itself—all are mysteries that the child must one day explore. But childhood is soon over, and a youth, now unguarded, moves swiftly and not too carefully toward a brightly lighted spot in the heart of the village. So hurried is his step and so eager is he to arrive that he does not read the signs; more than once he must retrace his erring footsteps from a dead-end street or an unexpected alley. Not until middle age does he reach the downtown area, only to find that its glitter has begun to dim, that its lure soon palls. True, the courthouse, the bank, and the village church are there—ready to secure and strengthen this erstwhile stranger. But there, also, are the windows of vacant buildings, dark and hollow-eyed reminders of broken dreams, faithless friends, a lost love. On into the other and older side of town the aging man makes his way, more slowly now and less eagerly. He has grown more observant and less prone to err. More often than not he is given to recollection. Here a neatly trimmed hedge reminds him of a deed well done; there an unkempt yard brings back a task long since begun but never finished. Gay blooms in a cheery window box recall his happy days; brittle leaves under-foot, the days that were filled with pain. He has walked long and far—this traveler through the village of life—and he begins to tire, of both his journey and his reverie. But the village has run out into green pastures, and the traveler, weary but unafraid, walks onward—through a valley and into a shadow.

8 SENTENCE STRUCTURE

A *sentence* is a unit of thought or a unit of feeling expressed through a logically related subject and predicate. Ordinarily the sentence serves as part of a larger unit, the paragraph, which in turn serves as part of a still larger unit, the whole composition. For the sake of simplicity, however, this chapter deals with the sentence as an independent unit, out of context of the paragraph and the whole composition.

Although it is the smallest of the units of thought or feeling important in theme-writing, the sentence is the largest of three kinds of word groups called grammatical units. The smaller grammatical units, the phrase and the clause, are explained and illustrated in Chapter 9, along with other points of grammar. The present chapter is chiefly concerned with the sentence as a whole. The early sections examine the basic kinds of sentences and the qualities that make them effective. Later sections suggest ways of preventing common errors and present a method of diagraming.

KINDS OF SENTENCES

A sentence is a means by which one person attempts to make clear to another what he thinks or feels. But since thoughts and feelings vary in kind, and since the reasons for communicating them differ, sentences are of different kinds also. What these kinds are can best be seen through a simple but orderly analysis. Like other plural subjects having common bases, sentences are classified for convenience in study. Just as, for instance, automobiles are classified according to body style, manufacture, and color (see p. 64), sentences are classified according to function, grammatical structure, and rhetorical form.

Sentences Classified by Function. Sentences are classified on the basis of *function* as declarative, interrogative, imperative, and exclamatory sentences. Although both the speaker and the writer use the declarative sentence most frequently, they find the other three types useful too. The speaker uses intonation to help make clear whether he is making a statement, asking a question, giving a command, or making an exclamation. The writer relies on punctuation to help make these distinctions.

Declarative Sentence. A *declarative sentence* is a single, complete statement. It is the kind of sentence that the writer almost always employs when his purpose is to convey information to his reader. He regularly closes the declarative sentence with a period.

Robins are not so aggressive as blue jays.

Although he was born in Kentucky, Abraham Lincoln spent most of his early life in Illinois.

Careful study of literary masterpieces compels the reader to feel compassion for humanity.

Interrogative Sentence. An *interrogative sentence* is a single, complete question. This is the kind of sentence the writer uses when he is seeking information for himself or trying to lead the reader into a consideration of possible answers. The writer helps to accomplish his purpose by closing the interrogative sentence with a question mark.

Questions frequently begin with words called interrogatives. In the first three examples the introductory words (*who, what, which*) function as subjects of verbs and are called interrogative pronouns (see p. 258).

Who called for a vote?   What happened to the ballots?
Which is correct, the first tally or the second?

In the next two examples the introductory words (*which, what*) modify nouns and are called interrogative adjectives (see p. 264).

Which state has the bluebonnet as its floral emblem?
What change in policy would you propose?

In the next example the introductory words (*when, where, how, why*) modify the verb *did join* and are called interrogative adverbs. (Ordinarily only one interrogative adverb, p. 265, begins a question.)

When, where, how, and why did Brutus join the conspiracy against Julius Caesar?

Questions sometimes begin with verbs or parts of verb phrases (see p. 297).

Has he any living relatives?   Does he have any living relatives?

Occasionally a question is written in the same order as a declarative sentence and is distinguished only by the question mark.

His grandfather was a duke.   His grandfather was a duke?

Imperative Sentence. An *imperative sentence* is a single, complete command or a single, complete request. It is a convenient kind of sentence for the writer who is giving directions or instructions. Unless it includes a negative term (*not, never*), the imperative sentence is a call for action. The writer usually closes it with a period but may occasionally use an exclamation point for emphasis.

The pronoun *you* is sometimes expressed but more commonly understood as the subject of an imperative sentence.

You lead the way.   Commence firing!

When you tour Colorado, be sure to visit Pike's Peak early in the morning and watch the sunrise.

Apply the cleaning fluid to the platen with a cloth; then rub the platen dry with a clean cloth.

Never apply the brakes suddenly when you are driving on ice!

Get on your mark! Get set! Go!

Occasionally the command or request is addressed to an audience through the use of an indefinite pronoun, a person's name, or a noun.

Everyone please stand and sing the school song.

Tom, help yourself to the candy and pass the box around.

Company, halt!

Exclamatory Sentence. An *exclamatory sentence* is a single, complete expression of sudden or strong feeling. Because of its tendency to make the writer seem unbecomingly emotional, this kind of sentence appears infrequently in good composition, especially on the formal level. It normally ends with an exclamation point but may end with a period.

What a boon the slide rule is to the engineer!

What a pleasant companion is a collie puppy!

Good grief! My billfold has disappeared!

How inconsequential yesterday's problem looks today.

Sentences Classified by Grammatical Structure. Sentences are classified on the basis of *grammatical structure* as simple, compound, complex, and compound-complex. All these types are used in good composition, but not indiscriminately.

The grammatical structure of a good sentence is always sound. It does not necessarily follow, however, that grammatical accuracy makes a sentence a good one. The structure should be not only correct but also appropriate for the particular idea being transmitted. If the idea is characterized by its singleness, for example, the appropriate grammatical form would be one independent clause. On the other hand, if the idea has a dual nature (for instance, if it is made up of two opposing or two complementary aspects of thought), the proper structure would be a pair of independent clauses joined by a co-ordinating conjunction that helps to clarify the relationship. These and other kinds of unison between idea and form are illustrated here. (See Chapter 9 for explanations of grammatical terms.)

Simple Sentence. A *simple sentence* consists of only one independent (also called *main* or *principal*) clause; that is, one subject and one predicate, either or both of which may be compound. (See "Grammatical Relationships" in Chapter 9.)

The children played games. (The sentence has a single subject, *children,* and a single predicate, *played games.*)

The children and the parents played games. (The sentence has a compound subject, *children and parents,* and a single predicate, *played games.*)

The children played games and sang ballads. (The sentence has a single subject, *children,* and a compound predicate, *played games and sang ballads.*)

The children and the parents played games and sang ballads. (Here both the subject, *children and parents,* and the predicate, *played games and sang ballads,* are compound; but the singleness of idea is maintained because the children and the parents formed one group and did the same thing at the same time.)

Compound Sentence. A *compound sentence* consists of two or more independent clauses. Ordinarily a co-ordinating conjunction joins the independent clauses. A comma precedes the co-ordinating conjunction when the subjects of the clauses differ, when the co-ordinating conjunction shows contrast, or when the clauses are fairly long. On the formal level in particular, it is safe practice to use the comma regularly to separate independent clauses joined by *for* or *but.* (See pp. 360–361.)

The children played games, and the parents sang ballads. (The two clauses show that two separate groups did different things. The comma is used because the subjects of the clauses are different.)

The sky darkened, but no rain fell. (Two events are recorded here, one affirmatively, one negatively. The comma is used with *but* to show contrast.)

Many animals were in hibernation, for winter had already begun. (The clauses state two facts that have a cause-and-effect relationship. The comma shows that *for* is a co-ordinating conjunction at the beginning of a new clause and prevents the reader's mistaking *for* as a preposition.)

If no co-ordinating conjunction joins the independent clauses, a semicolon usually separates them (see p. 369).

The committee met in closed sessions; it later published its findings. (The clauses relate two successive stages of action. The semicolon is necessary because no co-ordinating conjunction joins the clauses.)

The action throughout the story shows the main character struggling against an indifferent environment; furthermore, the end of the story shows that his struggle was futile. (The semicolon is necessary because the connecting word, *furthermore,* is a conjunctive adverb, not a co-ordinating conjunction.)

When the first clause of a compound sentence is a general introduction to a second clause that provides specific meaning, a colon serves better than a semicolon between the clauses (see p. 371). This is a very useful kind of sentence, one well worth mastering.

He felt that he was facing a dilemma: his choice was between deceiving his brother and offending his sister. (Here the second clause explains the first. Being a mark of anticipation, the colon helps the reader to expect an explanation.)

Complex Sentence. A *complex sentence* consists of one independent and one or more dependent clauses. Confining single ideas to simple sentences and putting equal-ranking aspects of an idea into the clauses of a compound sentence are fairly easy tasks. More difficult, and oftentimes more important, is the use of grammatical structure that reflects the relative significance of unequal parts of a complex idea. A young child puts almost all his thoughts into simple and compound sentences because he has not had enough discipline in thinking to recognize logical interrelationships. A small boy may report (in four independent clauses): "Tommy comes over to my yard on Saturdays, and he brings his baseball and glove, and we play catch, and we have fun." If he were to describe the same experience after he is a few years older, he would probably say (in one dependent and one independent clause): "When Tommy came over to my yard on Saturdays with his baseball and glove, we had fun playing catch." Whereas the former version, a long compound sentence, makes the four successive, loosely related ideas seem equally important, the latter version, a complex sentence, reserves the emphasis for the idea in the main clause, *we had fun playing catch,* and points out a time relationship between that idea and the one in the dependent clause. Here are additional examples of the complex sentence.

The girls chatted until they fell asleep. (*The girls chatted* is the independent clause. The dependent clause, *until they fell asleep,* is an adverbial clause modifying the verb *chatted* and pointing out a time limitation.)

The property owners who live in the suburb are opposing the plan for commercial zoning there. (*The property owners are opposing the plan for commercial zoning there* is the independent clause. The dependent clause, *who live in the suburb,* is an adjective clause modifying and restricting the noun *owners.* This clause makes an important qualification because it indicates that those particular persons who own property in the suburb and also live there are opposing the plan. Persons who own property there but live elsewhere are not included in the group opposing the plan.)

What the message meant remained a puzzle. (Here the whole sentence is the independent clause. *What the message meant* is a noun clause functioning as the subject of the verb *remained* in the independent clause.)

Compound-Complex Sentence. As its name indicates, a *compound-complex sentence* consists of two or more independent clauses (to make it compound) and one or more dependent clauses (to make it complex as well).

Soames Forsyte is the main character in Galsworthy's novel *The Man of Property;* Soames remains a character in some of the later stories which Galsworthy included in *The Forsyte Saga.* (The sentence contains two independent clauses separated by the semicolon. It also contains an adjective clause, the last seven words of the sentence, beginning with *which* and modifying the noun *stories.*)

The scientist knew that his experiment would succeed, but he avoided publicity until the final test was complete. (This sentence contains two independent clauses separated by the comma and joined by the co-ordinating conjunction *but.* The sentence also contains two dependent clauses: a noun clause, *that his experiment would succeed,* is the direct object of the verb *knew;* and an adverbial clause, *until the final test was complete,* modifies the verb *avoided.*)

Sentences Classified by Rhetorical Form. *Rhetorical form* here means the architecture of the sentence, the design or style that determines the effect of the sentence on the reader. Like a building, a sentence can be a monstrosity. The building may have the essential parts (foundation, walls, roof, etc.), all made of good materials, and yet shock and disturb the viewer. The sentence may have the necessary grammatical elements, even the appropriate number of independent and dependent clauses for the idea, and yet startle or distract the reader. If it does, its rhetorical form is poor. The sentence elements need to be controlled and grouped, the words chosen and arranged, so that the effect on the reader is as pleasing as possible. A sentence, like a well-designed building, can have an element of grace, of natural harmony. If it does, its rhetorical form is good. (See p. 212ff. for further discussion of effectiveness of sentences.)

Sentences are classified on the basis of *rhetorical form* as loose, balanced, and periodic sentences. The specific basis of this classification is the order in which the sentence elements are arranged. None of the sentences in this category is in itself better than the others. All three types are used in an interesting variety by competent writers.

Loose Sentence. A *loose sentence* is one in which the grammatical elements are arranged so that the main structure is complete before the end. Usually several optional parts follow the subject and predicate. Hence the loose sentence has a somewhat casual pattern. This pattern appears frequently in good composition—properly so, because it is not likely to become monotonous. The loose sentence has the effect of relaxing the reader, of helping him to grasp early the essence of the idea.

Grandmother was always pleased when her grandchildren came to visit her, especially when they came uninvited.

Remember the sabbath day, to keep it holy.—Bible

Balanced Sentence. A *balanced sentence* is a compound or compound-complex sentence in which the structure is parallel or nearly so. An important requirement is that the ideas be sufficiently similar or dissimilar to lend themselves to parallel structure. (See pp. 216–217 and pp. 225–227.) If its content is suited to its form, an occasional balanced sentence has almost certain appeal. It has the effect of temporarily satisfying the reader's fundamental need for symmetry.

When I want companionship, I visit with a friend or two in a quiet retreat; when I want solitude, I merge with a crowd of strangers in a noisy metropolis.

And therefore, if a man write little, he had need have a great memory; if he confer little, he had need have a present wit; and if he read little, he had need have much cunning, to seem to know that [which] he doth not.
FRANCIS BACON

Sometimes the effect of balance is sustained throughout a series of sentences, as in this passage.

The civilized man has built a coach, but has lost the use of his feet. He is supported on crutches, but lacks so much support of muscle. He has got a fine Geneva watch, but he has lost the skill to tell the hour by the sun.
EMERSON

Periodic Sentence. Unlike a loose or a balanced sentence, a *periodic sentence* is one in which grammatical structure becomes complete only with the last word. It has the effect of suspense, of making the reader wait as long as possible to know what the sentence means. In a short periodic sentence like "Let there be light," the suspense does not tax the reader. A long periodic sentence requires him to keep subordinate points in mind until he reaches the climax at the end. For this reason long periodic sentences should be used infrequently. A succession of them would exasperate rather than please the reader. Here are examples of varying length.

The tree that we planted last fall does not seem to be growing.

When the battle was over, neither of the two armies was able to call itself victorious.

During his first year in the one-room school, when he tried unsuccessfully to join the older boys at play, and when his efforts in reading and writing were often a source of merriment for them, Tim began to stutter.

As mentioned earlier, rhetorical form in the sentence is a matter of architecture. Certain basic patterns have been established and accepted, but they permit unlimited variety. Of the basic patterns, none would remain appealing if employed exclusively. The important thing for the writer—the architect of the composition—to remember is that by skillfully interspersing among his loose, casual structures a number of balanced, symmetrical units and a few carefully styled ones of varying sizes, he can create effective design in his organic whole composition.

EFFECTIVENESS OF SENTENCES

The *effectiveness* of any sentence is best measured in terms of how well it serves the purpose for which it was written. The general purpose of every sentence is to convey thought or feeling, or both, to an audience, and to do so convincingly and gracefully. But every sentence has also a particular purpose to serve, a special need to fill, which is determined largely by the context of the sentence, the character of the audience, and the motivation of the author. Whatever these special conditions may be, the sentence must satisfy them if it is to be effective. It should fit so well into the pattern set by surrounding sentences as to be an essential part of that pattern.

Effective sentences have certain qualities, such as unity, coherence, emphasis, economy, and variety, which help to convince and please the reader. These qualities usually do not just happen to appear in a sentence. They are the achievements of a writer who has studied and consciously applied the principles that underlie them. The inexperienced writer can achieve the same qualities by following the same principles.

These principles, along with illustrative sentences, form the subject matter of the next few divisions of this chapter.

Harmony Between Structure and Idea. What makes a sentence memorable? Why does a sentence written by a great author strike a responsive chord in the minds and hearts of many readers? It is probably not structure alone or idea alone that makes the lasting impression. More likely it is a subtle combination of the two that endures. The structure suits the idea and the idea suits the structure; the result is that harmonious blend which makes the sentence memorable.

These examples of appropriate relationship between form and idea are quoted at random from the works of Samuel Taylor Coleridge. In making a simple observation containing a comparison, Coleridge uses a direct statement characterized by simplicity and including an element of parallelism.

I have often thought what a melancholy world this would be without children, and what an inhuman world without the aged. (The memorable quality of this sentence stems from two pairs of parallel phrases and a skillful combination of like and unlike ideas. The *melancholy world* and the *inhuman world* would both be undesirable, but since they would be worlds *without children* and *without the aged,* respectively, they would be created by the absence of opposites. A warmth of feeling for the relatively helpless also pervades the sentence and corroborates for the reader what he already knows.)

In another situation, Coleridge makes a complex differentiation by means of elaborate sentence structure and considerably more space.

But a moment's reflection suffices to make every man conscious of what every man must have before felt, that the drama is an *imitation* of reality, not a *copy*—and that imitation is contradistinguished from copy by this: that a certain quantum of difference is essential to the former, and an indispensable condition and cause of the pleasure we derive from it; while in a copy it is a defect, contravening its name and purpose. (Here the author calls attention to his key words by using italics; but since knowledge of the distinction between an *imitation of reality* and a *copy* requires clear understanding of a fine point, he leads the reader up to that point and even introduces it with a colon. Then he uses specific, denotative words and phrases like *quantum of difference, indispensable condition and cause, defect,* and *contravening its name and purpose* to show that a certain deviation from reality is good in an imitation but bad in a copy.)

Doubtless the best illustrations of a happy relationship between form and content are sentences found in poetry. Oral reading of this stanza from Coleridge's "The Rime of the Ancient Mariner" permits one to hear the purposeful monotony of the first two lines and to see the static scene pictured by the last two lines. The calm is a lasting one: it goes on "day after day, day after day." It is total: the ship is "stuck." Certainly nothing could be more motionless or "idle" than a ship in a painting. Here is superb harmony between structure and idea.

> "Day after day, day after day,
> We stuck, nor breath nor motion;
> As idle as a painted ship
> Upon a painted ocean."

Unity. A sentence is by definition a unit—a unit of thought or a unit of feeling—expressed through a logically related subject and predicate. *Unity* or *oneness* is, therefore, an inherent quality of a good sentence. Every word in a good sentence is an integral part of the whole sentence. Every word contributes to the architectural form of the sentence and at the same time contributes to the expression of a single complete thought or feeling. In other words, a good sentence has both structural unity and logical unity, qualities so closely related that the sentence cannot have one without the other.

A sentence derives structural unity mainly from its subject and predicate. (See pp. 282–284.) If either or both of these parts are missing, the result is a sentence fragment—something less than a sentence, less than a unit. The italicized examples show how the fragment falls short of being a unit. (See also pp. 232–233.)

Like the family doctor, was a prominent part of the American panorama in the nineteenth century. (The fragment lacks a subject.)

The itinerant judge, like the family doctor, was a prominent part of the American panorama in the nineteenth century. (Addition of the subject *judge* for the verb *was* changes the fragment into a complete, unified sentence.)

The man carrying the new rod and reel. (The fragment lacks a predicate.)

The man carrying the new rod and reel was the game warden. (Addition of the predicate *was the game warden* changes the fragment into a complete, unified sentence.)

When my brothers and I were children, we were forever playing hide and seek. *Outdoors in the summertime, indoors in the wintertime.* (The fragment lacks both subject and predicate.)

When my brothers and I were children, we were forever playing hide and seek, outdoors in the summertime, indoors in the wintertime. (Attaching the fragment to the preceding construction makes a complete, unified sentence that has the subject *we* and the verb *were playing* in its main clause.)

The preceding illustrations show that the unified sentence must contain everything essential to the expression of a single complete thought or feeling. The next examples show that the unified sentence must contain nothing unrelated to the single complete thought or feeling. A sentence derives logical unity mainly from the interrelationship of the ideas suggested by its words. The introduction of an irrelevant idea disrupts the unity, causes the sentence to be more than a unit. In the first version below, certain details not used by the original author have been added.

Men were not intended to work with the accuracy of tools, *which have become more plentiful since the beginning of the Industrial Revolution,* to be perfect in all their actions. (The italicized clause introduces extraneous information and thus prevents logical unity.)

Men were not intended to work with the accuracy of tools, to be perfect in all their actions.—RUSKIN

The first version below contains more than one unit of thought and fails to clarify the interrelationship of ideas that the writer may have had in mind.

He learned English from a sailor and greatly admired the English language; he was a sailor too and he caught a tropical disease. (The idea about the tropical disease is irrelevant in a sentence about the subject's learning the English language. The relationship between his admiration for the language and his way of learning it is not sufficiently clear.)

He so admired the English language that he learned it from a fellow sailor. (The irrelevant idea about the tropical disease has been omitted. The sentence has been unified by a rewording that shows a cause-and-effect relationship between the subject's admiration for the English language and his way of learning it.)

Grammatical correctness helps to ensure unity in the sentence. Conversely, errors in structure, such as fused sentences, choppy sentences, dangling modifiers, and shifts in point of view (see pp. 235–242 for further explanation and for examples and corrections) represent serious breaches of unity. Fusing two sentences by omitting punctuation forces two units of thought to appear as one. Choppy sentences are so short and inadequately related that each contains only part of the unit of thought that the writer intends to communicate. A dangling modifier prevents unity in a sentence by implying a relationship that does not exist. An inconsistency in structure, such as a shift from one subject to another or from active voice to passive voice, destroys unity by bringing two points of view into the sentence. Clearly, then, grammatical errors have no place in a unified sentence. The writer who regularly unifies his sentences goes beyond grammatical accuracy, however, and observes the principles of coherence, emphasis, subordination, co-ordination, parallelism, and economy—principles which we shall now consider.

Coherence. *Coherence* in a sentence is a matter of relationships among its parts. The relationships should be logical, and they should be clear to the reader. Relationships can be clarified by proper arrangement of words, phrases, and clauses within the sentence and by the discriminating use of connectives. (See pp. 223–225 and pp. 277–281.) But the sentence must be sound otherwise (that is, it must be grammatically correct and have structural elements suited to its idea) before the arrangement and the connectives can do their work.

Important grammatical and structural aids to coherence are clear reference of pronouns, parallel structure for parallel ideas, and consistency in point of view. Violation of these obscures the relationship of sentence elements and hence destroys coherence. Other common causes of incoherence are dangling modifiers, mixed constructions, and incomplete constructions. The achievement of coherence in the sentence will be illustrated by the examples in this section.

A pronoun should refer clearly to a definite antecedent (see pp. 291–293).

AMBIGUOUS AND INCOHERENT: Barton Stone heard William Hodge speak at the Caldwell Academy, where he was studying law.
CLEAR AND COHERENT: Barton Stone heard William Hodge speak at the Caldwell Academy, where Stone was studying law.

INDEFINITE AND INCOHERENT: They have enormous wheat ranches in Montana.
DEFINITE AND COHERENT: Farmers have enormous wheat ranches in Montana.

Parallel grammatical form should be used to express parallel ideas (see pp. 225–227).

NONPARALLEL AND INCOHERENT: The insurance covered the cost of X-rays, medicine, and took care of the ambulance fee. (The predicate *took care of the ambulance fee* is forced into a series with two nouns, *X-rays* and *medicine*.)
PARALLEL AND COHERENT: The insurance covered the cost of X-rays, medicine, and ambulance service. (The noun *service* fits logically into the series with the other nouns. The modifier *ambulance* is an integral part of the noun phrase *ambulance service* and does not destroy the parallelism.)

NONPARALLEL AND INCOHERENT: He is old, miserly, and with a pessimist's outlook. (The prepositional phrase *with a pessimist's outlook* is forced into a series with two adjectives, *old* and *miserly*.)

PARALLEL AND COHERENT: He is old, miserly, and pessimistic. (The adjective *pessimistic* completes a series of parallel parts.)

A coherent sentence transmits its meaning to the reader without distracting him, without requiring him to pause and consider an idea from a second point of view before he has grasped it from a first point of view. For this reason the writer should usually keep such things as subject, tense, person, number, voice, and mood the same throughout the sentence. (See pp. 240–242.)

INCONSISTENT AND INCOHERENT: A young man gets interested in three or four vocations at the same time, and then you wonder where you are. (The point of view shifts from the third person *young man* to the second person *you.* The style also becomes more informal in the second clause.)

CONSISTENT AND COHERENT: A young man gets interested in three or four vocations at the same time and has difficulty making a choice. (The point of view remains in the third person, and the style remains on one level.)

CONSISTENT AND COHERENT: As a young man interested in three or four vocations at the same time, I find it difficult to choose one. (Here the idea is related from the point of view of the first person *I.* The original author was referring to a personal experience and could have properly used the first person.)

INCONSISTENT AND INCOHERENT: Stereophonic sound was discussed by the first speaker, and we also heard one on solar energy. (The subject changes unnecessarily from the noun *sound* in the first clause to the pronoun *we* in the second clause, and shifts from third to first person. The voice shifts from the passive *was discussed* to the active *heard.* The reference of *one* is ambiguous: *one* could refer to the antecedent *speaker* or to an unexpressed antecedent *speech.*)

CONSISTENT AND COHERENT: We heard one speaker discuss stereophonic sound and another discuss solar energy. (The sentence has one subject in the first person, one verb in the active voice, and no indefinite reference.)

In a coherent sentence all modifiers are logically and grammatically attached to other expressed elements. No modifiers dangle (see pp. 236–240).

DANGLING MODIFIER: *After finishing military service,* my former job was still waiting for me. (The introductory phrase seems to modify the noun *job* but cannot logically do so.)

COHERENT: After finishing military service, I found that my job was still waiting for me. (The phrase no longer dangles because it now has a word to which it can refer, the pronoun *I*—which names the logical agent to perform the action of finishing military service.)

COHERENT: After I had finished military service, my former job was still waiting for me. (The dangling phrase has been changed into an adverbial clause which clearly modifies the verb *was waiting*.)

DANGLING MODIFIER: *While negotiating,* the strike continued. (*While negotiating* is an elliptical clause which seems to modify the noun *strike* but cannot logically do so.)

COHERENT: While the leaders of the two sides were negotiating, the strike continued. (The fully expressed introductory clause clearly modifies the verb *continued* in the main clause. An elliptical clause is a clear modifier only if its understood subject or verb is the same as the subject or verb of the main clause. For examples: *While negotiating, the leaders of the two sides gradually became more affable. He is older than she.*)

A mixed construction destroys coherence by requiring the reader to adjust to a turn of thought that he is not expecting.

MIXED: I started reading *War and Peace* two weeks ago and when will I finish it? (The sentence begins as a statement and ends as a question.)

COHERENT: I started reading *War and Peace* two weeks ago. When will I finish it? (The reader has no problem of adjustment when the statement and the question appear as separate sentences.)

COHERENT: I started reading *War and Peace* two weeks ago but do not know when I will finish it. (The sentence is entirely declarative.)

MIXED: The cardigan sweater was named for the Earl of Cardigan, who wore a jacket of the type in the battle later became the subject of Tennyson's famous poem "The Charge of the Light Brigade." (This mixed construction doubtlessly resulted from carelessness and lack of revision. The writer was probably thinking of his second construction before he had quite finished his first.)

COHERENT: The cardigan sweater was named for the Earl of Cardigan, who wore a jacket of the type in the Battle of Balaclava in the Crimean War. The battle later became the subject of Tennyson's famous poem "The Charge of the Light Brigade."

COHERENT: The cardigan sweater was named for the Earl of Cardigan, who wore a jacket of the type in the battle that later became the subject of Tennyson's famous poem "The Charge of the Light Brigade."

MIXED: The reason the price dropped *was because* the supply increased. (This particular kind of mixed construction is gaining status because of its frequent use in speech and in informal writing. It should still be avoided on the formal level. The construction is a mixture of the two coherent versions which appear on the next page.)

COHERENT: The price dropped because the supply increased.
COHERENT: The reason the price dropped was that the supply increased.

Incomplete constructions are as disconcerting for the reader and therefore as destructive to coherence as mixed constructions are. The more common varieties, including incomplete comparisons, are illustrated here.

INCOMPLETE: George Washington always *has* and always *will be* an American hero. (The first principal verb is not completely expressed. The verb *be* cannot be understood after *has*.)
COHERENT: George Washington always *has been* and always *will be* an American hero.

INCOMPLETE: The enemy had broken promises, pacts, treaties, and others. (*Others* does not clarify what the things were.)
COHERENT: The enemy had broken promises, pacts, treaties, *and other agreements*.

INCOMPLETE: *As far as settling the dispute,* the last two meetings accomplished nothing. (A gap in thought needs filling after the introductory expression.)
COHERENT: *As far as settling the dispute is concerned,* the last two meetings accomplished nothing.

INCOMPLETE: Scientific knowledge of the Tonga Trench is *so limited.* (The intensive *so* needs to be followed by a phrase or clause showing result.)
COHERENT: Scientific knowledge of the Tonga Trench is *so limited that no definite conclusions about its contents are possible.*

INCOMPLETE: Children like comic books *better than parents.* (The construction is ambiguous: it does not say whether the comparison is between comic books and parents, or between children's tastes and parents' tastes.)
COHERENT: Children like comic books *better than parents do.*

INCOMPLETE: Alaska is *bigger than any* state in the Union. (The statement tries to compare Alaska with itself. The word *other* is needed to make the comparison logically complete because the things being compared are of the same class.)
COHERENT: Alaska is *bigger than any other* state in the Union.

If a sentence is free of grammatical errors and has the proper structural elements but is still incoherent, the cause is probably in the arrangement of its parts or in the lack of appropriate connectives and transitional expressions. The single words most likely to get misplaced are adverbs like *almost, nearly,* and *hardly.* An adverb should ordinarily be placed next to the word it modifies.

INCOHERENT: I have finished *almost reading* the book. (This sentence actually says that its author has finished his task with the book, and that the task consisted not of *reading* but of *almost reading*.)
COHERENT: I have *almost finished* reading the book.

INCOHERENT: We *nearly wrote* a thousand words every week in that class. (According to this statement the task with words was an odd one of *not quite writing*, or *nearly writing*.)
COHERENT: In that class we wrote *nearly a thousand words* every week.

INCOHERENT: I *hardly saw* him once a week all summer. (Here the writer says that what he did was *barely* or *hardly seeing*.)
COHERENT: I saw him *hardly once a week* all summer.

INCOHERENT: The *worst thing* these people need is education. (The student who made *worst* modify the noun *thing* in this sentence obviously caused his sentence to say something altogether different from what he intended. He should have made *worst* modify the verb *need*.)
COHERENT: The thing these people *need worst* is education.

A phrase should be so placed that its relation to the word it modifies is clear.

INCOHERENT: I wrote a statement of the purpose of my research *in the first paragraph of my paper*. (*In the first paragraph of my paper* seems to modify *research* but logically modifies *wrote*.)
COHERENT: In the first paragraph of my paper I wrote a statement of the purpose of my research.
COHERENT BUT SOMEWHAT STILTED: I wrote in the first paragraph of my paper a statement of the purpose of my research.
COHERENT AND ECONOMICAL: In the first paragraph of my paper I stated the purpose of my research.
COHERENT AND ECONOMICAL BUT SOMEWHAT STILTED: I stated in the first paragraph of my paper the purpose of my research.

An adjective clause should ordinarily be placed immediately after the word it modifies.

INCOHERENT: I heard the band play our school song *that led the parade*. (*That led the parade* seems to modify *song* but logically modifies *band*.)
COHERENT: I heard the band that led the parade play our school song.

INCOHERENT: The man dislikes the neighborhood pets *who built a fence around his yard*. (*Who built a fence around his yard* seems to modify *pets* but logically modifies *man*.)
COHERENT: The man who built a fence around his yard dislikes the neighborhood pets.

COHERENT, BUT DIFFERENT IN MEANING: The man who dislikes the neighborhood pets built a fence around his yard.

A modifier should not be allowed to "squint," that is, to modify either of two sentence elements between which it appears.

INCOHERENT: The store that had the big sale *recently* went bankrupt. (The reader cannot tell whether *recently* was intended to qualify the predicate *had the big sale* or the predicate *went bankrupt*.)
COHERENT: The store that recently had the big sale went bankrupt.
COHERENT: The store that had the big sale went bankrupt recently.

A connective that provides smooth transition from one part of the sentence to another strengthens both the unity and the coherence of the sentence. (Notice how the first of these sentences lacks unity and coherence and how the second sentence gains both these qualities from the subordinating conjunction *while*.)

Nero fiddled and Rome burned. (The two ideas seem unrelated. A reader might react by saying, "A man fiddled. A city burned. What is the connection?")

Nero fiddled while Rome burned. (Clarification of the time relationship gives a single meaning to the disparity of the two events: it must have been a colossally indifferent man who continued fiddling *at the same time* that the city was burning.)

Emphasis. An effective sentence, we have seen, has the two qualities of unity and coherence. It has a third quality: *emphasis,* the focus of attention on the most important part of the sentence. A writer often gains emphasis by placing important words at the beginning and at the end of the sentence, by using ascending order of importance in a series, by repeating certain words, by choosing the active voice instead of the passive, or by employing special punctuation.

Emphasis by Word Order. The two most emphatic positions in a sentence are at the beginning and at the end. Of these two positions the end is the more emphatic. When the reader approaches the end punctuation mark, he normally lessens his reading rate and thus automatically prepares to focus his attention on the last element in the sentence. As he begins to resume his speed at the beginning of the next sentence, he is only a little less willing to take notice if the writer offers an inducement. The sentence below is a good illustration of emphasis by word order because the most important word, "disinterestedness," occupies the conspicuous final position and the next most important word, "rule," occupies the slightly less conspicuous initial position.

The rule may be summed up in one word—*disinterestedness.*

MATTHEW ARNOLD (italics Arnold's)

Notice how much less emphatic the sentence would have been if Arnold had arranged his words in the following order.

In one word—*disinterestedness*—the rule may be summed up.

A writer does not have to make constant use of conspicuous positions in a sentence for the purpose of emphasis. The judicious writer injects pronounced emphasis only rarely, preferring instead an agreeable variety of the subtler shades of emphasis.

The climactic order gives an appropriate distribution of emphasis to the units in a series. Notice the increased effectiveness in the second version here.

The men in Company B were plagued by a cold rain, enemy gunfire, and a cigarette shortage. (The most important obstacle is in the middle of the series; the least important is last.)

The men in Company B were plagued by a cigarette shortage, a cold rain, and enemy gunfire. (The units in the series are in ascending order of importance.)

Emphasis by Repetition. Skillful and sparing use of *repetition* of words or structural elements makes for effective emphasis. Observe the repetition in these sentences.

The mountain trembled to its very base and the rock rocked.—POE

The Essays want no Preface: they are *all Preface.* A preface is nothing but a talk with the reader; and they do nothing else.—LAMB (capitalization and italics Lamb's)

And the opinions of the wise are good, and the opinions of the unwise are evil?   PLATO

Emphasis by Voice. The *active voice* is stronger and ordinarily more emphatic than the passive voice (see p. 270).

PASSIVE VOICE, UNEMPHATIC: The refreshments *were enjoyed* by the boys.
ACTIVE VOICE, EMPHATIC: The boys *enjoyed* the refreshments.

PASSIVE VOICE, UNEMPHATIC: His father's automobile *was washed* by Jim.
ACTIVE VOICE, EMPHATIC: Jim *washed* his father's automobile.

The *passive voice* is emphatic and desirable when the doer of the action is unknown or is less important than the receiver of the action.

PASSIVE VOICE, EMPHATIC: The records *were lost* a year ago. (The person or persons responsible for losing the records probably cannot be identified.)

PASSIVE VOICE, EMPHATIC: The car *was* not badly *damaged*. (The car is more important than the circumstance in which it received the slight damage.)

Emphasis by Punctuation. As we have already seen, the most conspicuous position in a sentence is just before the *end punctuation,* for it is here that the reader decreases his speed and concentrates his attention. He also notices the mark itself (period, question mark, or exclamation point) and thus determines whether the general function of the sentence is to state, command, inquire, or exclaim (see pp. 205–207). By keeping the reader's pace temporarily suspended, this end punctuation mark also helps to make the initial position in the next sentence important. *Internal punctuation* has a similar effect: it provides focal points within the sentence. Because they delay the reader just slightly, the internal marks (commas, semicolons, colons, etc.) provide positions of emphasis somewhat less important than the beginning or the end of the sentence. These internal positions vary in emphasis according to the strength of the marks that produce them. For example, a semicolon suggests a more definite pause for the reader than a comma does and therefore produces a more important focal point in the sentence than a comma does. Thus the words near a semicolon receive more of the reader's attention than do those near a comma.

Notice the emphasis gained by punctuation, word order, and repetition in this passage from Conrad's "The Lagoon."

"If you want to come with me, I will wait all the morning," said the white man, looking away upon the water.

"No, Tuan," said Arsat softly. "I shall not eat or sleep in this house, but I must first see my road. Now I can see nothing—see nothing! There is no light and no peace in the world; but there is death—death for many. We are sons of the same mother—and I left him in the midst of enemies; but I am going back now."

He drew a long breath and went on in a dreamy tone:

"In a little while I shall see clear enough to strike—to strike. But she has died, and . . . now . . . darkness."

Logical Subordination. One of the most important methods of securing emphasis for the main element in a sentence is the de-emphasis or subordination of the lesser elements. Only fundamental ideas belong in the subject and predicate of an independent clause—in other words, in the required parts of a sentence. Lesser ideas belong in modifiers (words, phrases, dependent clauses), in appositives, and in absolute expressions—in other words, in the elective parts of the sentence. Relegating the lesser ideas to the proper sentence elements is called *logical subordination*. The significance of logical subordination is that it lends emphasis to the important ideas by preventing the unimportant ones from attracting undue attention. Compare these pairs of examples.

ILLOGICAL: When I smelled smoke and realized that the house was on fire, I was getting the newspaper from the front porch. (This is an example of "upside-down" subordination: the main idea is in the introductory subordinate clause, and the subordinate idea is in the main clause.)

LOGICAL: When I was getting the newspaper from the front porch, I smelled smoke and realized that the house was on fire.

INEFFECTIVE: Becky Sharp is a character in a novel. The novel is Thackeray's *Vanity Fair*. Becky is a good example of the self-centered women in literature. She is also a good example of the pitiable women in literature. (The four separate sentences give equal prominence to the minor and the major ideas.)

EFFECTIVE: Becky Sharp, a character in Thackeray's novel *Vanity Fair*, is a good example of the self-centered but pitiable women in literature. (Here the incidental facts of identification are appropriately subordinated in an appositive, and the more important value judgments, combined for economy in words, get proper emphasis in the single main clause.)

INEFFECTIVE: Minds might be alike in strength, but that fact does not include this other idea. These minds are not necessarily alike in tastes and inclinations too. (The idea in the first half of the first sentence is subordinate to the idea in the second sentence and therefore should not be expressed in a main clause. The idea in the second half of the first sentence should not need to be expressed at all.)

EFFECTIVE: Minds, even if alike in strength, are not always alike in tastes and inclinations.—MONTAIGNE

Logical Co-ordination. The placing of equal-ranking ideas into equal-ranking elements of sentence structure is called *logical co-ordination*. A co-ordinating conjunction usually joins equal-ranking elements within a sentence and serves as a sign of their co-ordination. The co-ordinate elements may be words, phrases, or clauses. Here we shall be concerned with co-ordinate independent clauses, that is, with sentences that are either compound or compound-complex.

Every sentence must be a unit of thought or a unit of feeling. In other words, the ideas in the co-ordinate clauses that function together in a compound or a compound-complex sentence (see pp. 208–210) must be so related that they constitute a unified whole. The co-ordinating conjunction often helps to confirm this relationship. Notice how the italicized co-ordinating conjunction serves to clarify the relationship between the clauses in each of these sentences.

The first clown tossed out dozens of toy balloons, *and* the second clown was equally liberal with tin horns. (*And* suggests an addition, in this case an addition of an idea so similar to the first that a comparison results.)

You may read a novel, *or* you may read a collection of short stories. (*Or* indicates choice.)

I can enjoy society in a room; *but* out of doors nature is company enough for me.—HAZLITT (*But* shows contrast. Hazlitt's semicolon emphasizes the contrast; a comma would have been sufficient but not so emphatic.)

A conjunctive adverb, appearing in the second of a pair of co-ordinate independent clauses, serves in somewhat the same way as a co-ordinating conjunction in pointing out the relationship between the clauses. As a part of speech, however, a conjunctive adverb is classified as an adverb, not as a conjunction. For this reason a semicolon is necessary to separate independent clauses joined by a conjunctive adverb (the italicized word in each example below).

People in the West do much camping out; *therefore,* many of them are amateur astronomers. (*Therefore* anticipates a result.)

The rain is a treat for many persons; *moreover,* it is a boon to plant life. (*Moreover* points toward a supplementary idea.)

For many years the Sports had tried unsuccessfully to win the league pennant; last year, *however,* they won it easily. (*However* calls attention to a contrast.)

Sometimes the relationship between co-ordinate clauses is so close that no connecting word is necessary. Ordinarily a semicolon separates such clauses; a colon may be appropriate, but a comma would produce a comma fault. (See pp. 233–235 and 368–369.)

His face was dirty and unshaven; his hair looked as if it had not been combed for days.

The protagonist in Henry James's novel *The Beast in the Jungle* is blinded by self-interest: he does not even notice that his lifelong confidante is in love with him. (The colon is appropriate because the second clause illustrates the idea of the first clause. A semicolon would be acceptable but not so precise as the colon.)

Parallelism. *Parallelism* is the use of similar constructions to express similar ideas. Structure is parallel when a word, a phrase, or a clause is balanced by at least one other of its own type (an adverb is balanced by at least one other adverb, a prepositional phrase by at least one other prepositional phrase, etc.). Unless used excessively, parallel structure usually has a pleasing effect on the reader, and it shows him readily which ideas are of equal significance. (See pp. 208–211 and pp. 216–217.) It should not be employed for ideas that are not parallel, for then it would tend to mislead the reader. In these illustrations the ideas in the series are parallel and should be cast in parallel form.

NONPARALLEL: He likes to hunt, to fish, and swimming. (The gerund *swimming* is not parallel to the infinitives *to hunt* and *to fish*.)
PARALLEL: He likes to hunt, to fish, and to swim.
PARALLEL: He likes hunting, fishing, and swimming.

NONPARALLEL: She is gifted in speech, music, and she can do work in art. (The independent clause *she can do work in art* is not parallel to the nouns *speech* and *music,* which are used as objects of the preposition *in*.)
PARALLEL: She is gifted in speech, music, and art.

In the next example the author uses the intransitive verb *be* in a series with the two transitive verbs *do* and *believe;* nevertheless he achieves an effective degree of parallelism.

And in the meanwhile you must do something, be something, believe something.—R. L. STEVENSON

Jefferson used parallelism freely in the Declaration of Independence; the following sentence from it contains a series of dependent clauses and a series of terms used as the subject of one of those clauses.

We hold these truths to be self-evident, that all men are created equal, that they are endowed by their Creator with certain unalienable Rights, that among these are Life, Liberty, and the pursuit of Happiness.

Correlative conjunctions should be followed by sentence elements that are parallel in structure (see pp. 278–279).

NONPARALLEL: He *either* wanted to study chemistry *or* geology. (*Either* is followed by a verb and an infinitive phrase, whereas *or* is followed by only a noun used as an object of the infinitive.)
PARALLEL: He wanted to study *either* chemistry *or* geology.

NONPARALLEL: Every spring Miss Kelly entertains the children *both* with an Easter egg hunt *and* a Maypole dance. (*Both* is followed by a prepositional phrase, whereas *and* is followed by only an object of the preposition.)
PARALLEL: Every spring Miss Kelly entertains the children with *both* an Easter egg hunt *and* a Maypole dance.

Fully as important as using parallel form for equal-ranking ideas is careful avoiding of "false parallelism," or parallel structure for unparallel ideas. Such forced construction is illogical and misleading, as this example shows.

Although we once tried a League of Nations, and although we have had the United Nations since World War II, we still have not settled a number of serious problems arising out of that war. (The parallel structure of the two *although* clauses implies that the two concessions cited are equally related to the idea in the main clause; but the concession in the first *although* clause actually has nothing to do with the idea in the main clause and therefore ought not be in the sentence at all.)

Economy. *Economy* in a sentence means reasonable thrift in the use of words. It does not imply the omission of words essential to the thought or feeling or to the artistic form of the sentence. It signifies rather the avoiding of words that clutter the sentence and obscure its meaning. In each pair of examples below, the shorter version more readily communicates its meaning.

WORDY (28 words): I have known the Griffith boy—his name is Bob—ever since the time when he enrolled in college for the first time, which was three years ago.
ECONOMICAL (14 words): I have known Bob Griffith since his first enrollment in college three years ago.

TEDIOUS TO READ (31 words): It seems that in any unpleasant situation with which we are confronted in life, the experience is made to seem less painful to us if we have someone to encourage us.
EASY TO READ (10 words): Any unpleasant experience seems less painful if someone encourages us.

REPETITIOUS (24 words): In writing my term paper on the subject of aviation history, I chose this particular subject out of a personal interest in the subject.
CONCISE (13 words): For my term paper I chose a subject that interests me, aviation history.

WORDY AND INCOHERENT (31 words): Using the words "a set pattern of order" is telling that a company which follows same will not change the way it makes decisions in dealing with issues that come up.
ECONOMICAL AND COHERENT (15 words): A company that follows "a set pattern of order" decides issues according to a policy.

Variety. The flexibility of thought and language being what it is, an effective *variety* becomes almost automatic in a succession of correct, meaningful sentences supporting a central idea. The talented writer instinctively varies his sentences as he composes them. For the writer who is still striving for fluency, however, the conscious use of certain methods of varying the sentence structure and avoiding monotony is often necessary. These methods include (1) using different kinds of sentences, according to both grammatical structure and rhetorical form; (2) using different lengths of sentences; and (3) using different orders in the parts of sentences.

Variety in Kinds of Sentences. So far as grammatical structure is concerned, the complex sentence, because of its many possibilities for internal variety, is less likely to become monotonous than are the simple sentence and the compound sentence. For this reason the complex sentence should be used frequently, although of course no thought should be forced into an unsuitable structure merely for the sake of variety. The compound-complex sentence also offers many possibilities for variety, but because of its more involved structure should be used less frequently than the complex sentence.

The following paragraph from Macaulay's essay entitled "History" (1828) has an interesting and agreeable *variety in sentence structure*. Of the eleven sentences in the paragraph, six are complex and five are simple. Three of the complex sentences and all the simple sentences contain compound elements of one kind or another. Macaulay's paragraph appears in the left-hand column. In the right-hand column is a monotonous revision, which has been purposely written with no complex sentences. Of the seventeen sentences in this version, eleven are simple and six are compound. The number of compound elements within the simple sentences has been reduced. Note the weaknesses in meaning and the awkwardness in style resulting from lack of subordination.

EFFECTIVE VARIETY

A history in which every particular incident may be true may on the whole be false. The circumstances which have most influence on the happiness of mankind, the changes of manners and morals, the transition of communities from poverty to wealth, from knowledge to ignorance, from ferocity to humanity— these are, for the most part, noiseless revolutions. Their progress is rarely

INSUFFICIENT VARIETY

A history containing all true incidents can be written. Such a history may on the whole be false. Certain circumstances have the most influence on the happiness of mankind. These circumstances are the changes of manners and morals, the transition of communities from poverty to wealth, from knowledge to ignorance, and from ferocity to humanity. For the most part, these are noiseless

EFFECTIVE VARIETY (CONT.)

indicated by what historians are pleased to call important events. They are not achieved by armies, or enacted by senates. They are sanctioned by no treaties, and recorded in no archives. They are carried on in every school, in every church, behind ten thousand counters, at ten thousand firesides. The upper current of society presents no criterion by which we can judge of the direction in which the undercurrent flows. We read of defeats and victories. But we know that nations may be miserable amidst victories and prosperous amidst defeats. We read of the fall of wise ministers and of the rise of profligate favorites. But we must remember how small a proportion the good or evil effected by a single statesman can bear to the good or evil of a great social system.—MACAULAY

INSUFFICIENT VARIETY (CONT.)

revolutions. Their progress is rarely indicated by important events. At least the historians do not please to call the causes of these things important events. These things are not achieved by armies, and they are not enacted by senates. They are not recorded in archives. They are carried on in every school and in every church, behind ten thousand counters and at ten thousand firesides. The upper current of society presents no criterion for judging the direction of the undercurrent, and therefore we cannot judge that direction. We read of defeats, and we read of victories. We know two things. Nations may be miserable amidst victories, and nations may be prosperous amidst defeats. We read of the fall of wise ministers, and we read of the rise of profligate favorites. But we must remember one thing. The good or evil effected by a single statesman can bear only a small proportion to the good or evil of a great social system.

The preceding paragraphs illustrate that the proper subordination of minor ideas is the best means to an agreeable variety in sentence structure.

So far as rhetorical form is concerned, the loose sentence is the most natural and the most popular kind in modern composition. An occasional periodic or balanced sentence, then, provides effective variety. The writer's best criterion for deciding which form to use is this question: In which form can the sentence best serve its particular purpose? Other things being equal, however, he might be governed by the rhetorical form of other sentences in the context. These three sentences illustrate the different rhetorical patterns. (See pp. 210–212.)

LOOSE: My favorite indoor pastime is basketball, as you may have guessed by now. (The main structure is complete at the comma.)

PERIODIC: As you may have guessed by now, my favorite indoor pastime is basketball. (The grammatical structure becomes complete only with the last word.)

BALANCED: As you may have guessed long ago, my favorite indoor pastime is an athletic game; as you may have guessed by now, that game is basketball. (The structure following the semicolon parallels that preceding the semicolon.)

Variety in Length of Sentences. Just as in the whole composition it is important to avoid groups of very short or very long paragraphs (see p. 179), so within paragraphs it is important to avoid groups of very short or very long sentences. Neither kind, the short sentence or the long one, is necessarily better than the other. But sameness in length, no matter what that length is, of successive sentences, becomes tiresome for the reader. Moreover, *variety in the length of sentences* permits variety in structure appropriate to the ideas being communicated.

A good average for sentence length in expository composition is approximately twenty words, but the range in length may well extend from fewer than half to more than twice that number. In the paragraph from Macaulay (left column, pp. 228–229), the sentences average eighteen words and range from six to forty-one words in length. The sentences in the inferior revision of Macaulay's paragraph average only thirteen words and range from four to twenty-six words.

The following paragraph from a student composition would be more effective if the student had used more variety in the length of his sentences and correspondingly more variety in grammatical elements within the sentences. Here the average length of the sentences is thirteen words; the range, between ten and fifteen words.

The art of conversation in America began to decline over a century ago. The beginning of the decline can probably be attributed to the industrial revolution. Before the machine age a large percentage of the population lived on farms miles apart. As a result these people could not see their neighbors very often. But they did meet at specified times, and they did talk over their experiences. Job opportunities in the factory caused many people to move near the factory. Workers saw their neighbors at the factory almost every day. They were no longer eager for the privilege of conversation. Soon new inventions provided mass entertainment as a substitute for conversation. People went to movies or listened to the radio without saying much to one another. Now I go to visit a friend and am greeted by "Shh! *Gunsmoke* is on!"

Variety in the length of sentences is most noticeable when a relatively short sentence adjoins a relatively long one. The short sentence suggests finality. The two sentences which end a paragraph of Lincoln's "Second Inaugural Address" illustrate this point.

Both parties deprecated war; but one of them would make war rather than let the nation survive; and the other would accept war rather than let it perish. And the war came.

Variety in Order of Parts of Sentences. Unless the change hampers the meaning, an occasional *variation of the normal order of the parts within a sentence* is effective. Placing another sentence element before the subject is sometimes desirable. The writer must be careful, however, not to place emphasis on the wrong element merely for the sake of variety. In English sentences the normal order is subject—verb—complement or object; modifiers are as close as possible to the words they modify (modifying phrases and clauses normally follow the words they modify). Here are sentences illustrating common ways of varying the normal pattern.

NORMAL ORDER: The judge pronounced the sentence sternly but calmly.
VARIATION: Sternly but calmly, the judge pronounced the sentence. (Adverbs precede subject and predicate.)

NORMAL ORDER: An old soldier is among my best friends.
VARIATION: Among my best friends is an old soldier. (Prepositional phrase precedes inverted subject and predicate.)

NORMAL ORDER: The club will go on a picnic Saturday if the weather is pleasant.
VARIATION: If the weather is pleasant, the club will go on a picnic Saturday. (Adverbial clause precedes main subject and predicate.)

NORMAL ORDER: I still do not understand what the warning meant.
VARIATION: What the warning meant, I still do not understand. (Noun clause used as direct object precedes subject and verb.)

NORMAL ORDER AND EXPRESSION: Jerry gave a sigh of relief when his task was completed.
VARIATION: His task completed, Jerry gave a sigh of relief. (Absolute expression precedes subject and predicate.)

PREVENTION OF ERRORS IN SENTENCE STRUCTURE

Violation of the principle of unity is the major cause of errors in sentence structure. Among the most common errors are sentence fragments, comma faults, fused sentences, choppy sentences, dangling modifiers, and inconsistencies in point of view. These erroneous constructions do not conform to the definition of a sentence as a unit of thought or a unit of feeling expressed through a logically related subject and predicate.

Following is a discussion of these errors and of possible ways to correct them. A careful examination of these errors and an intensive review of sentence construction, as well as a thorough study of all phases of grammar (Chapter 9), are important for the person who wishes to avoid mistakes and to make his sentences increasingly effective.

Sentence Fragments. If a group of words lacks either of the required parts of a sentence—subject and predicate—or does not express a single complete unit of thought or feeling, that group of words constitutes not a sentence but a *sentence fragment*. This error is sometimes called a period fault because the period appears before the sentence is complete. Any dependent element (such as a phrase, an appositive, an absolute expression, or a subordinate clause), if written alone, is a sentence fragment. Generally speaking, in formal exposition sentence fragments are not conventional or acceptable.[1]

The illustrations that follow show how the most common types of sentence fragments can be corrected (1) by attaching them to adjacent sentences and thereby making them into integral parts of those sentences or (2) by changing them into separate sentences. The sentence fragments are italicized.

SENTENCE FRAGMENT (participial phrase): The volunteers who built the float for the parade found the task difficult. *Having had no experience in architecture.*

CORRECTION: Having had no experience in architecture, the volunteers who built the float for the parade found the task difficult. (The participial phrase has been made part of the adjacent sentence.)

CORRECTION: The volunteers who built the float for the parade found the task difficult. They had had no experience in architecture. (The sentence fragment has been changed into a separate sentence.)

SENTENCE FRAGMENT (prepositional phrase containing a gerund): Paul wins a merit badge every winter. *For feeding squirrels in the nearby timber during blizzards.*

---

[1] In certain contexts, particularly in informal narration, sentence fragments are sometimes appropriate. Fragmentary expressions like these, which are common in informal conversation, could be included in the dialogue of a narrative incident.

"Look! A telegram from Tom!"
"Good news?"
"Definitely."
"Coming home on leave?"
"Right. On the 12:00 noon flight tomorrow."

CORRECTION: Paul wins a merit badge every winter for feeding squirrels in the nearby timber during blizzards. (The prepositional phrase has been made part of the adjacent sentence.)

CORRECTION: Paul wins a merit badge every winter. He feeds the squirrels in the nearby timber during blizzards. (The sentence fragment has been changed into a separate sentence.)

SENTENCE FRAGMENT (appositive): As a grown man Jim Conway remembered his first bicycle. *The Christmas gift that had opened for him a whole new world of experiences.*

CORRECTION: As a grown man Jim Conway remembered his first bicycle, the Christmas gift that had opened for him a whole new world of experiences. (The appositive has been made part of the adjacent sentence.)

CORRECTION: As a grown man Jim Conway remembered his first bicycle. This Christmas gift had opened for him a whole new world of experiences. (The sentence fragment has been changed into a separate sentence.)

SENTENCE FRAGMENT (absolute expression): *The performance over and the crowd gone.* The cast began rehearsing a new opera.

CORRECTION: The performance over and the crowd gone, the cast began rehearsing a new opera. (The absolute expression has been made part of the adjacent sentence. An alternative correction could be made by inserting the verb *was* after the noun *performance* and thus changing the absolute expression into a separate sentence, but the result would not be so effective as the correction shown above.)

Comma Fault. A *comma fault* (*comma splice* or *comma blunder*) is the error in which a comma is used to separate two independent clauses not joined by a co-ordinating conjunction. The comma fault may be corrected in various ways, depending on the relationship between the ideas in the two independent clauses.

If the ideas are not sufficiently related to form a unit, the comma should be replaced by a period.

COMMA FAULT: Nancy hoped that the dormitory would be quiet so that she could read her new novel, she wanted to finish reading the novel and then give it to a friend.

CORRECTION: Nancy hoped that the dormitory would be quiet so that she could read her new novel. She wanted to finish reading the novel and then give it to a friend.

If the ideas are closely enough related to form a unit, the comma may be replaced by a semicolon. (See p. 225 and pp. 368–369.)

COMMA FAULT: Many friends called in person to congratulate the new governor, others sent him telegrams or letters.

CORRECTION: Many friends called in person to congratulate the new governor; others sent him telegrams or letters.

If the ideas are closely enough related to form a unit and if the second clause illustrates or provides specific meaning for the first clause, the comma may be replaced by a colon instead of a semicolon. (See p. 225 and p. 371.)

COMMA FAULT: Martha and Betty are much interested in science, they are both majoring in chemistry.
CORRECTION: Martha and Betty are much interested in science: they are both majoring in chemistry.

If the first clause asks a question and the second clause answers it, the comma should be replaced by a question mark.

COMMA FAULT: Why does a person mistreat his dog at the end of a strenuous day, he is using the dog as a scapegoat.
CORRECTION: Why does a person mistreat his dog at the end of a strenuous day? He is using the dog as a scapegoat.

If a co-ordinating conjunction can clarify the relationship of ideas, the conjunction should be added.

COMMA FAULT: My alarm clock is my worst enemy, it is also my best friend.
CORRECTION: My alarm clock is my worst enemy, but it is also my best friend.

If the comma fault occurs before a conjunctive adverb, the comma should ordinarily be replaced by a semicolon. (See p. 281, fn. 22 and p. 369.)

COMMA FAULT: He knew Norwegian customs from having been among the Norwegian pioneers in the Dakota Territory, furthermore, he had once lived in Norway.
CORRECTION: He knew Norwegian customs from having been among the Norwegian settlers in the Dakota Territory; furthermore, he had once lived in Norway.

If the idea of one clause clearly depends on that of the other clause, proper subordination should be used.

COMMA FAULT: The kitten sees herself in a mirror, she appears puzzled.
CORRECTION: The kitten appears puzzled whenever she sees herself in a mirror.

If a modifying phrase appears between the main clauses, punctuation should be supplied to show to which clause the phrase belongs.

COMMA FAULT: He thinks that the present system has long been outmoded, ever since last January, he has been wanting to suggest a change.

CORRECTION: He thinks that the present system has long been outmoded; ever since last January he has been wanting to suggest a change.

ALTERNATE CORRECTION (different meaning): He thinks that the present system has long been outmoded, ever since last January; he has been wanting to suggest a change.

Fused Sentences. When two sentences are run together with no punctuation between them, the sentences are said to be *fused*. This error is similar in type to the comma fault, but is an even more flagrant violation of the principle of unity in the sentence. The writer who finds that he is running sentences together should determine whether the cause is carelessness, hasty writing, or failure to recognize main clauses, and should concentrate on removing the cause. Also, he can help himself by proofreading his composition, preferably aloud, at least once for the specific purpose of finding any *fused sentences*. (Additional proofreadings to find other types of errors—one type at a time—are likewise advisable.)

The methods for correcting fused sentences are similar to those for correcting comma faults.

FUSED: Many writers have deplored what they describe as excessive conformity in modern society several have contended that individuality is almost non-existent.

CORRECTED: Many writers have deplored what they describe as excessive conformity in modern society. Several have contended that individuality is almost non-existent.

FUSED: The grain was ripening unevenly as a result the field was a mixture of green and gold.

CORRECTED: The grain was ripening unevenly; as a result the field was a mixture of green and gold.

FUSED: What will the population of the world be in 1990 any estimate is subject to error.

CORRECTED: What will the population of the world be in 1990? Any estimate is subject to error.

FUSED: He made a trip to England he wanted to study in the British Museum.

CORRECTED: He made a trip to England because he wanted to study in the British Museum.

FUSED: "Come back tomorrow," he said "my father will be home."

CORRECTED: "Come back tomorrow," he said. "My father will be home."

FUSED: "The temperature has gone above the freezing point," he explained "therefore the pond is no longer safe for skating."

CORRECTED: "The temperature has gone above the freezing point," he explained; "therefore the pond is no longer safe for skating."

Choppy Sentences. *Choppy sentences* are consecutive short sentences that have underlying relationships in meaning but do not adequately show these relationships. Because the sentences are unduly short and numerous, they give the same emphasis to minor ideas as to major ones. The way to avoid a series of choppy sentences is to combine related ideas, co-ordinating those of equal importance and subordinating the less significant ones (see pp. 223–225).

CHOPPY

In the center of the great city of London lies a small neighborhood. It consists of a cluster of narrow streets and courts. It consists also of very venerable and debilitated houses. It goes by the name of Little Britain.

EFFECTIVE

In the center of the great city of London lies a small neighborhood, consisting of a cluster of narrow streets and courts, of very venerable and debilitated houses, which goes by the name of Little Britain.

WASHINGTON IRVING

CHOPPY

Bodily labor is of two kinds. One kind a man submits to for his livelihood. The other kind he undergoes for his pleasure. The latter kind does not go by the name of labor. It goes by the name of exercise. It differs from ordinary labor in only one way though. It rises from another motive.

EFFECTIVE

Bodily labor is of two kinds, either that which a man submits to for his livelihood, or that which he undergoes for his pleasure. The latter of them generally changes the name of labor for that of exercise, but differs only from ordinary labor as it rises from another motive.

JOSEPH ADDISON

CHOPPY

I am writing a paper. I am interested in the relationships between history and economics. Therefore I am writing my paper on the Monroe Doctrine.

EFFECTIVE

Because I am interested in the relationships between history and economics, I am writing a paper on the Monroe Doctrine.

Dangling Modifiers. When a writer uses a modifier but fails to provide a definite word for it to modify (or through faulty arrangement fails to make the relationship clear), he leaves the modifier *suspended* or *dangling*. The modifiers that inexperienced writers most frequently leave in this dangling condition are verbal phrases, prepositional phrases, and elliptical clauses.

A point concerning the nature of verbals (participles, gerunds, and infinitives) is important here. Although verbals, unlike finite verbs, do not assert or affirm action or state of being (see pp. 274–277), they do *refer to* or *suggest* action or state of being. In the sentence "Barking loudly, the dog warned Jim," the verb *warned* in the main clause asserts the action of the noun *dog,* and the participle *barking* refers to action by the same agent or actor, the dog. Since the noun *dog* appears immediately after the participial phrase, there is no problem in modification: the reader can see easily that the phrase *Barking loudly* modifies the noun *dog.* But notice what happens when the sentence is written "Barking loudly, Jim was warned by the dog." This sentence is absurd: the participial phrase *Barking loudly* seems to modify the noun *Jim* but cannot logically do so. In other words, the participial phrase dangles because the noun it logically modifies, *dog,* is too far away and another noun, *Jim,* is adjacent to the phrase. It is important to remember (1) the general rule that the modifier and the word modified should be as near each other as possible (p. 219) and (2) the specific rule that the main clause following an introductory verbal modifier should begin with a subject which names the logical person or thing to do the act (or have the state of being) referred to by the verbal.

Note also that the reason the nouns *dog* and *Jim* are illogically placed in the absurd sentence above is that the main clause ("Jim *was warned* by the dog") is written in the passive voice. In the original sentence, where there is no dangling modifier, the main clause ("the dog warned Jim") is in the active voice. (See p. 270 and pp. 285–286 for further explanation of voice.) As other examples will show, many *dangling modifiers* result from overuse of the passive voice and can be corrected —or, preferably, prevented—by use of the active voice.

In general, the ways to correct introductory verbal phrases that dangle are (1) to give the main clause a subject to which the verbal phrase can refer and (2) to change the verbal phrase into a subordinate clause, adjusting the main clause as necessary to make the sentence structure consistent.

DANGLING PARTICIPIAL PHRASE: *Hurrying into the kitchen,* a jar of cookies was immediately noticed. (The participial phrase seems to modify the noun *jar* but cannot logically do so. The main clause does not contain a word that the phrase can logically modify; the sentence does not say who did the noticing or the hurrying.)

CORRECTION: Hurrying into the kitchen, he immediately noticed a jar of cookies. (The pronoun *he* denotes a logical doer of the actions affirmed by the verb *noticed* and referred to by the participle *Hurrying*. The main clause has assumed the active voice.)

ALTERNATE CORRECTION: As he hurried into the kitchen, he noticed a jar of cookies. (Here the entire structure has been revised: a subordinate clause has replaced the participial phrase, and the main clause has assumed the active voice. The adverb *immediately* has been omitted because the subordinate conjunction *As* shows that the actions of the two verbs were concurrent.)

DANGLING PARTICIPIAL PHRASE: *Sitting on our patio in the evenings,* airplanes can be seen and heard overhead. (The participial phrase has no word to modify, but the presence of the word *our* suggests that the author may have intended to use *we* as the subject of the main clause.)

CORRECTION: Sitting on our patio in the evenings, we can see and hear airplanes overhead. (The participial phrase clearly modifies the subject *we*, which denotes the logical agents of the actions asserted by the compound verb *can see and hear* and referred to by the participle *Sitting*. The main clause has assumed the active voice.)

ALTERNATE CORRECTION: When we sit on our patio in the evenings, we can see and hear airplanes overhead. (Here a subordinate clause has replaced the participial phrase, and the main clause has assumed the active voice.)

DANGLING PREPOSITIONAL PHRASE CONTAINING GERUND: *By casting the largest number of ballots in the history of the nation,* the new President was elected. (The introductory phrase dangles because the only person named in the main clause, the President, cannot logically have performed the action referred to by the gerund *casting*.)

CORRECTION: By casting the largest number of ballots in the history of the nation, the voters elected the new President. (The noun *voters* names the agents who cast the ballots and elected the President; the main clause has assumed the active voice.)

ALTERNATE CORRECTION: The voters elected the new President by casting the largest number of ballots in the history of the nation. (This revision is the same as the preceding one except that here the sentence elements appear in their normal order. Since the prepositional phrase containing the gerund —"by casting . . . nation"—is used adverbially to modify the verb *elected*, the normal position for the phrase is after the verb and its direct object.)

DANGLING INFINITIVE PHRASE: *To do a juggler's act,* exercises in rhythm must be practiced. (The sentence does not name an agent of the action asserted by the verb or of the action suggested by the infinitive.)

CORRECTION: To do a juggler's act, one must practice exercises in rhythm. (The pronoun *one* names the doer of the action of the verb *must practice* and that of the infinitive *to do*. The main clause has assumed the active voice.)

ALTERNATE CORRECTION: One who wishes to do a juggler's act must practice exercises in rhythm. (Here the same adjustments have been made as in the preceding correction, and in addition the infinitive has been put into a subordinate clause.)

Notice how the principles mentioned in the preceding corrections can be extended to an infinitive that suggests being instead of action.

DANGLING INFINITIVE PHRASE: *To be a juggler,* exercises in rhythm must be practiced. (The sentence does not name the person whom the infinitive refers to as existing or who could perform the action of the verb.)

CORRECTION: To be a juggler, one must practice exercises in rhythm. (The pronoun *one* names the person the infinitive refers to as existing and also serves as the subject of the verb, that is, names the agent of the action affirmed by the verb. The main clause has assumed the active voice.)

ALTERNATE CORRECTION: One who wishes to be a juggler must practice exercises in rhythm. (Here the same adjustments have been made as in the preceding correction, and in addition the infinitive has been put into a subordinate clause.)

In each example up to this point, the verbal and the verb have had a common agent. For example, in "Barking loudly, the dog warned Jim," the dog did both the barking and the warning. Such a common ground between verbal and verb often exists, but not always. A participle, for instance, may have a different agent from the subject of the verb. In such a case the sentence becomes preposterous when the subject of the verb seems to be also the agent of the action or being of the participle. Participial phrases of this kind dangle when the participle is too far away from the word it modifies. Notice how a change in word order removes the absurdity from this example.

DANGLING PARTICIPIAL PHRASE: *Dripping from the faucet all night long,* I heard the water. (The subject *I* cannot logically be the agent of the action referred to by the participle *Dripping* and therefore should not be in the position immediately following the participial phrase.)

CORRECTION: I heard the water dripping from the faucet all night long. (Only a change in word order has been made here. Now the agent—*water* —of the action suggested by the participle—*Dripping*—is clearly different from the subject—*I*—of the verb—*heard*.)

ALTERNATE CORRECTION: All night long I heard the water dripping from the faucet. (This is simply another possible rearrangement of the words with somewhat different meaning and emphasis.)

ALTERNATE CORRECTION: The water dripping from the faucet kept me awake all night long. (Here a change in wording alters the emphasis in still another way.)

A prepositional phrase indicating age dangles when it is not clearly related to the thing or person whose age the author had in mind.

DANGLING PREPOSITIONAL PHRASE: *At the age of sixteen* the law in my state allows a resident to apply for a driver's license. (The prepositional phrase seems to indicate the age of the law.)

CORRECTION: At the age of sixteen a resident of my state is legally old enough to apply for a driver's license. (The position of the subject *resident* makes the introductory phrase refer clearly to the age of the resident.)

ALTERNATE CORRECTION: The law in my state allows a resident to apply for a driver's license when he reaches the age of sixteen. (The prepositional phrase of age has been changed into a subordinate clause of time.)

DANGLING PREPOSITIONAL PHRASE: *In her old age* the child was a pleasant companion for Grandmother. (The introductory phrase seems to refer to the age of the child.)

CORRECTION: The child was a pleasant companion for Grandmother in her old age. (Placing the phrase adjacent to the word *Grandmother* clarifies the reference.)

ALTERNATE CORRECTION: In her old age Grandmother found the child a pleasant companion. (Placing the subject *Grandmother* adjacent to the introductory phrase clarifies the reference.)

An elliptical clause dangles when its understood subject and the subject of the main clause are not the same. (See p. 300.)

DANGLING ELLIPTICAL CLAUSE: *While trying to prolong peace,* a battle between the two countries was already under way. (The elliptical clause dangles because its understood subject cannot logically be *battle*, the subject of the main clause, and yet the present structure implies that this unseemly subject should be read into the elliptical clause.)

CORRECTION: While certain leaders were trying to prolong peace, a battle between the two countries was already under way. (The fully expressed introductory clause has a logical subject—*leaders*—different from the subject of the main clause—*battle*.)

ALTERNATE CORRECTION: While trying to prolong peace, certain leaders found that a battle was already under way between the two countries. (Here the elliptical clause does not dangle because its understood subject is *leaders*, the subject of the main clause; however, the meaning of this revision may be different from that intended by the author of the original sentence.)

Inconsistencies in Point of View. A shift in the grammatical structure of a sentence results in an *inconsistency in point of view*. When a sentence begins in the third person, for instance, the reader immediately adopts the third-person point of view and expects to grasp the whole idea from that viewpoint. If, then, the sentence suddenly shifts to second person, the effect is at best a distraction for the reader. If the distraction lasts long or occurs frequently, the reader may lose the idea or even lose confidence in the writer.

Keeping sentences consistent in viewpoint requires discipline in thinking and in writing. If the writer does not think through and control his ideas, he can easily shift from one grammatical pattern to another before he finishes composing a sentence. When he violates the structural unity of a sentence in one way, he may automatically do so in another. If he makes a shift in voice, for instance, he makes a shift in subject also. With each unnecessary shift he causes the reader the extra annoyance of adjusting to a new point of view.

The common shifts that mark careless writing and make for difficult reading are illustrated here. (See pp. 282–293 for additional examples. See Chapter 9 for explanation of grammatical terms.)

INCONSISTENCY IN PERSON AND SUBJECT: The student is an important member of society, and you should learn to assume civic responsibilities. (The point of view shifts from the third person *student* to the second person *you*. Since the words in question are subjects, there is an automatic shift in subject within the sentence.)
CORRECTION: The student is an important member of society and he should learn to assume civic responsibilities.

INCONSISTENCY IN SUBJECT: Timothy relaxed his hand, and his pencil dropped. (The subject shifts from *Timothy* to *pencil*.)
CORRECTION: Timothy relaxed his hand and dropped his pencil.

INCONSISTENCY IN NUMBER: A person should always have their identification papers with them. (The number shifts from singular to plural: from singular antecedent *person* to plural pronouns *their* and *them*.)
CORRECTION: A person should always have his identification papers with him.

INCONSISTENCY IN VOICE: Our team played the game hard and fair, but still the game was not won by our team. (The voice shifts from the active verb *played* to the passive verb *was won*. The subject shifts from *team,* the agent of the action, to *game,* the receiver of the action.)
CORRECTION: Our team played hard and fair but still did not win the game.

INCONSISTENCY IN MOOD AND SUBJECT: Wood is a useful product; for proof just examine the objects in any home. (There is a shift from the indicative mood of the verb *is* in the first clause to the imperative mood of the verb *examine* in the second clause, and a corresponding shift from the subject *Wood* of the verb *is* to the understood subject *you* of the verb *examine*.)

CORRECTION: Wood is a useful product, as the examination of the objects in any home proves.

OR: An examination of the objects in any home proves that wood is a useful product.

OR: You will find by an examination of the objects in any home that wood is a useful product.

INCONSISTENCY IN TENSE: The rain stopped for a few minutes and then starts again. (The tense shifts from past to present.)

CORRECTION: The rain stopped for a few minutes and then started again.

INCONSISTENCY IN TENSE: In the story Jacques tells Gertrude certain facts because he recognized her need for the truth. (The tense shifts from the present—*tells*—to the past—*recognized*. The "historical present" tense may be used in an account of narrative action; but if it is used at all, it should be used throughout the account. Narrating past events consistently in the present tense often makes them more vivid for the reader.)

CORRECTION: In the story Jacques tells Gertrude certain facts because he recognizes her need for the truth.

OR: In the story Jacques told Gertrude certain facts because he recognized her need for the truth.

PERMISSIBLE INCONSISTENCY IN TENSE: Before he started school he knew that gravity pulls objects toward the center of the earth. (The "universal present" tense is appropriate in statements of what is always true; in this example the verbs *started* and *knew* are consistently in the past tense, and the verb *pulls* is properly in the "universal present" tense.)

INCONSISTENCY IN SUBJECT AND PERSPECTIVE: The instructor stood surveying the class, and a few hands were beginning to go up timidly. (The subject shifts from *instructor* to *hands*. The perspective shifts from one part of the room to another, from the position of the instructor to that of the class.)

CORRECTION: As the instructor stood surveying the class, he noticed that a few hands were beginning to go up timidly.

INCONSISTENCY IN DISCOURSE: He asked me if I had a solution and are other solutions possible. (The shift is from indirect to direct discourse.)

CORRECTION: He asked me if I had a solution and if other solutions were possible.

OR: He asked me, "Do you have a solution? Are other solutions possible?"

DIAGRAMING OF SENTENCES

Diagraming is a brief graphic device for identifying and analyzing the grammatical relationships among the elements of a sentence. Because it calls attention to relationships within the sentence, diagraming has long been a useful tool for students of grammar and rhetoric.

Diagraming has two main purposes: (1) to aid the beginning writer in understanding the structure of effective sentences written by others and (2) to aid him in constructing effective sentences of his own.

Diagraming as an Aid in Understanding Effective Sentences. Writing correct and effective sentences requires constant awareness of the definition of a sentence and of basic grammatical principles. To master these principles, the beginner must study sentences in which they have been correctly applied. He needs frequently to analyze or break down a good sentence into its parts—subject, predicate, and optional elements. This is the place in his study where he finds diagraming a helpful device. He puts each part of the sentence in its assigned place; and when the diagram is complete he can see, without having to label them, how the words are related to one another. From the positions of the words on the lines, he can even tell the degrees of closeness in the relationships among the words. In the whole diagram he has a picture of the sentence as a unit—precisely what the definition says it should be.

Diagraming as an Aid in Constructing Effective Sentences. Once the beginner learns to diagram correct and effective sentences written by others, he can apply the same analytical method to his own sentence construction. The analytical study enables him to develop a consciousness of grammatical interrelationships and the principles underlying them. His experience in showing graphically the relationships among the elements in good sentences makes him aware that he should produce similar relationships as he composes sentences. When he has doubts concerning a given construction of his own, he can analyze it for accuracy and effectiveness. He will probably be able to discover, for instance, such a common error as the use of a co-ordinating conjunction between elements that are not co-ordinate (as in this example, where *and* joins a clause and a phrase, "The young author left college for two reasons: (1) he wanted to devote more time to writing fiction and (2) a dislike for his legal studies"). Also, by using the analytical method, he will probably be able to discover any incompleteness that exists in his own constructions.

Method of Diagraming. The *method of diagraming* illustrated here is a basic one. The subject and the verb appear on a horizontal base line; a vertical line extending above and below the base line separates them. The horizontal line branches out to provide places for the parts of compound subjects and verbs.

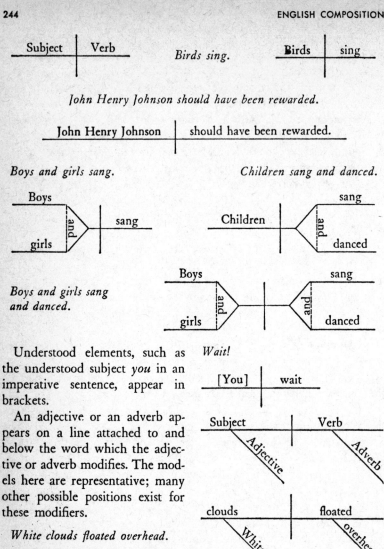

Understood elements, such as the understood subject *you* in an imperative sentence, appear in brackets.

An adjective or an adverb appears on a line attached to and below the word which the adjective or adverb modifies. The models here are representative; many other possible positions exist for these modifiers.

White clouds floated overhead.

Clouds, white and fluffy, floated here and there.

The subject complement, whether it is an adjective or a substantive, appears on the base line following the verb. A short line slanting toward the subject precedes the subject complement.

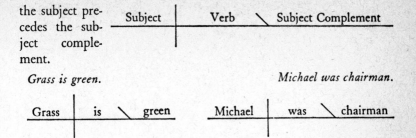

Grass is green.　　　　　　　　　　　　*Michael was chairman.*

The prepositional phrase appears on a broken line below the word the phrase modifies. The preposition appears on the slanted part of the broken line; the object of the preposition, on the horizontal part.

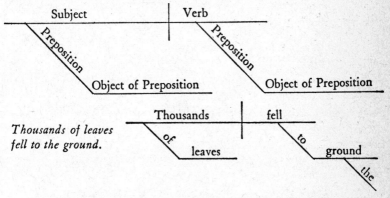

Thousands of leaves fell to the ground.

We walked to the white house at the end of the road.

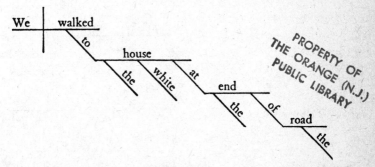

Any word or group of words not having a grammatical connection with the other parts of the sentence should be placed on a separate line above the main diagram. The expletive, the nominative of address, and the absolute expression come in this category, as does the subordinating conjunction *that* when it introduces a noun clause.

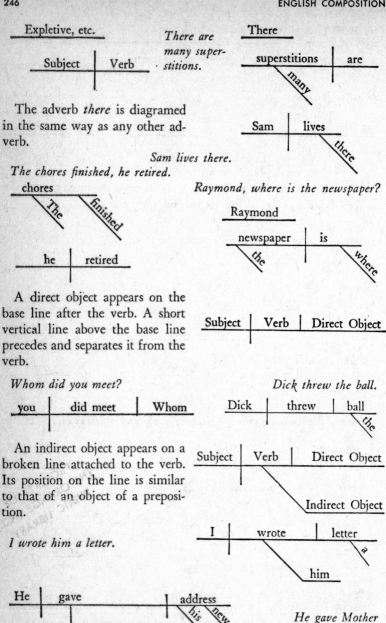

Expletive, etc.

There are many superstitions.

The adverb *there* is diagramed in the same way as any other adverb.

Sam lives there.

The chores finished, he retired.

Raymond, where is the newspaper?

A direct object appears on the base line after the verb. A short vertical line above the base line precedes and separates it from the verb.

Whom did you meet?

Dick threw the ball.

An indirect object appears on a broken line attached to the verb. Its position on the line is similar to that of an object of a preposition.

I wrote him a letter.

He gave Mother and me his new address.

An object complement, whether it is an adjective or a substantive, appears on the base line between the verb and the direct object. Preceding the object complement is a short line slanting toward the direct object.

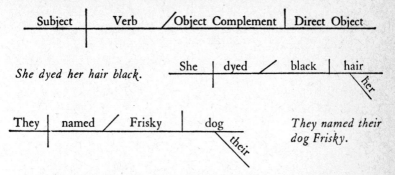

She dyed her hair black.

They named their dog Frisky.

An appositive appears in parentheses following the substantive which it renames or explains.

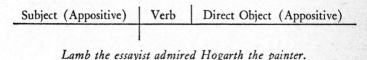

Lamb the essayist admired Hogarth the painter.

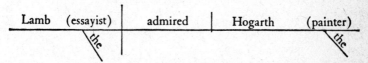

The man with Harry Kendall, the mayor, is John Allen, his friend.

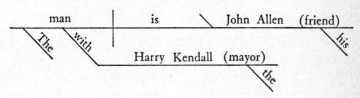

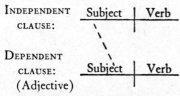

INDEPENDENT CLAUSE:

DEPENDENT CLAUSE: (Adjective)

An adjective clause, like an adjective, appears below the base line. The parts of the adjective clause and the elements of the independent clause are diagramed in the same way; each clause has its own base line, but they are connected by a dotted line running from a relative pronoun or relative adverb to the word which the adjective clause modifies.

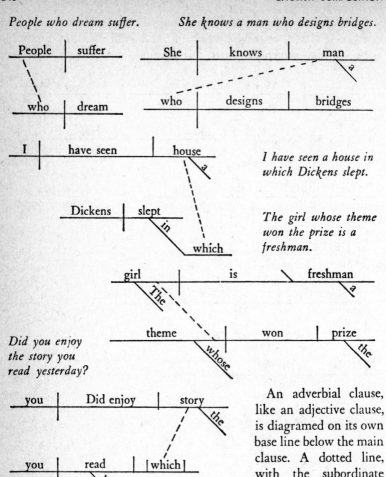

People who dream suffer.   *She knows a man who designs bridges.*

I have seen a house in which Dickens slept.

The girl whose theme won the prize is a freshman.

Did you enjoy the story you read yesterday?

An adverbial clause, like an adjective clause, is diagrammed on its own base line below the main clause. A dotted line, with the subordinate conjunction written on it, connects the adverbial clause to the main clause. This dotted line runs where the relationship is the strongest, usually between the verbs unless the adverbial clause shows comparison or degree.

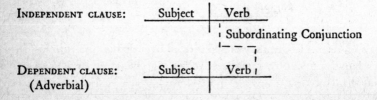

If you diagram carefully, you will understand grammatical relationships.

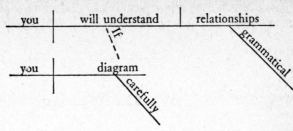

He is younger than I am.   *Susan was so happy that she almost cried.*

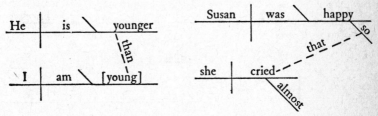

A noun clause appears on stilts in the position of the noun it replaces. A subordinating conjunction introducing a noun clause occupies a separate line above the noun clause.

Everyone knew where you had gone.

Her wish was that all wars would end.

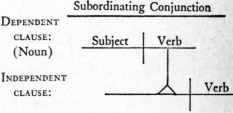

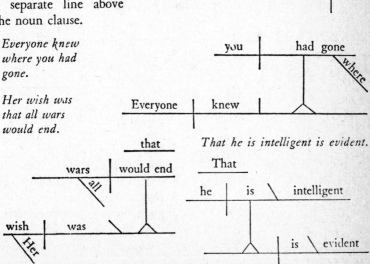

That he is intelligent is evident.

Compound sentences are diagramed as if each independent clause were a separate sentence. If a co-ordinating conjunction is expressed, it appears on the dotted line joining the verbs of the independent clauses.

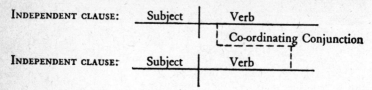

The sky darkened and the storm struck.

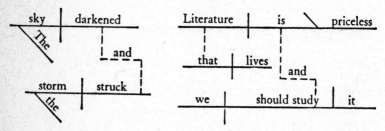

Literature that lives is priceless, and we should study it.

A combination of the methods used for diagraming a compound sentence and a complex sentence provides the method for diagraming a compound-complex sentence (above right).

A participle is diagramed below the word it modifies and at an angle so it occupies the slanting and the horizontal parts of a broken line.

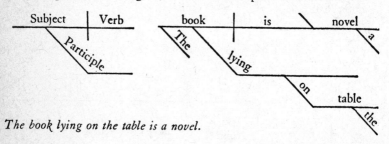

The book lying on the table is a novel.

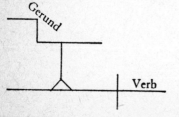

A gerund is diagramed on stilts and has a step in the line on which it rests, like the participle, at an angle. Adjective modifiers of the gerund appear to the left of the step; adverbial modifiers, to the right.

She enjoys painting land-scapes.

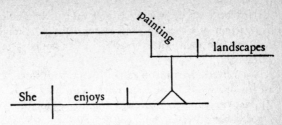

An infinitive is diagramed on the same kind of broken line employed for prepositional phrases. An arch drawn over the sign of the infinitive, *to,* distinguishes it from a preposition. An infinitive used as an adverb or an adjective appears below the base line of the diagram, and an infinitive used as a noun appears on stilts above the base line.

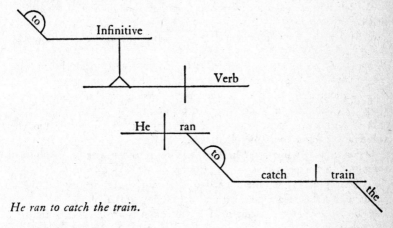

He ran to catch the train.

Exercises

1. Rewrite these sentences, making them less wordy and improving the word order where necessary.

a. There is a good deal of practical information scattered through the pages of a five-cent newspaper, such as the hints or suggestions on cooking, sewing, gardening, and building.

b. It was my curiosity that motivated me when I first began to read articles on nuclear physics.

c. The job of executioner in revolutionary France often stayed within a family, such as being passed on from father to son.

d. From that time on, every time I went to the library I used only one section, the section on airplanes, and this continued until I entered high school.

e. The driver admitted the fact that he had been exceeding the speed limit by driving twenty miles an hour faster than the law allows.

f. Any person who would not be aware of the participation of the bullet in the action of knocking the can from the post might be mystified and think that the man with the rifle had mysterious control over objects at a distance.

g. I received nine calls in response to my ad; three of the calls were from business firms and six of them were from individuals.

h. He was definitely interested in military glory, for with him it had been his goal since his early childhood.

2. Rewrite these sentences, correcting the errors in reference of pronouns.

a. After an airplane has crashed and burned, they can usually tell what the cause was.

b. Almost everyone in the group wanted to discuss their own problems first.

c. Each witness gave a report on what they thought had actually happened.

d. My uncle saw the president of the company when he was in Boston.

3. Supply the punctuation needed in these sentences to make the meaning immediately clear to the reader.

a. Without advertising our radio and television **stations would** not be readily available for announcements of public interest.

b. His encouragement produced good results for **many** people took his advice and became more useful citizens.

c. For a good while after he begins painting the novice may still have trouble with perspective.

d. After graduation time seemed to pass slowly for me, from June to September, I stayed on the farm and helped my grandfather.

e. The system is still inefficient for two channels are needed to transmit one program.

f. My uncle is paying for my educational needs, except for tuition, he does not expect to be reimbursed when I have an income of my own.

4. In each of these pairs of sentences, which is the better version and why?

a. (1) He is a good fielder and hits well also.
   (2) He is a good fielder and a good hitter.

b. (1) As far as a solution of the traffic problem is concerned, the removal of stop signs did no good.
   (2) As far as a solution of the traffic problem, the removal of stop signs did no good.

c. (1) Disputes continue to arise because some parents without dogs and some dog owners without children are so partial.
   (2) Disputes continue to arise because some parents without dogs and some dog owners without children are so partial that they do not consider opposite points of view.

d. (1) They renounced pleasure, identifying it with vice, and schooled themselves in temperance and self-control.

(2) They renounced pleasure, identified it with vice, and schooled themselves in temperance and self-control.

5. Rewrite these sentences, correcting the dangling modifiers. Explain briefly what each correction consists of and why it was necessary.

a. Crossing to the west side of Main Street, the bus station can be seen.

b. Shining brightly through the window, Patsy could see the sun.

c. By purring softly, the little girl was shown gratitude by the kitten.

d. To do an auditor's job, mathematical skill is needed.

e. To be an auditor, mathematical skill is needed.

f. Walking along the top of the hill, parts of the distant city can be seen.

6. Revise the paragraph on the art of conversation (p. 230), using appropriate subordination and variety in the sentences.

7. Rewrite these word groups, making each into a grammatically correct sentence. Explain briefly why each correction was necessary.

a. Raced down the track and cleared the hurdle easily.

b. Betsy Trotwood is an interesting character in the novel *David Copperfield* she has some eccentricities but also many good qualities.

c. Each student should bring their books to class.

d. He writes his theme and then studied his algebra lesson.

e. The melodious song of the cardinal.

f. The lecturer told several humorous stories, the audience seemed to enjoy them.

g. Whether by land or by sea or by air.

h. Every person has opportunities for mental growth, and you should make the best of them.

i. The teacher read the poem aloud, and the lesson was made interesting by him.

j. He studied hard all semester, therefore he was prepared for the examination.

8. Diagram these sentences.

a. The new student who joined our class today came from Nashville by train.

b. To whom did you lend the dictionary?

c. My roses usually bloom until Christmas, but the cold weather sometimes ruins them.

d. The salesman whom you met travels throughout the Southwest.

e. For three hours he studies the subject he likes best, and then he studies each of the others for thirty minutes.

9 GRAMMAR [1]

Grammatical terms are a kind of special vocabulary, like the technical terms used in natural science. When the physicist talks about matter and energy, he needs special words like *molecule, atom, proton,* and *electron.* When the grammarian talks about language, he too needs special words, such as *sentence, clause, phrase,* and *modifier.* Both the physicist and the grammarian desire maximum precision in discussing their subjects. It is important, therefore, to define these special words carefully and to understand their meanings clearly.

This chapter deals with grammatical terms in three general categories. First is the category of the parts of speech: terms applied to individual words to denote their grammatical functions. Second is the category of grammatical relationships: terms applied to words and word groups to denote their relationships to one another as parts of sentences. Third is the category of grammatical units: terms applied to different combinations of grammatical elements.

The principle of the levels of usage, briefly discussed in Chapter 1 and frequently invoked in Chapter 10, applies in some degree to grammar also. Where grammatical distinctions among the levels of usage are significant, the following account notes and illustrates them.

THE PARTS OF SPEECH AND THEIR INFLECTIONAL FORMS

The names of the *parts of speech,* as we have already seen, are terms applied to individual words to denote the kind of work they do in particular contexts. A word with one kind of function is a noun; with another, a verb; and so on. A single word in different contexts may represent different parts of speech: the word *iron,* for example, may be a noun (a steam iron), an adjective (an iron horseshoe), or a verb (we iron clothes). The criterion is always the function, the kind of work that the word is doing.

In the conventional classification there are eight parts of speech:

[1] For a much fuller treatment of this subject than is possible here, see George O. Curme, *English Grammar,* "College Outline Series" (New York: Barnes & Noble, Inc., 1947). This chapter gives an account of traditional grammar. There are other kinds, notably structural grammar and transformational-generative grammar, which have different systems of analysis and nomenclature.

noun, pronoun, adjective, adverb, verb, preposition, conjunction, and interjection. It makes clear the family relationships among them, however—and it is convenient—to regard the parts of speech not as eight separate items but as belonging to five classes. The following discussion classifies them as (1) substantives (nouns and pronouns), (2) modifiers (adjectives and adverbs), (3) verbs and verbals, (4) connectives (prepositions and conjunctions), and (5) interjections.

The discussion includes also an account of the various *inflectional forms* in which some of these parts of speech appear: forms with alterations—usually, though not always, at the end of the word—to denote distinctions between singular and plural number, present and past tense, and the like.

Substantives. *Substantives* are words that stand for persons or for things. A substantive may stand for one or more persons: *John, Doris, man, men, woman, women, children, mob, he, she, they, someone, anyone, who,* etc. It may stand for one or more things: these things may be concrete, tangible objects (*apple, building, ocean*); places (*city, New York, France, Asia, continent*); or abstract ideas, qualities, states of being, etc. (*truth, ugliness, absences*).

There are two kinds of substantives: nouns and pronouns.

Nouns. *Nouns* stand for persons or things by actually naming them. (The word *noun* is a derivative of the Latin word *nomen,* meaning *name.*) This naming may be particular, or it may have any degree of generality. Words in a sequence like *novel, narrative,* and *literature* show how the naming may have different degrees of generality.

Certain distinctions made among nouns relate to the things they name. A PROPER NOUN [2] names a particular person, place, or thing (*Shakespeare, England, Koran*); whereas a COMMON NOUN names a class or any member of a class (*writer, country, scriptures*). A CONCRETE NOUN names an object (*desk, tree, garage*); whereas an ABSTRACT NOUN names a concept, quality, or condition (*goodness, fear, poverty*). (For a brief discussion of the levels of abstraction, see p. 305.) A COLLECTIVE NOUN names a group of beings or things of the same kind (*audience, covey, herd, jury*). When the idea in the sentence concerns the group as a whole, a collective noun takes a singular verb and, if any appear, singular pronouns.

A covey of quail *was* nesting in the meadow.
The jury was ready with *its* verdict.

[2] A proper noun is always capitalized. (See pp. 378–381 for rules of capitalization.)

If, as occasionally happens, the idea concerns the individual members of the group, the collective noun requires a plural verb and, if any, plural pronouns.

The covey were trying to come together again after the gunshot had scattered *them.*

The jury [or *the members of the jury*] *were* still far from agreeing after *they* had argued all night.

Most nouns in English have different inflectional forms for number; a few, such as *deer, quail,* and *Chinese,* have the same form for both the singular and the plural. (See also p. 345.) Nouns have special forms for only one case, the possessive. A few nouns have special forms to distinguish masculine and feminine gender—*actor, actress; aviator, aviatrix*—but these are exceptional; there is no consistent inflection for gender. In certain instances a modifier rather than an inflectional form denotes gender: *male nurse, woman riveter.*

NUMBER. A noun is SINGULAR in *number* if it names one person or thing, PLURAL if it names two or more persons or things. The normal way to form the plural is to add *s* or *es* to the singular: *apple, apples; box, boxes.* (For other, special ways of forming plurals, see pp. 344–346.)

CASE. Case is the property of a noun or pronoun that indicates its relation to other words in the sentence. Modern English has three cases: (1) NOMINATIVE (or subjective), (2) POSSESSIVE (or genitive), and (3) OBJECTIVE (or accusative and dative combined). Since pronouns are more fully inflected for case than nouns, an illustrated explanation of the uses of the three cases appears in the section on pronouns (see pp. 260–264).

Nouns have special forms for the possessive case only. Almost all nouns become singular possessive with the addition of an apostrophe and *s* (*'s*)—*boy, boy's; carpenter, carpenter's*—and plural possessive with the addition of *s* and an apostrophe (*s'*)—*boy, boys'; carpenter, carpenters'.* (For occasional exceptions see pp. 381–382.)

Ordinarily we use the inflected possessive form of nouns which stand for animate beings. With nouns which stand for things, we commonly use a phrase consisting of the word *of* and an object: *the girl's hat,* or *the dog's collar;* but preferably *the plot of the story,* or *covers of books* (although the *story's plot* and *books' covers* are not incorrect). Occasionally we reverse the methods: we use an *of* phrase to show ownership by persons (as in *a friend of my brother,* or *the word of a gentleman*), and the inflected possessive form of nouns that name things (as in such frequently used phrases as *a day's work, money's worth,* and *the earth's surface*). In a few instances we combine the methods, making a double possessive (as in *a favorite saying of my father's*).

Pronouns. *Pronouns* stand for persons or things without actually naming them. The function of pronouns can be explained by its relationship to that of nouns: pronouns stand for persons or things indirectly, by taking the place of the nouns which name them directly. (The first part of the word *pronoun* is the Latin word *pro,* meaning "for," "on behalf of," or "instead of.") A pronoun usually takes the place of a noun that has appeared earlier; that is, the pronoun makes a repetition of the noun unnecessary. The noun is the *antecedent* of the pronoun. (In Latin, *antecedent* means "that which goes before.") Here is an example.

A fireman [noun, antecedent] came to the door; he [pronoun] was selling tickets for a benefit show.

Sometimes, however, pronouns have no antecedent: interrogative pronouns, for instance, in expressions like *"Who* is singing?" or *"What* did you say?" and indefinite pronouns like *someone, anyone.* (For an explanation of problems in relationships between pronouns and antecedents, see pp. 291–293.)

There are various classes of pronouns. The brief explanations given here show the common distinctions. Declensions of pronouns that frequently present grammatical problems because of their inflectional forms—the personal pronouns and the pronoun *who*—appear in the discussion of case (pp. 260–264).

The PERSONAL PRONOUNS (*I, you, he, she, it, we, they*) name persons who speak or write, their audiences, and their subjects. *It* is sometimes an IMPERSONAL PRONOUN used idiomatically without an antecedent, as in *"It* snowed ten inches last night."

A RELATIVE PRONOUN (*who, that, which, what, whoever, whichever, whatever*) takes the place of an antecedent, introduces a dependent clause (see pp. 289–299 and pp. 299–300), relates it to the antecedent, and functions grammatically in the dependent clause.

He *who* shirks loses self-respect. (The relative pronoun *who* refers to the antecedent *He* and functions as the subject of the verb *shirks* in the dependent clause, "who shirks.")

The house in *which* the Browns are living is for sale. (The relative pronoun *which* refers to the antecedent *house* and functions as the object of the preposition *in* in the dependent clause, "in which the Browns are living.")

I heard *what* the reporter said. (The relative pronoun *what* introduces the dependent clause, "what the reporter said," and functions as the direct object of the verb *said*. *What* differs from the other simple relative pronouns in that it does not have an expressed antecedent. *What* really means *that which*. If the sentence were written "I heard that which the reporter said," *that* would be the antecedent of *which*.)

Whoever places an order will receive a copy of the book. (The compound relative *Whoever* introduces the dependent clause, "Whoever places an order," and functions as the subject of the verb *places*. The compound relatives usually do not have expressed antecedents; in this example *Whoever* means *He who* or *One who*.)

An INTERROGATIVE PRONOUN (*who, which, what*) introduces a question and functions grammatically in the question, usually as the subject or object of the verb.

Who is calling?   *Which* of these books have you read?

A DEMONSTRATIVE PRONOUN (*this, that, these, those*) [3] stands for a clearly pointed out antecedent.

Some of the desks and bookshelves here in the office have been assigned to certain persons. *This* is Mary's desk; *that* is Bob's. *These* are John's bookshelves; *those* are unassigned.

The INDEFINITE PRONOUNS (singulars: *each, either, neither, one, other, another, anyone, someone, everyone, anybody, somebody, everybody, nobody, anything, something, everything, nothing, much;* plurals: *both, few, many,* [4] *others, several;* sometimes singulars, sometimes plurals: *all, any, none, some, enough, more*) stand for unidentified or unclearly identified persons, things, or groups.

Each of the children was getting restless. *Many* were sleepy.
The children were getting restless; *all* were tired.
The milk had been left unrefrigerated, and *all* of it was spoiled. (A pronoun like *all* is plural when its meaning concerns things that can be counted, but singular when its meaning concerns anything that cannot be measured in numbers.)

The REFLEXIVE and the INTENSIVE PRONOUNS are compounds formed by joining *–self* or *–selves* to certain personal pronouns (*myself, our-*

---

[3] *This here* and *that there* are vulgar, or subliterary, expressions unacceptable on even the colloquial level.

[4] *Many a* takes a singular verb and singular pronoun, if any: "*Many a man has* come to the aid of *his* country."

selves, yourself, yourselves, himself, herself, itself, themselves) [5] and to the indefinite *one* (*oneself* or *one's self*). These pronouns are REFLEXIVE when they direct the action of the verb back to the antecedent, which is usually the subject.

She surprised *herself.*
They gave *themselves* exercises in vocabulary development.

These same pronouns are INTENSIVE when they emphasize their antecedents.

I *myself* witnessed the accident.
They are doing the work *themselves.*

The compound personal pronouns should not be used without antecedents.

WRONG: Jim and *myself* built the patio.
RIGHT: Jim and *I* built the patio.

WRONG: The bills were addressed to my brother and *myself.*
RIGHT: The bills were addressed to my brother and *me.*

The RECIPROCAL PRONOUNS (*each other, one another*) are similar to reflexives but indicate a mutual rather than a self-directed relationship. On the formal level, *each other* refers to two, *one another* to more than two.

INFORMAL: His parents teased *one another.*
FORMAL: His parents teased *each other.*

INFORMAL: The members of Congress were questioning *each other.*
FORMAL: The members of Congress were questioning *one another.*

Not all pronouns have inflectional forms, but in general they are more fully inflected than nouns: the personal pronouns have separate forms to show distinctions of person, gender, number, and case; the compound personal pronouns, like *myself* and *yourself,* and the demonstrative pronouns *this* and *that* are inflected for number; and the relative and interrogative pronoun *who* shows case.

PERSON. In grammar, there are three "persons": the first person is that of the person or persons who are speaking or writing; the second, that of the person or persons spoken or written *to;* and the third, that of the person or persons, or thing or things, spoken or

---

[5] *Hisself, theirself,* and *theirselves* belong strictly to the vulgar level of usage.

written *about*. The personal pronouns have separate forms for these three: first person, *I;* second person, *you;* third person, *he.*

GENDER. In the third person singular, there are separate forms for the masculine, feminine, and neuter *genders: he, she,* and *it,* respectively.

NUMBER. In the first and third persons, the personal pronouns have separate forms for singular and plural: *I* and *we; he (she, it)* and *they.* (In the second person, the special singular and plural forms *thou* and *ye* are virtually obsolete except in special contexts—for instance, in certain religious services.) The demonstratives *this* and *that* have the plural forms *these* and *those* respectively. The plural forms of the compound personal pronouns in the three persons are *ourselves, yourselves,* and *themselves.*

CASE. With a few exceptions, the personal pronouns have separate forms for the nominative, possessive, and objective *cases:*

	Singular					**Plural**		
PERSON:	FIRST	SECOND	THIRD			FIRST	SECOND	THIRD
			M	F	N			
NOMINATIVE:	*I*	*you*	*he*	*she*	*it*	*we*	*you*	*they*
POSSESSIVE:	*my,*	*your,*	*his*	*her,*	*its*	*our,*	*your,*	*their,*
	mine	*yours*		*hers*		*ours*	*yours*	*theirs*
OBJECTIVE:	*me*	*you*	*him*	*her*	*it*	*us*	*you*	*them*

The pronoun *who,* whether used as a relative or an interrogative pronoun, is also inflected for case. The compound form *whoever,* which follows the same pattern, is included in the declension here.

NOMINATIVE:	who	whoever
POSSESSIVE:	whose	whosever
OBJECTIVE:	whom	whomever

Sentences illustrating nouns and pronouns used as various sentence elements will help to distinguish among the three cases. (See pp. 282–300 for grammatical relationships among sentence elements.)

The NOMINATIVE CASE is a property of a noun or pronoun used as (1) the subject of a finite verb, (2) a subject complement, (3) a nominative of address, (4) a nominative absolute, or (5) an appositive to any of these.

The subject of a finite verb is always in the nominative case.

My *brother* is coming home.   *Who* is coming home?
He is coming home.   *You* and *she* should be here then.

The subject of an understood verb is in the nominative case.

> He drives faster than *she* [drives].
> You are not so pessimistic as *I* [am].

When a whole dependent clause is the object of a preposition, the subject of that clause is still in the nominative case.

He will vote for *whoever* favors thrift.

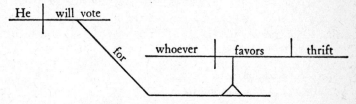

A noun or pronoun used as a subject complement is in the nominative case.[6]

> That was the *pilot*.   That was *he*.
> The only passengers were *she* and *I*.

When a whole dependent clause functions as the direct object of a verb, a subject complement in that clause is still in the nominative case.

I know *who* it was.

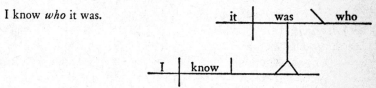

A nominative of address is in the nominative case.

Martha, please read the announcement.   *You*, the voters, have a duty.

A nominative absolute is in the nominative case.

The *storm* having ended, we continued driving.
Everyone in the audience having had an opportunity to ask questions, the speaker left the platform.

An appositive to a noun or pronoun in the nominative case is also in the nominative case.

Three cousins—*Pearl*, *Edith*, and *I*—planned the reunion.
The guests of honor will be the co-captains: *you* and *he*.

---

[6] In very informal conversation the use of the objective case (*me*, to a lesser degree *him*, but not *her*) as a subject complement is acceptable: "It is *me*" or "It is *him*." The speaker should keep in mind the audience whose approval he desires.

The POSSESSIVE CASE is a property of a noun or pronoun used to show ownership. (See pp. 256–257 and pp. 381–382 for discussions of the possessive forms of nouns.) A few of the indefinite pronouns have possessive forms similar to those of nouns (*one's, anyone's, another's, everyone's, anybody's,* the singular *other's,* the plural *others',* etc.), as do the reciprocals (*each other's, one another's*). The possessive forms of the personal pronouns and the pronoun *who* appear in the tables on page 260. It is important to remember that these possessive forms do not contain apostrophes; common errors are to confuse the possessive *its* with the contraction *it's* (*it is*) and the possessive *whose* with the contraction *who's* (*who is*).

WRONG: The program has lost *it's* appeal.
RIGHT: The program has lost *its* appeal.

WRONG: *Its* time for adjournment.
RIGHT (informal): *It's* time for adjournment.

WRONG: *Who's* plan was adopted?
RIGHT: *Whose* plan was adopted?

WRONG: *Whose* going to the convention?
RIGHT (informal): *Who's* going to the convention?

Several of the personal possessives (*my, our, your, her, his, its,* and *their*) are frequently called possessive adjectives, a logical designation since they act as modifiers (*my dog, your idea,* etc.). Certain illogical expressions which amount to double possessives, because they combine *of* and the possessive case of pronouns, have become established idioms in English (*a brother of mine, that idea of yours, this country of ours,* etc.).

On the formal level especially, the possessive case of pronouns (and less often nouns) is used before gerunds.

Many residents objected to the *city clerk's* ordering the removal of shade trees.

We enjoyed the *children's* singing and encouraged *their* practicing.

The OBJECTIVE CASE is the property of a noun [7] or pronoun used as (1) the direct object, retained object, or indirect object of a finite verb;

---

[7] Nouns in the objective case are used in two sentence elements where pronouns would be awkward: the object complement and the adverbial objective (adverbial noun).

We made him our *mascot.* (complement of direct object *him*)
We walked home. (adverbial noun, modifier of verb *walked*)

(2) the object of a preposition; (3) the subject of an infinitive, a subject complement following *to be* when *to be* has an expressed subject, and the object of any verbal; or (4) an appositive to any of these.

The direct object, retained object, or indirect object of a finite verb is in the objective case.

Do you remember *Janet Jones, whom* you knew in school? (direct objects of *do remember* and *knew*, respectively)

Janet now owns two *houses* (direct object)

She was given *them* by an uncle. (retained object)

He gave *her* the *houses* last year. (*her*, indirect object; *houses*, direct object)

The object of a preposition is in the objective case.

Whom should I talk to about the damages? [8]

I have a message for *him*.

A common error is the use of a pronoun in the nominative case as the last part of a compound object of a preposition.

WRONG: The children went to the concert with John, Mary, and *I*.
RIGHT: The children went to the concert with John, Mary, and *me*.

WRONG: Between you and *I*, the boss's plan is unrealistic.
RIGHT: Between you and *me*, the boss's plan is unrealistic.

The subject of an infinitive, a subject complement following *to be* when *to be* has an expressed subject,[9] and the object of any verbal are in the objective case.

I expected *him* to be early. (subject of infinitive *to be*)

At first I mistook *you* to be *him*. (*You*, subject of infinitive *to be*; *him*, subject complement following *to be* with an expressed subject.

I wanted *her* to introduce *him*. (*her*, subject of infinitive *to introduce*; *him*, object of infinitive *to introduce*)

---

[8] On the informal level, the nominative case *who* is sometimes acceptable as the object of a verb or a preposition when the pronoun is not adjacent to the verb or the preposition.

> *Who* do you know in Atlanta?
> *Who* should I talk to about the damages?

[9] When the infinitive *to be* has no expressed subject, the complement is in the nominative case on the formal level of expression but frequently in the objective case on the informal level.

> FORMAL: I should like to be *he*.
> INFORMAL: I should like to be *him*.

The lady accompanying *him* is his aunt. (object of participle *accompanying*)

I was surprised at his remembering *me*. (object of gerund *remembering*)

An appositive to a noun or pronoun in the objective case is also in the objective case.

He named three assistants: *you, John,* and *me*.
She called both of us—*Jane* and *me*—by telephone.

Modifiers. As their name implies, *modifiers* are words which limit or more exactly specify the meanings of other words. To "modify" is literally to make a mode or manner—to tell what manner of thing something is, or in what manner something happens. In grammar, the function of modifying covers a very wide range: from the minimal function of the indefinite article *a* in "a man's a man" to the radical effect of the negative *never* in "We shall never meet again." Both are modifiers.

There are two main classes of modifiers: adjectives and adverbs.

Adjectives. An *adjective* is the part of speech which modifies a substantive: *blue* sky, *good* idea, *no* luck; "he is *intelligent*." Grammatically, *a, an,* and *the* are adjectives; the first two are indefinite articles, the last one, a definite article. The sentence "Read a book; read an analysis" suggests any book and any analysis, whereas the sentence "Read the book; read the analysis" refers to definite materials.

DEGREES OF COMPARISON. Adjectives have three degrees: (1) positive, (2) comparative, and (3) superlative. When we wish merely to name a quality of a substantive, we use the POSITIVE degree: "Jane is *pretty*." Often we have occasion to distinguish between or among the degrees to which a particular adjective applies to two or more substantives: "Jane is *pretty,* but Ellen is *prettier;* of all the girls, Mary is *prettiest*." Most adjectives have forms to denote these distinctions. In comparing two persons or things, we employ the COMPARATIVE degree, normally formed by adding –*er* to the adjective; in comparing three or more, we use the SUPERLATIVE, normally formed by adding –*est.* Where the addition of these endings would be awkward, combinations with *more* and *most* are made instead: *beautiful, more beautiful, most beautiful; cautious, more cautious, most cautious.* In comparisons where diminishing degrees of a quality are indicated, we combine *less* and *least* with the adjective: *cautious, less cautious, least cautious.*

There is no definite rule stating when to use –*er* and –*est* and when to use *more* and *most* to form the comparative and superlative degrees.

Choosing the less awkward of these two methods is usually an adequate guide.[10] Combinations with *less* and *least* are appropriate regardless of the length of the word modified: *gay, less gay, least gay; preposterous, less preposterous, least preposterous.*

A few adjectives have irregular forms for comparison.

POSITIVE	COMPARATIVE	SUPERLATIVE
good	better	best
bad, ill	worse	worst
little (in amount)	less, lesser	least
many, much	more	most
far (in distance)	farther	farthest
far (in degree)	further	furthest

Strictly speaking, a few other adjectives, like *perfect* and *unique*, which do not logically admit degrees of comparison, have no such forms at all; but expressions like *nearly perfect, more nearly perfect,* and *most nearly perfect* are useful.

NUMBER. The demonstrative adjectives *this* and *that*, like the same words when they function as demonstrative pronouns, have separate forms for singular and plural. The adjective has the same number as the substantive which it modifies: *this* man, *these* men; *that* kind, *those* kinds.

Adverbs.[11] An *adverb* is the part of speech which modifies a verb, an adjective, or another adverb.

The ship sailed *smoothly*. (modifier of verb *sailed*)

Her motion was *very* smooth. (modifier of adjective *smooth*)

She sailed *almost too* smoothly. (*too*, modifier of adverb *smoothly*; *almost*, modifier of adverb *too*)

Many adverbs are formed by adding *–ly* to an adjective: *rapid*, adjective; *rapidly*, adverb. On the other hand, there are many adverbs which do not have the *–ly* form—like *very* and *too* in the examples above—and a number of adverbs are identical in form to the corresponding adjectives. The word *slow*, for instance, is correct as either adjective or adverb; the traffic signs which read "Go slow" are not ungrammatical. (*Slowly* is also correct as an adverb but not as an adjective.) Many

[10] Some grammarians say that all adjectives of one syllable and most adjectives of two syllables add *-er* and *-est* and that almost all adjectives of three or more syllables add *more* and *most* to form the comparative and superlative degrees.

[11] Adverbs in a special group, the conjunctive verbs, are discussed under "Connectives" (pp. 280–281), since they function not only as modifiers but also as connectives.

adjectives are formed by adding -*ly* to a noun (*leisurely, manly*) and in careful writing are distinguished from adverbs. When in doubt whether a particular word is proper as an adverb, the writer should consult a dictionary.

Adverbs tell such things as manner, place, time, and degree. Adverbs of MANNER indicate how something is done: "*How* does she sing?" or "She sings *well*." Adverbs of PLACE point out location or direction: "*Where* is the book?" or "The price went *down*." The idea of TIME is evident in adverbs like *now, then, soon, late*: "*When* did you notice the fire?" or "I noticed it *immediately*" or "We have to take the examination *now*." Common adverbs showing DEGREE are *almost, nearly, too, very*: "How *nearly* finished are you?" or "She types *very* fast" or "He was *almost* run over."

DEGREES OF COMPARISON. The degrees of comparison for adverbs are the same as for adjectives: (1) POSITIVE, (2) COMPARATIVE, and (3) SUPERLATIVE. As with adjectives, we often have occasion to distinguish between or among the degrees to which an adverb applies to two or more things: "The first ship sails *smoothly*, but the second sails *more smoothly*, and the third *most smoothly* of all." Most comparative and superlative degrees of adverbs are formed by combinations with *more* and *most* or *less* and *least*: *recently, more recently, most recently; hurriedly, less hurriedly, least hurriedly*. In some instances, where the result is not awkward, the endings *–er, –est* are used: *fast, faster, fastest; slow, slower, slowest; late, later, latest*. We may say that one ship sails *slow*, the second *slower*, and the third *slowest* of all.

ADJECTIVAL COMPLEMENTS AND ADVERBIAL MODI-FIERS. The distinction between *adjectival complements* and *adverbial modifiers* should be made at this point. Either of these two kinds of modifiers, in normal word order, may appear in a sentence immediately after the verb.

> The music sounds *beautiful*. (adjectival complement)
> She sang *beautifully*. (adverbial modifier)

The way to distinguish between them—to determine which kind is proper, in a particular context—is to apply as a criterion the different functions of adjectives and adverbs: adjectives modify substantives (nouns or pronouns), whereas adverbs modify verbs (or adjectives, or other adverbs). In the first example above, the modifier *beautiful* modifies the noun *music:* therefore it is an adjective, and the form *beautiful* is proper. In the second example, the modifier *beautifully* modifies the verb *sang;* therefore it is an adverb, and the adverbial form with *–ly* is proper.

In other words: when the modifier which follows the verb is an adverbial modifier, it normally modifies the verb itself; when the modifier is an adjectival complement, it modifies the subject of the verb. In the latter case, the verb is called a *linking* verb: [12] it links the subject with the complement which follows. Among the verbs which often perform this function of linking, some of the most common are the verb *to be* (as in "She was beautiful"), the verb *seem* ("He seems trustworthy"), and verbs of the five senses, as in the following examples:

SENSE	SUBJECT	LINKING VERB	ADJECTIVAL COMPLEMENT
sight:	The mountain	looks	high
hearing:	The motor	sounds	defective
smell:	The flower	smells	sweet
taste:	The pie	tastes	good
feeling:	The snow	feels	cold

Verbs and Verbals. A *verb* is a word the function of which is to denote action or being.

ACTION:	We *walk*.	Fish *are being caught*.
BEING:	You *will be* early.	Dinosaurs no longer *exist*.

A word which performs the full function of a verb is sometimes further characterized as a finite verb, in contradistinction to a verbal, which shares part of the function of a verb and also the function of some other part of speech.

Finite Verbs. A verb, we have said, denotes action or being. The function of a *true* or *finite verb* is to make a *predication;* that is, actually to affirm that the action or being occurs (or did occur, or will occur, or might occur), or to ask whether it occurs, or to direct that it shall occur. A finite verb is the essential element in making a statement, asking a question, expressing a wish or condition, or giving a command or request.

Finite verbs have different inflectional forms to indicate tense, voice, mood, person, and number. For some of these distinctions there are several different forms; for others there are only a few. Ordinarily all the inflectional forms can be constructed from the PRINCIPAL PARTS of the verb. These principal parts are, in the order found in the diction-

---

[12] Sometimes it is called a *copulative* verb; *copulative* is here synonymous with *linking*.

ary: (1) the INFINITIVE (for example, *like, sing*), (2) the PAST TENSE (*liked, sang*), (3) the PAST PARTICIPLE (*liked, sung*), and usually (4) the PRESENT PARTICIPLE (*liking, singing*).[13]

TENSE. Tense is the property of time, the property by which a verb denotes the time when events occur or conditions exist. There are six tenses: present, past, future, present perfect, past perfect, and future perfect. The names of the first three (the *simple* tenses) are largely self-explanatory. Even an explicit statement like "PRESENT TENSE denotes current being or action" admits variations, however; for words like *present* and *current* indicate a duration of time without specific limits. A statement in the present tense, "I *sing songs*," may mean "I *sing songs* from time to time" (not necessarily at the immediate moment), or it may mean "I sing songs regularly" (i.e., I am a professional singer).

The same statement in the PRESENT PROGRESSIVE FORM (made of the present participle of the principal verb and an auxiliary verb from *be*), "I am singing songs," points more definitely to the immediate context. Perhaps for this reason, the trend is toward more frequent use of the progressive forms (notice the progressive forms of the other tenses in the partial conjugation of the verb *ask* given below). The statement can occur also in the PRESENT EMPHATIC FORM (made of the infinitive form of the principal verb and the auxiliary *do*): "I do sing songs." (Only the present and the past tenses have emphatic forms of this kind.)

PAST TENSE denotes being or action finished at a past time that is not fused with the present. The sentence "I sang songs" expresses action that is definitely over; its effects are not lingering in the present.

FUTURE TENSE denotes being or action in the future; it speaks of action that has not yet started and says nothing of a time for completion: "I shall sing songs."

The three *perfect* tenses (made of the past participle form of the principal verb and auxiliary verbs from *have*) go beyond the simple tenses in showing relationships among points in time. The PRESENT PERFECT TENSE denotes being or action barely finished in the recent past and conceivably having effects that flow into the present. The statement "I have sung songs" (even more so, the progressive form, "I have been singing songs") suggests more recent action and more likelihood of its continuance than the past tense, "I sang songs" (or the past progressive, "I was singing songs"). A good test of the differ-

---

[13] Verbs like *like*, which form their past tense and past participle by adding *d* or *ed*, are called *weak* verbs; those like *sing*, which form these parts by a change in the stem, are called *strong* verbs.

ence between the present perfect tense and the past tense is the greater degree of solicitude we feel when a friend says, "I have been ill" than when he says "I was ill."

The PAST PERFECT TENSE denotes being or action finished at a time in the past before another time in the past. The sentence "I had sung songs" means that the action, compared to another past event, was over at a relatively remote time in the past. Perhaps I had sung songs as a child, even before I learned what the words really meant.

The FUTURE PERFECT TENSE denotes future being or action to be finished by a deadline in the future. The statement "I will have sung songs" indicates that my "singing" will be over when another event occurs; for instance, I will have sung certain songs before they are published.

A partial conjugation illustrates the tenses in this convenient table. Learn the auxiliary verb form.

Tense	Form
PRESENT:	I ask, *or* I am asking, *or* I do ask
PAST:	I asked, I was asking, I did ask
FUTURE:	I shall *or* will [14] ask, *or* be asking
PRESENT PERFECT:	I have asked, I have been asking
PAST PERFECT:	I had asked, I had been asking
FUTURE PERFECT:	I shall *or* will have asked, *or* have been asking

A few suggestions on *consistency in the use of tenses* and on the *proper use of sequence* are pertinent at this point. The general rule is that a unit of writing is most effective if it has no needless shifts in time to distract the reader. In most sentences the same tense is desirable in all clauses: "When he *was* [past] nineteen, he *went* [past] on a walking-tour of England." An indirect quotation follows this same pattern: "He *said* [past] that he *needed* [past] a storehouse of experience and observation." A direct quotation is logically in whatever tense the speaker has employed even when the verb that helps to introduce the quotation is in another tense: "He *said* [past], 'I *need* [present] a storehouse of experience and observation.'"

---

[14] In formal usage, the distinction between *shall* and *will* is still observed: For "simple futurity"—that is, simply to predict that something will happen—*shall* is used in the first person; *will,* in the second and third. To express determination on the part of the speaker, the forms are reversed: "Even if you try to dissuade me, I *will ask* him"; "Whether you want to or not, you *shall* ask him." This distinction is useful, but on levels lower than the formal it has largely disappeared. In speech the *shall-will* distinction is practically non-existent (unless the auxiliary is strongly stressed) because of the elision of *shall* and *will* to *'ll.*

The proper combinations of tenses to show sequence of events are (1) present with present perfect, (2) past with past perfect, and (3) future with future perfect.

When I *had defeated* (past perfect) my second opponent, I *was* (past) eligible for the semifinals.

Now that I *have lost* (present perfect) two successive nine-hole rounds to Hessemer, I *am* (present) no longer eligible to play in this year's tournament.

By next fall, when I *shall have had* (future perfect) considerably more practice, *I shall be* (future) in better condition to reach the finals.

There are two special kinds of present tense that may be used with other tenses when the subject matter warrants. The HISTORICAL PRESENT TENSE gives an aspect of immediacy to past events, especially in narrative accounts: "Shakespeare *uses* the witches to awaken Macbeth's dormant ambition, then quickly *brings* in new honors to give it impetus." The UNIVERSAL PRESENT TENSE is always appropriate for statements of general truth: "Water *consists* of hydrogen and oxygen."

A useful warning is that tenses may not always do what their names indicate. The simple present tense and the present progressive, for instance, when used with certain qualifying words, denote future time: "He *goes* into military service next month." "They *are sailing* in about three weeks." (See p. 242.)

VOICE. There are two *voices:* active and passive. A verb in the ACTIVE VOICE indicates that the subject performs the action of the verb; a verb in the PASSIVE VOICE, that the subject receives the action. (See pp. 222f.) The active forms of *ask* are on page 269; the passive in the six tenses, appear below. (Note that progressive forms occur only in the present and past tenses of the passive voice.)

Tense	Form
PRESENT:	I am asked, *or* I am being asked
PAST:	I was asked, I was being asked
FUTURE:	I shall *or* will be asked
PRESENT PERFECT:	I have been asked
PAST PERFECT:	I had been asked
FUTURE PERFECT:	I shall *or* will have been asked

Some verbs have no passive voice. These are verbs that cannot transmit action to the subject. Such verbs are called INTRANSITIVE in contradistinction to TRANSITIVE verbs, which do have passive forms. A few examples of intransitive verbs are *be, bloom, die, exist, seem.*

MOOD. The word *mood* as applied to verbs is in a sense figurative: it means something like what the word means when we say, "He was in a good mood." Figuratively, "mood" is the spirit or feeling of a verb; literally, it is "the manner in which the predication is conceived."

On the formal level, English has three moods: indicative, imperative, and subjunctive. (On other levels of usage, the subjunctive is seldom used.)

In the INDICATIVE MOOD a verb makes a statement or asks a question.

She *sang* three songs.   *Is* it *raining?*

In the IMPERATIVE MOOD a verb gives a command or makes a request.

Report to headquarters immediately. Please *close* the window.

In the SUBJUNCTIVE MOOD a verb expresses (1) a highly speculative wish, (2) a supposition, (3) a condition contrary to fact, (4) a concession, (5) a state of desirability or necessity (6) a request or demand, (7) a condition of possibility following *as if* or *as though,* (8) a condition of unlikelihood or improbability following *even if* or *even though,* (9) a condition contrary to the author's belief, (10) an idiomatic supplication, (11) an emphatic order or command, or (12) a formal resolution.

WISH: I wish I *were* in London.
SUPPOSITION: Suppose she *were* married already!
CONDITION CONTRARY TO FACT: If she *were* a young man, she would qualify for the job.
CONCESSION: *Be* that as it may, I shall read the book.
STATE OF NECESSITY: It is necessary that she *take* her medicine.
REQUEST: I request that he *explain* his action.
CONDITION OF POSSIBILITY: The dog trembled as if he *were* having a convulsion.
CONDITION OF IMPROBABILITY: Even if it *be* the last thing I do, I will solve this mystery.
CONDITION CONTRARY TO AUTHOR'S BELIEF (italics added):
          If this *be* error and upon me proved,
          I never writ, nor no man ever loved.—SHAKESPEARE
IDIOMATIC SUPPLICATION: Heaven *help* us.
EMPHATIC ORDER: The judge ordered that the defendant *do pay* the fine he was contesting and that he *do* not *appear* in traffic court again on penalty of a double fine.
FORMAL RESOLUTION: *Be* it *resolved* that any member delinquent in dues *forfeit* his right to vote or hold office.

No separate illustration of indicative forms is given here, since all the examples of inflectional forms given in this discussion of verbs, except where explicitly labeled otherwise, are indicative.

The usual imperative form is identical with the infinitive, the first principal part of the verb: *come* here; *be* yourself.[15]

The relatively few distinctive forms of the subjunctive occur in certain noticeable places. The third-person-singular form in the subjunctive is identical with the first- and second-person forms, whereas the third-person-singular in the indicative differs from the first- and second-person forms.[16]

INDICATIVE	SUBJUNCTIVE
I ask	I ask
You ask	You ask
He *asks*	He *ask*
I have asked	I have asked
You have asked	You have asked
He *has* asked	He *have* asked

Past indicative plural forms are used as present subjunctive forms with singular subjects in wishes and contrary-to-fact suppositions. (Notice the use of *were* in several of the illustrations on p. 271 and the italicized verbs here: "If he *knew* the truth, he would fret." "If we *worked* a few more hours we could finish the job.")

Another place where distinctive forms of the subjunctive appear is in the passive voice, which is formed with *to be*. Since the only present subjunctive form of this verb is simply *be*, the present passive subjunctive of all transitive verbs includes *be*.

INDICATIVE	SUBJUNCTIVE
I *am* asked	I *be* asked
You *are* asked	You *be* asked
He *is* asked	He *be* asked
We *are* asked	We *be* asked
You *are* asked	You *be* asked
They *are* asked	They *be* asked

Similarly, since the only past subjunctive form of the verb *to be* is *were*, the past passive subjunctive of all transitive verbs includes *were*. Thus,

[15] A perfect tense of the imperative may be formed with *have* and the past participle: "Have finished this work by tomorrow morning." This form is rather rarely used, however. The sense of it would ordinarily be expressed in a different kind of construction: for example, "Have this work finished by tomorrow morning."

[16] See the discussion below of inflectional forms to indicate person or number.

where the indicative includes *was* (in the first and third person singular), the subjunctive form is different.

INDICATIVE	SUBJUNCTIVE
I *was* asked, he *was* asked	I *were* asked, he *were* asked

PERSON AND NUMBER. All verbs are used in the first, second, and third persons in both the indicative and subjunctive moods. Verbs in the imperative mood are always in the second person; the subject is *you,* either explicitly expressed or, more often, understood: "You come with me, please," or simply "Come with me." In all three moods, all verbs are used in both the singular and the plural.

A verb must agree in *person* and *number* with its subject. (See also pp. 282–284.) There are relatively few distinctive inflectional forms, however, for person and number. These few occur chiefly in two places.[17] Ordinarily in the present active indicative a single form is common, except in the third person singular, where *s* or sometimes *es* is added.[18]

I
You
We   } *ask, do*   He
You   She   } *asks, does* [19]
They   It

Since the present passive and the past passive indicatives are formed by combination with parts of the verb *to be,* the passive has distinctive forms for person and number wherever the verb *to be* itself has them.

Present Passive		**Past Passive**	
SINGULAR	PLURAL	SINGULAR	PLURAL
I *am* asked	We *are* asked	I *was* asked	We *were* asked
You *are* asked	You *are* asked	You *were* asked	You *were* asked
He *is* asked	They *are* asked	He *was* asked	They *were* asked

Modal Auxiliaries. The *modal auxiliaries* are a special group of verbs (*may, might, can, could, shall, should, will, would, must, ought,* and

[17] Three, if we include the distinction for person between *shall* and *will* in the future and future perfect tenses; but see p. 269 fn.

[18] In earlier English there was a special form for the second person singular: I like, thou *likest.* This form and the corresponding form with *-eth* for the third person singular (he *liketh*) are now virtually obsolete except in special contexts.

[19] The corresponding third-person-singular form of the verb *have* (*has*) produces a parallel distinction in the present perfect tense, which is formed with *have* as an auxiliary.

sometimes *need* and *dare*) whose function is to assist other verbs: "I *may* go to Canada." "Ted *would* like to go." "He *must* stay here." Sometimes called "defective" verbs, the modal auxiliaries differ from regular verbs in three important ways: (1) Since they cannot perform the full function of stating, asking, or commanding, they never appear without a principal verb (expressed or implied): "*Can* the baby *walk?*" "He *can* [*walk*]." (2) They do not add *s* in the third person singular as regular verbs do; and they influence regular third person singular verbs that appear with them to drop the *s* (compare "He *can walk*" with "He *walks,*" or "He *must stay*" with "He *stays*"). (3) The modal auxiliaries have no participial forms and therefore cannot occur in progressive constructions or in the passive voice (for instance, since *could* does not add *–ing* and *–ed* endings, it cannot be substituted for *ask* in the progressive "I am asking" or in the passive "I am asked.").

Two of the words that ordinarily are modal auxiliaries, *can* and *will,* are sometimes regular verbs: "She *is canning* fruit." "He *willed* his estate to his children." Two other words, *need* and *dare,* are often regular verbs ("She *needs* work" or "He *is daring* me to a race") but sometimes modal auxiliaries ("She *need* not *walk* in the rain" or "He *dare* not *go* home now").

Distinctions among certain modal auxiliaries are appropriate in formal usage. In general, *should* and *would* follow the same pattern as *shall* and *will* (see fn. 14 in this chapter): "I *should* like to travel; so *would* you; so *would* he." Exceptions are that *should* appears with all persons in expressions of obligation ("I *should* keep promises; so *should* you; and so *should* he") or condition ("if I *should* happen to forget, or if you *should,* or he *should,* our plan will fail") and that *would* appears with all persons in expressions of customary action in the past: "I remember how I *would* build the campfire, you *would* cook the food, and then Jim *would* arrive." *Can* indicates ability; *may,* permission or possibility: "You *can* do the work if you try." "You *may* borrow my book, but you *may* want one of your own." *Could* and *might,* although they are past tense forms of *can* and *may,* usually refer to present or future action or state of being and show a more reserved attitude by the speaker or writer than *can* or *may:* "You *could* do the work if you tried." "You *might* want a book of your own."

Verbals: Inflected for Voice and for Tense. A *verbal* is a word which shares part of the function of a verb and also the function of another part of speech. A verbal shares with a verb the function of denoting action or being. Unlike a finite verb, however, a verbal does *not* make a predication. A verbal cannot by itself perform the full function of a finite verb in making a statement, asking a question, expressing a wish or condition, or giving a command or request.

In addition, a verbal shares the function of a substantive or a modifier. One kind of verbal, the infinitive, can share the function of either of these. The other two kinds, the gerund and the participle, are distinguished specifically on the basis of whether the other part of speech whose function they share is a substantive or a modifier: gerunds share that of a substantive, and participles that of a modifier.

Verbals have inflectional forms for active and passive voice, and for present and past tense. (In form, the past tense of verbals corresponds to the present perfect tense of finite verbs: it employs a part of the verb *to have*.) The tense-forms of a verbal represent time only *in relation to* the time indicated by the tense of the finite verb with which the verbal is associated. The past-tense form of a verbal represents time *before* that of the finite verb; the present-tense form represents time *the same* as that of the finite verb, or sometimes *after* that of the finite verb. Notice the time relationship in these examples (the verbals are printed in small capitals; the finite verbs in italics).

HAVING KNOWN him *is* an experience which I value. (past tense of verbal, representing time before that of the finite verb)

COMING up the walk, she *smiled* at me. (present tense of verbal, representing time the same as that of the finite verb)

He *hopes* TO GET a job this summer. (present tense of a verbal, representing time after that of the finite verb)

GERUNDS. A *gerund* shares the functions of a verb and a substantive. It stands for something by naming it; thus it functions as a noun. The thing which it names or denotes is action or being; thus it functions as a verb.

He earns extra money by *writing*.

Here the gerund *writing* names something, as a noun does. We could replace the gerund with a noun and make virtually the same statement.

He earns money by *authorship*.

The thing which the gerund *writing* names or denotes is the action or activity of writing. In its verb function the gerund can do some other things that verbs do; for example, it can take an object.

He earns extra money by writing *books*.

Note also that a gerund may be modified, like a noun, by an adjective; or, like a verb, by an adverb.

Good writing makes *easy* reading. (adjectives)
Writing *well* requires much practice. (adverb)

Gerunds are characterized by the ending *–ing*. In the present active gerund, this ending is added to the main word; in the other three forms, it is attached to one of the other words that enter into the combination.

PRESENT ACTIVE: *writing*   PAST ACTIVE: *having written*
PRESENT PASSIVE: *being written*   PAST PASSIVE: *having been written*

PARTICIPLES. A *participle* shares the functions of a verb and a modifier. It modifies a substantive; thus it functions as an adjective. It modifies by describing the substantive as performing or receiving action, or existing in a state of being; thus it functions as a verb.

The *beating* waves dashed against the rocks.

The participle *beating* describes the waves as performing the action of beating. A participle, like a verb or a gerund, can take an object.

The waves, beating the *boat* against the pier, threatened to cause serious damage.

Like both verbs and adjectives, whose function it shares, a participle can be modified by an adverb.

The waves, beating *fiercely,* made a rhythmic roar.

The *–ing* ending, characteristic of gerunds, appears in participles too, but not in all participles: in the passive forms the words *being* and *having been* are often omitted.

PRESENT ACTIVE: *beating*   PAST ACTIVE: *having beaten*
PRESENT PASSIVE: *being beaten*   PAST PASSIVE: *beaten* or *having*
   or simply *beaten*   *been beaten*

The form *beaten,* which is actually the past (passive) participle, may serve as either past or present passive. The context will normally make clear which tense is to be understood.

PAST: The ship, [having been] beaten by storms, finally arrived in port.
PRESENT: The ship, still [being] beaten by storms, slowly made her way around the Horn.

Note that when the participle is placed before the substantive which it modifies, the form used is always the simple one, without either *being* or *having been:* "Mix well, and add three *beaten* eggs."

INFINITIVES. An *infinitive* shares the functions of a verb and either a substantive or a modifier; the modifier may be either adjective or adverb. Thus the infinitive is the most versatile of the verbals in function. In each case it shares the function of a verb by denoting action or being.

INFINITIVE AS SUBSTANTIVE: They do not want *to leave.* (direct object of the verb *want*)

INFINITIVE AS ADJECTIVE: We found a way *to leave* without breaking up the party. (modifying the noun *way*)

INFINITIVE AS ADVERB: Our summer home was very hard *to leave.* (modifying the adjective *hard*)

An infinitive too can take an object, as in an altered version of the last example.

It was hard for us to leave our summer *home.*

An infinitive may be modified by an adverb.

It was hard for us to leave so *soon.*

Even though it may function as a substantive, an infinitive cannot be modified by an adjective.

The characteristic sign of the infinitive is the word *to.* The regular inflectional forms are listed here.

PRESENT ACTIVE: *to like*	PAST ACTIVE: *to have liked*
PRESENT PASSIVE: *to be liked*	PAST PASSIVE: *to have been liked*

In some uses, however, the infinitive appears without the *to.* The italicized words in these examples are infinitives.

Have you heard her *sing?*
What you should do is *see* him immediately.
I saw the parade *go* down Pennsylvania Avenue.
Agnes helped him *learn* the fundamentals of genetics.

Also, the first principal part of a verb, although it is the infinitive, is normally given without the *to:* simply *like, liked,* etc. (See examples of principal parts of verbs on p. 268; also see dictionary listing of principal parts of other verbs.)

Connectives. *Connectives,* as the name implies, are words whose function is to connect or join together words or sentence elements.

There are two major kinds of connectives: prepositions and conjunctions. In addition, the words usually called conjunctive adverbs perform the function of connectives and at the same time retain their adverbial properties too.

Prepositions. A *preposition* connects a substantive (or substantives) to another word or sentence element. The preposition and the substantive—which may have modifiers of its own, and which is called the object of the preposition—together form a modifying unit (see "Prepositional Phrase," pp. 294–295). The modified element may be a verb ("*walked* into the house"), a verbal ("a house *surrounded* by trees"), a noun ("the *house* on the hill"), or an adjective ("*impressive* in appearance").

Many common prepositions indicate direction or position, and yet each has its own meaning. If we imagine a dog going *into* a doghouse, *around* a doghouse, and *over* a doghouse, we get three different mental pictures. We can get other pictures of motion by substituting prepositions like *from, to, beyond, under,* and *through.* And we can see a variety of still scenes by imagining the dog lying *in, near, beside, on, behind,* and *in front of* the doghouse.

Several word groups regularly function as single prepositions: *according to* the report, *because of* the weather, *instead of* waiting, *in view of* circumstances, etc. Repeated use of such compound prepositions produces a cumbersome style: "an application *for* a job" is better than "an application *in regard to* a job"; "action *by* the manager" is better than "action *on the part of* the manager."

Conjunctions. *Conjunctions* are a more general and versatile kind of connective than prepositions: their function is to join together or connect words or sentence-elements which may have several different grammatical constructions. Sometimes the combination of a conjunction with one of the two elements which it joins produces a modifier; sometimes it does not.

Conjunctions may be divided into two classes: co-ordinating and subordinating conjunctions.

CO–ORDINATING CONJUNCTIONS. A *co-ordinating conjunction* connects two words or sentence elements of equal grammatical status. If two single words are joined by a co-ordinating conjunction, both represent the same part of speech; if two groups of words are joined, both are phrases, or both clauses. (See the discussion of grammatical units, pp. 293–301.) The chief co-ordinating conjunctions are *and, but, or, nor,* and *for.* Here are examples of co-ordinating conjunctions joining various elements.

JOINING SUBSTANTIVES: man *and* boy; John *and* he
JOINING MODIFIERS: cloudy *but* hot (adjectives); quickly *and* efficiently (adverbs)
JOINING VERBS: go *or* stay
JOINING PREPOSITIONS: above *and* beyond the call of duty
JOINING PHRASES: on the rug *or* on the floor
JOINING CLAUSES: I spoke up, *for* I knew the answer; they did not agree with me, *nor* did you.

A special group of co-ordinating conjunctions is that of the CORRELATIVE CONJUNCTIONS: *either . . . or, neither . . . nor, both . . . and,* and *not only . . . but also.* They almost always appear in these pairs. In formal usage, as with all co-ordinating conjunctions, the two elements which correlative conjunctions join must have the same or equal grammatical status or construction. In the first example each member of the correlative pair is followed by both a verb and an adverb.

You may *either* go now *or* go later.

In the next version each member is followed by an adverb only.[20]

You may go *either* now *or* later.

Similarly, each member may be followed by a verb and its object.

I *not only* like him *but also* like his brother.

Or, preferably, each member may be followed by the object only.

I like *not only* him *but also* his brother.

SUBORDINATING CONJUNCTIONS. Subordinating conjunctions are relatively specialized in function: at least one of the two elements which they join is always a dependent or subordinate clause, and the other is ordinarily an independent or main clause. (See "Grammatical Units," pp. 293–301.) In the example below, the subordinating conjunction *when* connects the independent clause "He will send for you" and the dependent clause "when he needs you." (The subordinating conjunction is considered a part of the dependent clause which it introduces.)

He will send for you *when* he needs you.

If, as often happens, the sequence of the clauses is reversed, the function of the subordinating conjunction is still to connect the two clauses.

---

[20] Actually, the latter version is preferable, for the conjunctions are placed, logically, immediately before the words to which they really apply. The latter version is also shorter.

When he needs you, he will send for you.

A subordinating conjunction may also connect two clauses which are both dependent.

Although he faltered *as* he walked, he reached his goal.

Here the subordinating conjunction *as* connects the dependent clause "as he walked" and the dependent clause "Although he faltered." The subordinating conjunction *although,* in turn, connects to the independent clause "he reached his goal" the whole group of words "Although he faltered as he walked." This group of words is in one sense a single dependent clause, even though it contains within itself the dependent clause "as he walked" as an internal modifier.

This list includes many of the common subordinating conjunctions and their special meanings. (See dependent clauses and their functions, pp. 289–290 and 298–300.)

CONDITION: *if, unless, provided that* [21]
MANNER: *as, as if, as though*
CAUSE OR REASON: *because, since, inasmuch as*
RESULT: *so that*
PURPOSE: *so that, in order that, lest*
CONCESSION: *though, although, even though, even if*
COMPARISON OR DEGREE: *than, as . . . as, so . . . as*
CONTRAST: *whereas*
TIME: *after, before, as, when, whenever, while, since, until*
PLACE: *where, wherever*

Conjunctive Adverbs. *Conjunctive adverbs,* as their name implies, function both as conjunctions and as adverbs; that is, they join two elements together, and they act as adverbial modifiers. They perform these two functions simultaneously.

The two elements joined by a conjunctive adverb are usually independent clauses; the adverbial function of the conjunctive adverb is to modify the verb in the second clause. Consider this example.

The firm was losing money; *therefore* the manager decided that expansion was impossible.

[21] Like certain prepositions, certain subordinating conjunctions are compound; that is, they consist of more than one word. Another, more confusing similarity is that certain words may be prepositions at one time, conjunctions at another; the difference is in the things they introduce or connect. (See punctuation before *for,* pp. 360–361.)

He left *before* dawn. (preposition)
He left *before* I was awake. (subordinating conjunction)

The conjunctive adverb *therefore* joins the two independent clauses "The firm was losing money" and "the manager decided that expansion was impossible"; at the same time, it modifies the verb *decided*.

Even if its position is within one of the clauses (in modern writing the preferable position) rather than actually between them, a conjunctive adverb still has the function of joining them.

The firm was losing money; the manager decided, therefore, that expansion was impossible. (Here *therefore* has the same two functions as described above.)

Among the most common conjunctive adverbs,[22] in addition to *therefore*, are *however, consequently, furthermore, likewise, moreover, nevertheless, otherwise,* and *accordingly*. (For the most part, these words have a formal quality and sound stilted in an informal or conversational context: "I was tired; *nevertheless,* I cleaned up the basement. *Moreover,* I gave the dog a bath.")

Interjections. An *interjection* is a word which is grammatically unrelated to the rest of the sentence in which it appears, and which has the function of expressing attitude or feeling. The same interjection (for example, the word *oh*) may express feeling either strong or mild, according to the context. Someone who has been injured might exclaim, "Oh! I am hurt!" On the other hand, someone who is asked a question and does not have an immediate answer might say, "Oh, I don't know." This latter person might go on, using as interjections the words which are here italicized, "*Now,* let me see. *Well,* there is one answer that I can give you. . . ." The interjection *alas* is more spe-

---

[22] Note that the term used here is *conjunctive adverbs,* not *adverbial conjunctions.* The term *conjunctive adverbs* indicates that as parts of speech the words are *adverbs,* not conjunctions (*adverbial conjunctions* is an appropriate designation for conjunctions like *when, if,* and *until,* which introduce adverbial clauses). The words that are here called conjunctive adverbs (*therefore, however,* etc.) are sometimes called *transitional expressions.* Both classifications are logical; the latter is simply broader (it does not specify a part of speech and it includes phrases like *on the other hand, in addition, in the second place*). The important point is that words like *therefore* and *however* are not really conjunctions and that when they connect independent clauses the clauses must be separated by a semicolon. Notice the punctuation in these examples. (See p. 234 and p. 369.)

CORRECT: The firm was losing money; the manager was worried.

CORRECT: The firm was losing money; therefore the manager was worried.

WRONG (comma fault): The firm was losing money, therefore the manager was worried.

CORRECT (because real conjunction *and* is present): The firm was losing money, and therefore the manager was worried.

cifically expressive of strong feeling—a feeling of grief—but this word is now almost exclusively "literary"; one almost never hears it actually said.

In common usage, interjections are sometimes not words in the strict sense at all, but rather simply exclamations that we make under particular circumstances: *whew, humph,* etc. Some interjections are essentially slang, but are widely used in actual speech: *gee, gosh, shucks.* Also, phrases of two or three words often function as single interjections: *good heavens! goodness gracious! upon my word!*

GRAMMATICAL RELATIONSHIPS

Words and groups of words are interrelated as parts of sentences. A complete sentence has a subject (expressed or understood) and a predicate, the latter always containing a finite verb. In addition to the verb, a predicate may include a subject complement, a direct object, a combination of direct and indirect objects, or a combination of direct object and object complement. The sentence may also contain a variety of modifiers, connectives, appositives, and absolute expressions.[23] Used with discretion, these optional elements provide not only agreeable variations in sentence structure but also logical positions for the ideas according to their relative importance.

Subject and Predicate. The two required parts of a sentence, the *subject* and the *predicate,* are irrevocably related in that the subject names a topic and the verb in the predicate says something about (or to) that topic. This naming-saying relationship may take the form of an assertion, a question, a command, or an exclamation. (See pp. 205–207.) Expressing the relationship may require few or many words. The one verb *Wait* (with the understood subject *you*) is a sentence: the single verb performs the entire task of predication, that is, commands the person represented by *you* to follow a certain course. In the sentence "Many ballads and plays have been lost through the years," the verb *have been lost* (see "Verb Phrase," p. 297) affirms a fact about an indefinite number of two kinds of things named in a compound subject, *ballads and plays,* which has a modifier, *Many.* The verb also has a modifier, *through the years,* but the modifier does not do any affirming. (A verb that performs the entire task of predication is either an intransitive verb, as *Wait* is, or a transitive passive verb, as *have been lost* is. See p. 270.)

---

[23] The absolute expression is mentioned as an optional sentence element but is not discussed in this section because it has no specific grammatical relation to any other sentence element (see p. 297).

An important requirement in the relationship between subject and verb is that they agree in number and person.[24] Here are rules and illustrations covering points that are frequently troublesome.

Two or more co-ordinate subjects joined by *and* usually take a plural verb. An exception is that a singular verb is correct if the co-ordinates combine in meaning to make one thing.

The ballad and the play [two things] *have* been lost.
Bread and water [one diet] *does* not satisfy the appetite.

A subject composed of singular co-ordinates joined by *or* or by *either . . . or* or *neither . . . nor* takes a singular verb.

John, Bob, or Bill [one person] *is* responsible.
Either a higher tax rate or a special assessment [one measure] *is* almost certain.

If in a sentence similar to the last example one co-ordinate is singular and the other is plural, the verb agrees with the nearer one.

Either a higher tax rate or special assessments *are* almost certain. (*Are* agrees with *assessments*.)

Modifiers or other words that appear between the subject and the verb have no bearing on the number of the subject and the verb.

The glow of multi-colored woods and fields *gives* testimony to autumn's warmth. (*Gives* agrees with *glow*.)
The papers I kept in a box on the bookshelf *are* missing. (*Are* agrees with *papers*.)

Except for the few that are sometimes singular and sometimes plural, the indefinite pronouns require verbs that agree with the convention-ally accepted number of the individual pronouns. (See p. 258 for a list that shows distinctions in number.) The indefinites that can be either singular or plural take their number from a qualifying term, usually the object of a preposition in a phrase that modifies the pronoun.

Some of the music *was* delightful. (*Some* is construed as singular because *music* is singular.)
Some of the children *were* noisy. (*Some* is construed as plural because *children* is plural.)

A relative pronoun takes its number from its antecedent.

[24] See pp. 269, 273–274 for choice of person with modal auxiliaries and pp. 255–256 for choice of number with collective nouns.

My dog is one of those nondescript mongrels who *make* exceedingly good pets. (The antecedent of *who* is the plural *mongrels*.)

"Snowball" is the only one, of the several pets we have had, that *has* seemed able to avoid violent mishap. (The antecedent of *that* is *one*.)

The number of the subject complement (see below) has no bearing on the agreement between subject and verb.

The annoying part of the experience *is* the interruptions. (*Is* agrees with *part*.)

The interruptions *are* the annoying part of the experience. (*Are* agrees with *interruptions*.)

The expletive *there* cannot name a topic; it is merely an introductory word, never a subject. In sentences that begin with the expletive *there*, the subject follows the verb.

There *are* several reasons for the change. (*Are* agrees with *reasons*.)

There *is* a robin or two pigeons on the fence almost every morning. (*Is* agrees with the nearer co-ordinate, *robin*.

Subject, Verb, and Subject Complement. The predicate of a sentence may consist of the verb and a subject complement.[25] Here the interrelationship is that the *subject complement,* which is a substantive or an adjective, renames or describes the subject, and the verb links those two elements. (See linking verbs, p. 267.) The word *complement,* from the Latin *complementum,* means "that which fills up or completes"; the subject complement "fills up or completes" the predication that the linking verb initiates. Without the complements, the first two examples below would be identical; with the complements to "fill up" the affirmation about the subject, the sentences say different things.

The flowers are *violets*. (The predicate noun *violets* renames the subject *flowers*. The intransitive verb *are* links the complement and the subject.)

The flowers are *blue*. (The predicate adjective *blue* describes the subject *flowers* by pointing out an attribute. The intransitive verb *are* links the attribute to the subject.)

---

[25] *Subject complement* is a general term. More specifically, this construction is called a *predicate nominative* (if it is a noun or pronoun); even more specifically, it is called a *predicate noun* (if it is a noun), a *predicate pronoun* (if a pronoun), or a *predicate adjective* (if an adjective).

He is a *realist*. (predicate noun)

The lucky person could be *you*. (predicate pronoun)

She seemed *unhappy*. (predicate adjective)

The culprit was *she*. (The predicate pronoun *she* renames the subject *culprit*. The intransitive verb *was* links the subject and its complement. See case of pronouns, pp. 260–264.)

Subject, Verb, and Direct Object. A predicate may consist of the verb and a direct object. When a direct object is present, the interrelationship of grammatical units is this: the *direct object,* which is a substantive, completes the meaning of the verb and names the receiver of the action performed by the subject and expressed through the verb. (In such a sentence the verb is transitive active. See p. 270.) Here are examples to clarify the relationships.

Jerry hit *Bill*. (The direct object *Bill* names the person who received the blow that the person named in the subject *Jerry* gave. The transitive active verb *hit* expresses the action that goes across from subject to object, that is, from actor to receiver.)

He is building a *birdhouse*. (The direct object *birdhouse* names the thing that is being acted upon by the person named in the subject *He*. The transitive active verb *is building* tells that the action is in process—see progressive form of present tense, p. 268—and is going across from subject to object.)

In determining the interrelationship of subject, verb, and direct object it is helpful to read the subject and verb and then ask the question "What?" or "Whom?" The direct object answers the question. In the illustrations above, *Bill* answers the question "Jerry hit whom?" and *birdhouse* answers the question "He is building what?"

Subject, Verb, Direct Object, and Indirect Object. Occasionally a predicate that includes a direct object includes also an indirect object. If so, the interrelationship of grammatical elements consists in that the *indirect object,* which is another substantive, helps the direct object complete the meaning of the verb and tells *to whom* or *for whom* or *to what* or *for what* the subject performs the action of the verb. (Here again, the verb is transitive active, indicating that the action is transmitted from subject to direct object and then on *to* indirect object.)

The news gave *him hope*. (The indirect object *him* indicates the person to whom the subject *news* brought the emotion named in the direct object *hope*. The transitive active verb *gave* tells what the action was and the direction in which it went.)

The secretary sent each *member* a notice. (The indirect object *member* names the person to whom the person named in the subject *secretary* transmitted the thing named in the object *notice*. The transitive active verb tells that the action was one of sending and that it went across from the agent to the thing acted on, the notice, so that that thing could get *to* the member.)

In checking the relationships in these two examples, we can use this question-and-answer sequence: "The news gave what?" *Hope.* "The news gave hope to whom?" *To him.* "The secretary sent what?" *A notice.* "The secretary sent a notice to whom?" *Each member.* As this procedure suggests, the indirect object is somewhat like the object of a preposition not expressed in the sentence.

Subject, Verb, Direct Object, and Object Complement. Occasionally, too, a predicate that includes a direct object includes also an object complement, which, like the subject complement, can be a substantive or an adjective. When an *object complement* is present, the grammatical relationship is that the object complement assists the direct object in completing the meaning of the verb, renames or describes the direct object, and indicates the result of the action that has been performed by the subject, expressed through the verb, and received by the direct object. In the sentence "We named John captain," the object complement *captain* tells what John has become as a result of the action; he is still John, but he is also a captain now. If the object complement is an adjective, it names a new attribute that the direct object has acquired as the result of the action. When Jack Spratt and his wife had "licked the platter clean," they still had the same platter, but it had the new attribute of cleanness.

The paint made the room *attractive.* (The object complement, the adjective *attractive,* mentions the effect the paint had on the room; that is, it names the new attribute the object has acquired as a result of the action by the subject through the verb.)

The chairman appointed Mr. Jenkins *parliamentarian.* (The object complement, the noun *parliamentarian,* renames Mr. Jenkins in his new capacity now that the action of appointing has been done by the chairman.)

(As in any other sentence that has a direct object, the verb here is transitive active.)

Object complements most commonly follow verbs like *call, choose, name, elect, appoint, make,* and *find.* It is possible to insert the words *to be* between the direct object and its complement without distorting the meaning of the sentence: "The paint made the room [to be] attractive." "The chairman appointed Mr. Jenkins [to be] parliamentarian."

Modifier and the Thing Modified. The effect of a *modifier,* which may be a word, a phrase, or a dependent clause, is to qualify or limit that grammatical element of the sentence to which it is related. Regardless of its length, each modifier functions as a single part of speech: an adjective or an adverb.

Words as Modifiers. The *one-word modifier* is ordinarily an adjective, which modifies a substantive; a participle, which also modifies a substantive; or an adverb, which modifies a verb, an adjective, or another adverb. Sometimes a general statement can be made specific by the inclusion of a few informative one-word modifiers. In the first of the pair of sentences below, certain one-word modifiers employed by the original author have been purposely omitted; without them the precise image intended by the author can hardly be experienced by the reader.

He complied of course, and stood shading his face in the sunlight of the window, looking as if he had been summoned from the grave.

He complied of course, and stood shading his *haggard* face in the *unwonted* sunlight of the *great* window, looking as *wan* and *unearthly* as if he had been summoned from the grave.—DICKENS (italics added)

With the author's modifiers restored, the sunlight, the window, and the character's face take specific form and the whole image becomes clear.

Phrases as Modifiers. The phrase, a group of words which contain no subject-predicate relationship but which are related in another sense, is similar in effect to the one-word modifier but has the advantage of greater length. *Phrasal modifiers* are of two chief kinds: prepositional phrases and verbal phrases.

A PREPOSITIONAL PHRASE (see pp. 294–295) has the effect of a single adjective (if the thing modified is a substantive) or a single adverb (if the thing modified is a verb, an adjective, or an adverb). The prepositional phrase enriches the meaning of the element it modifies by supplying a bit of specific information. In the first of these two sentences, the prepositional phrases included by the author have been purposely omitted; the result is a more general, less meaningful statement than the original.

I have called the perfection or virtue philosophy, philosophical knowledge, enlargement, or illumination; terms which are not commonly given.

In default of a recognized term, I have called the perfection or virtue *of the intellect* . . . philosophy, philosophical knowledge, enlargement *of mind,* or illumination; terms which are not commonly given *to it by writers of this day.*—NEWMAN (italics added)

There are three kinds of VERBAL PHRASES (see pp. 295–296); only one kind, the participial phrase, is always a modifier, and one other, the infinitive phrase, is sometimes a modifier. The *participial phrase,* which modifies a substantive, has an effect similar to that of an adjective or an adjectival prepositional phrase; but because it has certain properties of a verb, the participial phrase is somewhat more flexible than these other modifiers. Compare the effect of the modifiers in these three sentences.

The portrait *covered with dust* is a family heirloom. (participial phrase)
The portrait *with dust on it* is a family heirloom. (prepositional phrase)
The *dusty* portrait is a family heirloom. (adjective)

The writers of these other examples used participial phrases in typical ways to add specific meaning to their sentences.

Having played her violin in her senior recital, the girl was one step nearer to a degree in music. (Without the participial phrase the reader would know less about the girl and would not know at all how she had gone the "step nearer to a degree.")

The author, *being a realist,* gave his characters a mixture of good and bad traits. (Here the participial phrase supplies information about the author that the reader might have surmised but could not have been positive of from the rest of the sentence.)

Its flexibility as a modifier makes the participial phrase very useful. If not handled carefully, however, it can easily become a dangling modifier (see pp. 236–240).

The *infinitive phrase,* when it is a modifier, can function as either an adjective or an adverb. The infinitive phrase that modifies a substantive assists in describing or identifying or limiting the substantive. In the sentence "Here is the money *to spend on household needs,* and here is the money *to put in the bank,*" the two infinitive phrases describe in such a way as to make a distinction between the things they modify. Here are other examples showing infinitive phrases qualifying substantives.

We could not find a hotel *to stay in for even one night.* (The infinitive phrase restricts the meaning of *hotel;* instead of meaning any hotel, the word means a hotel that would serve a given purpose.)

His chance *to answer the question* was soon gone. (The infinitive phrase identifies a particular chance and lets the reader infer that the person spoken of will probably have many chances to do other things; just the identified chance is gone.)

As an adverbial modifier, the infinitive phrase modifies the same parts of speech and answers the same kinds of questions that simple adverbs do (see pp. 265–266). Here are examples.

He went *to see whether the mail had come.* (The infinitive phrase modifies the verb *went* and answers the question *Why?* and possibly, by implication, the question *Where?*)

She traveled in the Far East *to get information for a report.* (The infinitive phrase modifies the verb *traveled* and answers the question *Why?*)

He is unable *to sleep in a warm room.* (The infinitive phrase modifies the adjective *unable* and gives it specific meaning by answering the question *To do what?* or *In what way?*)

The distance is too far *to walk in an hour.* (The infinitive phrase modifies the adjective *far* and answers the question *For what purpose?* or *In what way?*)

Dependent Clauses as Modifiers. There are three kinds of dependent clauses (see pp. 299–300), but only the two that function as modifiers are discussed here. These are the adjective clause and the adverbial clause.

An ADJECTIVE CLAUSE modifies a substantive. The clause is usually introduced by a relative pronoun (such as *who, which,* or *that*) or by a relative adverb (such as *when* or *where*) which helps to clarify the relationship between the clause and the substantive it modifies. Sometimes the connectives are understood.

The leader *whom we chose* is a good one. (The adjective clause modifies the noun *leader* and to a certain extent has the effect of identifying the person. The adjective clause is introduced by the relative pronoun *whom,* but the relationship would be clear if the connective were understood: "The leader we chose is a good one.")

Do you remember the time *when you lost your keys?* (The adjective clause modifies the noun *time* and limits the general meaning of that term to a specific point in time. The adjective clause is introduced by the relative adverb *when* [at which]. The relationship would be clear without the connective: "Do you remember the time you lost your keys?")

Personnel managers like to find employees *who are efficient in their work and considerate of other persons.* (The adjective clause modifies the noun *employees* and performs the double function of describing and limiting it. Here the relative pronoun *who* is essential because it serves as the subject [a required element] of the dependent clause.)

An ADVERBIAL CLAUSE modifies a verb, an adjective, or an adverb and qualifies its meaning in any of a number of different ways. The subordinating conjunction, the kind of connective that has the special function of joining the adverbial clause to the word it modifies, has a particular meaning which helps in the function of qualifying. (See list of subordinating conjunctions and their special meanings, p. 280). Here are sentences that illustrate common relationships between the adverbial clause and the element it modifies.

CONDITION: *If frost damages the trees,* fruit will be scarce.
CONDITION: *Had he been here,* he would have helped us. (Subordinating conjunction *if* omitted)
MANNER: She spoke *as if she were tired.*
CAUSE: *Because an election was in progress,* many voters were discussing political problems.
RESULT: We were *so* busy *that we were unaware of the passing of time.*
PURPOSE: Leave before the rush hour *so that you will not be delayed by heavy traffic.*
CONCESSION: *Although they were unsupervised,* the children played quietly.
COMPARISON: The puppy is not *so* playful *as I expected him to be.*
CONTRAST: Tom earned money on the trip, *whereas Martha spent her savings.*
TIME: The warning was given *after the storm was over.*
PLACE: Nancy lives *where ocean breezes blow.*

Restrictive and Nonrestrictive Modifiers. The relationship between a so-called *restrictive modifier* and the thing modified is a close one: a restrictive adjectival modifier is necessary to identify the substantive it modifies ("The portrait *covered with dust* is a family heirloom"); a restrictive adverbial modifier is necessary to point out *when, why, how, where, under what condition, with what result,* etc., the action or quality of the modified element prevails ("We were *so* busy *that we were unaware of the passing of time*"). The relationship between a so-called *nonrestrictive modifier* and the thing modified is a loose one: a restrictive adjective modifier is not necessary for identification but is informative in a parenthetical way about the substantive it modifies ("My dog Rover, *covered with dust,* stood up and shook himself"); a nonrestrictive adverbial modifier does not essentially clarify the modified verb or descriptive word but merely adds parenthetical comment ("The whole night had gone by, *although I did not realize it*").

Because nonrestrictive modifiers can be omitted without affecting the essential meaning of the words they modify and without disrupting basic sentence structure, they are set off by commas (see pp. 362–363).

Appositive and the Thing Explained. The relation of an *appositive* to the sentence element it renames or explains is that it does the renaming or explaining without the assistance of an intervening verb. The appositive, which is always a substantive explaining another substantive, can be made into a subject complement if the two substantives are removed from the context of the sentence and an appropriate form of *to be* is placed between them. Illustrations will clarify the relationship.

Mr. Grayson, the *secretary,* is reading the minutes. (Mr. Grayson [is] *secretary.*)

He enjoys his two hobbies, *bowling* and *golfing.* (Hobbies [are] *bowling* and *golfing.*)

James White, a *contemporary* and *friend* of Charles Lamb, befriended the chimney sweeps of London. (James White [was] *contemporary* and *friend.*)

She memorized Shelley's poem *"Mutability."* (Poem [is] "Mutability.")

Like modifiers, appositives may be restrictive or nonrestrictive and are punctuated accordingly (see pp. 363–364).

Pronoun and Antecedent. A *pronoun,* unless it is an indefinite pronoun (see p. 258), usually takes the place of an earlier substantive, or *antecedent.* The relationship between the pronoun and its antecedent should be clear and definite.

Reference. A pronoun should refer to a single-word antecedent, not to several possible words or to a whole clause.

WRONG: John and his father both used the car, and it was not always available when *he* wanted it. (The pronoun *he* has two possible antecedents, *John* and *father.*)

RIGHT: John and his father both used the car, and it was not always available when *John* (or, depending on the writer's intended meaning, *John's father,* or *one or the other of them*) wanted it.

WRONG: Birds cannot find enough food during a snowstorm, *which* is why people should feed them. (The pronoun *which* refers generally to the whole preceding clause instead of to a single-word antecedent.)

CORRECT: Because birds cannot find enough food during a snowstorm, people should feed them.

Oftentimes, as the preceding examples suggest, the best way to prevent vagueness in the *reference of a pronoun* is to express the idea without the pronoun. (Inexperienced writers tend to overwork pronouns in constructions where nouns would be more meaningful.) Here are other typical examples of vagueness and clarity in reference.

Vague: Montana is an important grain-producing state. *They* grow wheat on large ranches there. (The pronoun *They* has no antecedent.)
Clear: Montana is an important grain-producing state. *Farmers* there grow wheat on large ranches.

Vague: My father said I had acted wisely in reporting the incident. *That* made me feel better. (The pronoun *That* refers vaguely to the preceding sentence.)
Clear: My father said I had acted wisely in reporting the incident. His approval made me feel better.

Agreement. A pronoun should agree with its antecedent in number, gender, and person. The part of this rule most frequently violated is that requiring a pronoun to be of the same number as its antecedent. To avoid errors of this type remember that when a pronoun takes a singular verb it requires other pronouns that refer to it to be singular also. (See agreement between subject and verb, pp. 282–284, and list of indefinite pronouns differentiating between singulars and plurals, p. 258.) Here are examples.

Wrong: Everyone is doing *their* best.   Right: Everyone is doing *his* best.

Wrong: Each child in the neighborhood seems to have a habit of leaving *their* toys in my yard.
Right: Each child in the neighborhood seems to have a habit of leaving *his* toys in my yard.

Wrong: Anyone takes chances when *they* drive.
Right: Anyone takes chances when *he* drives.

Wrong: Either of them is sure to have plenty of work of *their* own.
Right: Either of them is sure to have plenty of work of *his* own.

The most common error in person is a shift from third person (especially from the third person *one*) to the second person *you*.

Wrong: When one shops on Saturdays, *you* are likely to find the stores crowded.
Correct (but stilted): When one shops on Saturdays, *one* is likely to find the stores crowded.
Correct: When one shops on Saturdays, *he* is likely to find the stores crowded.
Correct: A person who shops on Saturdays is likely to find the stores crowded.

The masculine form is appropriate in reference to an antecedent designating either sex.

AWKWARD: Each member of the congregation puts *his or her* contribution in an envelope.

PREFERABLE: Each member of the congregation puts *his* contribution in an envelope.

Co-ordination and Subordination. In good composition the ranks of ideas in their relationships with one another are clarified for the reader through *co-ordination* and *subordination*. (For discussions of these topics, see "Connectives" in this chapter and "Logical Subordination" and "Logical Co-ordination" in Chapter 8.)

GRAMMATICAL UNITS

Every sustained piece of exposition is made up of units of varying nature and size. A large work may consist of several volumes, each dealing with a separate phase of the general subject. Virtually every expository work of book length, whether part of a larger work or complete in itself, is divided into parts, usually called chapters—although there may be larger parts, each containing a number of chapters. Ordinarily each chapter is divided, perhaps into sections which are groups of paragraphs, and in any case into paragraphs themselves. The usual paragraph, in turn, includes a number of sentences. We can carry the subdivision down to different groups of words within the sentence, to individual words, and even to individual sound-elements or letters.

In this section we are concerned with the range of units from the sentence down to, but not including, individual words; we are concerned with different groups of words within a sentence. The units within this range are specifically *grammatical units*.

The nature of the larger units, from the book or set of books down to the paragraph, is primarily a matter of logic and the broader tactics of organization. The nature of grammatical units, on the other hand, is fixed precisely by grammatical principles.

The basic grammatical units are the phrase, the clause, and the sentence.

The Phrase. A *phrase* is a group of closely related words not including a subject and finite predicate.

Phrases may be classified in two ways: (1) *by structure,* that is, by the part of speech which is the principal or most characteristic element of the phrase, and (2) *by function,* that is, by the part of speech whose function the phrase as a whole performs.

Phrases Classified by Structure. Phrases may be classified by structure as noun, verb, prepositional, gerund, participial, and infinitive phrases.

NOUN PHRASE. A *noun phrase* consists of a noun and one or more modifiers.

They are building *a large new* HOUSE.[26]
We tried to find *some ripe* BLUEBERRIES.
A short, fat MAN entered the room.

VERB PHRASE. A *verb phrase* consists of a verb and one or more auxiliary ("helping") verbs. (See pp. 273–274.)

He *is working*.   They *have been hurrying*.
The job *will have been completed* by tomorrow.

PREPOSITIONAL PHRASE. A *prepositional phrase* consists of a preposition and its object or objects, with their modifiers if any. The most characteristic element in such a phrase is the preposition itself.

The men have gone TO *war*.   Mice hide IN *holes and corners*.
Kitty jumped OFF *the chair*.   We live IN *a large new house*.

Note, as indicated in the last example above, that a prepositional phrase may include a noun phrase within itself. The noun phrase "a large new house" consists of the object *house* of the preposition *in,* plus the modifiers of *house: a, large,* and *new*.

The preposition joins its object,[27] which always contains one or more substantives, to a sentence element which may be a substantive, a modifier, or a verb or verbal. In any case, the prepositional phrase as a whole functions as a modifier of this element. If this is a substantive, the prepositional phrase is an adjectival modifier.

the girl ON *the porch*   the one WITH *the green hat*

("On the porch" modifies the noun *girl;* "with the green hat" modifies the pronoun *one.*) If the modified element is itself a modifier, or a verb or verbal, then the prepositional phrase is an adverbial modifier.

---

[26] In the examples where the phrase is composed of two or more elements, the principal or most characteristic element (the noun in a noun phrase, the preposition in a prepositional phrase, etc.) is printed in small capitals, and the rest of the phrase in italics. If the whole phrase is one element, it is printed entirely in italics.

[27] In English statements, the object virtually always follows the preposition. There are a very few exceptions; for example, the object sometimes precedes the preposition *notwithstanding:* "The storm notwithstanding, we decided to set sail." In questions, especially spoken ones, the object frequently appears earlier than the preposition: "What are you doing that for?"

ADJECTIVE MODIFIED: It was difficult FOR *me*.
VERB MODIFIED: Come WITH *me*.
VERBAL MODIFIED: Walking UP *the steps,* he stumbled.

GERUND PHRASE. A *gerund phrase* consists of a gerund and one or more other elements, such as an object or objects of the gerund, and modifiers. (See pp. 275–276.)

SOLVING *problems* is a good way to develop facility in mathematics.

His favorite sport is FISHING *for trout*. (Here the gerund phrase includes within itself the prepositional phrase "for trout" as a modifier.)

We were delighted to hear of *his* WINNING. (Here the gerund phrase is included within the prepositional phrase "of his winning")

Note carefully, in the last example, that the gerund *winning* is modified by *his*. This kind of modifier with a gerund, indicating the person or thing that performs the action, is sometimes called the *subject of the gerund*. On the formal level, a pronoun used for this purpose is regularly in the *possessive case*. The use of the objective case of a pronoun in such a context ("We were delighted to hear of him winning") has until recently been considered ungrammatical, or characteristic of the vulgate level of usage. It is now being given some status on the informal level, but is still avoided by many careful writers. A noun used as the subject of a gerund, on the other hand, is frequently not in the possessive case, especially if the noun is plural or there are intervening modifiers: "We sometimes hear of *persons* with much intelligence doing foolish things."

PARTICIPIAL PHRASE. A *participial phrase* consists of a participle and one or more other elements, such as an object or objects of the participle and modifiers. (See pp. 276–277.)

HAVING CAUGHT *the ball,* he threw it quickly to first base.

He saw the books *neatly* ARRANGED *on the shelves*. (Note that the participial phrase includes the prepositional phrase "on the shelves" as a modifier.)

Misuse of a participial phrase results in the common error called a dangling modifier. (See pp. 236–240.)

INFINITIVE PHRASE. An *infinitive phrase* consists of an infinitive and one or more other elements, such as subjects, objects, and modifiers. (See p. 277.)

I am too tired TO DRIVE *now*.

TO READ *easily in a foreign language* is one of his objectives. (The infinitive phrase includes the prepositional phrase "in a foreign language" as a modifier.)

We wanted *him* TO SING *a song*. (The subject of an infinitive, as illustrated by *him* in this example, is always in the objective case.)

Phrases Classified by Function. Phrases may be classified by function as substantive, adjective, adverbial, verb, and absolute phrases. Phrases which belong to different groups in the classification by structure may belong to the same group in the classification by function; and conversely, phrases which belong to the same group in the classification by structure may have different functions. To illustrate this point, some of the examples from the preceding subsection are repeated here.

SUBSTANTIVE PHRASE. A *substantive phrase* functions as a noun. Phrases classified by structure as noun phrases and gerund phrases always function as nouns, and those classified as infinitive phrases sometimes do.

A short, fat man entered the room. (noun phrase functioning as substantive phrase, subject of verb *entered*)

His favorite sport is *fishing for trout*. (gerund phrase functioning as substantive phrase, subject complement after the linking verb *is*)

I want *to go now*. (infinitive phrase functioning as substantive phrase, direct object of the verb *want*)

ADJECTIVE PHRASE. An *adjective phrase* modifies a noun or other substantive. Phrases classified by structure as prepositional phrases, participial phrases, and infinitive phrases may function as adjective phrases.

The flowers *in the garden* are beautiful. (prepositional phrase functioning as adjective phrase, modifying the noun *flowers*)

Startled by the noises, the girl looked up. (participial phrase functioning as adjective phrase, modifying the noun *girl*)

Now is the time *to decide*. (infinitive phrase functioning as adjective phrase, modifying the noun *time*)

ADVERBIAL PHRASE. An *adverbial phrase* modifies a verb, an adjective, or an adverb. Phrases classified by structure as noun phrases, prepositional phrases, and infinitive phrases may function as adverbial phrases.

We lived there *half a year*. (noun phrase functioning as adverbial phrase, modifying the verb *lived*)

We lived *in that house*. (prepositional phrase functioning as adverbial phrase, modifying the verb *lived*)

He is able *to learn quickly*. (infinitive phrase functioning as adverbial phrase, modifying the adjective *able*)

VERB PHRASE. A *verb phrase* functions as a finite verb. Unlike other phrases, a verb phrase includes words of only one part of speech: all the words in a verb phrase are verbs. The function of the verb phrase is simply to express different modal and inflectional forms of a verb.

She *is talking.*   You *will see* him.   He *may go.*
He *might be* able to do it.   I *do like* you.
They *should have arrived* an hour ago.
Our clothes *will have been soaked* by then.
A change *has been suggested.*   A change *will be put* into effect.

ABSOLUTE PHRASE. An *absolute phrase* has no specific grammatical connection to any particular element in the rest of the sentence; its effect is to modify the predication as a whole. Characteristically, an absolute phrase consists of a substantive (or substantive phrase) modified by a participle (or participial phrase). (See also p. 364.)

His voice being somewhat hoarse, the speaker paused and took a drink of water.

Sometimes the participle is omitted; the participle *being* is understood by the hearer or reader:

His voice somewhat hoarse, the speaker paused and took a drink of water.

The Clause. A *clause* is a group of closely related words forming a sentence or part of a sentence and *including* a subject and a finite predicate.

Clauses may be classified in three ways: (1) by *degree of dependence;* (2) by *function* (only dependent clauses can be classified by this criterion); and (3) by *degree of completeness.*

Clauses Classified by Degree of Independence. Clauses are classified as independent clauses (sometimes called main or principal clauses) and dependent clauses (sometimes called subordinate clauses). The different names for each kind are synonymous; they are simply different terms used by various grammarians to denote the same things.

INDEPENDENT (MAIN, PRINCIPAL) CLAUSE. An *independent clause* is one which could stand alone, as a separate sentence.

It conveys a unit of meaning which might be complete in itself; it does not imply to the hearer or reader that something else must necessarily be added to complete the sense. Consider the sentence,

I know him well, and *I recommend him highly.*

In this sentence each of the italicized group of words is an independent clause. Each has a subject (*I*), and each has a finite predicate (the remainder of each clause). Each could stand alone, as a separate sentence:

I know him well.   I recommend him highly.

Similarly, the independent clauses in these examples might stand as separate sentences.

I do not know much about the play, but *I am going to see it anyway.*
Their plan is a good one; furthermore, they have the ability to carry it out.
The light will not go on; the bulb may be burned out.

Two independent clauses may be separated in three ways: (1) by a comma and a co-ordinating conjunction, like *but* in the first of the three examples immediately above (the conjunction is not regarded as being part of either clause); or (2) by a semicolon and a conjunctive adverb, like *furthermore* in the second example (this conjunctive adverb *is* regarded as being part of the clause in which it appears); or (3) by a semicolon alone, as in the third example. (See pp. 208–209, 368–369.) Independent clauses may *not* be separated by a comma alone (see pp. 233–235).

DEPENDENT (*SUBORDINATE*) CLAUSE. A *dependent clause* is one which, although it includes a subject and finite predicate, could *not* stand alone as a separate sentence. It does not convey a complete unit of meaning; by its form it *does* imply to the hearer or reader that something else must be added to complete the sense. Here is an example.

If they had seen her, they would have spoken to her.

The italicized group of words is a clause: it includes a subject (*they*) and a finite predicate (*had seen her*). If someone heard or read only the words "If they had seen her," he would be waiting for something else to complete the sense. Similarly, the dependent clauses in these examples could not stand alone.

Here they come, *as I knew they would.*
This is the house *where I used to live.*

Here is the book *which I recommended to you.*
I do not know *who he is.*   That is the road *we ought to take.*
Tell me *how I should do it.*   I remember the time *I last saw her.*

A dependent clause may be introduced by (1) a subordinating conjunction, like *as* in the first example immediately above; [28] or (2) a relative adverb or an interrogative adverb, like *where* and *how* in the second and fifth examples respectively; or (3) a relative pronoun or an interrogative pronoun, like *which* and *who* in the third and fourth examples respectively; or (4) a relative pronoun or relative adverb actually omitted but understood, as in the two examples: "That is the road [which] we ought to take." "I remember the time [when] I last saw her." The word that introduces a dependent clause (even a word that does not actually appear, but is only understood) is regarded as being part of the clause. (See pp. 279–280.)

Dependent Clauses Classified by Function. Dependent clauses are further classified by function, that is, by the part of speech whose function the clause as a whole performs. By this criterion there are three kinds of dependent clauses: substantive (also called noun clauses), adjective, and adverbial clauses.

SUBSTANTIVE (NOUN) CLAUSE. A *substantive clause* functions as a noun. (See pp. 255–257.)

That you say so is enough for me. (The noun clause is the subject of the verb *is.*)

They wanted to learn *where the treasure was.* (The noun clause is the direct object of the infinitive *to learn.*)

The question is *whether we should go or not.* (The noun clause is the subject complement after the linking verb *is.*)

ADJECTIVE CLAUSE. An *adjective clause* modifies a noun or other substantive. Most adjective clauses are introduced by relative pronouns. (See also pp. 257–258, 289.)

The children, *who by this time were hungry,* were glad to arrive at home. (The adjective clause modifies the noun *children.*)

My feet are always the ones *that get stepped on.* (The adjective clause modifies the pronoun *ones.*)

---

[28] The subordinating conjunction *that* is sometimes omitted: "I know they will come" is used instead of "I know that they will come." Also, *if* is sometimes omitted, and the conditional meaning conveyed by inverted word order: "Had they seen her, they would have spoken to her."

Do you remember the corner *where we made a left turn?* (The adjective clause modifies the noun *corner.*)

ADVERBIAL CLAUSE. An *adverbial clause* modifies a verb, an adjective, or an adverb. (See also pp. 279–280, 289–290.)

As he approached the intersection, he applied his brakes. (The adverbial clause modifies the verb *applied.*)

Be sure to get enough food *so that no one will have to go hungry.* (The adverbial clause modifies the adjective *enough.*)

Clauses Classified by Degree of Completeness. Clauses are classified by degree of completeness as complete clauses and elliptical clauses. *Elliptical* in this context is synonymous with *incomplete.*

COMPLETE CLAUSE. A *complete clause* is one in which both the essential elements, the subject and the finite predicate, are explicitly expressed. Nothing is left to be filled in by the hearer or reader; that is, nothing is left to be understood as part of the meaning, even though it is not actually included.

All the examples of clauses given thus far are complete clauses. Here are two more examples, designed specifically for comparison with the examples of elliptical clauses given in the next paragraph.

Mary arrived at three o'clock; Helen arrived an hour later. (two complete independent clauses)

While he was walking along the street, he heard an engine backfire. (one complete dependent clause followed by one complete independent clause)

ELLIPTICAL CLAUSE. Although a clause does by definition include a subject and a finite predicate, sometimes part or all of either the subject or finite predicate is not explicitly expressed but is left to be filled in by the hearer or reader; that is, to be understood even though it is not actually included. Sometimes, even, the whole subject and also part of the predicate are left out. A clause from which any of the normally essential elements has been thus omitted is called an *elliptical clause.* Here are examples.

Mary arrived at three o'clock; *Helen, an hour later.* (One complete independent clause followed by one elliptical independent clause: the finite verb *arrived* has been omitted from the predicate of the second.)

While walking along the street, he heard an engine backfire. (One elliptical dependent clause followed by one complete independent clause: omitted from the former are the subject *he* and also the first word, *was,* of the finite verb phrase.)

The Sentence. The *sentence* is the largest grammatical unit. It always includes at least one independent clause; it may include one or more additional independent clauses, and one or more dependent clauses. (For a discussion of the sentence as a whole, see Chapter 8, "Sentence Structure.")

Exercises

1. a. Give the indicated form of the personal pronoun. Example: second person singular, possessive: *your, yours.*
  (1) third person singular, neuter, possessive.
  (2) first person plural, objective.
  (3) second person singular, objective.
  (4) third person singular, feminine, nominative.
  (5) first person singular, possessive.
  (6) third person singular, masculine, objective.
  (7) second person plural, possessive.
  (8) third person plural, nominative.
  b. (1) Give the objective case of the relative and interrogative pronoun *who.*
  (2) Give the plural of the demonstrative adjective *that.*

2. Write an expression consisting of a personal pronoun as subject and a verb or verb phrase to represent each of the following combinations of person, number, tense, voice, and mood. Example: first person plural, past active indicative of the verb *throw: we threw.*
  a. first person singular, present passive indicative of *send.*
  b. second person singular, future active indicative of *know.*
  c. third person plural, present perfect passive indicative of *teach.*
  d. first person plural, future perfect active indicative of *sing.*
  e. third person singular, present active indicative of *fix.*
  f. second person plural, present active imperative of *hurry.*
  g. first person singular, past passive subjunctive of *give.*
  h. first person plural, present passive subjunctive of *dismiss.*
  i. second person singular, future active indicative of *say.* (Write the form which in formal usage indicates determination on the part of the speaker.)
  j. third person singular, present active subjunctive of *do.*

3. a. In the following sentences find and label the participles, gerunds, and infinitives; also list the function of each verbal—or phrase containing a verbal—as a part of the sentence.
  (1) Do you prefer reading a play or seeing the performance?
  (2) To master the art of swimming in a year is an achievement.
  (3) He crossed the street without stopping.

(4) The chair standing in the corner needs repairing.

(5) The surprised janitor frowned at the mud lying on the floor.

b. In the following sentences find and label these parts: (1) the verbs, (2) the simple subjects, (3) the direct objects, (4) the indirect objects, (5) the subject complements, (6) the object complements, (7) the objects of prepositions, and (8) the appositives.

(a) His first impromptu theme was excellent.

(b) The most valuable player on the team is ill.

(c) Mr. Brown told me a fascinating story.

(d) On the track he is an expert.

(e) Dora's uncle, a painter, gave the school a picture of the sea.

(f) The class elected Rodney president.

(g) Julius was the chairman of the committee for a year.

(h) Did you know that speeding is dangerous?

(i) He painted the fence white.

(j) Miss Jones, the teacher, gave us a long assignment.

4. Find the subordinate (dependent) clauses in the following sentences. Label each subordinate clause to show its use as a part of speech (noun, adjective, or adverb).

a. David thought that the lesson was interesting.

b. The class was dismissed when the bell rang.

c. How do you like the plan which he explained?

d. If the program is given in the evening, the chorus will participate.

e. What the student learns now will be useful to him later.

f. The library is the place where we should study.

g. He left early because he was sleepy.

h. The person who works diligently will probably succeed.

i. Give the book to whoever needs it.

j. Sam Houston, about whom many interesting stories are told, liked good literature.

5. Correct the errors in agreement between subject and verb or between pronoun and antecedent. State briefly why each correction was necessary. A few sentences are already correct (mark them correct).

a. Neither my uncle or my aunt are free to make the trip.

b. Is she the girl who I saw yesterday?

c. The quality of the magazines on the stands varies.

d. The best part of the game were the home runs.

e. Everyone should prepare their own report.

f. More of this kind of entertainment is to come.

g. Is he one of the seven men who has been selected for training?

h. Either the superintendent or both of his assistants are going to the convention.

i. Neither of them have tried to increase their reading speed.

j. There is several reviews of the book available.

k. The letter, along with several pamphlets, have disappeared.

l. Each of the children should have their own supplies.

m. Whom do you think will be there?

n. I am certain she is younger than me.

o. The agreement is strictly between you and I.

p. Three friends—Bob, Ted, and me—will be leaving at the same time.

q. I mistook him to be you, for I felt certain of your arriving early.

r. She has never approved of him working at the bakery after school.

s. There was a stack of books on the table.

t. The books on the approved reading list are good choices for whoever has time to read them.

10 DICTION

Diction is the selection of words to express ideas. Good diction is the choice of words effective and appropriate in meaning, as well as suitable to the subject, audience, and occasion. (See Chapter 1, the discussion of "The Levels of Usage.") The selection of appropriate words, important in all types of communication, is especially important in writing, which must convey ideas and attitudes without facial expression, intonation, or gesture. Thus, this chapter is designed to help the writer choose words that will express his meaning with clarity and precision.

The chapter is divided into four main parts. First is a brief survey of the basic functions of words and the kinds of meanings that words convey. Second is an account of the qualities of good diction, and third is a discussion of the principal means of attaining it. The final section offers some suggestions for avoiding common errors or improprieties in diction.

BASIC FUNCTIONS OF WORDS

A *word* is a number of things. It is a sound, or a combination of sounds. It is a pattern of marks on a page, or—since individual letters are such patterns—it is usually a combination of patterns.

Words as Symbols. The most important thing that a word is, is a *symbol;* that is, it stands for something which is not itself. A house has walls and a roof; the word *house* does not have these things. The most important function of the word *house* is to stand for a house. We call the word *house* a symbol; we call the thing with walls and a roof the *referent* of the symbol. The relationship between the two is one of *reference*.

Specific Reference: Denotation. *Denotation* is a *specific reference* between the word and the thing which it represents. That is, their relationship is such that the symbol stands for a single referent, clearly defined and limited; it does not in itself suggest a number of other things which are in some way connected or associated with the referent. The word *house* denotes the thing with walls and a roof; ordinarily this is *all* that it stands for or calls to mind.

MULTIPLE MEANINGS. Of course a word may stand for a number of different things. The word *spring,* for example, is the symbol for a kind of leap or bound, a season of the year, a piece of coiled wire, or a source of water. It stands for only one of these at a time, and we know which one from its context—from the other words around it. One of these specific meanings is clear in each of these sentences.

The tiger crouched for its spring.   Spring is late this year.
I need a spring for my watch.   Water ran from a tiny spring.

Thus, if the word stands for only one thing at a time, without suggesting others, its relationship with each one of its referents is still denotation. A word such as *spring* simply has a number of *different denotations,* or denotative meanings.

LEVELS OF ABSTRACTION. In denotation a word stands for only one thing at a time, but that one thing may have very narrow or very broad scope—or any breadth of scope in between. The word *John,* for example, would ordinarily stand for one "thing"—that is, one person. The word *man* stands for one "thing" too; but this word may stand for any one of a great number of persons, or even, in an expression like "Man is mortal," for all persons. We say that *man* represents a higher *level of abstraction* than *John,* because it stands for a whole class of things which have certain characteristics in common. Clearly, the level may be higher than that of *man:* the word *animal* stands for a class which includes man and many other members too; the expression *every living thing* includes animals and also plants. Therefore, when we say that in denotation a word stands for one thing, we must remember that this one thing may itself be a whole class of great or small scope, or any member of such a class.

Suggestive Reference: Connotation. Sometimes the relationship between a word and its referent is richer and more complex. The word may still stand for some one thing primarily, but at the same time the word itself suggests and therefore really signifies some other things which are associated with the principal referent. If the word *house* means the thing with walls and a roof, what does the word *home* mean? It too may stand for a house, but its meaning does not stop there. It suggests also comfort and warmth and love—parents and children, shared experience, security. This kind of relationship between a word like *home* and the whole atmosphere which it implies to the mind is called *connotation.* For an example of the difference between denotation and connotation, suppose that the author of "Home, Sweet Home" had written

> 'Mid pleasures and palaces though we carouse,
> Be it ever so humble, there's no place like a house!

The effect is almost ludicrous. Clearly, we cannot substitute a comparatively "flat" word like *house* in a context which requires the rich connotation of *home*. On the other hand, on many occasions the clarity and directness of denotation are essential; the emotional suggestiveness of connotation would be out of place. Such occasions would include, for example, the writing of most kinds of reports, or of any objective factual account like the explanation of a process or a set of instructions for operating a mechanical device.

COMMON CONNOTATIONS. A great many connotations are part of the tradition of language. They are universally recognized and understood, because they are based on common or "public" experience. For every person who speaks English the word *home* has some connotation. In no two cases perhaps are the connotations identical: one person may think of a glowing fireplace with a dog on the hearth; another may think of a television set in the living room. But there is enough in common in virtually all persons' experience with this word so that the connotation is useful for purposes of communication. We all know what is meant by "There's no place like home." Skillful writers and speakers make effective use of *common connotations*. Some particular types of communication would be scarcely possible without them: poetry, for instance, and other kinds of imaginative literature; sermons of devotion or of exhortation; and also all kinds of propaganda, from political oratory to ordinary advertising.

UNIQUE CONNOTATIONS. Certain connotations are not common property. In one family the word *umbrella* may suggest, say, Aunt Fanny, because Aunt Fanny always carries an umbrella. These *unique* or "private" *connotations* are not so important as the common ones, for an obvious reason: they have no value for communication to any audience wider than the group in which the association is familiar.

Extended Reference: Figurative Language. Usually a house is something with walls and a roof; but what is it in a context like this?

> If the heats of hate and lust
>> In the house of flesh are strong,
> Let me mind the house of dust
>> Where my sojourn shall be long.[1]

Clearly it is something else: "the house of flesh" is the living human body, and "the house of dust" is the dead body in the grave. It might

[1] Reprinted with permission from A. E. Housman, "When I Watch the Living Meet," lyric number 12 in his collection of poems called *A Shropshire Lad* (New York: Henry Holt & Co., Inc.).

be said that in a sense the word *house* still stands for a house, but that the house itself—the thing with walls and a roof—has now in turn become a kind of symbol, standing for something else: in this case the human body living and dead. In effect, then, the word *house* now stands for the human body. This use of words which extends their meaning beyond their ordinary sense we call *figurative language* [2] in contradistinction to the *literal* language in which words have only their normal meanings. A single expression involving extended reference is called a *figure of speech*.

Provided that it is used appropriately, figurative language can contribute to the effectiveness of the writing in which it appears. The excessive use of such language may produce an impression of artificiality; and in certain kinds of writing, where the straightforward, matter-of-fact expression of literal language is suitable, figures of speech should be used only sparingly if at all. In the proper context, however, a figure of speech has a number of advantages. It usually makes a direct appeal to the reader's senses; it is more concrete than a literal expression and therefore more vivid. At the same time, it is almost always *shorter* than the corresponding literal expression would be. Even the simple figure "You are my sunshine" would require for a literal translation something like "You represent happiness in my life; you give me a sense of security and contentment." At the other end of the emotional scale, the literal statement "He is a vicious, treacherous, contemptible character" might be replaced by the figurative "He is a rat."

Briefly, the most common figures of speech may be grouped in three categories: figures of comparison, figures of contrast, and figures of association.

FIGURES OF COMPARISON. The *figures of comparison* are simile, metaphor, and personification. A *simile* is a figure in which a comparison is stated explicitly: "The child is like a flower." In this simplest kind of figure there is not actually any extended reference; the flower is still just a flower, and we understand simply that the child is like it in certain respects, such as beauty and purity. In a *metaphor,* on the other hand, the comparison is not stated explicitly but implied. For example, an expression like "Oh, she is a flower!" does not actually state a comparison, although of course the comparison

[2] Sometimes the expression *metaphorical language* is used to mean the same thing. Since the word *metaphorical* really refers to one particular kind of figure, however (see below), the phrase *figurative language* is preferable for this meaning.

is understood by implication. In a metaphor there *is* extended reference: the child is not literally a flower. In such a statement the word *flower* may in one sense still stand for a flower, as the word *house* in "the house of dust" still means a house; but the flower itself now stands for "something" with the beauty and purity of a flower. A special kind of metaphor is *personification*, in which some non-human thing is compared by implication to a human being. When the poet says, "The Moon doth with delight look round her," he is implying a comparison between the moon and a woman.

There are two requirements to be observed in connection with the figures of comparison. The first, which pertains chiefly to the simile, is that the comparison must be drawn between things of different classes, like the child (human being) and the flower (plant). Otherwise the language is not figurative at all. If we say, for instance, that a love seat is like a sofa, except that the former has room for only two people, we are comparing two things of the same class (furniture). This is not a simile but a purely literal expression. The second requirement, pertaining chiefly to the metaphor, is that if the comparison is extended, it must be carried out consistently. Otherwise the result is likely to be what is called a *mixed metaphor*. In "Hitch your wagon to a star, and step on the gas!" a life or career is compared by implication first to a vehicle which is pulled by something else, and then to an automobile. The effect of such inconsistency is incongruous and often unintentionally humorous.

FIGURES OF CONTRAST. The *figures of contrast* are irony, overstatement, and understatement. *Irony* as a figure of speech represents a particular kind of extended reference: extension in a direction opposite to the normal one. That is, a word or expression used ironically takes on a meaning which sharply contrasts with or even in effect contradicts its ordinary meaning. For example, if we look out the window in the morning and see dull clouds and rain, we may exclaim, "Oh, don't you just love this kind of day for a picnic?"—and the word *love* will of course convey a meaning something like that of *hate*. In the other two figures of contrast there is a lesser degree of difference between what the words mean literally and what meaning they convey by implication. In *overstatement* (*hyperbole*) and *understatement* (*litotes*), as the names imply, the difference between the literal and the extended meaning is simply that in overstatement the words appear to say more than what is actually meant; in understatement, less. "We just died laughing" and "I was frightened out of seven years' growth" are examples of overstatement. A familiar example of understatement is the old sailor's comment on a violent storm at sea: "There's a wee bit of a blow."

The figures of contrast function in accordance with the psychology of implication (see Chapter 5). Their use requires the reader to be alert, to discern the difference between what is said and what is meant. If he does discern it, he has in a sense participated in the total sending-and-receiving process of communication more fully than would be necessary in the absence of any figures of contrast. The net result of their successful use is to intensify the expression of the basic meaning and heighten its effectiveness.

FIGURES OF ASSOCIATION. The *figures of association* are metonymy and synecdoche. In *metonymy,* the meaning of a word is extended from its ordinary referent to something associated with that referent. For example, the proverb "The pen is mightier than the sword" really means that writing is more powerful than fighting; or, extending the reference one step farther, that ideas exert more influence than does physical strength or violence. Voltaire once used one of these examples of metonymy, together with another: "I have no sceptre [royal power and authority], but I have a pen." In *synecdoche* the association is of a particular kind: a part of something is made to stand for the whole, or the whole for the part—a chorus of fifty *voices* for fifty *members* or *persons,* or "the mellow year" for autumn.

Words as Things-in-Themselves. Although by far the most important and the most frequent function of a word is to stand for something which is not itself, sometimes we have occasion to talk about words themselves. This usage of *words as things-in-themselves* is an exception to the rule that words function as symbols. We say that the word *house* contains five letters, or that in pronouncing the word *building* we put the accent on the first syllable. Here we are discussing not the house nor the building for which the word ordinarily stands; we are discussing the word itself.

Words used in this special way—as things-in-themselves—are distinguished by being printed in italic type; in handwriting or typescript they are underlined. An alternative method is to enclose them in quotation marks. These two sentences illustrate both methods.

The word *kindergarten* comes from the German.
The word "kindergarten" comes from the German.

QUALITIES OF GOOD DICTION

Good diction, we have said, is the choice of words that serve the writer's purpose with maximum effectiveness. Such words are precise in denotation, appropriate in connotation, and as specific and concrete as is suitable to their context; also, they are judiciously varied to avoid monotonous repetition.

Precision in Denotation. The first requirement of an effective word is that its denotation, its specific meaning, be *precisely* what the writer intends at that point to express. For this reason, he must distinguish carefully among synonyms: words of similar, but virtually never of identical, meaning. There may be a number of synonyms which at least approximate the meaning that the writer wants to convey. Frequently *only one* expresses it precisely. The writer should not be content with any approximation, but should consider the synonyms carefully to determine which one is *the* word for his purpose.

Suppose that a writer is explaining his interpretation of a character in a story which he has read. In revising his first draft, he comes upon the sentence, "My first concept of the character was that he was a moral weakling." The writer pauses; he is not quite satisfied with the word *concept.* Do we have a *concept* of an individual human being, whether real or fictional? The word does not seem just right. What other word might fit this context better? The writer begins to think of synonyms and refers to his dictionary. For synonyms of *concept* he finds a reference to *idea;* under *idea* he finds listed as synonyms not only *concept* but also *conception, thought, notion,* and *impression.* Is one of these the right word for this context?

Idea itself is a little too general; *thought,* a little too specific. Both *concept* and *conception,* according to the dictionary, commonly apply to "any idea of what a thing should be" [3]; but the writer wants a word that will apply to his first idea of what the character actually was. *Notion* implies some degree of "vagueness or caprice"; the vagueness might possibly be appropriate to the writer's meaning here, but not the caprice. Finally he reads that *impression* refers to "an idea stimulated by something seen, heard, read, etc." This word implies just that specific qualification of *idea,* then, which fits the context; it is the right word. The writer revises his sentence to read, "My first impression of the character was that he was a moral weakling." The little time he has spent on this revision was fully worth while: he now has the best word for his purpose.

Examples could be multiplied indefinitely, but they would all illustrate the same point. The writer should be determined always to find

[3] Reprinted with permission from *Webster's New Collegiate Dictionary* (Springfield, Mass., G. & C. Merriam Company, 1960, publishers of the Merriam-Webster Dictionaries).

the word with the *precise denotation* for the context; he should not
be satisfied with one that fits almost, but not exactly.

Control of Connotation. The second requirement of an effective
word is that its connotation be properly controlled. That is, the associations which the word suggests, in addition to its central and primary
meaning, should be appropriate to the context and to the writer's intention. A knight in shining armor may ride a *horse* or, perhaps even
more suitably, a *steed;* unless he is Don Quixote (i.e., unless an effect
of deliberate incongruity is to be produced), he ought not to ride on a
nag.

In certain kinds of writing, the *control of connotation* is really the
elimination of connotation, insofar as possible. In purely objective, impersonal, factual writing, suggestive associations or imaginative over-
tones would be out of place; the diction should be restricted to words
with little or no connotation. Scientific writing, in which objectivity
is essential, is characterized by the use of special terms which have
precise denotation but no connotation at all. The zoologist will use
not *steed* or *nag* but *horse* or even the technical terms *equidae* and
equus caballus for the genus and species, respectively.

In all except the purely objective and impersonal types of writing,
the inclusion of some connotative words is usually desirable. And
whenever such words are selected, the control of connotation is a positive, rather than a negative, principle. It means being careful that the
things associated with a word are appropriate to the effect which the
writer intends. For instance, we may consider a little more closely
the words *horse, steed,* and *nag. Horse* is relatively neutral in connotation; it would be suitable in any context where no particular
atmosphere is being developed, no special coloring of attitude or
feeling: "In the farmyard were two cows, a dozen chickens, and a
horse."

Steed and *nag* are both more highly connotative than *horse.* But
steed and *nag* differ widely from each other and from *horse* in the
kinds of their connotation; the associations which they suggest are
almost diametrically opposite. *Steed* is a "romantic" word; its connotations, then, would be appropriate to an effect of excitement or
glamor. A steed might be a wild horse, a creature of spirit and mettle,
with flowing mane—the leader, perhaps, of a herd. A steed would
scarcely be tame, under any circumstances (the connotations of *steed*
and *tame* are incongruous), but he might be civilized to the service of
man. If so, he wears a rich harness and trappings; he neighs and paws
the ground. As suggested above, he may bear a knight in armor; he

may march in a gorgeous procession. He may draw a state coach, or better still a chariot, but certainly never a cart or a wagon. In each case the connotations of *steed* work together with those of *knight, armor, chariot,* to build up a consistent effect. Obviously, words like *steed* and *wagon* would work against each other.

On the other hand, a nag might perfectly well pull a wagon; most appropriately, perhaps, a wagon filled with trash. *Nag* is a homely word; its connotations are such as to be useful in developing an effect, say, of squalor. There are other words, too, that still denote a horse, words that would also be appropriate to such an effect. *Hack,* for example, is closely similar to *nag* in connotation; *jade* is reasonably close, although it connotes some viciousness of temper as well as decrepitude. As a heritage from the times when transportation was largely horse-drawn, we have these several words for horses, words that suggest different associations and attitudes.

Specificity and Concreteness. A third requirement of an effective word is that ordinarily it be as *specific* as the context will allow. Closely related to this requirement is the value of *concreteness* in diction. In common usage, the words *specific* and *concrete* are both opposed to *abstract,* although in these two oppositions the word *abstract* has two somewhat different meanings. As opposed to *specific, abstract* has the sense of *general;* that is, *inclusive:* an abstract term applies to a relatively large class of things (e.g., *trees*), or any member of such a class (*tree*). As the class becomes smaller (*pines* or *pine, white pine*), the word becomes more specific; it is most specific when it refers to one unique thing (*the white pine tree in my back yard*). This is the meaning which the word *abstract* has in the discussion of the levels of abstraction (see p. 305).

As opposed to *concrete, abstract* means "referring to an intangible idea or quality" (e.g., *truth, falsehood, beauty, ugliness*). A *concrete* word, on the other hand, refers to something immediately perceptible by one or more of the five senses (*dog, bark, bread, perfume, snow*). In this context the word *tree* is not abstract but concrete, because a tree may be seen, felt, and sometimes heard and smelled.

Specific vs. Abstract or General Words. Whenever the context allows, a *specific word* that refers to a particular thing is preferable to an abstract or general expression.

RELATIVELY ABSTRACT:	RELATIVELY SPECIFIC:
The garden was full of lovely flowers.	In the garden there were snapdragons, tulips, and red roses.

RELATIVELY ABSTRACT:	RELATIVELY SPECIFIC:
On the table was a book.	On the table was a copy of D. C. Somervell's abridgment of Arnold Toynbee's *A Study of History*.
He went to get some tools.	He went to get a hammer and a pair of pliers.

MORE SPECIFIC: He went to get a claw hammer and a pair of round-nosed pliers.

Sometimes we do have occasion to make broad and general statements; for these, words which represent a high level of abstraction are entirely proper. If what we want to express, for instance, is that all living things are characterized by growth, then these are the words to use. In such a context we should *not* be more specific and say, "The white pine tree in my back yard grew eighteen inches last year" because, clearly, this is not what we mean. The inexperienced writer often tends to generalize, to use abstract terms, when he might effectively be more specific. He is more likely to err in the direction of over-generalization than of over-particularization. What he should work for, then, is the maximum appropriate specificity; he should try consciously and deliberately to select words that are highly individualized.

Concrete Words vs. Words Referring to Intangibles. Where either kind of word will fit the context and convey the writer's meaning, a *concrete word* is preferable to one that is abstract in the other sense, of referring to something intangible.

INTANGIBLE:	CONCRETE:
Nothing else aroused his indignation so intensely as falsehood.	Nothing else aroused his indignation so intensely as a lie.
She was keenly susceptible to beauty.	She was profoundly moved by watching the lovely sunset.
The spirit of our municipal government is epitomized by democracy.	The spirit of our municipal government is epitomized by the town-meetinghouse in the square.

We do have occasion to use words which are abstract in the sense of referring to intangibles. Abstract ideas and qualities are important; often we wish to speak or write about them, and we cannot get along without the words which denote them. It would be impossible in concrete words to convey the meaning of "And now abideth faith, hope, charity, these three" all of which are abstract. But where it *is* possible for the writer adequately to express his meaning in concrete words, he should do so.

Variety. A fourth requirement of effective words is that they be judiciously varied to avoid monotonous repetition. This requirement applies primarily to *words* rather than to any single word, for of course *variety* cannot be a quality of a single word.

The most obvious danger of monotonous repetition is the danger that the writer may injudiciously repeat his own words too often, in short space. There is another possibility, however: that he may use expressions which have already been repeated too often in common usage and have thereby become stale and trite; thus he may in effect injudiciously repeat an expression although he uses it only once himself.

Repetition: Pro and Con. Some *repetition* is perfectly proper; it is only monotonous or injudicious repetition that the writer needs to avoid. It is not true that he should never use one word more than once on a page, or even more than once in a paragraph. If one particular word is the precise word for his purpose, then that is the word to use, even if it does recur frequently in short compass. Here is a passage by a careful writer of prose.

The disparagers of culture make its motive curiosity; sometimes, indeed, they make its motive mere exclusiveness and vanity. The culture which is supposed to plume itself on a smattering of Greek and Latin is a culture which is begotten by nothing so intellectual as curiosity; it is valued either out of sheer vanity and ignorance or else as an engine of social and class distinction, separating its holder, like a badge or title, from other people who have not got it. No serious man would call this *culture,* or attach any value to it, as culture, at all. To find the real ground for the very different estimate which serious people will set upon culture, we must find some motive for culture in the terms of which may lie a real ambiguity; and such a motive the word *curiosity* gives us.[4]

The word *culture* appears seven times in this paragraph. It might seem that for the sake of variety the writer could have replaced this word with synonyms like *cultivation, enlightenment, refinement;* but these would not have represented his meaning accurately. For this writer, *culture* has a precise meaning which no other word will convey. Variety in word choice is desirable, but it is less important than precision.

[4] Matthew Arnold, *Culture and Anarchy,* the first paragraph of Chapter I, "Sweetness and Light."

Often, however, the writer does not have to choose between variety and precision; he can have both. Many times, there are synonyms or synonymous expressions which will represent his meaning just as accurately as a word which he has already used. Under these circumstances he should not repeat the word but should substitute the synonymous expression. In the following passage the word *students* (or *the students*) might conceivably have been repeated in place of each of the italicized words and phrases. Here the repetition would have been awkward; the use of the synonymous expressions is obviously preferable.

Students in their first year participate in a planned schedule of activity. For example, *as a group they* attend weekly non-denominational services in the Chapel; after each of these meetings *they all* proceed to a special luncheon in the Commons, with some program arranged by a committee of *class members*. Sometimes two or three of *the freshmen* themselves address *their classmates* on some topic of current interest.

As we have seen, synonyms should not be used indiscriminately. In passages like this one, however, where no confusion or distortion of the meaning will arise, the writer should observe the principle of variety and use varied synonymous expressions rather than repetitions of a single word.

Avoiding Clichés. The other principal danger of injudicious repetition is that the writer will use expressions which have been repeated too often already, by other writers and speakers, and which are therefore trite and ineffective. Such an expression is called a *cliché* (the French word means literally "stereotyped"). Ordinarily clichés are phrases rather than single words; the effect of staleness arises from the frequent use of a particular group of words together.

Many clichés are figures of speech, especially the figures of comparison (see pp. 307–308), simile ("busy as a bee," "sober as a judge") and metaphor ("shadow of a doubt," "sands of time"). Often the comparisons were highly effective in their original contexts; "at one fell swoop," for example, occurs in Shakespeare's *Macbeth,* in the scene where Macduff, on hearing the news that his wife and children have been murdered by Macbeth, compares the latter to a hellish bird of prey swooping down and killing several victims at once. The originally powerful vividness of such expressions is itself the reason why they have been quoted again and again, both consciously and unconsciously, until they have become stale and lost their effectiveness.

To avoid clichés entirely is an ideal difficult to achieve. They are heard and read a great deal; almost everyone uses some of them occasionally. The writer can at least approach the ideal—he can minimize his own use of these hackneyed expressions—by developing his awareness of them, his ability to recognize them when he meets them or when he is on the point of using one of them himself. This development is a continuing process; it is furthered by the writer's general experience with words—by extensive reading and by practice in writing. There is no shortcut to this goal, but acquaintance with this list may increase one's consciousness of many of the most common clichés.

acid test
after all is said and done
among those present
animal cunning
at one fell swoop
bated breath
bitter end
blind as a bat
broad daylight
brown as a berry
burn the midnight oil
calm and collected
clear as a bell
colorful spectacle
commune with nature
conspicuous by its absence
cool as a cucumber
crack of dawn
crying need
doomed to disappointment
dotted landscapes
drunk as a lord
each and every
fast and furious
Father Time
few and far between

finer things of life
flowing with milk and honey
generous to a fault
goodly number
hang in the balance
hit the nail on the head
honest as the day is long
humble opinion
hungry as a bear
imposing structure
in the final analysis
in this day and age
irony of fate
last but not least
life of the party
like a bolt from the blue
method in his madness
nip in the bud
none the worse for wear
plot thickens
point with pride
powers that be
precarious existence

pretty as a picture
proud parents
proud possessor
pure and simple
rank outsider
raving beauty
rough diamond
sedulously avoid
sigh of relief
slow as molasses
smart as a whip
stands to reason
stark naked
taken aback
tale of woe
tired and/but happy
too numerous to mention
unvarnished truth
veritable mine of information
view with alarm
watery grave
well-rounded person
wend one's way
white as snow
with a dull thud
wits' end
yield to no man

TOOLS AND TECHNIQUES FOR ATTAINING GOOD DICTION

Several suggestions regarding ways to attain particular qualities of good diction have been given in the preceding section of this chapter.

In the present section a few more suggestions are given; they are somewhat broader and more basic and have to do with the development not only of good diction but of general competence in dealing with language. Their principal application, however, is still in the area of diction. These suggestions apply to using dictionaries, to vocabulary building, and to listening and reading.

Dictionaries and Their Uses. The best way to learn about dictionaries is not to read about them but to use them. It is important to own a good dictionary, to refer to it regularly, to become thoroughly familiar with it. One ought actually to read, as continuous discourse, the introductory explanatory sections. From this material one will learn about the special features of the dictionary [5] and also about the symbols and abbreviations employed.

Types of Dictionaries. *Dictionaries* may be classified in three principal types: unabridged, abridged, and special-subject dictionaries.

UNABRIDGED DICTIONARIES. An *unabridged dictionary* is one which theoretically includes all the words in a language. We say "theoretically" because actually such all-inclusiveness is impossible. Language is always changing; and in the time required to compile or even to revise an unabridged dictionary, at least a few new words will have come into existence which the dictionary will not include. A good unabridged dictionary, however, is inclusive enough for all practical purposes.

This type may be subdivided into two subtypes: dictionaries concerned primarily with current usage, and those with greater emphasis on the historical development of the language and its vocabulary. The first subtype—more widely used and adequate for all ordinary occasions—is represented in this country by *Funk and Wagnalls New Standard Dictionary* and by *Webster's New International Dictionary*. The second subtype—indispensable if for any reason the user needs a full account of the history of a word—is represented by the *Dictionary of American English on Historical Principles* and especially by the thirteen-volume *Oxford English Dictionary* (edited in England).

ABRIDGED DICTIONARIES. An *abridged dictionary* is one which includes a *selection* of the words in a language. The selection may be small or large; accordingly, there are abridged dictionaries of varying scope, from "vest-pocket" editions with only a few thousand words up to substantial volumes. A good abridged dictionary includes all words in common usage, plus a great many more which are less

---

[5] For example, in some dictionaries biographical and geographical information appears in separate sections, not with the main alphabetical listing.

common. Under normal circumstances it will serve practically all the needs of a writer—although he ought still to have access to an unabridged dictionary for dealing with special problems.

Among the good abridged dictionaries, ordinarily adequate for college writing or for other writing on general topics, are *Webster's New World Dictionary*, the *American College Dictionary*, and *Webster's New Collegiate Dictionary*.

SPECIAL–SUBJECT DICTIONARIES. The *special–subject dictionary* is actually a particular type of abridged dictionary: it too includes a selection of the words in a language. Its distinguishing feature is that the criterion of selection is relevance to one special area of knowledge; for example, Grove's *Dictionary of Music and Musicians*. Such compilations usually contain a far smaller total number of words than general-purpose abridged dictionaries of comparable scope; but they include some technical or special terms that would otherwise appear only in an unabridged dictionary and often biographical or historical entries which would not be found even there. Also, many of the definitions, discussions, and illustrations are likely to be more extensive than those in any general-purpose dictionary. (For further material concerning reference works of this nature, see Appendix, pp. 408–409.)

Uses of a Dictionary. From a dictionary we can often get five or six different kinds of information about a word: its meaning(s), spelling and syllabication, pronunciation, and derivation; sometimes a list of its synonyms or examples of its use in idiomatic expressions, or both.

MEANING. We look to the dictionary for definitions explaining the *meaning* or *meanings* of a particular word. If the word may be used as more than one part of speech, its meanings in each category are included. If the meaning of the word has changed, earlier as well as current meanings may be given.

SPELLING AND SYLLABICATION. The dictionary indicates the *correct spelling* of a word; if more than one spelling is correct (e.g., *theater, theatre*), both versions are given, with the more usual or preferred spelling first. Also, the dictionary indicates how the word is divided into *syllables*. When the writer is in doubt about where he ought to divide a word at the end of a line, he can find out by looking it up.

PRONUNCIATION. By means of phonetic symbols, the dictionary shows the proper *pronunciation* of a word. The particular symbols vary among different dictionaries, but within each one the method is consistent. One should familiarize himself with the system employed in his own dictionary. In pronunciation as well as in spelling, acceptable alternatives are indicated; for example (in the symbols used in *Webster's New Collegiate Dictionary*), pĭ·ăn′ĭst; pē′á·nĭst.

DERIVATION. Often the dictionary gives the *source* of the English word: the language from which it came, and the form and meaning of the word in the original. Thus we learn that *physical* comes ultimately from the Greek *physis,* meaning *nature*. For native English words, the dictionary usually provides the earlier form, in Old or Middle English; for instance, *stone* was previously *stan* and *ston*.

SYNONYMS. For certain words the dictionary enumerates *synonyms,* sometimes with a brief discussion of their various shades of meaning. The separate alphabetical entry for each of the synonyms will carry a cross reference to this discussion. For an example of the use of a synonym reference, see "Precision in Denotation," page 310.

IDIOM. An *idiom* is an expression of an idea in a particular phrasing or combination of words characteristic of a language or, sometimes, characteristic of one group using a language. For instance, in American English we say that one thing is different *from* another; in British English the idiom is usually different *to*. If the writer is faced with a question of idiom—for example, if he is wondering whether he should speak of comparing one thing *with* or *to* another—he can find the answer in his dictionary. (In this example, he will find under *compare* that both idioms are proper, but that they have somewhat different meanings.)

Vocabulary Building. The better one's vocabulary—the more words he knows and the better he knows them—the more readily he can attain distinction in diction. Precision in denotation, appropriateness in connotation, specificity and concreteness, variety—the qualities of good diction all depend for their achievement upon the writer's having a large stock of words at his command, so that he can choose the best among them. This section, therefore, is devoted to suggestions for vocabulary building.

Up to a point, *vocabulary building* is an entirely natural process. We all do acquire at least a minimum working vocabulary of the words we need in our everyday life. We become familiar with them by encountering them repeatedly, in settings in which their meaning is apparent, either immediately or after repetition or explanation. We learn our first words by hearing them spoken; later we learn some in this way and others by reading them. Most of these words we soon come to speak and write ourselves, although there is some difference between the number of words we can recognize and understand (our *passive* vocabulary) and the number that we ourselves use (our *active* vocabulary). This process takes place rapidly in our early years; later it slows down somewhat, and sometimes it stops altogether.

For anyone who is concerned to improve his vocabulary—and the writer must be thus concerned—the best thing he can do is to foster and encourage this natural process in himself, to make sure that for him it does not stop but continues. How can he do this? *He must learn every new word he encounters.* (By a new word is meant either one that is unfamiliar to him, or one that is only partly familiar.) He must never let a new word slip by unlearned, never be satisfied because he has an approximate understanding of a passage, if it contains a word he does not know. With all new words, his policy should be "They shall not pass" without investigation.

Particular Suggestions. These principles, though easy to state, require scrupulous care and attention to apply. Here are a few specific suggestions.

1. Unless you are using material which it would be improper for you to mark (e.g., library books), circle, check, or underline any new words you read. If you understand the general sense of what you are reading, it may be best for you *not* to investigate these words immediately, and thereby break the line of thought; but when you have finished reading, or arrived at the end of a paragraph or topic discussion, you can go back and consider carefully every word you have marked.

2. Take full advantage of any assistance afforded by the *context* of a new word—by the surrounding passage in which it appears. Usually this does afford at least some clue to the meaning of the word. Occasionally, in fact, it makes the meaning clear: only one meaning would fit the context. But usually some question about the word will remain—about its precise shade of meaning, perhaps, or about its pronunciation. If you are in any doubt at all, consult the dictionary.

3. Keep a dictionary at your regular place for reading and studying. This may occasionally be impossible, in a library reading room, for instance; but even there you can take a seat near the dictionary so you may refer to it easily.

Many other suggestions may be made for the purpose of vocabulary building. One may use prepared lists of words on the outer fringe of a basic vocabulary. Lists of this kind, with short tests to be self-administered, appear rather often even in newspapers and magazines as well as in textbooks. One may make similar use of a list which he compiles for himself, recording every new word he meets, with a brief definition and perhaps a sample context. One may make a point of using recently-learned words in writing as well as speaking. One may apply the adage "Use a word three times and it is yours" as a means of adding new words to his active as well as his passive vocabulary. And one may always enlist the assistance of his instructors and friends in determining the precise meaning of a difficult word.

Principles of Word-Formation. There is another consideration useful enough in vocabulary building to warrant discussion here: a consideration of some of the ways in which English words are *formed*. These include the principle of compounding, and the use of foreign words and word-elements as ingredients of English words.

COMPOUNDING: ROOT, SUFFIX, AND PREFIX. Compounding is the putting together of separate words or word-elements to make other words.[6] If one knows the meaning of the separate ingredients, he can often infer the meaning of the compound. For a simple example, we put together *work* and *man* to make *workman*. By adding further elements we may get *workmanlike* and *unworkmanlike*.

The words and word-elements which make up compounds are classified in three groups: roots, suffixes, and prefixes. A ROOT is simply an uncompounded word or word form: in the example above, the words *work* and *man*. A SUFFIX is an element added at the end of a word (*workman*LIKE), and a PREFIX, an element added at the beginning (UN*workmanlike*). Suffixes and prefixes may have the form of independent words (the suffix *–like*, the prefix *self–*), or they may be elements which could not stand alone (the suffix *–ness,* as in *self-consciousness,* and the prefix *un–*). A word or word-element is a suffix or prefix if it is used at the end or beginning of a large number of compounds and is thus a standard compounding unit.

Compounds are formed by the combination of two or more roots, or of a root or roots with one or more other elements.

Root plus **root** equals **compound,** plus **root** equals **compound.**
door   bell   doorbell   button   doorbell-button
Root plus **suffix** equals **compound,** plus **suffix** equals **compound.**
leisure   –ly   leisurely   –ness   leisureliness
Root plus **prefix** equals **compound,** plus **prefix** equals **compound.**
conscious[7] *self–   self-conscious   un–   unself-conscious*

[6] The word *compound* is sometimes restricted to combinations of distinct words. It is here used in its broader sense, to include also combinations of a distinct word with other elements.

[7] Strictly speaking, *conscious* is not actually a root but itself a compound; see the following subsection.

Root plus **root** equals **compound,** plus **suffix** equals **compound.**
work   *man*   *workman*   *–like*   *workmanlike*
    plus **prefix** equals **compound.**
        un–   *unworkmanlike*

In compounding, the whole may sometimes be more than, or at least different from, the sum of its parts. A *workman* may be simply a man who does work—that is, the word need not imply any value judgment —but with *workmanlike,* an attitude of approval enters into the meaning of the compound. A workmanlike product is not simply like the product of a workman; it is like the product of a workman who does his work well. Despite such modifications in meaning, the fact remains that knowledge of the parts of a compound will almost always aid in understanding the compound itself. It is worth while, therefore, to know as many roots, suffixes, and prefixes as possible.

USE OF FOREIGN WORDS AND WORD–ELEMENTS. The vocabulary of English is an amalgamation of words from many sources. English is basically a Germanic language (like modern German, Dutch, Flemish, and the Scandinavian languages), and most words of Germanic origin are therefore in a real sense native. But a very great many of the words in modern English have come into the language, through the centuries, from foreign sources: most especially from Greek, from Latin directly, and indirectly from Latin through French. A background in one or more of these languages will often help in the interpretation of new English words; similarly, a knowledge of how English words have been formed from these sources may be advantageous.

Certain words have been taken into English intact; that is, in their original foreign form. Thus *cosmos* and *genesis* are Greek words, *auditorium* and *appendix* are Latin, *capable* and *courier* are French (ultimately from a Latin origin).

Knowing only this much might not be of great value; the real value lies in observing how the *basic elements* (chiefly roots) *of foreign words* like these enter into numerous combinations. The meaning of each element remains constant, or varies through only a relatively small range; a knowledge of its meaning, therefore, contributes toward an understanding of all its compounds. The Greek root *cosm* of *cosmos* means "order or harmony," often specifically "the ordered universe or the world"; this meaning is preserved in *cosmopolitan, microcosm.* The *gen* of *genesis* means "development, origin, or birth"; compare *genealogy, genetics, eugenics.* Latin *aud* means "hear," as in *audience, audi-*

ble, audition; the *pend* of *appendix* means "hang," as in *impend, depend;* in the variant form *pens* it appears in *pensive* and *suspense.* The *cap* of French *capable* is actually a Latin root meaning "take or contain," as in *capacious, capacity;* the *cour* of *courier* is the French form of the Latin *cur(s),* meaning "run," as in *precursor, concur,* and (with the French form again) *concourse.* Selected lists of Greek and Latin roots, suffixes, and prefixes appear on the next few pages.

Greek Root	Original Meaning	English Derivative
ANDR	man (specif. male)	polyandry
ANTHROP	human being	anthropology
CHROM	color	chromatic
CHRON	time	synchronize
DEM	people	epidemic
DERM	skin	pachyderm
DYN	power	dynamic
GEO	earth	geology
GNOS	know, distinguish	diagnosis
GRAPH, GRAM	write	telegraph, epigram
GYN	woman	misogynist
HYDR	water	hydrant
LOG	word, study	sociology
MIS	hate	misanthropic
PATH	suffer	sympathy
PHAN, PHEN	appear	diaphanous, phenomenon
PHIL	love	philanthropic
POD	foot	tripod
POLI	city	metropolis
PSYCH	mind [8]	psychopathic
PYR	fire	pyrotechnic
TELE	far, distant, end	telephone, teleology
THANA	death	euthanasia
THE	god	theology
TOM	cut	appendectomy

Greek Suffix [9]	Meaning	English Example
−ARCH	ruler, leadership	monarch, oligarchy
−IC(s)	pertaining to	athletic, physics
−ISM	system	communism
−IST	agent or doer	hedonist

[8] Originally, *butterfly,* which came to symbolize the mind.

[9] Some of the forms listed here, like *-arch* and *-meter,* are actually roots in Greek; but in English they function chiefly as suffixes. The meanings given represent their usual signification in English; their original meanings vary somewhat.

Greek Suffix	Meaning	English Example
—ITIS	inflammation	appendicitis
—IZE	make, render	sterilize
—METER	measure	chronometer

Greek Prefix	Meaning	English Example
A—, AN—	(negative)	atheist, anhydrous
ANTI—	against	antidote
AUTO—	self—	automobile
DI—	two	dipodic
DIA—	through, across	diameter
EPI—	upon	epitaph
EU—	good, well	euphemism
HYPER—	above, over	hypersensitive
HYPO—	beneath, under	hypodermic
MACRO—	large	macrocosm
MICRO—	small	microscope
MONO—	one, single	monomania
NEO—	new	neologism
PAN—	all	pandemonium
PARA—	beside	paraphrase
PERI—	around	peripatetic
POLY—	many	polygamous
PRO—	before	prologue
PSEUDO—	false	pseudonym
SYN—, SYM—	with	synchronous, sympathy

Latin Root	Original Meaning	English Derivative
ALT	high	altitude
ANIMA	mind, spirit	magnanimous
BIB	drink	imbibe
CANT, CHANT (Fr.)	sing	incantation, enchant
CED	go, yield	accede
COR(D), COUR (Fr.)	heart	cordial, courage
CRED	believe	credible
CRESC, CRU (Fr.)	grow	crescent, accrue
DIC(T)	speak	diction
DUC(T)	lead	reduce, conduct
FER	carry	transfer
GRAV	heavy	grave, aggravate
GRAD, GRESS	go, move	retrograde, congress
JECT	throw	reject, adjective
JUNCT, JOIN (Fr.)	connect, join	conjunction, rejoin
JUR	swear	jury, adjure

Latin Root	Original Meaning	English Derivative
LOQU, LOCUT	speak	eloquent, locution
MAGN	great, large	magnificent
MANU	hand	manual
MIT, MISS	send	remit, mission
NOMEN, NOMIN	name	cognomen, nominal
PED	foot	pedal
PORT	carry	transportation
REG, RECT, ROY (Fr.)	rule, straight	regal, rectangle, royal
RUPT	break, destroy	corruption
SCRIB, SCRIPT	write	subscribe, prescription
SEQU, SECUT	follow	consequent, persecution
SPIC, SPECT	look, regard	conspicuous, perspective
SPIR	breath, breathe	spirit, inspiration
SUM, SUMPT	take, accept	resume, assumption
TEN (Fr.), TAIN	hold	tenacious, maintain
TRACT	pull, draw	attract, traction
VEH, VECT	bear, carry	vehicle, convection
VEN(T)	come	intervene, prevent
VERT, VERS	turn	convert, reverse
VID, VIS	see	invidious, vision
VOC	call	vocation, invoke
VOLV, VOLUT	roll	revolve, convolution

Latin Suffix	Meaning	English Example
−ANT		important
−ENT		prevalent
−ANCE	performing, or the performance of, an action	insurance
−ENCE		inadvertence
−ANCY		redundancy
−ENCY		impudency
−CIDE [10]	the killing of	homicide, parricide
−C(U)LE	(diminutive)	animalcule, cubicle
−ESCE	become	coalesce, deliquesce
−FY [10]	make, render	purify
−ITY	condition of being	verity
−IVE	having the nature of the doer of an act	active, receptive
−TOR		victor
−TUDE	state of being	turpitude

Latin Prefix	Meaning	English Example
AB−	from, away	absent, abject
AD−	to, toward	adjacent, admission

[10] Actually a root, functioning in English as a suffix.

Latin Prefix	Meaning	English Example
ANTE–	before	antecedent
BENE–	good, well	beneficial
BI–	two	bilateral
CIRCUM–	around	circumference
CON– [11]	with, together	conscious, convention
CONTRA–	against	contravene
EX– [11]	out, out of	exhale
JUXTA–	beside	juxtapose
MAL–	bad, evil	maleficent
MULTI–	many	multiply
POST–	after	postpone, posterity
PRO–	in behalf of	pronoun, protest
RETRO–	backward	retrospective
SUB– [11]	under, below	subtype, subjection
SUPER–	over, above	supersede
TRANS–	across	transition

Even without actual study of a classical language, the writer can add to these lists by noting elements which recur in many compounds. For instance, what must the Greek root *bio* mean (*biology, biography, symbiosis*)? Notice that in compounds including foreign elements, as in native compounds like *workmanlike*, there is sometimes an extension or a change of meaning; it is a long way, for instance, from *reduce,* "lead back," to an eighteen-day diet. Usually, however, there is a discernible relationship between the original meaning of the foreign element and the meaning of the English compound. A knowledge of the foreign elements, therefore, is very useful in vocabulary building.

Listening and Reading. There is yet another way in which the writer can help himself to attain good diction: he can make a point of *listening,* whenever possible, to good spoken English, and of *reading* well-written material in magazines and books. By comparison with making regular use of a dictionary and with following specific suggestions for vocabulary building, the method of listening and reading is somewhat indirect. But, put to full use, it can be very effective.

The writer should look for occasions when he can hear excellent English spoken. Such opportunities are not always immediately at hand. Not that most of what he hears is *bad* English; but the kind that is good enough to be really valuable in the development of good

---

[11] The last letter of *con-* and *sub-* is often changed to agree with the first letter of the root in the compound (*commotion, colloquial, correct; suggest, support, sufficient*); the *x* in *ex-* sometimes disappears (*elapse, elicit, educate*).

diction, he may not be able to hear whenever he likes. From whom *can* he hear this kind? Some leaders in government use excellent English in their public addresses. Some radio and television commentators speak very well indeed; so too do some clergymen. If the writer is on a college campus, where in certain courses formal lectures are given, the language of these will probably be very good English. A number of stage plays and films have excellent dialogue; for example, most of the plays of George Bernard Shaw. There *is* good English to be heard at times.

Good written material is available always. Wide reading is the best way of all for the writer to develop his general skill in dealing with language. Of course such reading is valuable for many other reasons too; most often, perhaps, the assistance which it gives the writer in improving his own work is a side effect, subsidiary to other values. But it does serve this specific purpose. Benjamin Franklin tells in his *Autobiography* how he was able to benefit in his own writing, chiefly in style and diction, by reading the best English essayists of his time. To cite only one other, more recent example, Somerset Maugham recounts a similar experience in his autobiographical work called *The Summing Up*. Searching deliberately for material which might help him write better, he read a number of different authors. Some were of greater assistance to him, and some were of less; but the net result of his reading was distinctly beneficial. The inexperienced writer will discover the same thing for himself: not everything which he reads will be very helpful to him, but certain things will be—and the more good writing he reads, the greater will be his benefit.

AVOIDING COMMON IMPROPRIETIES

For the attainment of good diction, the positive principles outlined in the preceding sections of this chapter are more important and ought to be more useful than any list of negative suggestions. There is some value also, however, in the writer's being specifically aware of certain common improprieties—expressions involving poor or at least questionable diction—so that if one of them occurs to him as he is writing, he will recognize it as improper and avoid using it. These expressions occur in some of the English that we read and in more of what we hear, and even in some that most of us use occasionally ourselves when we are not being careful. To be realistic, sometimes it is all right for us not to be careful, or in any case it is probably inevitable that we shall not always be. But at other times it is not all right; sometimes it is inappropriate and results in ineffective communication. At these times, clearly, we should exert care. It is for this purpose that knowledge of particular expressions to be avoided is especially useful.

Notice one qualification in connection with the list given below. Some of these expressions are improper on the formal or high informal level only; they are acceptable on the low informal or colloquial level. Perhaps even the worst of them are acceptable on the vulgar level— indeed they are characteristic of it—but since it is only very rarely appropriate for a writer to employ the vulgar level, these worst expressions should be avoided always. Reference to a distinction among levels is made occasionally in the list which follows.

This list is highly selective; for a comprehensive presentation, see Harry Shaw, *Errors in English and Ways to Correct Them,* "Everyday Handbooks" (New York: Barnes & Noble, Inc., 1962).[12]

A Short Glossary of Usage

ACCEPT, EXCEPT. These two words should be pronounced and spelled carefully in order to avoid confusion. *Accept* is a verb approximately synonymous with *take* or *receive; except* is a preposition synonymous with *but,* or a verb meaning to *rule out* or *eliminate.*

AFFECT, EFFECT. These two words should not be confused. *Affect* is almost always a verb, meaning to *influence.*[13] *Effect* as a verb means to *bring about* (a doctor may *effect* a cure); it is used more commonly as a noun meaning *result.* One thing may *affect* another; or one thing may produce an *effect.*

AGGRAVATE. This word is improper in the sense of *irritate* or *annoy:* "He aggravated me by interfering with my work." It is proper in the sense of *intensify* or *make worse:* "His interference aggravated my difficulty."

ALL RIGHT, "ALRIGHT." Only the first of these two forms is proper; the second is a misspelling.

AROUND. *Around* in the sense of *approximately* ("He makes *around* ten thousand dollars a year") is questionable usage above the colloquial level.

AS FAR AS . . . IS (ARE, WAS, etc.) CONCERNED. The latter part of this construction should not be omitted. Sometimes a writer forgets how he has begun this construction and leaves it incomplete: "As far as the circumstances—the weather, the condition of the field, the spirit of the team and of the rooters in the grandstand—it is a good time for the game." Properly, *are concerned* should appear before or after the expression set off by dashes.

AWFUL, AWFULLY. On the formal or high informal level, *awful* is proper only in the meanings *full of awe* and *inspiring awe,* and *awfully* in the

[12] For further information, the standard reference work on this subject is H. W. Fowler, *A Dictionary of Modern English Usage* (London: Oxford University Press, current revision 1937).

[13] There is a rather rare noun *affect* (with the accent on the first syllable), meaning *feeling;* it is largely restricted to psychological terminology.

corresponding adverbial senses. The use of either one as an intensive meaning *very,* or in the sense of *very bad(ly),* is colloquial in status.

BETWEEN. As a preposition, *between* properly takes just two objects, or a plural object which denotes just two things: "between you and me," or "between the two brothers." On the formal or high informal level, it is improper to use *between* when the objects are more than two: "between you and me and him," or "between all the members of the football team." In these latter examples the right word to use is *among.*

Note also that two objects of *between* should be joined by *and:* between five *and* (not *to*) ten," "between one possibility *and* (not *or*) another."

BRING OUT. Though not actually improper, this expression is used to excess, and often in a vague sense, by inexperienced writers, especially in paraphrasing the views of someone else: "The author brings out that conditions at this time were unfavorable." Usually in such a context some other, more precise expression is preferable: the author *shows* or *demonstrates* or *indicates* or *proves* or even simply *says.*

CAN, MAY. In formal English, the auxiliary verb *can* means to *be able to;* the corresponding sense of *may* is to *have permission to.* The use of *can* has spread into this second sense, the one proper to *may* (e.g., "Can I go now?"); but this encroachment is questionable usage above the colloquial level. "May I go now?" is preferable.

CAN'T HELP BUT. Logically, this expression includes three negatives: the adverb *not,* the verb *help* (here meaning *avoid*), and the preposition *but* (meaning *except* or *besides*). "I can't help but feel angry" logically means "I can't avoid (doing something else) besides feeling angry"; that is, "I can't feel angry." On levels lower than the formal, the "can't help but" construction is sanctioned by widespread usage, and it will normally be understood in the intended positive meaning, even though it is logically negative. On the formal level, the writer should use the logically positive expression, with just two negatives that cancel each other: "I cannot help feeling angry."

CAN'T SEEM. This expression involves what is actually a misplaced negative modifier. If I say, "I can't seem to do it," what I mean is probably "It seems that I cannot do it." That is, the negative properly applies not to the seeming but to the doing: I can *seem,* all right, but I cannot *do* it— whatever the task may be. A good way to avoid this kind of difficulty is provided by an expression like "I seem unable to do it."

CASE. Though of course perfectly proper in specific senses like that of a *case* in a law court or a *case* of ginger ale, this word is too often used in vague, roundabout, unnecessarily wordy expressions: "In the case of a professional actor, calm nerves are essential." Usually such expressions can be simplified and improved by omitting the *case* phrase: "A professional actor must have calm nerves."

COME UP WITH. In the sense of *ascertain* or *arrive at,* this construction is improper above the low informal or colloquial level. It is proper for a pearl diver to come up with an oyster, but not, in careful usage, for some-one investigating a problem to "come up with" a solution.

COMPLECTED. According to *Webster's New Collegiate Dictionary,* this substitute for *complexioned* is characteristic of dialect rather than of stand-ard usage. Probably the best alternative to the questionable "He was dark-complected" is "He had a dark complexion."

CONTACT. As a verb meaning to *get in touch with* a person, contact has only colloquial status. "Why not communicate with the president?" is better usage than "Why not contact the president?"

COULD OF. See *Of.*

CUTE. This word is very widely used in the colloquial language of the campus. Even in this context it may be objectionable because of triteness, but no one could question its being sanctioned by usage on this level. On the higher levels, however, the word properly means "attractive by reason of daintiness or picturesqueness, as a child" (*Webster's New Collegiate Dictionary*). Clearly, then, the application of this adjective, say, to a football player is improper except in colloquial language.

DATA. This word is plural; the singular is *datum. Data,* therefore, when it is a subject, requires a plural verb; when it is modified by an adjective that shows number, it requires the plural form of the adjective: "*These* data *are* important."

DISINTERESTED. Although there is some sanction for the use of *disinter-ested* in the sense of *having no interest or concern,* many writers use only *uninterested* in this sense, and save *disinterested* to mean *impartial:* "The dispute should be adjudged by a disinterested third party." This distinction is worth keeping.

DON'T. This form is the contraction for *do not,* not for *does not.* It is ungrammatical, therefore, with a third-person singular subject, as in "He don't know any better." On the informal level, it is proper to use *doesn't* in the third-person singular and *don't* elsewhere; on the formal level, of course, it is proper to avoid contractions altogether.

EFFECT. See *Affect, effect.*

ENTHUSE. This form is improper except in colloquial usage. On the higher levels, the correct expression is to *be* or *make enthusiastic.*

ETC. This is the abbreviation for two Latin words (*et cetera*) meaning "and others"; *and etc.,* therefore, means "and and others," and is improper because it is redundant and illogical.

Notice also that it is illogical to end either with "etc." or with "and (many) others" a series introduced by "such as." The expression "such as" itself clearly implies that of all the pertinent items only a representative number will be cited, that there are more such items than will appear in the enumeration. A final "etc.," therefore, is superfluous.

EXCEPT. See *Accept, except.*

FELLOW. As an adjective meaning *sharing a status, fellow* is sometimes used redundantly. "My fellow classmates" is redundant, for example, because the *–mates* part of *classmates* is itself sufficient to indicate the sharing of status. "My fellow citizens," on the other hand, is not open to this objection and is perfectly proper.

Fellow as a noun, in the sense, usually, of *young man*—"a few of the fellows from the office"—is colloquial in usage.

FINE. *Fine* is often employed as an adjective approximately synonymous with *very good,* or indicating general favor or approval. This usage is established and entirely proper in certain familiar contexts: to the casual greeting "How are you?" the customary response "Fine, thank you" is certainly acceptable. In other contexts, however, the word in this sense is too vague to be very expressive: "We took a fine trip," "We had a fine time," "We saw a great deal of fine scenery." Other words, at least somewhat more specific, are ordinarily preferable. In the examples above, "enjoyable," "exciting," and "beautiful" respectively would represent some improvement.

INFER. This word is sometimes used improperly where the context calls for *imply. Imply* is proper in the sense of *hint, suggest,* or *indicate indirectly;* to *imply* is the act of a person who, by speaking or writing, is *making* a communication. To *infer* means to *deduce* or *gather;* it is the act of the person *receiving* the communication. In talking to me you may imply (*not* infer) something; in hearing you I may infer an ulterior meaning in what you say.

INGENIOUS, INGENUOUS. These two words should not be confused. *Ingenious* is approximately synonymous with *clever; ingenuous* means *frank, open, artless.* The noun which corresponds to *ingenious* is *ingenuity;* to *ingenuous, ingenuousness.*

IS BECAUSE (also IS WHEN, IS WHERE). These expressions are often used improperly. The most common misuse of *is because* occurs in the context "The reason is because . . ."; the other two expressions are most often misused in statements that look like definitions: "A foul is when you break a rule"; "A grade crossing is where a railroad crosses a road." It is worth noting that the basic fault here lies in the grammar: *is,* a linking verb, is properly followed by a noun or a noun construction (as in "That man is my brother"), whereas clauses introduced by *because, when,* and *where* are ordinarily adverbial. The thing to do, therefore, is to use a noun construction instead of the adverbial clause: "The reason for his fatigue is *that he has been working hard*" (noun clause); "A foul is *an infraction of the rules*" (noun phrase); "A grade crossing is *the point at which a railroad intersects a road*" (noun with adjective-clause modifier).

ITS, IT's. These forms should not be confused. *Its* is the possessive of the pronoun *it; it's* is the contraction for *it is:* "The cat is chasing its tail; it's an amusing creature to watch."

LESS. *Less* is the right word to indicate a smaller quantity of something which is *not* regarded as consisting of individual items: "I have less money in the bank now than I had last week." Where there *are* individual items which might be numbered, the right word is *fewer:* "I have fewer dollars now than I had last week."

LET, LEAVE. *Let* means to *allow; leave,* to *go away from* or *abandon.* To use *leave* in the sense of *let,* as in "Leave me do it my own way," is a vulgarism.

LIABLE. *Liable* is proper in the sense of *responsible* or *answerable* (liable for a debt), or in that of *exposed* to a danger (liable to prosecution); it is improper as a general synonym for *likely,* as in "The rain is liable to stop soon."

LIE, LAY. *Lie* is an intransitive verb meaning to *recline* or *repose:* "The books lie on the table." *Lay* is a transitive verb meaning to *put* or *place:* "Please lay the books on the table." One reason these two verbs are sometimes confused is that the past tense of *lie* is *lay:* "The books lay on the table yesterday." Anyone who has difficulty with these words should make a point of learning the principal parts of both.

Present	Past	Past Participle
lie	lay	lain
lay	laid	laid

LIKE. It is questionable usage to employ *like* as a conjunction, to introduce a dependent clause: "Do like I tell you"; "They acted like they had seen a ghost." Formerly condemned as improper in virtually any context, this usage now has some sanction on the informal or colloquial level. On the formal level, however, it is still preferable to use the orthodox *as, as if,* or *as though:* "Do as I tell you"; They acted as though they had seen a ghost."

The use of *like(d) to* as an equivalent of *almost*—"He like to died laughing" or "We liked to never got there"—is a vulgarism.

LINE. This word is overworked in expressions like *in* or *along the line of.* It is usually preferable to replace *line* with another, more specific word like *manner, area, subject, field,* or sometimes to omit the phrase entirely. "I plan to work in advertising" is better than "I plan to work in the line of advertising." ("In the line of duty" is acceptable as an established idiom.)

LOAN. Some writers use *loan* as a noun only and *lend* as a verb: "I asked him for a ten-dollar *loan,*" but "I asked him to *lend* me ten dollars." This distinction is one which is worth keeping, on the formal level anyway, even though the dictionary authorizes the use of *loan* as a verb also.

LOT(s). In formal English it is better to use *very much* or *a great deal* than *a lot* or *lots of* to mean the same thing: "I admire her very much" rather than "I admire her a lot"; "He has a great deal of money" rather than "He has lots of money."

MOST. On any level higher than the colloquial, the writer should use *almost* rather than the shortened form *most* as an equivalent: "It took us *almost* (not *most*) an hour to get there."

MYSELF (HIMSELF, YOURSELF, etc.). The pronoun forms with *–self* are properly restricted to two functions: (1) the intensive, in which they are always used together with a noun or another pronoun (*"John himself* will be there"; "It is He that hath made us, and not *we ourselves"*); and (2) the reflexive, in which they are always objects of a verb or a preposition ("I hurt myself"; "He told himself to be brave"; "She found out for herself"). These forms should not have any other grammatical function; for example, they should *not* be used as subject of a verb: "Paul and George and myself were there." (In "John himself will be there," the subject is not *himself* but *John.*)

NICE. *Nice,* like *fine,* is sometimes used as an adjective indicating general favor or approval: "It's a nice day"; "They are nice people"; "We had a nice time." Though such expressions are acceptable in casual conversation, in careful usage the meaning can be better represented by words like *pleasant, charming, agreeable.*

NOT TOO. Expressions like "She is not too bad a cook," "The team is not too good this year," though not technically improper, are open to two objections. For one thing, they are used too often. Actually, they are examples of a dead figure of speech, dead because of its triteness in these expressions. (The figure of speech is litotes, or understatement, p. 308.) The second objection is that they are vague or unprecise. A perversely literal-minded reader might take "She is not too bad a cook" to mean "She is just bad enough"—presumably, to give her guests ptomaine poisoning.

OF. Basically as a result of careless pronunciation, *of* is sometimes misused for *have* (or for the contracted form *'ve*), especially in verb phrases: "I could of (misused for *could have*) done it easily"; "Is this what you would of (for *would 've*) expected?" Sometimes, by extension, the *of* creeps in where even the *have* would be improper: "If only I had of known!" Both these misuses of *of* are vulgarisms.

ON ACCOUNT OF. This phrase should not be used as a subordinating conjunction, to introduce a dependent clause, as in "We had to postpone our trip, on account of it rained." It would be proper to say, "on account of the fact that it rained," but it would be better to say simply, "because it rained."

PARTY. The use of *party* to represent an individual person is proper only in legal terminology (e.g., "party of the first part"); elsewhere it is slang: "John is a tight-fisted old party."

PLENTY. It is improper to use *plenty* as an adverb meaning *very:* "We had to be plenty careful to get through safely."

PREDOMINATE. Proper only as a verb, *predominate* is sometimes misused as an adjective. The adjective form is *predominant:* "Hoopskirts were a predominant (*not* predominate) fashion of the time." The adverb is *predominantly:* "The population is predominantly (*not* predominately) Chinese."

PREJUDICED TOWARD. This expression is ambiguous. Since a prejudiced attitude may be either favorable or unfavorable, the writer should make clear which kind he means by using *prejudiced in favor of* or *prejudiced against*.

Notice that *prejudiced* is spelled with a final *d;* it is improper to write "He was prejudice against red-haired women"—and improper for two reasons to write "He was prejudice toward them."

PRINCIPAL, PRINCIPLE. *Principal* is either an adjective meaning *most important,* or a noun meaning *chief person* or *head officer* or *sum of money earning interest:* "This is the principal danger we must guard against"; "Allow me to introduce our new principal, Mr. Jones"; "The bank has increased its principal." *Principle* is a noun meaning *rule, doctrine, ideal:* "The physics teacher explained the principle of the conservation of energy"; "I agree with you in principle."

QUITE. On the colloquial or informal level, it is acceptable to use *quite* in the sense of *rather* or *somewhat:* "It is quite warm today." On the formal level, however, the word should be used only in the sense of *entirely, wholly, absolutely.* On this level, "I am quite sure" means that I am absolutely positive. Note that this formally proper meaning is the one which the word always carries in a negative context: "not quite" always means in effect "not entirely."

REAL. It is incorrect to use *real* as an adverb, as in "I was real tired." The writer should use the adverbial form *really,* or else some other modifier: "I was very tired."

SHOULD OF. See *Of.*

SIT, SET. *Sit* and *set* are analogous to *lie* and *lay* respectively. *Sit* is most commonly an intransitive verb; *set,* a transitive verb meaning *put, place, lay:* "Set it down on the floor." There are some proper intransitive senses of *set* (e.g., the sun sets), and a few, rather rare transitive meanings of *sit* (e.g., to sit a horse); but it is improper to say "She was setting in the chair" or "Sit it down on the floor."

SO. Two precautions should be observed in the use of *so.* First, it should not be overused as a loose kind of co-ordinating conjunction: "I was tired, so I decided to go home, so I got my hat and coat." The second precaution is that *so* as an adverb of degree ordinarily requires a *result clause* to complete its meaning: "I was so tired *that I could hardly walk.*" The use of *so* as an intensive, with no result clause following (simply "I was so tired!"), is questionable, on the formal level anyway.

SUCH AS. See *Etc.*

SURE. It is improper to use *sure* as an adverbial intensive, as in "I was sure glad to see him." Either "I was very glad" or "I surely was glad" would be an acceptable substitute.

SWELL. *Swell* in the sense of *stylish* or *fashionable* is colloquial: "Her clothes were very swell." In the sense of *very good,* it is slang: "We had a swell time"; "She is a swell person." A good policy is not to use *swell* as an adjective at all.

TITLES: SIR, HONORABLE, REVEREND. It is improper to use any of these titles with a surname only, as in *Sir Churchill, the Honorable Jones, the Reverend Smith.* Good usage requires the inclusion of a first name or at least of initials; or, with *Honorable* and *Reverend,* of an additional title: *Sir Winston Churchill* (or *Sir Winston*), the *Honorable George Jones, the Reverend H. L. Smith, the Honorable Mr. Parker, the Reverend Dr. Albert Stone.*

USE(D) TO. Sometimes the idiom *used to* is misspelled *use to,* as a result of careless pronunciation: the initial *t* of *to* swallows up the final *d* of *used.* The proper form is illustrated in "I used to (*not* use to) see him often."

WHO'S, WHOSE. *Who's* is the contraction for *who is; whose,* the possessive form of the pronoun *who:* "Who's knocking at whose door?"

WOULD OF. See *Of.*

YOU'RE, YOUR. *You're* is the contraction for *you are; your* the possessive form of the pronoun *you:* "You're doing good work in your studies."

Exercises

1. In each of the following groups, arrange the words and expressions in ascending order of the levels of abstraction.

   a. (1) literature (2) novel (3) *David Copperfield* (4) fiction.
   b. (1) sweater (2) cardigan (3) garment.
   c. (1) food (2) pumpernickel (3) bread.
   d. (1) firearm (2) revolver (3) weapon (4) pistol.
   e. (1) periodical (2) New York *Times* (3) newspaper.

2. In each of the following pairs, indicate which word or expression is the richer in connotation.

   a. odor, aroma
   b. God, Deity
   c. water, H_2O
   d. window, casement
   e. coat, cloak
   f. children, offspring
   g. feather, plume
   h. trepidation, alarm
   i. hero, protagonist
   j. mother, female parent

3. Identify the figures of speech in the following expressions:

   a. It rained the whole week, and the car broke down twice. We had a *wonderful* trip!
   b. a fleet of fifty sail
   c. We simply *perished* with the heat!
   d. The car rode as smoothly as a ship in calm waters.
   e. His ruin began when he took to the bottle.
   f. She found success and happiness to be not at all unpleasant.
   g. "Nature never did betray the heart that loved her." (Wordsworth)
   h. ". . . the honorable men whose daggers have stabbed Caesar." (Shakespeare)
   i. "Life's a walking shadow." (Shakespeare)

j. "Thou from whose unseen presence the leaves dead
    Are driven, like ghosts from an enchanter fleeing . . ." (Shelley)

4. Substitute something more specific for each of these italicized expressions:

a. Last night we went to see *a play*.

b. She was wearing a beautiful *piece of jewelry*.

c. My parents gave me *a present* for graduation.

d. The final course was *a delicious dessert*.

e. The setting sun made a display of *gorgeous colors*.

5. Rewrite the following sentences, eliminating the clichés. Stay as close as you can to the presumptive meaning; try to express it more effectively. (There may be a few clichés here which do not appear in the list on page 316; try to recognize and eliminate them anyway.)

a. There is a crying need for more engineers.

b. Central has defeated Parkhurst, and we have beaten Central; it stands to reason that we will win the game with Parkhurst.

c. In my humble opinion, you are wrong; the Parkhurst game will really be the acid test for our team.

d. I think I had better see the Dean and get an approval from the powers that be.

e. The coach really laid down the law; when he finished speaking, you could have heard a pin drop.

6. List five native English suffixes and five prefixes other than those included in the examples on pages 321–322.

7. As accurately as you can, infer the meaning of the root which recurs in each of the following sets of words:

a. astrology, astronomy, astrophysics

b. temporal, temporary, contemporaneous

c. exclamation, declamation, reclamation

d. restriction, constriction, district

e. factor, artifact, manufacture

8. Find out from your dictionary and indicate the language or languages from which each of the following words came into English:

       apricot, campus, chief, dollar, dun,
       homonym, poltergeist, seraph, sky, theater

9. Indicate the number of meanings listed in your dictionary for each of the following words. (It is recommended that you use one of these: *The American College Dictionary, Webster's New Collegiate Dictionary,* or *Webster's New World Dictionary.* In the first of these, all meanings are numbered consecutively. In the other two, there is a separate enumeration for each part of speech; if you use either of them, you will want to add the totals of the separate enumerations to arrive at the grand total.)

a. drift   f. log
b. fellow   g. proof
c. image   h. property
d. iron   i. stand
e. law   j. voice

10. Rewrite the following sentences, improving the diction or usage. Assume that you are writing on the formal level.

a. The intramural athletic program includes competition in such sports as tennis, softball, touch football, and etc.

b. A *faux pas* is when you break some rule of etiquette.

c. He is not too good a teacher, but he is a nice man.

d. I can't help but think that she is prejudice toward me.

e. Not having heard him distinctly, I do not really know, but I am quite sure the teacher inferred that the next assignment would be difficult.

11 SPELLING [1]

As has been pointed out in Chapter 1, correct spelling is important for two very good reasons: it helps the writer keep the respect of his readers, and it is sometimes actually essential to his saying what he means. Either of these reasons justifies any expenditure of effort by the writer in learning to spell acceptably. If he loses his readers' respect, he can hardly sustain their interest in what he is saying. If he says one thing but means another (for instance, if he writes "The report describes a personal problem" when he means "The report describes a personnel problem"), he defeats the purpose of communication.

Anyone who is willing to try can become reasonably proficient in spelling the words he is likely to use in composition. Spelling is largely a matter of habit; therefore, improvement means forming good habits and breaking bad ones. Mastering a few basic rules and other aids, such as associational devices, also leads to accuracy in spelling. As an extra precaution, however, it is always advisable for the writer to proofread his composition expressly for spelling and, whenever he is in doubt, to consult a good dictionary. (See pp. 406–407 in the Appendix for a list of standard, desk-size dictionaries.)

This chapter contains suggestions on developing good spelling habits; the most helpful spelling rules in simple, analytical form; a number of other aids; and several lists of commonly misspelled words.

SPELLING AS A MATTER OF HABIT

Doubtless one writes hundreds of words again and again without ever misspelling any of them. These are the words he already spells correctly by habit. When he writes these words, he no longer needs to concentrate on how to arrange the letters, just as the experienced driver of an automobile no longer needs to concentrate on how to shift the gears or apply the brakes. How did the writer make the correct spelling of these words habitual? He did so by practice, much as the driver learned to shift gears and apply brakes; if the writer regularly misspells certain other words, he has confirmed these errors by practice also. To improve his spelling, he must make a special study of any

---

[1] For a more comprehensive presentation of the subject, see Harry Shaw, *Spell It Right!* "Everyday Handbooks" (2nd ed.; New York: Barnes & Noble, Inc., 1965).

word he misspells and learn the correct form so thoroughly that he can add that word to the store of words he habitually spells correctly.

Responsibility for Spelling. A mature person is responsible for accurate spelling in all his writing. The person who accepts this responsibility soon finds that the more words he masters, the abler he becomes in handling written assignments. On the other hand, the person who spells carelessly or relies on others to correct his errors risks losing the esteem of his readers. A good approach is to recognize that good habits in spelling, as in anything else, can be developed by conscious effort.

Sensory and Muscular Recall. Early in life everyone develops a sense of responsibility for spelling his name correctly, and almost as early he trains his senses to reproduce his name automatically. He *sees, hears,* and *says* his name with special care, and he *writes* it without error. The good speller trains his senses to reproduce accurately in this same way as many other words as possible. Steps for training the senses to reproduce words accurately are outlined in the following sections.

The Visual Method: Seeing the Word. Look carefully at a word you are learning to spell, being sure to pay specific attention to any difficult part (for example, cat*e*gory, par*all*el, p*er*form, temper*a*ment). Look at the word until you can close your eyes and visualize it as clearly as you can visualize your name. Follow this same procedure with new words you meet in your reading.

Many persons read without actually *seeing* the specific forms of words. A college student once read Thomas Hardy's novel *The Return of the Native,* passing over the name *Eustacia Vye* dozens of times in so doing; he participated intelligently in a class discussion on the characters in the novel; then on an examination paper he wrote, fifteen times, *Yustasha Vi.* That student had not really seen *Eustacia Vye* on the printed page or in his mind.

Persons who do not observe words carefully often mistake one word for another. As a result many words that have superficial similarities but important distinctions in meaning appear in lists of words frequently misspelled. (For a good exercise in visualization, turn to the lists of "Homonyms" and "Words Similar in Sound or Form" later in this chapter. Be sure to associate the proper meaning with each word you visualize.)

The Phonetic Method: Saying the Word. Pronounce correctly a word you are learning to spell. Practice pronouncing and visualizing the word at the same time until you can see the letters in sequence as clearly as you can see those in your name. By following this procedure you will learn which words are spelled phonetically, that is, spelled as they are sounded; and you will probably be surprised at how many trouble-some words are spelled phonetically.[2]

Of course some words are not spelled phonetically, and similar sounds can be represented by different letters. The student who wrote *Yustasha Vi* for *Eustacia Vye* had *heard* and *said* the name correctly. He was "ear-minded" enough; but because he was not "eye-minded" also (because he did not *see* the letters of the name in sequence), his attempt at phonetic spelling ended in error.

When you misspell a word, find out immediately from your instructor or from a dictionary whether your misspelling is the result of mispronunciation. If so, practice saying the word until the correct pronunciation becomes automatic. Listen critically to your own speech whenever you can. Also, make use of opportunities to listen to and to imitate the pronunciation used by expert speakers: performers in legitimate drama, speech instructors, distinguished lecturers or clergymen, perhaps your favorite news analyst. (For a special exercise in pronunciation, turn to the list of "Words Frequently Mispronounced" and follow the directions given there.)

The Muscular Method: Writing the Word. Write a word you are learning to spell. You may need to write certain words only once—others a dozen times—but write them you must before you can consider them words which you have mastered. The muscular motion is part of the total process of spelling a word by habit. When you have trained your muscles to make your pencil glide unerringly through a group of words while your mind is busy phrasing the next idea, then you have learned to spell those words by habit.

Muscular practice may lead to bad spelling habits also, if you begin with the wrong spelling of a word. The student who misspelled *Eustacia Vye* confirmed his error by writing the wrong form fifteen times. Learning the correct spelling was then a more difficult task for him than it would have been if he had not written the name at all.

The first time you misspell any word, practice writing that word correctly until you find that you can spell it as automatically as you spell your name.

---

[2] Caution is necessary in the use of simplified spelling, which on the whole attempts to make the spelling of words conform to sound. Certain forms sometimes seen in advertisements (e.g., *enuf, naborhood, nite*) are unacceptable in most kinds of composition. A few of the simplifications (e.g., *tho, altho, thru*) have won a greater degree of acceptance, especially in informal writing. (See the most recent edition of a good dictionary for the current status of variant spellings.)

AIDS TO ACCURATE SPELLING

The effectiveness of various aids to accurate spelling varies with the individual and the intensity with which he uses them. Because different persons learn to spell in somewhat different ways, and because each person learns to spell in a variety of ways, no single method of learning can be set up as a panacea for spelling problems. The methods analyzed in the following sections of this chapter, however, have been tested and found effective in most instances where the individual was willing to make a serious effort to follow them.

Rules. A spelling rule is helpful if it is simple and if it has many applications and relatively few exceptions. In each of the following rules [3] *all* the requirements must be satisfied before the rule is applicable.

Final Silent e.

FIRST REQUIREMENT: The word ends with a silent *e*.
SECOND REQUIREMENT: The suffix to be added to the word begins with a vowel.
RULE: Drop the final silent *e*.

Examples:

admire, admiration	love, lovable *
desire, desirous	note, notable
dine, dining	plume, plumage
guide, guidance	precede, preceding
imagine, imaginary	true, truism
like, likable *	write, writing

(* *Likable* and *lovable* are preferred to *likeable* and *loveable*.) *Notable exceptions: acreage, mileage.*

Retention of the silent *e* distinguishes the words *dyeing, singeing, swingeing,* and *tingeing* from the words *dying, singing, swinging,* and *tinging.*

Because in the English language *c* and *g* are hard (that is, pronounced respectively like *k* and like the *g* in *gap*) before *a* and *o*, the silent *e* is kept to preserve the soft sound (the sound of *s* for *c*, and the sound of *j* for *g*) in the following words: *advantageous, changeable, courageous, manageable, marriageable, noticeable, outrageous, peaceable, replaceable, serviceable, traceable.*

[3] The rules given here are, for the most part, modifications of the most helpful of Noah Webster's spelling rules.

*Examples of words to which the rule is not applicable
because the second requirement is not satisfied:*

amuse, amusement	like, likeness
awe, awesome	love, lovely
care, careful	move, movement
excite, excitement	safe, safety
hope, hopeless	sincere, sincerely

Notable exceptions (words in which the final silent *e* is dropped even though the second requirement is not satisfied): *abridgment* (preferred to *abridgement*), *acknowledgment* (preferred to *acknowledgement*), *argument, awful, duly, judgment* (preferred to *judgement*), *ninth, truly, wholly.*

Final Consonant.

FIRST REQUIREMENT: The word has one syllable or has the accent on the last syllable.

SECOND REQUIREMENT: The last three letters of the word are *consonant, vowel, consonant* (or a two-letter word consists of a *vowel* and a *consonant,* respectively).

THIRD REQUIREMENT: The suffix to be added to the word begins with a vowel.

RULE: Double the final consonant.

Examples:

bag, baggage	infer, inferring
begin, beginning	occur, occurrence
compel, compelled	plan, planned
control, controlling	prefer, preferred
defer, deferred	quit, quitter *
drop, dropping	refer, referring
equip, equipped *	run, running
forbid, forbidden	sit, sitter
get, getting	stop, stopped
in, inner	up, upper

(* *U* after *q* is a consonant, equivalent to *w*.)

Notable exceptions: chagrined, gaseous, gasify.

In each of the following derivatives the accent has been shifted to an earlier syllable than the one that was accented in the base: *deference, inference, preferable, preference, referable, reference.* (*Referrable* and *referrible* are accepted forms, but in these forms the accent remains on *fer,* the syllable that was accented in the base.)

*Examples of words to which the rule is not applicable
because the first requirement is not satisfied:*

benefit, benefited	orbit, orbiting
happen, happening	profit, profitable
offer, offered	prohibit, prohibited

Notable exceptions: crystallize, handicapped.

*Examples of words to which the rule is not applicable
because the second requirement is not satisfied:*

appear, appearance	shout, shouted
ask, asking	train, training
box, boxed *	treat, treated
need, needed	warm, warmer

(* *X* is in effect a double consonant, equivalent to *ks*.)

*Examples of words to which the rule is not applicable
because the third requirement is not satisfied:*

allot, allotment	man, manly
glad, gladness	spot, spotless

Final y.

FIRST REQUIREMENT: The word ends with *y*.

SECOND REQUIREMENT: The letter preceding the final *y* is a consonant.

THIRD REQUIREMENT: The suffix to be added to the word begins with any letter except *i*.

RULE: Change the final *y* to *i*.

Examples:

beauty, beautiful	lady, ladies
cry, cried	mercy, merciless
early, earlier	modify, modifier
envy, envious	pity, pitiable
irony, ironical	study, studious

Notable exceptions: babyhood, citylike, dryness, ladylike, ladyship, shyness.

*Examples of words to which the rule is not applicable
because the second requirement is not satisfied:*

buy, buyer	employ, employment
chimney, chimneys	enjoy, enjoyable
delay, delayed	monkey, monkeys
donkey, donkeys	obey, obeyed

Examples of words to which the rule is not applicable
because the third requirement is not satisfied:

baby, babyish	cry, crying	pity, pitying
beautify, beautifying	lobby, lobbyist	study, studying

Ie or ei.

First Requirement: The combination *ie* or *ei* is pronounced *ee*.
Second Requirement: The letter *c* does not precede the combination.
Rule: Use *i* before *e*.

Examples:

believe	fiend	relief	thief
chief	grief	retrieve	wield
field	niece	siege	yield

Notable exceptions: The exceptions are contained in this easily memorized nonsensical statement: *Neither financier seized either species* of *leisure* on the *weird weir*.

Examples of words to which the rule is not applicable
because the first requirement is not satisfied:

eight	neighbor	sleigh	vein
feign	reign	sleight	weigh

Examples of words to which the rule is not applicable
because the second requirement is not satisfied:

ceiling	conceive	deceive	receipt
conceit	deceit	perceive	receive

Formation of Plurals. Consult the dictionary for plural forms whenever you are in doubt. In addition, you will find these rules helpful.[4]

(1) Form the plural of most nouns by adding *s* to the singular, especially when the addition of *s* does not create an extra syllable: *flower, flowers; girl, girls; home, homes; scholar, scholars.*

(2) Form the plural of nouns ending in a sibilant—the sound of *s, x, j, z, ch, sh*—by adding *es* (by adding *s* if the word ends with a silent *e*) to the singular and creating an extra syllable: *boss, bosses; fox, foxes; wedge, wedges; buzz, buzzes; church, churches; wish, wishes; case, cases; maze, mazes.*

(3) Form the plural of common nouns ending in *y* following a con-

---

[4] The first five rules given here on the formation of the plurals of nouns apply also to the formation of the third person singular of verbs: rule 1 (*hit, hits; run, runs*); rule 2 (*pass, passes; place, places*); rule 3 (*try, tries; play, plays*); rule 4 (*woo, woos; go, goes*); rule 5 (*chafe, chafes; stuff, stuffs*).

sonant by changing the *y* to *i* and adding *es: baby, babies; cry, cries; daisy, daisies; lady, ladies; library, libraries.*

Form the plural of proper nouns ending in *y* following a consonant by adding *s* to the singular: *Mr. and Mrs. Murphy, the Murphys; Mr. and Mrs. Perry, the Perrys.*

Form the plural of nouns ending in *y* following a vowel by adding *s* to the singular: *boy, boys; buy, buys; key, keys; tray, trays; valley, valleys; Mr. and Mrs. Wiley, the Wileys.*

(4) Form the plural of nouns ending in *o* following a vowel by adding *s* to the singular: *cameo, cameos; curio, curios; radio, radios; trio, trios; zoo, zoos.*

Form the plural of certain nouns ending in *o* following a consonant (including musical terms, many of them borrowed from Italian) by adding *s* to the singular: *alto, altos; canto, cantos; kimono, kimonos; piano, pianos; solo, solos; soprano, sopranos.*

Form the plural of certain other nouns ending in *o* following a consonant by adding *es* to the singular: *echo, echoes; hero, heroes; Negro, Negroes; potato, potatoes; tomato, tomatoes.*

Form the plural of a few nouns ending in *o* following a consonant by adding either *s* or *es* to the singular. The preferred plural form immediately follows the word in each instance: *buffalo, buffaloes* or *buffalos* (or *buffalo*); *lasso, lassos* or *lassoes; motto, mottoes* or *mottos; volcano, volcanoes* or *volcanos.*

(5) Form the plural of most nouns ending in *f, fe,* or *ff* by adding *s* to the singular: *belief, beliefs; handkerchief, handkerchiefs; roof, roofs; safe, safes; cuff, cuffs; sheriff, sheriffs.*

Form the plural of some nouns ending in *f* or *fe* by changing the *f* or *fe* to *ves: calf, calves; half, halves; leaf, leaves; life, lives; wife, wives.*

Form the plural of a few nouns ending in *f* by adding *s* or by changing the *f* to *ves.* Here the preferred plural form immediately follows the word cited: *beef, beefs* or *beeves; hoof, hoofs* or *hooves; scarf, scarves* or *scarfs; turf, turfs* or *turves.*

(6) Use the same form of certain nouns for both singular and plural: *athletics, athletics; Chinese, Chinese; deer, deer; moose, moose; politics, politics; sheep, sheep; trout, trout* (and other names of fish).

(7) Form the plural of some nouns in an irregular way by changing internal vowels: *chairman, chairmen; Englishman, Englishmen; foot, feet; goose, geese; louse, lice; man, men; mouse, mice; tooth, teeth; woman, women.*

(8) Form the plural of some nouns in an irregular way by adding *en* (sometimes *ren*) to the singular: *child, children; ox, oxen.*

(9) Keep the foreign plurals of certain nouns borrowed from foreign languages: *alumna, alumnae; alumnus, alumni; analysis, analyses; basis, bases; crisis, crises; datum, data; hypothesis, hypotheses; Mr., Messrs.; Mrs., Mmes.; phenomenon, phenomena; thesis, theses.*

Use either the foreign plural or the English plural of certain nouns borrowed from other languages. The preferred plural form appears first in each instance in the following list: *appendix, appendixes* or *appendices; beau, beaux* or *beaus; curriculum, curriculums* or *curricula; criterion, criteria* or *criterions; formula, formulas* or *formulae; index, indexes* or *indices; medium, mediums* or *media; memorandum, memorandums* or *memoranda; radius, radii* or *radiuses; stratum, strata* or *stratums; syllabus, syllabuses* or *syllabi.*

(10) Form the plural of most compound nouns by pluralizing the principal part: *brother-in-law, brothers-in-law; editor-in-chief, editors-in-chief; passer-by, passers-by.*

Pluralize the end of a compound noun considered as a single word: *handful, handfuls; football, footballs; spoonful, spoonfuls.*

Pluralize both parts of some compound nouns: *manservant, menservants; gentleman-commoner; gentlemen-commoners.*

(11) Form the plural of figures, signs, letters, and words talked about as such by adding *s* or *'s: 3s* or *3's; +s* or *+'s; Cs* or *C's; too many ifs* or *too many if's.*

Affixing of Prefixes and Suffixes. To determine whether the last consonant of a prefix appears double in a word to which that prefix is affixed, apply the mathematical principle or $1 + 1 = 2$ or $1 + 0 = 1$. Notice that in the following words the consonant in question appears double only when the basic word begins with that same consonant.

dis + appear	= disappear		dis + satisfy	= dissatisfy
dis + appoint	= disappoint		dis + similar	= dissimilar
mis + take	= mistake		mis + spell	= misspell
un + usual	= unusual		un + necessary	= unnecessary

To determine whether the first consonant of a suffix appears double in a word to which that suffix is affixed, apply the mathematical principle of $0 + 1 = 1$ or $1 + 1 = 2$. Notice that in the following words the consonant in question appears double only when the basic word ends with that same consonant.

evident + ly	= evidently		formal + ly	= formally
former + ly	= formerly		literal + ly	= literally
frank + ness	= frankness		drunken + ness	= drunkenness
quiet + ness	= quietness		sudden + ness	= suddenness

Certain endings (for example, *-able, -ible; -ance, -ence; -ant, -ent; -sion, -tion, -xion*) cause difficulty because they are pronounced alike but spelled differently. Since no rules apply to the use of such endings, learn to spell the individual words and, when in doubt, consult the dictionary. Here are examples of words with the above endings.

-able		*-ible*	
acceptable	imaginable	audible	feasible
advisable	justifiable	compatible	gullible
available	movable	convertible	legible
dependable	sizable	credible	tangible
desirable	suitable	discernible	terrible

-ance		*-ence*	
abundance	extravagance	coincidence	obedience
acceptance	reluctance	competence	persistence
accordance	repentance	confidence	preference
balance	resemblance	excellence	residence
endurance	resistance	insistence	reverence

-ant		*-ent*	
attendant	intolerant	coherent	innocent
defendant	irritant	competent	insistent
defiant	observant	confident	intelligent
distant	radiant	existent	precedent
extant	vigilant	expedient	recurrent

-sion		*-tion*	
collision	fusion	attrition	mention
collusion	impression	condition	mutation
division	incision	creation	radiation
extension	lesion	fiction	retention
fission	tension	location	rotation

-xion	
complexion	crucifixion

(For further information on prefixes and suffixes, see Chapter 10. For rules on the form of compound words, see Chapter 12.)

Grammar. A knowledge of grammar is an invaluable aid to spelling. For example, you can avoid confusing these words if you know that *advise, devise, breathe, clothe,* and *prophesy* are verbs and that *advice, device, breath, cloth,* and *prophecy* are nouns. Knowing the principal parts of common verbs will also help you choose the correct forms. Fourteen of the troublesome ones appear on page 348.

Infinitive	Past Tense	Past Participle
bring	brought	brought
burst	burst	burst
dive	dived	dived
hang (execute)	hanged	hanged
hang (suspend)	hung	hung
lay	laid	laid
lie (recline)	lay	lain
lie (tell a falsehood)	lied	lied
raise	raised	raised
rise	rose	risen
set	set	set
sit	sat	sat
steal	stole	stolen
teach	taught	taught

Grammar and meaning are closely related in the proper use of certain spellings, such as the correct choice between *anyone* and *any one,* *everyone* and *every one,* or *already* and *all ready.* For example, in "I think *anyone* who is qualified should vote," *anyone* is an indefinite pronoun correctly written as one word; whereas in "I think *any one* of the symptoms is reason for alarm," *any* is an adjective modifier of the pronoun *one,* and the two separate words are necessary. (For more information on grammar see Chapter 9.)

Association Devices. Many persons use memory devices [5] (sometimes called *mnemonics*) as aids to accurate spelling. Probably the most helpful of such associations of ideas, serious or nonsensical, are those the individual makes up for his own purpose. Here are a few devices that apply to particular words: a *shepherd* has a *herd; environment* contains *iron; definite* has something *finite; ma* is in *grammar; pa* is in *separate;* there is *science* in *conscience;* and there is *air* in the middle of *prairie.*

Special Marks. Care in the use of *special marks* is necessary for precise spelling of certain words borrowed from foreign languages. The cedilla, which shows that the letter *c* is pronounced like *s,* is required in "façade," for example. The diaeresis, which indicates that the second of two successive vowels is pronounced in a separate syllable, is still preferred though not required in words like "naïve" and "Chloë." The two dots are regularly used over a vowel affected by umlaut in

[5] For further suggestions on the use of memory devices, see James D. Weinland, *How To Improve Your Memory,* "Everyday Handbooks" (New York: Barnes & Noble, Inc., 1957).

words borrowed from the German, for example, "kümmel." (For correct use of these and other special marks, consult a good dictionary.)

Word Lists for Special Study. Study the following lists according to the directions that precede them.

Homonyms. *Homonyms* are words that are identical in pronunciation but different in meaning and, usually, in spelling. Make sure that you can distinguish between the homonyms in the following list. Learn the meanings along with the spelling. Comparing the derivations given in the dictionary will help you remember the distinctions.

aisle, isle	foul, fowl	scene, seen
altar, alter	hear, here	shone, shown
arc, ark	heard, herd	sole, soul
bare, bear	hole, whole	stake, steak
berth, birth	its, it's	stationary, stationery
brake, break	lead, led	steal, steel
buy, by	lessen, lesson	straight, strait
canvas, canvass	mantel, mantle	tail, tale
capital, capitol	marshal, martial	their, there, they're
cereal, serial	medal, meddle	threw, through
cession, session	passed, past	throne, thrown
chord, cord	peace, piece	to, too, two
cite, sight, site	plain, plane	troop, troupe
coarse, course	principal, principle	vain, vane, vein
die, dye	rain, reign, rein	waist, waste
dying, dyeing	right, rite, wright,	weak, week
faze, phase	write	who's, whose
fiancé, fiancée	ring, wring	your, you're
forth, fourth	role, roll	

Be sure not to confuse nominative and possessive forms that sound alike. Here are a few examples:

NOMINATIVE PLURAL	POSSESSIVE SINGULAR	POSSESSIVE PLURAL
actors	actor's	actors'
brothers	brother's	brothers'
guardians	guardian's	guardians'
ladies	lady's	ladies'
secretaries	secretary's	secretaries'

(For rules on the formation of possessives, see Chapter 12.)

Words Similar in Sound or Form. The words in the following groups, despite similarities in sound or form, have important differences in pronunciation, spelling, and meaning.[6] Study these words carefully, using the dictionary whenever necessary, until you are certain that you will not confuse them. Using a few of the words at a time, practice visualizing, pronouncing, and writing them.

accept, except	costume, custom	marital, martial
adapt, adept, adopt	council, counsel, consul	moral, morale
advice, advise	dairy, diary	of, off
affect, effect	decent, descent, dissent	personal, personnel
alley, ally	desert, dessert	poor, pore, pour
allusion, illusion	device, devise	prophecy, prophesy
angel, angle	dining, dinning	quiet, quite, quit
author, Arthur	dual, duel	respectfully,
bases, basis	elicit, illicit	respectively
bath, bathe	emigrant, immigrant	sense, since
born, borne	eminent, immanent,	speak, speech
breath, breathe	imminent	statue, stature,
Calvary, cavalry	ever, every	statute
casual, causal	farther, further	suit, suite
censor, censure	foreword, forward	than, then
choose, chose	formally, formerly	though, thorough,
close, clothes, cloths	holly, holy, wholly	through
cloth, clothe	hoping, hopping	trail, trial
collar, color	human, humane	vary, very
coma, comma	later, latter	wander, wonder
complement,	loath, loathe	weather, whether
compliment	loose, lose, loss	woman, women

Words Frequently Mispronounced. Mispronunciation begets misspelling. The person who fails to pronounce the *a* in *temperament* is likely to omit that letter when he writes the word, and the person who carelessly inserts an extra syllable when he says the word *athlete* is likely to write this two-syllable word incorrectly in three syllables. Likewise, the person who transposes the *e* and the *r* when he pronounces the first syllable of *perform* or *pertain* is likely to misspell the word.

The following list contains words that are frequently misspelled by persons who pronounce them in a slovenly manner. If you will pronounce the list for a reliable critic, mark all the words that you do not say correctly the first time, and then study carefully the dictionary

---

[6] In a few of the groups, two words are pronounced alike (for example, *holy* and *wholly*) and a third word (*holly*) is pronounced differently, but each has its separate meaning.

markings of those words, you will find the spelling easy to learn along with the pronunciation.

accompanist	college	hindrance	particularly	remembrance
antarctic	disastrous	hungry	perform	similar
arctic	divide	identity	perspire	sophomore
athlete	divine	jewelry	pertain	studying
athletics	drowned	kindergarten	poem	suppress
attacked	escape	mathematics	portray	surprise
barbarous	evidently	mischievous	practically	temperament
burglar	February	nowadays	probably	temperature
candidate	government	pamphlet	quantity	undoubtedly

Words Frequently Misspelled. The following list supplements preceding ones so that together they include most of the words misspelled by college students. The words in this list are almost all common ones, for it is usually the common words that give the most difficulty in spelling.

Try to master the entire list at the rate of at least twenty words a week. You may eliminate, of course, the words you already know, but only if you are certain of pronunciation and meaning as well as spelling. When you come to a word of which you are uncertain, proceed through the following steps: (1) Observe the word carefully, paying special attention to any difficult parts. (2) Pronounce the word distinctly as a whole, then more slowly by syllables. Consult the dictionary for the pronunciation if necessary. (3) Think of the meaning of the word and envision the word in a sentence. Consult the dictionary for the meaning if necessary. (4) Write the word several times, pronouncing it distinctly by syllables as you do so. (5) Check your knowledge of the word after a week and perhaps at later intervals.

absence	across	altogether	annual
accidentally	actually	always	answer
accommodate	address	amateur	antecedent
accompanying	adolescent	ambitious	apparent
accomplish	aesthetics,	among	appearance
accumulate	esthetics	amount	appreciate
accustomed	against	analogous	approach
achievement	aggression	analogy	appropriate
acknowledge	allotted	analysis	approximately
acquainted	all right	analyze,	argument
acquire	already	analyse	article

ascend	before	British	careless
assassination	beginning	Briton	carriage
assistant	belief	buoyant	carries
association	believe	bureau	carrying
attendance	benefit	business	category
audience	benefiting	busy	cemetery
auxiliary	boundary	calendar	certain
basically	brilliant	captain	challenge
because	Britain	career	changeable
becoming	Britannica	careful	characteristic
characterize	commit	conceivable	considerably
chauffeur	committed	conceive	consistent
chieftain	committee	condemn	continuous
clarify	community	conjunction	control
collegiate	comparable	connoisseur	controlled
colloquial	comparison	conscience	controversial
colonel	competition	conscientious	convenience
column	competitor	conscious	convincingly
coming	completely	consensus	copyright
commercial	concede	consider	corps
corpse	curriculum	definite	destroy
courageous	curtain	definitely	destruction
courteous	dangerous	definition	determined
courtesy	daughter	democracy	difference
cried	dealt	describe	difficulty
cries	deceased	description	disappear
criticism	deceive	desirable	disappoint
criticize	decide	desire	discipline
cruelty	decision	despair	disease
curiosity	deferred	desperate	disillusion
dissatisfied	efficient	entirely	excel
distinction	eighth	environment	excellent
doctor	eligible	equip	excitement
dominant	eliminate	equipment	exercise
dormitory	embarrass	equipped	exhausted
drunkenness	embarrassment	equivalent	existence
during	emphasize	erroneous	experience
easily	enough	especially	experiment
ecstasy	enter	exaggerate	explanation
efficiency	entertain	exceed	extraordinary

extravagant
extremely
facility
fallacy
familiar
family
fascinating
fictitious
field
fiery

finally
financial
financier
first
forehead
foreign
foremost
forty
frantically
fraternity

friend
friendliness
fulfill,
  fulfil
fundamental
gaiety,
  gayety
gauge,
  gage
generally

ghost
governor
grammar
grammatical
guarantee
guard
handsome
happening
happiness
height

heinous
heroes
hesitancy
horror
huge
humor,
  humour
hurriedly
hurrying
hypocrisy

hypocrite
hysterical
illogical
imagination
immediately
impossible
inadequate
incident
incidentally
incredible

independence
indispensable
inevitable
influence
influential
ingenious
initiative
intelligence
interesting
interfere

interference
interpretation
interrupt
invariably
irrelevant
irreverent
itself
judgment,
  judgement
knowledge

laboratory
laid
laurel
legitimate
leisure
length
library
lieutenant
likely
liqueur

liquor
literally
literature
livelihood
lively
loneliness
lonely
losing
lovely
luxury

magazine
magnificent
maintenance
maneuver,
  manoeuvre
many
marriage
material
maybe
meant

mechanical
medicine
medieval,
  mediaeval
merely
miniature
minute
mischief
misspelled
modifying

mountain
naïve,
  naive
naturally
necessarily
necessary
necessity
Negro
Negroes
nevertheless

nickel
niece
night
nineteenth
ninety
ninth
noisily
noticeable
noticing
notorious

obstacle
occasionally
occur
occurred
occurrence
occurring
omission
omitted
operate
opinion

opponent
opportunity
optimist
ordinarily
organization
original
paid
parallel
parliament
pastime

peculiar
perceive
perhaps
permanent
permissible
permitting
perseverance
persistent
persuade

persuasion
philosophy
physical
physician
planning
playwright
pleasant
politician
possession

possibility
prairie
precede
preceding
preference
preferred
prejudiced
preparation
prevalent

previous
primitive
privilege
probable
procedure
proceed
profession
professor
prominent

pronunciation
propaganda
prove
psychology
publicly
pursue
pursuit
ready
realize
really

realm
reason
receipt
receive
recognize
recommend
reference
referred
regretted
rehearsal

relevant
relieve
religion
remember
reminiscent
renaissance
renascence
renowned
repetition
representative

resource
response
responsibility
restaurant
rhyme, rime
rhythm
ridiculous
roommate
sacrifice
sacrilegious

safety
sarcasm
satire
satirical
scarcely
schedule
seize
semester
sentence
separate

separation
sergeant
several
shepherd
shining
significance
sorority
soliloquy
source
specifically

specimen
sponsor
strength
strenuous
stretched
substantial
subtle, subtile
succeed
successful
summarize

superintendent
supersede
suppose
surrounding
suspense
syllable
symbol
symbolism
sympathetic
synonymous

technical
tendency
theory
therefore
those
thought
throughout
together
tolerance
tragedy

transferred
tried
tries
truly
Tuesday
twelfth
unanimous
unnecessary
until
unusual

usage
usually
variety
various
vengeance
victim
view
village
villain
visible

volume
Wednesday
weird
where
writer
writing
written
yacht
yield
zoology

Exercises

1. Add the suffixes *ed* and *ing* to each of the following words:

admit	drop	locate	occur	treat
benefit	guide	maintain	plan	try
dine	like	occupy	refer	vacate

2. Insert *ie* or *ei* into each of the following:

ach—ve	ch—ftain	f—rce	l—sure	r—gn
bel—f	dec—ve	fr—ght	n—ce	s—ge
c—ling	f—ld	gr—f	p—ce	s—ze

3. Choose the correct word from within the parentheses.

a. Columbus is the (capital, capitol) of Ohio.

b. An (emigrant, immigrant) is one who comes into the country.

c. He would not (prophecy, prophesy) a successful trip to Mars.

d. The boy spoke (respectfully, respectively) to his uncle.

e. Sir John Gielgud appeared in the (role, roll) of Hamlet.

f. How long has it been (sense, since) you wrote the letter?

g. He is older (than, then) his sister.

h. The machinery in the shop is (stationary, stationery).

i. The sailors (threw, through) (their, there, they're) caps in the air.

j. Can you tell (who's, whose) (advice, advise) will have the greatest (affect, effect) on (your, you're) plans?

4. Write the plural forms of the following:

airstrip	belief	hero	loss	salesman
alley	box	hobby	manservant	seven
ally	C	house	mouse	sheep
alumna	chairman	index	ox	sister-in-law
alumnus	child	Kelly	potato	sky
army	Chinese	knife	problem	solo
baseball	dish	leaf	quarterback	spoonful
basis	echo	library	radio	

5. Keep a cumulative list of the words you misspell. Use the spelling principles in this chapter to help you analyze and master each word when you enter it on your list. Have a friend dictate the list to you at intervals. When you have spelled a word correctly on three different occasions, remove it from the list.

12 PUNCTUATION AND MECHANICS

Punctuation is a system of devices which writers use in a conventional way to clarify the relationships among words and groups of words. The devices, commonly called "punctuation marks" or "symbols," have their own meanings; these meanings supplement the meanings of words.[1] The purpose of punctuation, therefore, is practical, not ornamental. A careful writer may sometimes take liberties with conventional punctuation, but he does so only when he knows that such liberties will not mislead or confuse his readers. He keeps in mind that his reason for punctuating what he writes is to make his meaning clear.

Closely related to punctuation are other conventions, such as capitalization and the use of italics; these other conventions, also, have standardized meanings, which careful writers employ and careful readers observe.

PUNCTUATION [2]

Because punctuation plays a vital part in the transfer of ideas from the mind of the writer to the mind of the reader, the writer who punctuates discriminately is better able to inform, convince, delight, or otherwise influence his readers than is the writer who punctuates haphazardly. How does a writer learn to punctuate with discrimination? He does not memorize a set of rules; instead he seeks to understand the meanings and functions of the various punctuation marks so that he can choose the proper mark whenever the need for punctuation arises in his composition.

Period. The *period* indicates the end of a complete unit or sentence. Strictly speaking, the function of the period is to designate the end of an idea.[3]

---

[1] For a more comprehensive discussion of the meaning of each punctuation mark, see Harry Shaw, *Punctuate It Right!* "Everyday Handbooks" (New York: Barnes & Noble, Inc., 1963).

[2] The punctuation devices explained in this chapter are standard on the formal level of usage; as writing becomes less formal, punctuation conventions are less strictly applied.

[3] The uses of the abbreviation point and the decimal point, identical in form to the period, are explained later in this chapter.

Closing a Sentence. Use a period at the end of a declarative sentence, an imperative sentence, or a request in interrogative form (an indirect request).

DECLARATIVE SENTENCE: Ducklings are good swimmers.

IMPERATIVE SENTENCE: Please sharpen the pencil.

REQUEST IN INTERROGATIVE FORM (indirect request): Will you please forward my mail to my new address.

Following Numerical and Alphabetical Symbols. Place a period after each symbol (number or letter) in a formal outline or in a list.

I. Exposition	1. England
II. Argument	2. France
A. Logical	3. Germany
B. Psychological	4. Italy
III. Description	
A. Technical	a. Bach
B. Emotional	b. Beethoven
IV. Narration	c. Brahms

Question Mark. The *question mark* points out the end of a query. The function of a question mark is to indicate a question or suggest a doubt.

As End Punctuation. Use a question mark after an interrogative sentence (that is, after a direct question, but not after an indirect question [4]); after a question quoted within a sentence; or after each interrogative element within a sentence, for emphasis.

INTERROGATIVE SENTENCE: When did Queen Elizabeth II make her first tour of the British Empire?

QUESTION QUOTED WITHIN A SENTENCE: "Who is at the door?" she asked.

INTERROGATIVE ELEMENTS WITHIN A SENTENCE: Is the composition good in form? style? meaning?

As Indication of Uncertainty. Use a question mark, ordinarily enclosed in parentheses, to indicate uncertainty or doubt.

We studied the poems of Chaucer, who lived from 1342 (?) to 1400.

As a device suggesting irony as well as doubt, the question mark is weak.

The truant gave a foolproof (?) explanation of two of his ten absences.

---

[4] An indirect question is part of a declarative sentence and is therefore followed by a period.

WRONG: John asked whether I could operate the machine?

RIGHT: John asked whether I could operate the machine.

Exclamation Point. The *exclamation point* indicates the end of an emotional expression. The function of the exclamation point is to show emphasis, usually emphasis of feeling rather than of idea. Careful writers use the exclamation point sparingly: they are aware that the writer who tries to stress everything, like the speaker who gushes, really emphasizes nothing.

As End Punctuation. Place an exclamation point after an emphatic interjection [5] or an exclamation (a word, phrase, or sentence showing strong feeling).

Alas! I had burned my old costume only a few minutes before Mary asked for it.

Help! Robbers! Police!

What a transportation problem arises during a heavy snowstorm!

As Indication of Irony. Use an exclamation point to indicate irony if the emphasis provided by the exclamation point helps to achieve the purpose of the irony. Keep in mind, however, that irony is usually more effective without a label than with one, and that the label is hardly a compliment to the reader's intelligence or imagination. Compare the effectiveness of the following two sentences:

I once spent a pleasant (!) night out of doors in a rain-drenched bedroll.

I once spent a pleasant night out of doors in a rain-drenched bedroll.

Single Comma. A *single comma* ordinarily means that a word or a group of words has been omitted but can easily be understood at the point where the comma appears. The function of the single comma is usually to warn the reader that he must supply the omitted element.

A comma combined with a co-ordinating conjunction between independent clauses has a special significance: this mark signifies the end of one independent clause and the beginning of another.

The single comma is also used to prevent misreading; to follow the salutation of a friendly letter and the complimentary close of any letter; and to separate co-ordinate, consecutive adjectives preceding the noun they modify.

Separating Terms in a Series. Use the comma to separate several words or phrases in a series; that is, to indicate the omission of a co-ordinating conjunction between the terms.

---

[5] A weak interjection is followed by a comma rather than an exclamation point.

Oh, I feel certain that you can depend on your memory.

Well, the change in policy was hardly a surprise.

The leaves were red and gold and green and brown.
The leaves were red, gold, green, and brown.

Among the treasures in his den he still kept a few Indian flints and a well-worn baseball glove and a small air rifle.
Among the treasures in his den he still kept a few Indian flints, a well-worn baseball glove, and a small air rifle.

When the terms contain internal commas and thus require a stronger mark of separation, use the semicolon.

The leaves were red, sprinkled with green; gold, blended with brown; green, etched with gold; and brown, dappled with red.

Among the treasures in his den he still kept a few Indian flints, reminders of his grandparents' farm; a well-worn baseball glove, a relic of his sand-lot experiences; and a small air rifle, his first hunting weapon.

The comma preceding the co-ordinating conjunction *and* or *or* between the last two terms in a series is optional. Because this comma is oftentimes necessary for the sake of clarity, many writers use it regularly. The punctuation of the first of the following two sentences readily shows that the writer intended to name four dishes, but the punctuation of the second sentence does not actually indicate whether the writer intended to name three dishes or four.

CLEAR: Bill ordered steak, potatoes, strawberries, and milk.
AMBIGUOUS: Bill ordered steak, potatoes, strawberries and milk.

Words or phrases used in pairs are usually joined by a conjunction and therefore require no punctuation between them. If the conjunction is omitted, the single comma takes its place.

As a child she was temperamental and unruly.
As a child she was temperamental, unruly.

Papers were strewn in the streets and on the sidewalks.
Papers were strewn in the streets, on the sidewalks.

Indicating Understood Verb or Other Element. Use a single comma to indicate the omission of a verb or other element understood from an earlier part of the sentence. In the first sentence below *has* is understood after *Sam.* In the second sentence the words "came running as fast as possible" are understood after *Jim,* after *Edward,* and after *Bob.*

Ted has two collies and one cocker spaniel; Sam, one collie and two cocker spaniels.[6]

[6] The understood verb must be identical to the verb that appears earlier in the sentence. In the following sentence, for instance, the singular verb *has* needs

The boys came running as fast as possible from different places: Jim, from the attic; Edward, from the den; and Bob, from the basement.

Preceding a Co-ordinating Conjunction Between Independent Clauses. Use a comma and a co-ordinating conjunction between independent clauses that are closely enough related to constitute a unit of thought and that do not contain a number of internal commas. Remember that the place to use this combination of comma plus coordinating conjunction is in the middle of a compound sentence.

Coleridge was an unhappy man, and some of his poems treat the subject of his dejection.

You must transplant the trees soon, or they will be too large for you to handle.

If the independent clauses are short, especially if they have the same subject, omit the comma before the co-ordinating conjunction.

Seasons come and seasons go.

Yesterday Tom had fever and today he has chills.[7]

The regular use of a comma before the co-ordinating conjunction *but* joining two independent clauses promotes the idea of contrast.[8]

Alexander Pope had a brilliant career as a writer, but he was never quite satisfied with the plaudits of his readers.

The local baseball team is leading the league, but the second-place team is only two games behind.

The regular use of a comma before the co-ordinating conjunction *for* prevents confusion with the preposition *for*.

---

to be expressed after *Sam* because the plural verb *have,* used earlier in the sentence, cannot logically be understood after *Sam:* "The Smiths have two dogs; Sam has one cat."

[7] In modern usage the comma is frequently omitted before a co-ordinating conjunction joining independent clauses much longer than those shown here. The important point is that no ambiguity should result from the omission of the comma. For instance, if the example used above is reworded as follows, a comma becomes necessary to make the meaning immediately clear.

AMBIGUOUS: Tom had fever yesterday and today he has chills.

CLEAR: Tom had fever yesterday, and today he has chills.

[8] The comma lends emphasis to other types of parallel expressions also.

The longer she waited, the more frightened she became.

The greater the demand, the higher the price.

The children were enjoying a party, for Linda was celebrating her birthday.

Roy waited a long time, for many of his classmates had told him to come early.

Serving Other Purposes. The single comma has several other conventional uses, the most common of which are for immediate clarity; in letters; and between co-ordinate, consecutive adjectives.

FOR IMMEDIATE CLARITY. Place a comma wherever necessary to make the meaning of the sentence immediately clear to the reader (that is, use the comma for clarity, even when no further specific reason can be cited). Notice how the clarity of these sentences is improved by the use of commas.

AMBIGUOUS: When Jane left the room was suddenly quiet.
CLEAR: When Jane left, the room was suddenly quiet.

AMBIGUOUS: Outside the cars were speeding along the road.
CLEAR: Outside, the cars were speeding along the road.

IN LETTERS. Place a comma after the salutation of a friendly letter and following the complimentary close of any letter.

Dear Polly,	Sincerely yours,
Dear Grandmother,	Very truly yours,

BETWEEN CO–ORDINATE, CONSECUTIVE ADJECTIVES. Use a single comma to separate co-ordinate, consecutive adjectives preceding the noun they modify. Compare the following sentences, and notice that the comma in the second sentence indicates the omission of the co-ordinating conjunction *and*.

The actress spoke in a low and cynical tone of voice.
The actress spoke in a low, cynical tone of voice.

Do not use a comma to separate consecutive adjectives when they are not co-ordinate, that is, when the first adjective modifies the idea represented by both the second adjective and the noun. Notice that in the following two sentences *congenial* modifies the idea represented by *old man,* and *small* modifies the idea represented by *white rabbit.*

He is a congenial old man.
A small white rabbit hopped across the path.

Pairs of Commas. The normal order of the English sentence is subject-verb-complement. (See Chapter 8.) A *pair of commas* usually means that the word, phrase, or clause set off by the commas interrupts this normal order. In addition, the pair of commas usually functions as a signal to the reader that the element that appears between the commas is a nonessential interrupter which can be omitted without impairing the grammatical structure of the sentence. In fact, more often than not the omission of the interrupter simplifies and solidifies the sentence structure.[9]

The pair of commas is the most frequently used interior mark of punctuation. Mastering the use of this mark, though possibly time-consuming, is essential for every competent writer.

Setting Off Nonrestrictive Modifiers. Use a pair of commas to set off [10] a nonrestrictive, or loose, modifier. A nonrestrictive modifier is a word, phrase, or clause not needed to identify or limit the meaning of the word it modifies. Unlike a restrictive modifier, which is needed to identify or limit the meaning of the modified word and therefore is not set off by commas, the nonrestrictive modifier merely furnishes additional descriptive details. The nonrestrictive element may be either an adjective modifier or an adverbial modifier. Each modifier set off by a pair of commas in the following sentences could be omitted without affecting the essential meaning of the word it modifies and without disrupting the basic sentence structure.

RESTRICTIVE ADJECTIVE PHRASE: Any territory *with rich natural resources* appeals to a pioneer-spirited person.
NONRESTRICTIVE ADJECTIVE PHRASE: Texas, *with its rich natural resources,* appeals to a pioneer-spirited person.

RESTRICTIVE PARTICIPIAL PHRASE: An historical figure *sufficiently popularized by adults* becomes a hero for children.
NONRESTRICTIVE PARTICIPIAL PHRASE: David Crockett, *popularized by adults from time to time,* remains a constant hero of small boys.

RESTRICTIVE ADJECTIVE CLAUSE: A man *who spends much time lecturing* recognizes the value of audience appeal.
NONRESTRICTIVE ADJECTIVE CLAUSE: William Shakespeare, *who was a capable businessman as well as a brilliant playwright,* understood the value of audience appeal.

---

[9] Generally speaking, the interrupting elements set off between commas are parenthetical expressions, but most of them have other, more specific grammatical names also. Although these elements interrupt normal order, their use is not considered incorrect.

[10] Whereas *separating with a comma* calls for a single comma, *setting off with commas* calls for a pair of commas unless, of course, one of the two commas is suppressed because the element to be set off appears at the beginning or the end of the sentence.

RESTRICTIVE ADVERBIAL PHRASE: He waited *in the rain.*
NONRESTRICTIVE ADVERBIAL PHRASE: All through the night the condemned man waited, *without quailing,* for the executioner to arrive.

RESTRICTIVE ADVERBIAL CLAUSE: He always sounds the horn *when he drives through a tunnel.*
NONRESTRICTIVE ADVERBIAL CLAUSE: *Whether you are an English major or not,* you will need to master the fundamentals of effective composition.

An element that is nonrestrictive is set off virtually always; one that is out of normal order, usually (one that is both would be covered by the first principle.) [11]

Setting Off Nonrestrictive Appositives. Use a pair of commas to set off a nonrestrictive appositive. Do not set off a restrictive appositive, one necessary to identify the term with which it is in apposition.

RESTRICTIVE APPOSITIVES:
   The word *convenient* is frequently misspelled.
   She memorized Shelley's poem *"Mutability."*
   Shakespeare's *Twelfth Night* is a play based on mistaken identities.

[11] The following pairs of sentences illustrate the usual practice of setting off a modifier when it is moved out of its normal position:

ADJECTIVE IN NORMAL POSITION: A *vicious* lion sprang from the underbrush.
ADJECTIVE OUT OF NORMAL POSITION: An enraged lion, *vicious,* sprang from the underbrush.
PARTICIPLE IN NORMAL POSITION: After the game the *exhausted* team headed for the showers.
PARTICIPLE OUT OF NORMAL POSITION: After the game the entire team, *exhausted,* headed for the showers.
ADVERB IN NORMAL POSITION: George Washington *earnestly* warned the nation against entangling alliances.
ADVERB OUT OF NORMAL POSITION: George Washington warned the nation, *earnestly,* against entangling alliances.
ADVERBIAL CLAUSE, NORMAL SENTENCE ORDER: I will order the book *if you will share the cost with me.*
ADVERBIAL CLAUSE, INVERTED SENTENCE ORDER: *If you will share the cost with me,* I will order the book.

A modifier is not always set off by commas when it is moved out of its normal position. The sentences in each of the following pairs are equally acceptable without commas:

ADVERB IN NORMAL POSITION: He *suddenly* remembered his father's advice.
ADVERB OUT OF NORMAL POSITION: *Suddenly* he remembered his father's advice.
ADVERBIAL PREPOSITIONAL PHRASE IN NORMAL POSITION: The two old friends reminisced *throughout the afternoon.*
ADVERBIAL PREPOSITIONAL PHRASE OUT OF NORMAL POSITION: *Throughout the afternoon* the two old friends reminisced.

NONRESTRICTIVE APPOSITIVES:

Mark Twain, *a famous American author,* immortalized the Mississippi River.

The red rose, *my very favorite flower,* blooms most freely in the springtime.

Softball, *a modified form of baseball,* is a popular game.

Setting Off Nominatives of Address. Use a pair of commas to set off a name or other substantive used in direct address.

You know very well, Patrick, that your driver's license expired last September.

Where are you going, my friend?

Setting Off Yes or No. Use a pair of commas to set off *yes* or *no* or any other expression that modifies the whole sentence.

He is working, yes, even though he is not receiving a salary.

No, the storm did not follow the course predicted.

Unfortunately, the request to disband came too late. (The comma here is optional.)

The typewriter is to be discarded because, in the first place, it is old and, in the second place, it is in need of repair.

Setting Off Parenthetical Expressions. Use a pair of commas to set off a parenthetical expression that serves as a commentary, a parenthetical expression that is a transitional device within a clause, or a parenthetical expression that appears in the form of an absolute phrase.

PARENTHETICAL COMMENTS:

Your policy, *it seems to me,* is a wise one.

The decision of the judges, *no doubt,* will be final.

PARENTHETICAL TRANSITIONS WITHIN CLAUSES:

Sir Walter Scott assumed the responsibility for paying a large debt; he worked very hard, *consequently,* for many years.

Bob gardens after sundown almost every evening; he tries, *in this manner,* to stay physically fit without getting sunburned.

PARENTHETICAL ABSOLUTE PHRASES:

His chores finished, Silas went into the house for breakfast.

The dog slunk from the room, *his tail drooping,* after his master had scolded him.

Setting Off Short Direct Quotations. Use a pair of commas to set off a short direct quotation or to set off the words which introduce such a quotation.

The spectators chanted, "We want a touchdown," until the game ended.

"I had just begun to read the newspaper," complained Mr. Jordan, "when the telephone rang."

Be careful to use a period (or a semicolon) after an expression like *he said* which separates complete sentences (or main clauses not joined by a conjunction) of one person's speech.

"I have no further use for this road map," he said; "you are welcome to it."

"Is this your book?" she asked. "I found it on the floor."

Setting Off Introductory Verbal Phrases. Use a pair of commas to set off an introductory participial phrase, an introductory phrase containing a gerund, or an introductory or a parenthetical infinitive phrase, especially if the phrase is fairly long.

PARTICIPIAL PHRASE: *Apparently intrigued by the novelty of the production,* several persons stayed through two showings.

PHRASE CONTAINING GERUND: *By going to summer school for three consecutive summers,* Patsy earned twenty-four semester hours of credit.

INFINITIVE PHRASE OF PURPOSE: *To get to school on time on Monday mornings,* he ran all the way.

PARENTHETICAL INFINITIVE PHRASE: I am positive I left my umbrella on the bus although, *to tell the truth,* I cannot recall where I left my hat.

Setting Off Long Introductory Phrases and Clauses. Use a pair of commas to set off a long phrase or clause, whatever its grammatical nature, which precedes a main clause.

LONG PREPOSITIONAL PHRASE PRECEDING MAIN CLAUSE: *In his final report on the various problems in the plant,* the engineer recommended the installation of new equipment.

LONG NOUN CLAUSE PRECEDING MAIN CLAUSE: *That Philip Nolan was homesick for the United States,* no reader could deny.

LONG ELLIPTICAL CLAUSES PRECEDING MAIN CLAUSES: *Though not a frequenter of movie houses,* he is familiar with the roles of many popular stars; and, *though not a regular viewer of television programs,* he knows which stars have made their television debuts.

Setting Off Each Item After the First in Addresses and Dates. Use a pair of commas to set off each item after the first in an address or a date. Notice that the last item in an address or a date should have a comma following it unless, of course, that item is at the end of the sentence.

Ronald addressed the letter to 2402 Emily Drive, San Francisco 16, California, and mailed it immediately.

He left Dallas, Texas, on Wednesday, August 24.

Setting Off Titles or Initials Following Names. Use a pair of commas to set off a title or similar expression following a name.

Charles Carey, M.D., has opened a new clinic.

The bibliography lists Smalley, Donald, as the author of a book on Browning.

John visits Washington, D.C., almost every summer.

I should like to visit Barnes & Noble, Inc., in New York City.

Professor C. J. Stowell, of McKendree College, presided at the mathematicians' convention.

Setting Off Mild Exclamations. Use a pair of commas to set off an exclamation too mild to require an exclamation point.

Well, your guess was almost right.

True, we did have a shower after the clouds had been seeded.

Please buy an eggplant and, oh, about a pound of onions.

Setting Off Expressions Used in Contrast. Use a pair of commas to set off an expression showing contrast.

Some parking meters take a dime, not a nickel, for an hour of parking.

The Churchills are British, not French.

Setting Off Particular Introductory and Concluding Expressions. Ordinarily use a pair of commas to set off an expression like *for example, namely,* or *that is* introducing an explanation or illustration. Also, use a pair of commas to set off an expression like *etc., and so on,* or *and the like* concluding a series.[12]

I have recently reread some interesting comedies, for example, Sheridan's *The School for Scandal.*

The protasis, that is, the first two acts, of a five-act play introduces the characters and presents the problem.

Writers generally use I, II, III, IV, etc., to designate the main divisions of an outline.

The ballad singer entertained the group by singing "Sir Patrick Spens," "Lord Randal," "The Douglas Tragedy," and the like, for an hour.

[12] Use a comma before but not after the expression *such as* introducing one or more examples.

Meteorologists use women's names, such as *Connie, Diane,* and *Maria,* to distinguish storms.

Setting Off Idiomatic Questions. Use a pair of commas to set off an idiomatic question, that is, a question which lacks the force of an independent clause but implies the answer expected.

You are going home, aren't you, when your brother goes?
The new organ is attractive, isn't it?   The river isn't high now, is it?
You might go to Europe, might you not, when you are graduated from college?

Unnecessary Commas. Because they obscure rather than clarify the meaning of a sentence, unnecessary commas should be avoided. Commas should not be used between a short subject and its verb, between a verb and a subject complement, between a verb and its object, between an adjective and the word it modifies, before the first or after the last unit of a series, before a co-ordinating conjunction joining two words or phrases, or after a co-ordinating conjunction joining clauses.

Between a Short Subject and Its Verb. Do not use a comma between a short subject and its verb.

WRONG: The grass under the trees, grew more slowly than that in the sunny part of the yard.
RIGHT: The grass under the trees grew more slowly than that in the sunny part of the yard.

Between a Verb and a Subject Complement. Do not use a comma between a verb and a subject complement.

WRONG: His difficulties were, lack of time and scarcity of material.
RIGHT: His difficulties were lack of time and scarcity of material.

Between a Verb and Its Object. Do not use a comma between a verb and its object.

WRONG: Wave recorders on the coast of California can detect, tropical storms south of the equator.
RIGHT: Wave recorders on the coast of California can detect tropical storms south of the equator.

A common error is the use of a comma either before or after the subordinating conjunction *that* introducing a noun clause used as the object of a verb.

WRONG: The lecturer remarked, that the theories on space and time are very complex.
WRONG: The lecturer remarked that, the theories on space and time are very complex.

RIGHT: The lecturer remarked that the theories on space and time are very complex.

Between an Adjective and the Word It Modifies. Do not use a comma between an adjective and the word it modifies.

WRONG: He gave only a short, evasive, answer to each question.
RIGHT: He gave only a short, evasive answer to each question.

Before the First or After the Last Unit of a Series. Do not use a comma before the first or after the last unit of a series.

WRONG: The bacteria were found in, milk, butter, and cheese.
RIGHT: The bacteria were found in milk, butter, and cheese.

WRONG: Mice, rats, and people, have certain characteristics in common.
RIGHT: Mice, rats, and people have certain characteristics in common.

Before a Co-ordinating Conjunction Joining Two Words or Phrases. Do not use a comma before a co-ordinating conjunction joining two words or phrases unless you wish to emphasize contrast.

WRONG: Ocean waves are caused by wind, or earthquakes.
RIGHT: Ocean waves are caused by wind or earthquakes.

WRONG: In the audience were many young children, and their parents.
RIGHT: In the audience were many young children and their parents.

RIGHT: She went to the appointed place but not at the appointed time (*or* She went to the appointed place, but not at the appointed time).

After a Co-ordinating Conjunction Joining Clauses. Do not use a comma after a co-ordinating conjunction joining clauses unless an interrupting element requires setting off.

WRONG: George enjoyed attending lectures, but, he disliked doing his homework.
RIGHT: George enjoyed attending lectures, but he disliked doing his homework.
RIGHT: George delayed his homework for several hours, but, once he got started, he found the assignment interesting (*or* George delayed his homework for several hours; but, once he got started, he found the assignment interesting).

Semicolon. The *semicolon* means that a major point of separation within a sentence is at hand. Actually, the semicolon is a hybrid, a cross between a period and a comma. The function of the semicolon, therefore, is to signify a less definite break in structure and meaning than a period indicates and a more definite break in structure and meaning than a comma indicates.

Between Independent Clauses. The semicolon, because of its hybrid nature, is a convenient mark for a writer to use between independent clauses that he wishes his readers to understand as one large unit of thought.

WITHOUT A CO-ORDINATING CONJUNCTION. Use a semicolon between independent clauses not joined by a co-ordinating conjunction.

Jonathan Swift published *Gulliver's Travels* in a somewhat mysterious manner; he realized that the political satire in the story could provoke resentment against him.

Jane leaves for work at eight o'clock almost every morning; she usually returns home at five in the evening.

WITH A CO-ORDINATING CONJUNCTION. Place a semicolon between long independent clauses joined by a co-ordinating conjunction if internal punctuation appears in one or both of the clauses.

Carol found biology, chemistry, and algebra the most interesting courses in college; but her twin sister, Caroline, preferred English to all the other subjects.

When I watched the sunrise from Pikes Peak, I thought I was seeing the grandest sight in the world; but at that time I had not yet seen a sunrise from Virginia Beach, Carolina Beach, or Miami Beach.

WITH A CONJUNCTIVE ADVERB. Use a semicolon between independent clauses if a conjunctive adverb (*accordingly, besides, consequently, furthermore, hence, however, in addition, likewise, meanwhile, moreover, nevertheless, therefore, thus,* etc.) serves as a transitional device between the clauses no matter at what position the conjunctive adverb appears.[13]

Terry had lost his textbook and his notebook; consequently he had difficulty preparing his assignment.

The guest of honor was ill; the hostess decided, therefore, to postpone the luncheon.

Between Long and Complicated Subordinate Clauses. Put semicolons between long subordinate clauses which contain internal commas and therefore require a stronger mark of separation.

[13] The tendency of modern writers is to defer the conjunctive adverb, placing it at an inconspicuous place within the clause rather than at the beginning.

He wrote a simple topic outline for his research paper before he attempted to write a comprehensive sentence outline, make a speech on his topic, or write the rough draft of his paper; but not until he had prepared a bibliography, read several books and articles on his topic, and taken many notes.

The damage was intensified because the tornado, which struck the city after midnight, came without warning; because darkness hampered rescue operations; and because heavy rain, hail, and strong winds continued for several hours afterward.

Between Internally Punctuated Terms in a Series. Use semicolons between terms in a series if the terms contain internal commas.

Jack was stationed at United States Air Force bases near Columbus, Ohio; Detroit, Michigan; Great Falls, Montana; Shreveport, Louisiana; San Antonio, Texas; and Rantoul, Illinois.

The letters were dated May 4, 1959; June 10, 1960; and August 1, 1961.

Between Figures Which Must Be Kept Distinct. Place semicolons between groups of figures which contain other internal marks and must be kept distinct.

She quoted Genesis 2:1–9; 3:1; 4:1–10.

He memorized three speeches from *Hamlet* (II:ii:575–634; III:i:56–87; and III:ii:1–16).

Before Introductory Expressions. Use a semicolon (or colon, or dash, or period) between main clauses the second of which begins with such an expression as *for example, that is,* or *namely.*

Charles Lamb wrote most convincingly at some distance in time from the experiences he recorded; for example, he based his famous *Essays of Elia* on events that had occurred several decades earlier.

Many a thinking person changes his philosophy of life; that is, he revises his basic beliefs from time to time.

Colon. The *colon* signifies that specific information is to follow. The function of the colon is to anticipate any of the following: a series used as an appositive, an explanation or a question, a long or formal quotation, a secondary title, a lesser part of a numerical group, the body of a formal speech or business letter, or the initials of a stenographer.

Anticipating a Series Used as an Appositive. Use a colon to anticipate a series if, and only if, the series serves as an appositive to an earlier part of the sentence.

The class studied four Shakespearean plays: *Twelfth Night, Julius Caesar, Othello,* and *Hamlet.*

The class studied the following: *Twelfth Night, Julius Caesar, Othello,* and *Hamlet.*

The class studied *Twelfth Night, Julius Caesar, Othello,* and *Hamlet.*

Be careful not to use a semicolon when the sentence structure requires a colon.

WRONG: The course includes an introduction to three types of literature; short stories, plays, and poetry.

RIGHT: The course includes an introduction to three types of literature: short stories, plays, and poetry.

Anticipating an Explanation or a Question. Use a colon to anticipate a specific explanation of a general statement or to anticipate a particular question following a preface.

The members of the varsity baseball team are hitting well this season: the batting averages of the regular players range from 300 to 350.

He proceeded as follows: first he washed the automobile with warm water and mild soap; then he rinsed off the suds with clear water; finally he dried and polished the clean surface with a soft cloth.

Here is one of the issues which the residents of a certain rural area are considering: Will annexation to the nearby city end the water shortage in the area?

Anticipating a Long or Formal Quotation. Place a colon before a long or formal quotation.

As John Henry Newman explained it in "Knowledge and Learning," enlargement of mind is something more than acquisition of facts: "That only is true enlargement of mind which is the power of viewing many things at once as one whole, of referring them severally to their true place in the universal system, of understanding their respective values, and determining their mutual dependence."

The lecturer quoted from Pope's *Essay on Man* the well-known words: "Whatever is, is right."

Anticipating a Lesser Part of a Numerical Group. Use a colon to anticipate a lesser part of a numerical group.

The ship sailed at 10:30 this morning.
The minister discussed Corinthians 2:6.
The students enjoyed dramatizing *Macbeth* I:i:1–12.

Anticipating a Secondary Title. Place a colon before a secondary title.

I have enjoyed reading John Herman Randall, Jr., and Justus Buchler's *Philosophy: An Introduction* ("College Outline Series").

Anticipating the Body of a Formal Speech or Business Letter. Use a colon following the salutation, that is, anticipating the body, of a formal speech or business letter.

Mister Chairman, Ladies, and Gentlemen: Dear Mr. Conway:

Anticipating the Initials of a Stenographer. Use a colon to anticipate the initials of a stenographer following those of the signer of a letter.[14]

JN:BR   JN:br   JN:r

Parentheses. The pair of marks called *parentheses* indicates that the element enclosed is a nonessential interrupter, one less closely related to the rest of the sentence than is an interrrupter set off by a pair of commas. The interrupter enclosed by parentheses has no grammatical relation to the rest of the sentence. As far as meaning is concerned, this enclosed element is an extra bit seemingly thrown in for good measure. It is the function of the parentheses to notify the reader of the nonessential nature of the enclosed element.

Enclosing Supplementary Information or Comment. Use parentheses to enclose a word, phrase, or clause that gives supplementary information or comment but is structurally unrelated to the sentence.

Immanuel Kant (1724–1804) was a German philosopher.
The word *villain* (see dictionary) has degenerated in meaning.

A common error in bibliographical references is the use of a comma before parentheses. Notice that in this correctly punctuated reference there is no comma before the parentheses and that the comma following the parentheses has no relation to the parentheses; that comma would be needed even if the parenthetical element were not there.

An interesting paragraph on the subject of vocabulary appears in *College English,* VI (May, 1945), 453.

A question mark or an exclamation point may appear as end punctuation inside parentheses.

Back in 1944 (or was it 1945?) that song was popular.
He spent six months looking for a new job (what a loss of time!) and then returned to his old job.

---

[14] The last two uses of the colon listed here are really conventions of letter writing, not punctuation devices.

A period may appear as end punctuation inside the parentheses only if the parenthetical sentence is not included in a larger sentence.

Harold has been a salesman most of his life. (I do not like saleswork.) He has sold hardware for the same company for twenty years.

If the parenthetical sentence is included in a larger sentence, no period follows the parenthetical sentence. The period closing the larger sentence appears outside the parentheses.

Where the climate is mild, the early autumn is a good time for planting daffodils (September may be considered the early autumn).

Bill was going to law school (he was a graduate student) when I first met him.

Enclosing Symbols in Enumerations. Use parentheses to enclose figures or letters enumerating terms in a series.

The advertisement in the newspaper lists four household items for immediate sale: (1) a rug, (2) a bookcase, (3) a cedar chest, and (4) a radio.

The speaker discussed the following events as examples of the relationship between economy and migration: (a) the Crusades, (b) the Irish Famine, and (c) the Gold Rush.

Enclosing Confirmatory Figures. Use parentheses to enclose figures which confirm numbers or sums expressed in words; remember, however, that the trend is toward less frequent use of this device.

Mr. Miller ordered eight (8) boxes of candy.

According to the invoice he owes thirty-four dollars and twenty cents ($34.20).

Brackets. The pair of marks called *brackets* indicates that the element enclosed is an editorial insertion within a quoted passage or that the element enclosed is a parenthetical expression within another parenthetical expression already enclosed by parentheses. The brackets signify the addition of the words of one writer to those of another or the insertion of one parenthetical element into another.

Within Quotations. Use brackets to enclose an explanation, a comment, or a correction which you as editor insert into a passage you are quoting.

Samuel Butler describes undue self-esteem in one of his characters in *The Way of All Flesh,* "He [George Pontifex] had a good healthy sense of *meum,* and as little of *tuum* as he could help."

In Galsworthy's *The Man of Property* young Jolyon discusses Forsyteism with Bosinney: "As a Forsyte myself, I have no business to talk. But I'm a kind of thoroughbred mongrel [an apt paradox]; now, there's no mistaking you. You're as different from me as I am from my Uncle James, who is the perfect specimen of a Forsyte. His sense of property is extreme, while you have practically none."

Use the Latin word *sic,* which means *thus,* inside brackets to show that you are reproducing a misspelled word or other error exactly as you have found it in the original.

The student closed his theme with a flourish: "Whoa [*sic*] unto the college freshman who does not know his grammar!"

Within Parentheses. Use brackets to indicate parentheses within parentheses.

The famous dagger scene in *Macbeth* (II:i:33–64 [pp. 851–852 in the Oxford edition]) illustrates the workings of a disturbed mind.

Clifton Fadiman wrote an interesting article on Herman Melville (see *The Atlantic Monthly,* CLXXII [October, 1943], 88 ff., for the complete text).

Single Dash. A *single dash* ordinarily means that an incomplete construction stops suddenly and the sentence continues in a different form. The dash often represents an unexpected turn of thought. The usual function of the dash, therefore, is to announce a sudden change in thought or sentence structure. Another function of the dash is to indicate the omission of words or of letters in a word.

Indicating Sudden Change in Thought or Sentence Structure. Use a single dash to indicate an unexpected shift in thought or point of view or an abrupt change in sentence structure.

Patsy mused, "I believe I shall translate a hundred more lines before I—no, I'm going to eat lunch now."

The bachelor chortled, "Marriage is an honorable institution, and I sometimes think of—but who wants to live in an institution?"

Blue, green, red, and yellow—these are the colors the decorator selected.

Coleridge, Wordsworth, Byron, Shelley, and Keats—these five writers are important Romanticists.[15]

[15] Notice that in the last two examples the dash anticipates a general term that has already been illustrated by a series of specific terms. If the sequence were reversed, that is, if the generalization came first, a colon would be used to anticipate the specific terms.

These are the colors the decorator selected: blue, green, red, and yellow.

These five writers are important Romanticists: Coleridge, Wordsworth, Byron, Shelley, and Keats.

Indicating Omission of Words or Letters. Use an en dash [16] to indicate the omission of the words *to and including* between dates and
page numbers. Use a two-em dash to indicate the omission of letters to
complete a word or of words to complete a sentence.[17]

1961–1970 (1961 *to and including* 1970)

pp. 16–20 (p. 16 *to and including* p. 20)

William H—— is a favorite essayist of mine.

He continued patiently, "But I'm trying to explain that I ——"
"You're just making excuses!" she interrupted.

Pair of Dashes. A *pair of dashes* means that the intervening material
is strongly parenthetical and is not grammatically related to the rest of
the sentence. The sentence structure begins according to a certain pattern, suddenly stops to allow an emphatic interrupter to appear, and
then resumes the original pattern. A somewhat more dramatic device
than a pair of commas, a pair of dashes shows a more distinct break
in thought or structure than a pair of commas shows. Because of
their dramatic nature, dashes, like exclamation points, are most effective when used sparingly. A good plan is to avoid using dashes unless
the need for them is very clear.

Use a pair of dashes to set off a decidedly parenthetical element,
especially one that is structurally independent.

A trip through the Black Hills—the Black Hills in South Dakota are
especially picturesque—is a memorable experience.

Poe's "The Raven"—every student of Poe should read "The Raven" aloud
—has a haunting kind of rhythm.

Quotation Marks. *Quotation marks,* always used in pairs, signify
that the element enclosed comprises the exact wording of another person or the exact title of a short printed work. The primary purpose

---

[16] The *en dash* and the *em dash* get their names from the letters *n* and *m*,
respectively, used as units of measure for printed matter. An *en* is half the width
of an *em*. In typewriting, the en dash is represented by a single hyphen, ordinarily not preceded or followed by a space; the em dash is represented by a
double hyphen, preferably not preceded or followed by a space; and the two-em
dash is represented by four hyphens, with a space preceding or following if
necessary to show ordinary separation between words. The em dash (double
hyphen) is the regular dash, the one used as a punctuation device.

[17] Strictly speaking, the use of dashes to indicate omissions is a matter of
mechanics rather than of punctuation.

of quotation marks is to give credit to the person whose words are cited.

Enclosing Direct Quotations. Use double quotation marks to enclose the exact words of another person.

"I like to watch all the animals at the zoo," said Molly, "but I especially like to watch the elephants."

Lord North remarked of the British generals sent to oppose the American colonists in the Revolutionary War, "I don't know whether they frighten the enemy, but I am sure they frighten me."

Most Americans believe in "government of the people, by the people, for the people."

Use single quotation marks to enclose a quotation within a quotation.

Judith reported gleefully, "Mother, I just overheard Aunt Lucy say to Uncle Jim, 'Let's surprise Judith on her birthday.'"

Do not use quotation marks to enclose an indirect quotation, one in which the exact words of a speaker do not appear.

DIRECT QUOTATION: Ruth said, "I returned Mary's book."
INDIRECT QUOTATION: Ruth said that she had returned Mary's book.

Enclosing Titles of Short Printed Works. Use double quotation marks to enclose the title of any printed work which is too short to be bound separately and therefore is ordinarily published along with other pieces in a volume; in other words, use double quotation marks around the title of an essay, a magazine article, a short story, a one-act play, a short poem, a chapter, or a short musical composition. (See pp. 383–384 for information on italicizing titles.)

The reading assignment included William Hazlitt's essay "On Going a Journey," Joseph Conrad's short story "The Lagoon," and Robert Herrick's poem "To Blossoms."

"My Wild Irish Rose" is Pat's favorite song.

Use single quotation marks to enclose the title of a short printed work when that title appears within a quotation.

The teacher explained, "Galsworthy's 'Quality' reflects the problems of industrialization."

Enclosing Words of Special Status. Use quotation marks to enclose slang expressions, provincialisms, and technical terms which appear unconventionally in formal writing.

The girls agreed that Bob's automobile is "cool," that his conversation is "neater than neat," and that Bob himself is "the most."

Residents of San Antonio expect at least one "blue norther" before Christmas.

Many a person has tried in vain to "liquidate" intolerance.

Use quotation marks to enclose a word being defined, or italicize the word. (See the explanation of italics later in this chapter. See Chapter 10 for a discussion of words as things-in-themselves.)

The word "panacea" means a remedy for all problems.
The expression "Basic English" means a restricted vocabulary of English words used internationally.

Follow the established practice of using only one other mark of punctuation with quotation marks at the end of a quotation. For instance, drop the comma or the period that you might logically expect to use after a question mark or an exclamation point at the end of a quotation.

UNCONVENTIONAL (therefore incorrect usage):
"Would you like to dance?", Rex asked.
Nora answered, "Yes, indeed!."

CONVENTIONAL (therefore correct usage):
"Would you like to dance?" Rex asked.
Nora answered, "Yes, indeed!" (The last comma is optional.)

Also, follow the American printers' convention, not logic, in always placing a comma or a period inside the closing quotation marks. Place any other mark of punctuation where it logically belongs, inside the closing quotation marks if it belongs with the quotation and outside the closing quotation marks if it belongs with the whole sentence or with a sentence element which is larger than the quotation.

"Rover is a clever dog," said Della.
Joe countered, "Rover is not clever at all."
Della repeated, "Rover is a clever dog"; and Joe still disagreed.
But did Joe follow Della's lead and ask, "Why do you say Rover is clever"? He did not.
After a brief silence Joe remarked, "We have had smarter dogs": he was referring to Rusty and Prince.
Then Della asked, "Have you seen Rover do his new trick?"
Joe scoffed, "Did someone say, 'Rover knows a new trick'?"
Della commanded Rover, "Play dead!"
What a surprise Joe had when Della told Rover to "play dead"!

If a direct quotation consists of more than one paragraph, place quotation marks at the beginning of each paragraph and at the end of only the last paragraph. Or, follow the common practice of using especially wide margins (and single-spacing in otherwise double-spaced typescript) to take the place of quotation marks around a quoted passage of some length.[18] In print such a passage usually appears in contrasting small type with less space between the lines as well as with extra-wide margins. (See Chapter 6 for explanation and illustration of the handling of quoted passages in the research paper.)

MECHANICS

A writer uses, in addition to punctuation, certain other conventions to aid in making his meaning clear to his readers. Just as punctuation involves the use of marks with special meanings and functions, so these other conventions involve the use of symbols that both writer and reader must understand if the maximum transfer of ideas is to take place. The nonpunctuational symbols include the capital letter (which can be considered a punctuation device at the beginning of a sentence), the apostrophe, the hyphen, italics (underlining), the abbreviation point, the decimal point, and the numeral, each of which serves one or more standard purposes in effective composition. The writer who employs these nonpunctuational devices in the standard way makes his composition more intelligible to the reader than it would otherwise be.

Capitalization. A *capital letter* lends significance to the word of which it is a part. The capital letter might mean that the word introduces a unit of thought or a metrical unit, or that the word itself is important, or that the word is an important element within a given construction.

First Word of Sentence, Direct Quotation, or Verse. Capitalize the first word of an ordinary sentence, of a directly quoted sentence, or of a line of poetry.[19]

He expected a feeling of depression to follow his gay mood.

Susan coaxed, "May I go swimming just once more this week?"

"This labor-saving gadget," explained the salesman, "has been our most popular item all year."

---

[18] Some writers use the special arrangement for four or more lines of quoted prose or two or more lines of quoted poetry. Other writers reserve the special form for much longer quotations.

[19] In contemporary poetry the convention of capitalizing the first word in each line is sometimes not followed.

> To hear an oriole sing
> May be a common thing,
> Or only a divine.—EMILY DICKINSON

Proper Nouns and Derivatives. Capitalize all proper nouns and their derivatives, no matter where they appear in the sentence.

NAMES OF DEITY, SACRED WRITINGS, AND RELATED WORDS. Capitalize names of Deity and words pertaining to Deity: Allah, the Almighty, the Bible, Christ, the Creator, God, His Holy Word, in His Name, the Holy Ghost, the Holy Spirit, the Holy Virgin, Jehovah, Jesus, the Koran, the Logos, the Lord, Messiah, the Mishnah, the Redeemer, the Saviour, the Talmud, the Ten Commandments, the Veda, Yahweh.

NAMES, NICKNAMES, AND EPITHETS OF PERSONS. Capitalize the given names, family names, nicknames, and epithets of persons: Edward Jones, Babe Ruth, Stonewall Jackson, Alfred the Great.

TITLES WITH PROPER NAMES. Capitalize titles or abbreviations used with proper names of persons: Senator Bright; Sergeant Jenkins; the Reverend J. E. Foster; Dean Madison; L. R. Henderson, Professor of German; Henry Adams, Jr.; Walter Lindsay, M.D.; Dr. Lindsay.

TITLES WITHOUT PROPER NAMES. Capitalize titles of high-ranking governmental officers when such titles designate particular persons without the use of the proper names of those persons: the President, the Secretary of State, the Chief Justice, the Prime Minister, the Queen, the Shah.

WORDS INDICATING KINSHIP. Capitalize words indicating kinship if they are used with personal names or if they are used instead of personal names. Do not capitalize words of kinship that are modified by possessives.

I met Uncle Will and Father at the station.
I met my uncle and my father at the station.

NAMES OF PLACES. Capitalize the names of particular places: Augusta, Mobile, Arizona, Ohio, Ireland, Australia.

NAMES OF REGIONS. Capitalize words that designate geographical sections of the country or regions of the world, but do not capitalize words that indicate directions: the South, the Southwest, the Midwest, the Orient, the Far East, flying north, traveling westward.

NAMES OF RACES AND LANGUAGES. Capitalize the names of races of people and the names of languages: Caucasian, English, French, Italian, Latin, Negro, Polish, Teutonic.

DERIVATIVES OF PROPER NAMES. Capitalize the derivatives of proper names: Babbittry, Byronic, Elizabethan, Gallicism, Hitlerite.

NOUNS MODIFIED BY PROPER ADJECTIVES. Capitalize or do not capitalize nouns following proper adjectives, but be consistent throughout a whole composition: American History, English Literature, Vicksburg Hotel; or American history, English literature, Vicksburg hotel.

NAMES OF DAYS, MONTHS, SPECIAL HOLIDAYS. Capitalize the names of the days of the week, the months, special civic holidays, and particular days of religious observance; but do not capitalize the names of the seasons or the centuries: Sunday, Thursday, February, November, New Year's Day, Veterans' Day, Christmas, Easter, Feast of the Assumption, Passover, Yom Kippur, winter, summer, fifteenth century, twentieth century.

NAMES OF SPECIFIC COURSES, CLASSES, INSTITUTIONS, AND ORGANIZATIONS. Capitalize the names of specific courses, classes, institutions, and organizations; but do not capitalize these same words when they name members of general classifications: Chemistry 3D, the Sophomore Class of Harlandale High School, Deaconess Hospital, Pi Kappa Delta Forensic League, University of Illinois, my university, a course in chemistry, a sophomore in high school, a hospital, a debating club.

NAMES OF HISTORICAL DOCUMENTS, EVENTS, AND PERIODS. Capitalize the names of particular historical documents, special historical events, and definite historical periods: the Declaration of Independence, the Magna Charta, the Battle of Bunker Hill, the Deluge, World War II, Middle English, Pleistocene, the Renaissance.

NAMES OF GOVERNMENTAL BODIES. Capitalize the names of governing bodies and other official organizations: Congress, Parliament, Bureau of Engraving and Printing, Chicago City Council, Federal Reserve System, United Nations, United States Air Force.

PERSONIFICATIONS. Capitalize all personifications, whether of inanimate objects or of abstract ideas:

> Sport that wrinkled Care derides,
> And Laughter holding both his sides.—JOHN MILTON

First Word and All Important Words in Titles. Capitalize the first word (except the initial article in the name of a newspaper or a magazine) and each important word in the title of a literary work, a non-literary publication, or a musical composition. Ordinarily do not capitalize prepositions and conjunctions within a title unless they consist of four or more letters: "Of Wisdom for a Man's Self," "A Valediction Forbidding Mourning," *Caught Between Storms*, *The Return of the Native*, the *Times Literary Supplement*, the *Saturday Evening Post*, *Better Homes and Gardens*, *The Moonlight Sonata*, *The Pirates of Penzance*. (See pp. 375–376 and 383–384 for use of quotation marks and italics, respectively, with titles.)

The Words I and O. Capitalize the personal pronoun *I* and the poetic exclamation *O* (but not the interjection *oh*) wherever they appear in a sentence.

We thank Thee, O Lord, for Thy blessings.

I expected the place to look the way I remembered it, but oh, what a change I found!

Words in Special Parts of Letters. Capitalize the first word and all nouns in the salutation of a letter (or a speech) and the first word only in the complimentary close of a letter.

My dear Madam: Yours very truly,

Apostrophe. The *apostrophe* is a mark used to indicate the possessive case of most nouns and of the indefinite pronouns, the omission of one or more letters or figures, and certain plural forms.

Possessive Forms. To form the possessive singular of any noun that names an animate being, add an apostrophe and *s*: baby, baby's; boss, boss's; boy, boy's; dog, dog's; Harvey Johnson, Harvey Johnson's; leader, leader's; man, man's; woman, woman's.

Usage varies in the formation of the possessive of singular nouns already ending in an *s* or a *z* sound. A common practice is to add both the apostrophe and *s* to such nouns of one syllable (Burns, Burns's; James, James's; lass, lass's; Tess, Tess's), but to add only the apostrophe to such nouns of two or more syllables (Dickens, Dickens'; Moses, Moses'; Ulysses, Ulysses'; witness, witness'). As the first examples show, adding both the apostrophe and *s* creates an extra syllable.

Ordinarily use an *of* phrase rather than an apostrophe and *s* to form the possessive (singular or plural) of a noun that names an inanimate thing. Say *the hand of the clock*, not *the clock's hand*; but say *the boy's hand*, not *the hand of the boy*, unless sentence structure requires otherwise.

In forming the possessive plural of a noun, be sure first to spell correctly the plural form of the word in the nominative case. Then, if this plural spelling does not end in *s*, add an apostrophe and *s* to form the possessive plural: child, children, children's; man, men, men's; one sheep, two sheep, two sheep's wool; woman, women, women's. If, however, the nominative plural ends in *s,* add only an apostrophe to form the possessive plural: baby, babies, babies'; boss, bosses, bosses'; girl, girls, girls'; lady, ladies, ladies'; Eisenhower, the Eisenhowers, the Eisenhowers'; Kennedy, the Kennedys, the Kennedys'.

Ordinarily, to form the possessive singular of a compound noun add an apostrophe and *s* to the last word in the compound: brother-in-law, brother-in-law's; Prince of Wales, Prince of Wales's; stand-in, stand-in's. To form the possessive plural of a compound noun, first pluralize the most important word in the compound; then add the necessary sign of the possessive to the last word of this pluralized compound: one brother-in-law, two brothers-in-law, two brothers-in-law's assistance; one Prince of Wales, two Princes of Wales, two Princes of Wales' opinions; one stand-in, two stand-ins, two stand-ins' costumes.

To show individual ownership, place an apostrophe and *s* after each of two or more names in a group: Clark's and Anderson's horses, Jim's and Danny's toys. To show joint ownership, use an apostrophe and *s* with only the last of two or more names in a group: Clark and Anderson's horses, Jim and Danny's toys.

To form the possessive of indefinite pronouns, follow the principles for forming the possessive of nouns: anyone, anyone's; everyone, everyone's; someone, someone's; other, other's (singular), others' (plural).

Do not use an apostrophe with the possessive form of any personal pronoun or with the pronoun *whose,* which is sometimes a relative pronoun and sometimes an interrogative pronoun: his, hers, its, ours, theirs, whose, yours. (Note that *it's* is a contraction for *it is* and that *who's* is a contraction for *who is.*)

Contractions. Use an apostrophe to indicate the omission of a letter or letters in a contracted word or phrase: can't, didn't, ne'er, they're, you've. Use an apostrophe to indicate the purposeful omission of the first or the last letter in a word: 'gainst, somethin'. (Remember that contractions are appropriate only on or below the informal level of usage.)

Also, use an apostrophe to indicate the omission of figures from dates: Class of '61, back in '30.

Plural Forms of Figures, Symbols, Letters, and Words as Things-in-Themselves. Ordinarily use an apostrophe and *s* to form the plural of a figure, a symbol, a letter, or a word as a thing-in-itself. The growing tendency is to omit the apostrophe where ambiguity is unlikely: 8's (*or* 8s), 1950's (*or* 1950s), +'s, &'s, a's, I's, and's (*or* ands).

Hyphen. The *hyphen,* which is half the length of the regular dash, is a mark used to join the parts of a compound word or to indicate the break of a word divided between syllables at the end of a line. Thus the hyphen is a mechanical device which, used correctly, becomes a mark of precision in spelling.

Compound Words. Various writers and publishers follow quite different practices in the use of compound words. Although the best procedure is to consult a dictionary for the form of particular compounds, here are a few helpful general principles.

Hyphenate two or more words which function together as one adjective modifier of a noun they precede: a well-known theory, an eight-hour day, an up-to-date laboratory, forty-eight end-of-the-month reports.

Hyphenate compound numbers from twenty-one to ninety-nine, inclusive: thirty-three (thirty-third), sixty-two (sixty-second).

Ordinarily hyphenate fractions unless either the numerator or the denominator already contains a hyphen: one-third, five thirty-sixths, twenty-one fortieths.

Hyphenate a compound made up of a prefix and a proper noun or derivative thereof: anti-Asiatic, pro-Canadian, non-European.

Syllabication. Use a hyphen to indicate division between syllables at the end of a line. Place the hyphen at the end of the first line concerned, not at the beginning of the second.

If you are not certain where the syllables of a word begin and end, follow the syllabication given in a dictionary. However, do not place a syllable of only one letter at the end of a line and do not place a syllable of fewer than three letters at the beginning of a line.

The logical point of division of a word containing a prefix or a suffix is between the prefix or the suffix and the rest of the word; but the division is permissible only if the prefix consists of two or more letters, or the suffix consists of three or more letters. The logical dividing point of compound words is between their main parts.

A good practice is to divide as few words as possible and not to divide short words at all. It is also important not to divide words that are already hyphenated.

Italics. Italic type is print in which the letters slope to the left at the bottom and to the right at the top. In handwritten or typewritten manuscript, a single straight line under a word means that the word, if printed, should appear in italics.

Titles of Long Printed Works. Italicize the titles of books, magazines, newspapers, or other printed works that are long enough to be bound separately: *Vanity Fair, The Plantation, Scribner's Magazine, Newsweek,* the *New York Times* (or the New York *Times*), *Romeo and Juliet, Evangeline.* (See p. 376 for use of quotation marks with titles.)

Names of Ships, Trains, and Airplanes. Italicize the names of particular ships, trains, and airplanes: the *Admiral,* the *Queen Mary,* the *Texas Special,* the *Columbine.*

Names of Paintings and Musical Compositions. Italicize the names of paintings and the titles of long musical compositions: Millet's *The Gleaners,* Hogarth's *The Rake's Progress,* Gilbert and Sullivan's *The Mikado,* Puccini's *Madama Butterfly.*

Words and Expressions as Things-in-Themselves. Italicize (or enclose in quotation marks) words or expressions used as things-in-themselves. (See the explanation of quotation marks earlier in this chapter. See Chapter 10 for a discussion of words as things-in-themselves.)

The word *definite* is frequently misspelled.

Murmur and *scream* have different connotations.

Have you ever heard the expression *get away with* used as a substitute for *embarrass?*

Foreign Words and Expressions. Italicize foreign words and expressions which have not been naturalized (that is, adopted into standard English usage) when you use them in an English text: *au naturel, Deo favente, Gesundheit, laborare est orare, mens sana in corpore sano, Weltansicht.*

Words Needing Emphasis. Italicize words which need particular emphasis, but use this device sparingly.

The other boys were still wearing their skates when they reached the opposite side of the frozen lake; Michael was *carrying* his.

Falstaff *impersonates* royalty; Hal *is* royalty.

Abbreviation Point. The *abbreviation point,* a mark identical in form to the period, is a spelling device used to save time in the writing of certain words. In composition on the formal level, abbreviations should appear infrequently. Here are the most common uses of the abbreviation point.

Titles Preceding Names. Use an abbreviation point after a group of letters that stand for a title preceding a name: Dr. Murphy Bounds, Mrs. R. E. Clayton.

Do not abbreviate the titles *Professor, Honorable,* and *Reverend;* if you use only the surname with either of the last two of these titles, you should include also the title *Mr.*: Professor Daniel Hodge, Professor Hodge; the Honorable Richard Wells, the Honorable Mr. Wells; the Reverend C. A. Langston, the Reverend Mr. Langston.

Titles and Other Limiting Expressions Following Names. Place an abbreviation point after each letter or group of letters substituted for a word in a title or other limiting expression following a name: Alfred Tillman, M.D.; Ralph Dudley, Esq.; Bradley and Jones, Inc.

Expressions of Time. Place an abbreviation point after each letter standing for a word in conventional abbreviations referring to time: A.M. (*or* a.m.), P.M. (*or* p.m.), A.D., B.C.

Ordinarily use an abbreviation point after each initial capital letter that stands for a word in the abbreviation of a term consisting of more than one word: A.B., M.A., Y.W.C.A. You may choose, especially for informal writing, to follow the current trend to omit abbreviation points from standardized abbreviations: AAA, DNB, TVA, UN, UNESCO (*or* Unesco).

Decimal Point. The *decimal point,* a mark identical in form to the period or the abbreviation point, is a spelling device used to precede a decimal fraction expressed in Arabic numerals: 3.7 (three and seven-tenths), .9 (nine-tenths), .03 (three hundredths), $4.75.

Numbers. Except in certain instances, numbers should appear in word form rather than as figures. This is especially true when a figure appears first in a sentence: "Forty children played in the yard at one time."

Dates and Other References to Time. Use figures in dates (except in formal social notes) and in references to time which include *a.m.* or *p.m.*

The play represents the historic events of October 12, 1492.
At 3:30 a.m. he was awakened by a single rap on the door.

Street Addresses. Use figures in street addresses and other designations (such as telephone numbers, chapter numbers, page numbers, and measurements) where figures are more convenient for reference than are words: 8104 Braddock Avenue; Garfield 7–6377; Chapter 5, page 68; a room 22 feet long, 12 feet wide, and 8 feet high.

Sums of Money. Use figures to represent sums of money that would require more than a word or two: $7.55; $9,582.10.

Statistics. Use figures to express statistics that would require more than two words.

Plans for the picnic included 432 sandwiches and 648 glasses of lemonade for 216 children.

Bibliographical References. Bibliographical references commonly contain figures, Roman as well as Arabic. (For illustrations see pp. 118, 133–134, 160, and 405–417.)

Exercises

1. Supply appropriate end punctuation for the following sentences. State the reason for each mark.
 a. In which direction were the geese flying
 b. She explained why she prefers Beethoven to Bach
 c. How far is it from Paris to Rome
 d. The question for discussion concerned whether or not a new expressway should be built
 e. How absurd it is to think that mankind is perfect
 f. I wondered why he was running down the street
 g. Will you please hand me the dictionary
 h. The police questioned the suspects for an hour

2. Use commas to set off the nonrestrictive appositives and modifiers in the following sentences. Do not punctuate the restrictive elements.
 a. He learned to distinguish the word *allusion* from the word *illusion*.
 b. The victim's father who saw the accident occur testified in court.
 c. The *Skate* a famous submarine came to the surface through the ice at the North Pole.
 d. Anyone who likes social drama will probably enjoy Ibsen's plays.
 e. Ghana located in West Africa and Kenya located in East Africa are both on his itinerary.
 f. Tom lives in the house built of California redwood.
 g. He read Joseph Conrad's novel *Victory*.
 h. *Victory* a novel by Joseph Conrad is a story which concerns an individual's detachment from society.

3. Supply commas where they are needed for clarity in the following sentences:
 a. The crowd shouted for the quarterback had just scored a touchdown.
 b. High above the jet plane streaked through the sky.
 c. Just when she tried to swallow the dentist began drilling on her tooth.
 d. The class continued to wait patiently for the professor had explained that he might be detained.

4. The following sentences contain more commas than they need. Copy the sentences, keeping only the necessary commas. State your reason for omitting or for keeping each comma.
 a. The store on the corner, has been vacant since Monday, October 20.
 b. He decided, that he would enroll in three courses in day school, and two courses in night school.

c. He bought, apples, bread, coffee, and cream.

d. For as long as I can recall, the neighborhood has been a quiet, peaceful, one.

5. Certain commas in the following sentences need to be replaced by semicolons or colons. Correct as necessary and state the reason for each correction.

a. Janet plays four instruments, the piano, the harp, the flute, and the violin.

b. The meanings of some words ameliorate, the meanings of other words pejorate.

c. The chairman presided at every meeting, however, he did not participate in the voting.

d. He had three duties when he worked in the library, answering the telephone, shelving books, and operating the microfilm machine.

e. During the tour they stopped at Grant's Farm, where they saw several Clydesdale horses, Forest Park, where they visited the zoo, and Lambert Field, where they watched the airplanes take off and land.

f. When he entered college last year, Bob had already studied trigonometry, analytic geometry, and calculus, but Harry, who is already a junior in college, is only now studying trigonometry.

6. Supply quotation marks where they are needed in the following sentences. Be sure to follow convention in placing the quotation marks before or after other marks.

a. Did you call me? asked Nora.

b. If you wish, said the instructor, you may write two short papers instead of one long one.

c. The short story entitled Brooksmith is one of my favorite stories, said John.

d. The officer said, Mrs. Jones, you were speeding; but Mrs. Jones insisted that she was not.

7. Punctuate the following sentences with whatever marks they need. State the reason for each mark you use.

a. Father brought in a tree from the timber we children decorated it with cranberries popcorn and pictures.

b. We went fishing on hot humid days.

c. Miss Brown how soon will you need my book asked Ruth.

d. The children are looking forward to a party for Judith will celebrate her birthday next week.

e. All night long the snow fell and the wind blew consequently many roads were drifted the next morning.

f. The boys carried blue banners the girls white balloons.

g. She ordered the following supplies ink paper and pencils.

h. Goodness beauty truth these qualities continue to influence the development of civilization.

i. Thomas DeQuincey 1785–1859 was an English author.

j. William Shakespeare who was an actor as well as a playwright must have led a busy life.

8. Supply capitals and indicate italics or use quotation marks where necessary in the following sentences:

a. A group of tourists guided by professor kent larson sailed from new york on the queen elizabeth in July.

b. She went to grade school in the south, high school in the midwest, and college in the east.

c. Chapter 10, the technical report, in the book english communication is part of the assignment.

d. Students of central high school had a holiday the day before thanksgiving.

e. Tom's course of study includes english, latin, algebra, biology, and history.

f. Matthew arnold's poem dover beach and john henry newman's essay the educated man are both in the anthology entitled adventures in english literature.

9. In the following exercise pay careful attention to spelling as well as to possessive forms.

a. Write the possessive singular and the possessive plural of each of the following nouns:

adult	Davis	governess	man	son-in-law
albatross	deer	horse	Negro	student
bird	donkey	Irishman	passer-by	Swede
child	editor-in-chief	laborer	poet	woman

b. Write the following pronouns in the possessive case:

another	he	one	someone	who
anyone	it	she	they	you

APPENDIX

Letter Writing

Letter writing is, and is likely to remain, a very important means of communication between individuals and between organizations. The eagerness and care with which we all look in our mailboxes and open the letters that have come first class suggests the significance of both personal and commercial correspondence. We may not be so eager to write letters as to receive them; but then, most of us are not so eager to write essays or stories as we are to read those that others have written. When we do write a letter, we have an opportunity to use the basic skills we have acquired from our study of composition.

The twelve chapters of this book explain and illustrate the main principles of effective composition. *We should apply these same principles in writing letters.* It is a mistake to think that writing a composition is one thing and that writing a letter is an altogether different thing. The body of a letter *is* a composition. It may sometimes be a miniature composition; but if it accomplishes its purpose, it is a whole composition.

Without going into detail again, we shall consider some of the fundamentals of good composition, then summarize the chief conventions of letter writing and present a few examples of common types of letters.[1]

COMPOSITION IN LETTER WRITING

Although the other parts of the letter are either adaptations or reproductions of strict conventional patterns, the body is a created organic unit of composition. The body of an effective letter is complete, clear, and grammatically correct. It has a pleasing style and an appropriate tone.

Completeness. *Completeness* requires that the writer of a letter, as of any other form of composition, select and organize according to basic techniques all the information that is pertinent to his purpose. Completeness does not mean undue length; in fact, a business letter

---

[1] For a more fully illustrated explanation of letter writing, see Alfred Stuart Myers, *Letters for All Occasions,* "Everyday Handbooks" (New York: Barnes & Noble, Inc., 1957).

For a detailed coverage of business letters in particular, with examples of both ineffective and effective letters for special purposes (inquiry, order, credit, collection, adjustment, sales, application, etc.), see also J. Harold Janis, Edward J. Kilduff, and Howard R. Dressner, *Business Writing.* "College Outline Series" (New York: Barnes & Noble, Inc., 1956).

should be concise, though never perfunctory; its paragraphs are often justifiably short. A business letter may have one or more specific purposes: to make or answer an inquiry, to order merchandise, to state or settle a claim, to sell a product or an idea, to collect a payment, to grant or refuse credit, to apply for a job, to transmit a report, and so on. Whatever its purpose, the letter that includes the relevant details and excludes the irrelevant will succeed better than one that contains only generalizations. A simple order letter, for instance, is obviously incomplete if it elicits a response like "We are sorry that we cannot fill your order for a plastic garden hose until you specify the length you want and send us a check or money order in payment or authorize us to send the hose C.O.D." Nor is a letter of application that gives no data on the applicant's age, education, and experience likely to secure him a job or even an interview.

A personal letter may also have a specific purpose—such as expressing gratitude, congratulations, or sympathy—or the more general purpose of informing and entertaining a friend. Whether long or short, a letter that accomplishes any of these purposes requires thoughtful planning and the enrichment of concrete materials. A personal letter that develops a central topic or a nucleus of related topics is usually interesting to the reader. An unexplained statement like "I had an exciting spring vacation" will puzzle a student's parents, but details on a four-day glee club tour and the winning of a contest will let them share the excitement.

Clarity. *Clarity* in a letter, as elsewhere, calls for simple, direct prose. There is no special language reserved for letter writing. It is much better to say simply, "As we agreed, I am enclosing two copies of the lease for you to sign," than to use such hackneyed phrasing as "Pursuant to our agreement, please find enclosed two copies of the lease, and I beg the favor of your signature on same." And it is far more appropriate to write to a friend, "I had fun staying awake all night at your slumber party," than to cause doubt by overdoing the diction, as in "Please accept my profound gratitude for the recreation you provided at your incomparable slumber party."

Grammatical Correctness. *Correct grammar* is essential in both personal and business letters. Sentences should be interestingly varied in structure, but without distracting shifts in point of view. Paragraphs should be unified and coherent. All these devices of good composition are useful in maintaining the reader's interest because they help him understand the message clearly. To keep the reader's respect as well as his interest, spelling and punctuation in the letter must be flawless.

Pleasing Style and Appropriate Tone. When a letter has a degree of formality or informality consistent with its subject and with the relationship between the sender and the recipient, we say it has *pleasing style*. If its *tone* is consistent with its purpose, we call the tone *appropriate*. Professional or business correspondence on serious subjects usually requires the dignified, but unstilted, style and the sober tone of a good formal essay. Letters between friends, on the other hand, are more like informal essays—ranging from the whimsical and sprightly to the nostalgic and meditative. But informality does not admit hasty or careless composition. With most writers, a letter that has the effect of spontaneous, charming conversation is the result of painstaking selection and organization of ideas and then of careful writing and even rewriting. Finally, a good letter is sincere and courteous.

CONVENTIONS OF LETTER WRITING

Certain well-established conventions should be observed in letter writing. These concern the parts of the letter and their arrangement on the page, the materials, and the folding.

Parts of the Letter. The business letter (see example on p. 398) has six conventional parts—heading, inside address, salutation, body, complimentary close, and signature—and several optional parts. The personal letter has all the conventional parts except the inside address.

Heading. The *heading* includes the writer's mailing address and the date, and, except on letterhead paper, appears near the upper right-hand corner on the first page of the letter. On letterhead paper the writer adds only the date, either in the center at least two spaces under the letterhead, as in the example on page 398, or in a right-hand position, as in this example.

BARNES & NOBLE, Inc.

BOOKSELLERS & PUBLISHERS
105 FIFTH AVENUE   NEW YORK, N. Y. 10003   TELEPHONE: 212-255-8100

October 20, 1965

In handwritten or typed headings, abbreviations should be avoided, and the date written as shown above or 20 October 1965 (but not 10/20/65). Two styles, the block form without end punctuation and the indented form with end punctuation, are shown below. Modern usage favors the former because it is easier to type.

Heading in block *form without* *end punctuation*	3216 West Olive Street Baltimore, Maryland 21008 November 10, 1965
Heading in indented *form with end* *punctuation*	3216 West Olive Street, Baltimore, Maryland 21008, November 10, 1965.

Inside Address. The *inside address,* a conventional part of the business letter but not of the personal letter, contains the name and mailing address of the recipient. The inside address begins at the left-hand margin and at least a space below the date line.

The inside address is reproduced on the envelope (that is, unless a window envelope is used, in which case the letter is folded so that the inside address shows through the window). For consistency the inside and outside addresses, including the return address, should follow the style of the heading. Here are examples.

Professor J. Edwin Whitesell Managing Editor, The Explicator University of South Carolina Columbia, South Carolina	*Inside address in* *block form without* *end punctuation*
Professor J. Edwin Whitesell, Managing Editor, The Explicator, University of South Carolina, Columbia, South Carolina.	*Inside address in* *indented form with* *end punctuation*

The name of the state may be placed on a separate line. For clarity, abbreviations of place names should be avoided in addresses. *Mr., Mrs.,* and *Dr.* are the only acceptable abbreviations of personal titles.

Salutation. The *salutation,* or greeting, begins at the left-hand margin, two or more spaces below the inside address of a business letter or the heading of a personal letter. The first word and all nouns in the salutation are capitalized. The salutation of a business letter is regularly followed by a colon; that of a personal letter, by a comma. The salutation should be consistent with the body and the complimentary close in degree of formality. Here are examples of conventional salutations arranged to show decreasing degrees of formality.

For Business Letters

Sir: Madam: (*to a public official*)
My dear Sir: My dear Madam:
Dear Sir: Dear Madam:
Gentlemen: Mesdames: Ladies: (*to a company or group*)
My dear Mr. Hill: My dear Mrs. Hill: My dear Miss Hill:
Dear Mr. Lee: Dear Mrs. Lee: Dear Miss Lee:

For Personal Letters

```
My dear Mr. Hill,  My dear Mrs. Hill,  My dear Miss Hill,
Dear Mr. Lee,   Dear Mrs. Lee,   Dear Miss Lee,
Dear Michael,   Dear Elizabeth Ann,
Dear Mike,   Dear Liz,
```

Body. The *body* of a typewritten letter begins two spaces below the salutation. Unless an office style sheet prescribes otherwise, the paragraphs should be single-spaced with double-spacing between them. The paragraphs may be indented a uniform number of spaces (usually five or eight spaces) or typed in block form. The paragraphs of a hand-written letter should be indented about an inch; no space is necessary between them.

(For suggestions on how to compose the body of a letter, see "Composition in Letter Writing," pp. 391–393.)

Complimentary Close. The *complimentary close* begins slightly more than half way across the page (if spacing permits, directly below the beginning of the heading) and two spaces below the last line of the body of the letter. Only the first word of the complimentary close is capitalized, and the last word is regularly followed by a comma. The complimentary close should be consistent in tone with the salutation and the body but independent in form (closings like "Hoping to hear from you soon, I remain, Yours truly" are no longer acceptable). Here, arranged to show decreasing degree of formality, are examples of complimentary closes now in use.

For Business Letters

```
Respectfully yours,        Yours respectfully,
Very truly yours,          Yours very truly,
Yours truly,
Very sincerely yours,      Yours very sincerely,
Sincerely yours,           Yours sincerely,
Cordially yours,           Yours cordially,
```

For Personal Letters

```
Very sincerely yours,      Yours very sincerely,
Sincerely yours,           Yours sincerely,
Cordially yours,           Yours cordially,
Sincerely,                 Cordially,
```

Signature. The *signature,* always handwritten of course, appears under the complimentary close. (If a firm assumes responsibility for a letter, the name of the firm appears above the signature of the sender.)

In a typewritten business letter the name and, when necessary to indicate authority, the official title of the writer are typed under the signature. Here are examples of acceptable forms.

For Business Letters

An officer
of a firm

Very truly yours,
D. M. Henderson
D. M. Henderson
Treasurer

A firm assuming
responsibility
for the letter

Very truly yours,
NATIONAL LEADER, INC.
T. W. Baker
T. W. Baker

An individual
writing in his
own behalf

Very truly yours,
Edward E. Wilson
Edward E. Wilson

A married
woman

Very truly yours,
Frances Tucker
(Mrs. William Tucker)

A married woman
using her own name in
business or profession

Very truly yours,
Ruth Shaw Carson
(Mrs.) Ruth Shaw Carson

An unmarried
woman

Very truly yours,
Janice Jordan
(Miss) Janice Jordan

For Personal Letters

A new acquaintance

Sincerely yours,
John Parker

A good friend

Sincerely,
Beth

Optional Parts. At the left-hand margin a few spaces below the signature on a business letter may appear any of these *optional* notations that are applicable: an inscription showing initials of dictator and stenographer (EMH/bn *or* EMH:BN); a notation on enclosures (Encl. *or* Encls.: 3); a notation naming recipients of carbon copies of the letter (Copy to Mr. Harter *or* cc to Mr. Harter). If a letter requires more than one page, the name of the addressee, the date, and the page number should appear in a line at the top of each succeeding page, several spaces above the continuation of the body (Mr. R. W. Thompson, April 15, 1960, page 2). These *optional parts* of a letter are useful for identification and reference. For specific reference to the subject treated in a letter, the writer may use *Re* followed by a colon and a brief label in the space above and to the right of the salutation (see the letter on p. 399).

Materials. Most modern business letters are typed on white bond paper, $8\frac{1}{2}$ by 11 inches in size. Half sheets, $5\frac{1}{2}$ by $8\frac{1}{2}$ inches, are appropriate for brief messages. The paper and envelopes should be of good quality. Letterhead paper is used for only the first page of a letter, and a similar quality of bond paper is used for any additional pages.

The typing should be clear and even, with no strikeovers or obvious erasures. Margins that give the effect of balance, and double-spacing between single-spaced paragraphs help to make a letter attractive. Although most commercial correspondence is typed nowadays, a neat, clear pen-written business letter is still acceptable.

Typing a letter to a friend is no longer considered a discourtesy, but most personal letters are still handwritten. Care in the writing and in the selection of materials adds grace to a personal message. It is always a courtesy to write legibly. It is always in good taste to use a conservative color of ink (blue, blue-black, or black) and a good quality of paper, preferably white or off-white, with matching envelopes.

Folding. A business letter is *folded* approximately in thirds horizontally (to fit into a long envelope) or approximately in half horizontally and then in thirds vertically (to fit into a small envelope). A personal letter is folded to fit into the matching envelope: the book-type paper usually needs to be folded once horizontally; the club type, twice horizontally. Every letter should be neatly and precisely folded.

TYPES OF LETTERS

So far in this appendix we have made the general distinction between business letters and personal letters. A somewhat more representative cross section of modern letter writing includes two other kinds, the combination business and personal letter, and the social note.

Business Letter. The example on the next page is a letter of transmittal-summary written to accompany the report on pages 82–84 of this book. The purpose of this *business letter* is to convey the report to the person who had requested it and to provide him with a concise summary of the report for ready reference. The first paragraph identifies the report and makes clear who had requested and authorized it; the second establishes the qualifications of the author and explains his

STANDARD CLEANING COMPANY

1436 East Main Street

Morrisville 2, Illinois

April 15, 1960

Mr. R. W. Thompson, President
Standard Cleaning Company
1436 East Main Street
Morrisville 2, Illinois

Dear Mr. Thompson:

The attached report concerns three stores now vacant and
for rent north of Tenth Street and west of Cedar Avenue,
the area in which you have proposed that Standard Cleaning
Company open a branch service shop. The report is the result of a study which you requested and Mr. David Cochran,
Chairman of the Board of Directors, authorized at the development meeting on April 1.

As I did last year in finding the location for our Central
Avenue branch, I have (1) personally inspected the vacant
stores, including a check on parking facilities; (2) con-
sulted each owner or manager on rental terms; (3) visited
City Hall to determine the zoning rules in each neighborhood and the predominant occupations of the residents; and
(4) observed the location of competitors in each neighborhood. The details of my findings appear in the report.

Of the available stores (called A, B, and C in the report),
I believe that Store B, on the ground floor of the York-
Hanley Apartment Hotel, 429 State Street, offers the best
opportunities for us. Its chief disadvantage, meter parking, is largely offset by the proximity of potential customers. Store A, at 600 Wilson Avenue, would have more
overhead than any of our present branches. And Store C,
at 7842½ Berry Road, despite its newness and wealth of
parking space, would not be good for our purpose because
most of the residents in that area wear working clothes
which are laundered in their homes. Just the opposite is
true of the professional people in the State Street area
near Store B. The obviously great volume of business being
done by all three of the laundry and dry cleaning establishments already located on State Street indicates that a
fourth one could compete.

I shall be happy to explain more fully any points in this
letter and the accompanying report or, at your request, to
pursue the study further. (According to Mr. E. J. Cook,
Manager, the Western Auto Store at 2210 Pine Street will be
vacated early in 1961. If Standard's expansion continues,
that might be a logical location for still another branch.
The Pine Street address is about equidistant from our
plant, our Central Avenue branch, and Store B.)

Respectfully submitted,

John J. Graham

John J. Graham
Field Representative

JJG/nc

W. R. BENDY CEMENT ENGINEERS

1530 PAGE INDUSTRIAL BLVD.
ST. LOUIS 32, MO.

June 8, 1960

Mr. W. F. Fellows
Assistant Vice President, Engineering
Illinois Portland Cement Company
2068 South Grand
Chicago
Illinois

Re: Raw Grinding Department

Dear Mr. Fellows:

This is in reply to the last paragraph of your letter of
June 1, in which you asked for a tentative engineering
schedule for improvements to the raw grinding department.

We have already started work on the design of the sampling
equipment. But for the leaching system, various tests are
required before we can accurately size the equipment. The
necessary tests were described in our letter of May 16 to
your Mr. Winkler, who is having them carried out. In the
meantime, we sent you drawings of the proposed arrangement
on May 27 and are awaiting your comments.

We plan to start work on the raw grinding mill itself on
June 13 and anticipate that drawings will be available in
about a month, or about the middle of July.

To summarize, the last of the preliminary drawings for the
several portions of this work should be in your hands by
about July 18. We shall advise you of a firm completion
date on or before June 22.

Yours very truly,
W. R. BENDY CEMENT ENGINEERS

W. R. Bendy

WRB/bh

cc: Mr. A. N. Winkler

methods; the third summarizes and interprets briefly his findings and
recommendations; and the last makes a courteous offer of further
service. The letter, which uses first and second person pronouns (*I, our,
us, you, your*), is less formal than the report, which uses the third
person ("the writer believes," etc.).

In the above letter [2] a consulting engineer answers with specific detail
a customer's request for information on services in progress.

[2] Printed with permission of the writer, Mr. W. R. Bendy.

Emporia, Kansas
September 14, 1920

My dear Edna:

...We had a beautiful summer, Sallie and I, in Colorado.... We had some company, an average of nine, I think, at the table was our rule, sometimes it ran up to fourteen, but never lower than seven. Bill and Mary were both there. I suppose it will be Bill's last all-summer trip in the Park. He is going to work next summer. Just at the moment Bill is in Lawrence at the University of Kansas..., but he is going to Harvard next week, and he thinks he will go to work next summer on the paper. He has been working now for three or four years, and he makes a pretty fair fist as a reporter....

Mary seems to have come into a new era in her life. Last year and the year before she was mighty carefree, as you know, but this year she is...doing all sorts of stunts, taking five subjects and clamoring to take six; has an ambition to make grades and is tremendously impressed with the idea of going to Wellesley. She has forgotten all about the horse, except in odd moments, when the horse complex returns, but it only holds her attention a few minutes a day. The horse and all that goes with the horse is in the past with her. She is reading serious books. She got her great stimulus to work at the Y.W. conference at Estes Park, where she did remarkably well and met a lot of girls from different colleges, mostly eastern colleges.... She reads all sorts of tremendously serious, high-brow stuff, and at the same time she does love to put pins in the teacher's chair....

...I didn't take the cover off my typewriter while I was in the West. I left all my letters unanswered, as you have reason to suspect, and just naturally loafed. Bill drove us around in the car a good deal....

As a result of my summer's siesta, I feel quite fit and want to go to work. I have the Roosevelt thing on the block and will probably get rid of it right away....[3]

Personal Letter. The example of *personal letter* writing quoted here is from a letter by William Allen White to Edna Ferber. White, as editor of the Emporia, Kansas, *Gazette* from 1895 to 1944, had an active public life; but he was singularly devoted to his family and friends, as his many personal letters show. Edna Ferber was an intimate friend of the White family. If she could have had a conversation with White on the day he wrote this letter, she might very well have asked him the questions that he anticipated and answered. (Sallie in the letter is Mrs. White; Bill and Mary are the White children.)

Combination Business and Personal Letter. *Combination business and personal letters* are often exchanged by writers who are personal

[3] Reprinted with permission from W. L. White and Walter Johnson, ed., *Selected Letters of William Allen White* (New York: Henry Holt and Company, 1947), pp. 208–209.

3310 Hamilton Avenue
Chicago, Illinois 60022
June 14, 1964

Dear Bob,

Thank you for your letter of June 10, outlining the
tentative agenda for the Get-Out-the-Vote Committee Meeting
at the Jaycee Convention in St. Louis next week. I shall
try to have several appropriate ideas in mind to use as
entering wedges when you call for discussion. The agenda
as it stands covers very thoroughly, I believe, the work
specifically assigned to our committee this year. I have
just one suggestion, concerned more with continuity than
with present duties: I recommend adding an item on the
need for keeping the committee active next year, when there
will not be the automatic impetus of a Presidential election. A pooling of ideas now on ways to sustain the general interest in voting would give the members who remain
on the committee, and indirectly the new members, a basis
from which to work. No doubt such ideas will emerge incidentally from the discussion, but the point seems important
enough to have a place on the agenda. Perhaps it could be
the last item.

Carol and I are all set to go conventioning. Nick
and Bobby are at camp; the parakeets are vacationing in a
friend's apartment; and our own place, suddenly, is in a
state of hush. Carol has a dozen tours--all woodsy--on
her convention agenda. She plans to explore places like
the Missouri Botanical Garden, Grant's Farm, and Forest
Park. (Carol has turned forester, or "forestrix." Early
this spring she started raising a tree in a tub on the
balcony of our third-floor apartment, and she's having such
good luck that we're beginning to wonder what to do when
the tree outgrows the tub.)

We're both looking forward to seeing you and Linda in
St. Louis. We're sorry that Linda won't be there the whole
week but agree that it's a good chance for her to visit her
family in Kansas City. It's been almost two years, you
know, since we were all in K.C. and our living rooms were
half a block instead of half a continent apart. As you
suggested, we're saving Friday, when Linda gets in (and the
convention should be over), for a private picnic. By that
time Carol will have discovered a perfect site.

Cordially,
Chuck

friends as well as professional or business associates. A common practice is to deal with the business in the first part of the letter and to
make that part relatively formal, then to shift to an informal style and
write a personal message in the last paragraph or two. The example
above shows a combination of this kind. The style becomes more con-

versational at the beginning of the second paragraph. The language becomes more informal (people are going "conventioning," parakeets are "vacationing," tours are "woodsy"), but it is not slipshod. A word is coined, but it is a logical coinage ("forestrix" may remind the reader of "aviatrix"). The incident of the tree in the tub creates an image, and other details provide concreteness in this part of the letter, but the convention theme remains to unify the whole.

Social Notes. *Social notes* include invitations and replies and various other brief messages, such as thank-you notes and expressions of congratulation or sympathy. Unless engraved, social notes should always be written by hand on a good quality of paper. They range from very informal to very formal.

There is no rigid pattern for informal social notes. The writer's address and the date usually appear at the left margin slightly lower than the signature. It is important that the informal note, however brief, contain enough thoughtful detail to show the writer's sincerity. Examples of an informal invitation and reply begin on this page and continue on the next.

Dear Susan,

Ann Collins will be in town for a few days next week. I'd like you to come to a patio supper for her Thursday at seven. I'm asking Janet Dobson and Tina Kramer, and we'll make the occasion a reunion for our erstwhile bowling team. I do hope you can come. If you need a ride, please let me know, and Mother and Dad will be happy to come by for you.

Love,
Joan Miller

3525 Holly Lane
August 14, 1965

Dear Joan,

I'm delighted with your invitation to the patio supper next Thursday and with your reunion idea. It will be fun seeing you and Ann again and recalling those Tuesday night bowling sessions when we could never get our scores up on a plane with our spirits. Since Janet and Tina live in my neighborhood and I have reserved the family car for next Thursday evening, we'll all drive over together.

Love,
Susan

2206 Jennings Avenue
August 16, 1965

Formal invitations and replies follow a definite pattern. They are written in the third person without heading, inside address, salutation, complimentary close, or signature. The writer's street address and the date appear in the lower left-hand corner. Dates and hours are written out as shown in these examples. Formal invitations may be specially engraved, but formal invitations and replies are never typed.

Mr. and Mrs. John W. Forbes
request the pleasure of
Miss Kathleen Grayson's
company at dinner
on Thursday evening
May the fifteenth
at eight o'clock

*1*220 Maryland Place
May the sixth

Whether or not a formal invitation includes a request for a reply (usually *r.s.v.p.,* an abbreviation for a French phrase meaning *please reply*), formal invitations are almost always answered, and promptly.

Miss Kathleen Grayson
accepts with pleasure
the kind invitation of
Mr. and Mrs. John W. Forbes
to dinner on Thursday evening
May the fifteenth
at eight o'clock

1266 Greenview Drive
May the seventh

A reply refusing a formal invitation appears on the following page.

Miss Kathleen Grayson
regrets that she is unable to accept
the kind invitation of
Mr. and Mrs. John W. Forbes
to dinner on Thursday evening
May the fifteenth
at eight o'clock

1266 Greenview Drive
May the seventh

Reference Books and Indexes

The typical large American library has the major reference books and indexes available on open shelves in a special reference room (often the main reading room). These materials are indispensable in research. Self-explanatory directions to aid the researcher usually appear on the introductory pages.

REFERENCE BOOKS

Reference books provide information ranging from the very general to the very specific and often contain selected bibliographies. The works listed here are among the most useful.

Encyclopedias. These are helpful general encyclopedias.

Collier's Encyclopedia. 20 vols. New York: P. F. Collier & Son Corporation, 1960. Annual printing. New in 1950, *Collier's Encyclopedia* has since been kept up-to-date by continuous revision. There has been a *Collier's Year Book* (not always with the same title) since 1939.

Columbia Encyclopedia. 3rd ed. New York: Columbia University Press, 1963. The *Columbia* (in one volume) is a very useful, concise encyclopedia for quick reference.

Encyclopedia Americana. 30 vols. New York: Americana Corp., 1960. Annual printing. The *Americana* is in process of continuous revision. Since 1923 the issue of the *Americana Annual* has kept this reference work up-to-date. The *Americana* treats almost all phases of human knowledge—especially modern science, industry, business, politics, government, history, and literature—in short, authoritative articles, many of which include bibliographies. The last volume contains an index.

Encyclopaedia Britannica. 24 vols. Chicago: Encyclopaedia Britannica, Inc., 1960. Annual printing. Of the fourteen numbered editions, the 9th [–10th] edition (1875–1889) and the 11th edition (1911) and the 13th (1926) are the most scholarly. The 14th edition was published in 1929. Edition statements do not appear on the title page in printings since 1936. The *Britannica* is continuously being revised and since 1938 has had an annual supplement, the *Britannica Book of the Year.* The most extensive work of its kind, the *Britannica* contains full, reliable essays dealing with nearly all areas of human knowledge. The essays, most with substantial bibliographies, are the contributions of experts from many different countries. The last volume contains a general index and an atlas.

New International Encyclopaedia. 23 vols. 2nd ed. New York: Dodd, Mead & Co., 1922–1930 (now distributed by Funk & Wagnalls Co.). The *New International Encyclopaedia,* although not recently revised, is still useful for subjects on which up-to-date information is not important. The *New International Year Book* (now published by Funk & Wagnalls Co.) has been published annually since 1907.

English Language Dictionaries. The most valuable general dictionaries of the English language are listed here.

Century Dictionary and Cyclopedia. 12 vols. New York: Century Company, c. 1911. This is the most comprehensive American-made dictionary of the English language. It shows word usage in different periods of American history. It has had partial revisions but not a complete one and is therefore not up-to-date on usage.

Craigie, Sir William A., and Hulbert, James R., eds. *Dictionary of American English.* 4 vols. 2nd ed. Chicago: University of Chicago Press, 1960. This work traces the use of words in the United States. Each word appears in context in a series of chronologically arranged quotations from the works of American writers.

New Century Dictionary of the English Language. 2 vols. New York: Appleton-Century-Crofts, Inc., 1948. This is a shortened and rewritten version of the 12-volume *Century Dictionary and Cyclopedia.*

New Standard Dictionary of the English Language. 1 vol. New York: Funk & Wagnalls Co., 1959. This popular unabridged dictionary emphasizes current rather than historical information on English words.

Oxford English Dictionary. 12 vols. and supplement. Oxford: The Clarendon Press, 1933 (originally *A New English Dictionary on Historical Principles.* 10 vols. and supplement. Oxford: The Clarendon Press, 1888–1933). The *Oxford English Dictionary,* an authoritative work edited by A. H. Murray and others, traces the changes in form and meaning of words in the English language. Each word appears in context in a series of chronologically arranged quotations from the works of English writers.

Shorter Oxford English Dictionary. 2 vols. 3rd ed. Oxford: The Clarendon Press, 1944. This is the authorized abridgment of the *Oxford English Dictionary.*

Webster's New International Dictionary of the English Language. 2nd ed. Springfield, Mass.: G. & C. Merriam Co., 1959. This is probably the most widely used unabridged dictionary in the United States. This dictionary contains a section of new words which grows with each printing. *Webster's Third New International Dictionary,* 1961.

Here are desk-size dictionaries, one of which every student needs to have within reach.

The American College Dictionary. Text ed. New York: Random House, 1964. This is not an abridgment but an original desk-size dictionary.

Webster's New Collegiate Dictionary. Springfield, Mass.: G. & C. Merriam Co., 1965. This is an abridgment of *Webster's New International Dictionary of the English Language,* 3rd ed., cited earlier.

Webster's New World Dictionary of the American Language. College ed. Cleveland: The World Publishing Company, 1964. This desk-size dictionary is based on a 2-volume encyclopedic edition by the same name published in 1951.

Special Wordbooks. Special wordbooks such as these are not substitutes for general dictionaries but are often auxiliary devices.

Crabb, George. *Crabb's English Synonyms.* Rev. and enl. ed. New York: Grosset & Dunlap, Inc., 1945. This book lists words alphabetically according to the first word of each group of synonyms and contains cross references.

Evans, Bergen, and Evans, Cornelia. *A Dictionary of Contemporary American Usage.* New York: Random House, 1957.

Fernald, James Champlin. *Standard Handbook of Synonyms, Antonyms, and Prepositions.* Rev. ed. New York: Funk & Wagnalls Co., 1947. This book arranges words according to significance and contains an alphabetical index.

Fowler, H. W. *A Dictionary of Modern English Usage.* 2nd ed. Oxford: The Clarendon Press, 1965.

Horwill, H. W. *A Dictionary of Modern American Usage.* Oxford: The Clarendon Press, 1944.

Kenyon, John Samuel, and Knott, Thomas Albert. *A Pronouncing Dictionary of American English.* 2nd ed. Springfield, Mass.: G. & C. Merriam Co., 1953. By means of the phonetic alphabet this book shows the varying pronunciations used by educated Americans in different sections of the country.

Mathews, M. M. *A Dictionary of Americanisms on Historical Principles.* London: Oxford University Press, 1951.

——. *American Words.* Cleveland, Ohio: The World Publishing Company, 1959.

Partridge, Eric. *Dictionary of Slang and Unconventional English.* 6th ed. New York: The Macmillan Co., 1967. A comprehensive coverage of words and phrases in the lower levels of usage.

——. *Usage and Abusage; A Guide to Good English.* 5th ed. rev. and enl. London: Hamilton and Company, 1957.

Roget's International Thesaurus. 3rd ed. New York: Thomas Y. Crowell Company, 1962. This book lists synonyms and antonyms in categories based on idea—helpful in vocabulary building. Lewis, Norman, ed. *The New Roget's Thesaurus.* New York: G. P. Putnam's Sons, 1964.

Webster's Dictionary of Synonyms. Springfield, Mass.: G. & C. Merriam Co., 1951. This book explains shades of meaning and contains helpful illustrations of connotative differences.

Wentworth, Harold. *American Dialect Dictionary.* New York: Thomas Y. Crowell Company, 1944. This book uses quotations to show dialects peculiar to different regions of the United States.

Wright, Joseph. *English Dialect Dictionary.* 6 vols. London: Frowde, 1898–

1905. This work records dialects used in different parts of the British Isles in the eighteenth and nineteenth centuries.

Yearbooks. Besides the annual supplements to the leading encyclopedias, these are a few of the more useful yearbooks.

American Year Book. New York: Thomas Nelson & Sons, 1910–1919, 1925 to 1950. The *American Year Book* contains signed articles written under the direction of national learned societies in such fields as American government, history, and science (to 1950).

Kieran, John, ed. *Information Please Almanac.* New York: The Macmillan Co., 1947 to date. The *Information Please Almanac,* now edited by Dan Golenpaul, contains informative summaries of outstanding events of the year.

International Year Book and Statesmen's Who's Who. London: Burke's Peerage, Ltd., 1953 to date. This relatively new annual publication reports on events and persons of international note.

Statesman's Year-Book. London: The Macmillan Company, 1864 to date. The *Statesman's Year-Book* contains data, classified by countries, on government, defense, industry, agriculture, trade, and other related topics.

United States Bureau of the Census. *Statistical Abstract of the United States.* Washington: U. S. Government Printing Office, 1878 to date. This book is the standard summary of statistics on the industrial, social, political, and economic organization of the United States.

World Almanac and Book of Facts. New York: *World-Telegram & The Sun,* 1868 to date. This is a compact storehouse of miscellaneous information—the most popular yearbook of its kind.

Yearbook of the United Nations. Lake Success, N. Y.: United Nations Secretariat, 1946 to date. This yearbook, published somewhat irregularly, reviews the development and proceedings of the United Nations and its agencies.

Biographies. These are useful biographical works.

Current Biography: Who's News and Why. New York: H. W. Wilson Co., 1940 to date. *Current Biography* is a monthly publication, with annual cumulations. The emphasis is on notable living Americans.

Dictionary of American Biography. 20 vols. and index. New York: Charles Scribner's Sons, 1928–1937. Supplement One, 1944. Supplement Two, 1958. *DAB,* edited by Allen Johnson and Dumas Malone, is the standard biography of notable Americans who are dead. The articles include good bibliographies.

Dictionary of National Biography. Main work and 1st Supplement, 63 vols. London: Smith, Elder and Company, 1885–1900. Reissued in 22 vols.,

1908–1909. 2nd Supplement, 1912. 3rd–6th Supplements by Oxford University Press, 1927, 1937, 1949, 1957. *DNB,* edited by Leslie Stephen and Sidney Lee, is the standard biography of notable Britons who are dead. The articles include good bibliographies.

Kunitz, Stanley J., and Haycraft, Howard. *American Authors,* 1600–1900. New York: H. W. Wilson Co., 1938.

——. *British Authors Before 1800.* New York: H. W. Wilson Co., 1952.

——. *British Authors of the Nineteenth Century.* New York: H. W. Wilson Co., 1936.

——. *Twentieth Century Authors.* New York: H. W. Wilson Co., 1942 (also supplement, 1955). This work gives concise biographies of leading American, British, and other authors of the twentieth century and includes bibliographies of their main writings. The supplement features autobiographies as well as biographies.

Webster's Biographical Dictionary. Springfield, Mass.: G. & C. Merriam Co., 1943, 1953, 1956, 1958, 1964. This pronouncing dictionary contains biographies of notable persons, living and dead, of all countries.

Who's Who. London: A. and C. Black, Ltd., 1849 to date annually. *Who's Who* contains brief biographies of notable living persons, mainly Britons.

Who's Who in America. Chicago: The A. N. Marquis Co., 1899 to date every two years. *Who's Who in America* contains brief biographies of notable living citizens of the United States.

Who's Who in ——. There is a special *Who's Who* for each of a number of different subjects and geographical sections—for instance, *Who's Who in American Art, Who's Who in the Major Leagues, Who's Who in the Midwest, Who's Who in the East* and *Who's Who of American Women.* The card catalogue lists on separate cards whatever such books the library has on its reference shelves.

Reference Works by Subjects. The reference works listed here, many of which contain useful bibliographies, provide information on particular subjects.

AGRICULTURE

Bailey, Liberty H. *Cyclopedia of American Agriculture.* 4 vols. New York: The Macmillan Co., 1907–1909.

——, and Bailey, Ethel Zoe. *Hortus Second.* New ed. New York: The Macmillan Co., 1941.

Owen, Wyn F. *American Agriculture: The Changing Structure.* Boston, Mass.: D. C. Heath & Co., 1969.

United States Department of Agriculture. *Agricultural Statistics.* Washington: Government Printing Office, 1936 to date annually.

——. *Yearbook of Agriculture.* Washington: Government Printing Office, 1894 to date annually.

ARCHITECTURE

Architectural Publication Society. *Dictionary of Architecture.* 6 vols. London: Richards, 1852–1892.

Fletcher, Sir Bannister F. *History of Architecture on the Comparative Method for Students, Craftsmen, and Amateurs.* 17th ed. New York: Charles Scribner's Sons, 1961.

Hamlin, Talbot. *Architecture Through the Ages.* Rev. ed. New York: G. P. Putnam's Sons, 1953.

———, ed. *Forms and Functions of Twentieth Century Architecture.* New York: Columbia University Press, 1952.

ART

Adeline, Jules. *Art Dictionary.* Translated from the French and enlarged. New York: Appleton, 1891.

Bryan, Michael. *Bryan's Dictionary of Painters and Engravers.* 5 vols. New York: The Macmillan Co., 1903–1905.

Fielding, Mantle. *Dictionary of American Painters, Engravers, Sculptors.* New York: The Macmillan Co., 1945.

Gilbert, Dorothy B., ed. *American Art Directory.* 43rd ed. New York: R. R. Bowker Co., 1967.

Encyclopedia of World Art. 15 vols. New York: McGraw-Hill, 1959–1968.

Larkin, Oliver W. *Art and Life in America.* Rev. ed. New York: Rinehart & Co., 1960.

BUSINESS AND ECONOMICS

Clark, Donald T., and Gottfried, Bert A. *University Dictionary of Business and Finance.* New York: Thomas Y. Crowell Company, 1957.

Coman, E. T. *Sources of Business Information.* Rev. ed. Berkeley and Los Angeles: University of California Press, 1964.

Encyclopedic Dictionary of Business. New York: Prentice-Hall, Inc., 1952.

Greenwald, Douglas, and Others. *Dictionary of Modern Economics.* New York: McGraw-Hill, 1965.

Larson, Henrietta M. *Guide to Business History.* Cambridge, Mass.: Harvard University Press, 1948.

Manley, Marian C. *Business Information: How to Find and Use It.* New York: Harper & Brothers, 1955.

Munn, Glenn G. *Encyclopedia of Banking and Finance.* 6th ed., by Ferdinand L. Garcia. Boston, Mass.: Bankers Publishing Co., 1962.

Rand McNally Commercial Atlas and Marketing Guide. Chicago: Rand McNally & Co., 1911——.

Sloan, Harold S., and Zurcher, Arnold J. *Dictionary of Economics* ("Everyday Handbooks"). 5th ed. New York: Barnes & Noble, Inc., 1970.

United Nations Statistical Office. *Statistical Yearbook.* Lake Success, N. Y., 1948 to date.

United States Bureau of the Census. *Statistical Abstract of the United States.* Washington, D. C.: U. S. Government Printing Office, 1878 to date annually.

EDUCATION

Harris, Chester W., ed., *Encyclopedia of Educational Research.* 3rd ed. New York: The Macmillan Co., 1960.

Monroe, Paul, ed. *Cyclopedia of Education.* 5 vols. New York: The Macmillan Co., 1911–1913.

Monroe, Walter Scott. *Encyclopedia of Educational Research.* Rev. ed. New York: The Macmillan Co., 1950.

Review of Educational Research. Washington: American Educational Research Association, 1931 to date, five issues annually.

Rivlin, Harry N., ed., and Schueler, Herbert, assoc. ed. *Encyclopedia of Modern Education.* New York: Philosophical Library, Inc., 1943.

World Survey of Education. Vol. I: *World Handbook of Educational Organization and Statistics.* Vol. II: *Primary Education.* Vol. III: *Secondary Education.* Vol. IV: *Higher Education.* Paris UNESCO, 1952——.

GEOGRAPHY

American Guide Series. Comp. by Federal Writers' Project, later called Writers' Program. Various publishers, 1937–1949.

Columbia Lippincott Gazetteer of the World. New York: Columbia University Press, 1962.

Times Atlas of the World. 5 vols. London: *Times,* 1955——.

Webster's Geographical Dictionary. Rev. ed. Springfield, Mass.: G. & C. Merriam Co., 1966.

GOVERNMENT AND POLITICS

Congressional Directory, 1809——. Washington: Government Printing Office, 1865——. (Private printers before 1865.)

McLaughlin, A. C., and Hart, A. B., eds. *Cyclopedia of American Government.* 3 vols. (First issued by Appleton, New York, in 1914.) Gloucester, Mass.: Peter Smith.

Smith, Edward C., and Zurcher, Arnold J. *Dictionary of American Politics* ("Everyday Handbooks"). 2nd ed. New York: Barnes & Noble, Inc., 1968.

Stebbins, Richard P., and Amoia, Alba, eds. *Political Handbook and Atlas of the World.* New York: Published for the Council on Foreign Relations by Simon & Schuster, 1970.

Theimer, Walter. *Encyclopedia of Modern World Politics.* New York: Rinehart & Company, Inc., 1950.

United States Government Organization Manual. Washington: Government Printing Office, 1935——.

Zimmerman, Joseph F. *State and Local Government.* ("College Outline Series"). 2nd ed. New York: Barnes & Noble, Inc., 1970.

HISTORY

Adams, James Truslow, ed. *Dictionary of American History*. 5 vols. and index. 2nd ed. New York: Charles Scribner's Sons, 1942.

Cambridge Ancient History. 12 vols. and 5-vol. atlas. Cambridge: Cambridge University Press, 1923–1939.

Cambridge Mediaeval History. 8 vols. and 8-vol. atlas. Cambridge: Cambridge University Press, 1911–1936.

Cambridge Modern History. 13 vols. and 1-vol. atlas. Cambridge: Cambridge University Press, 1902–1926. (A 14-volume *New Cambridge Modern History,* edited by Sir George Clark, is in process.)

Harvard Guide to American History. Compiled by Oscar Handlin, Arthur M. Schlesinger, and Others, eds. Cambridge, Mass.: Belknap Press (of Harvard University Press), 1954.

Historical Atlas of the World. New York: Barnes & Noble, Inc., 1970.

Langer, William L., ed. *An Encyclopedia of World History* (based on Ploetz's *Manual of Universal History*). Rev. ed. (H. W. Gatzke, ed.) Boston: Houghton Mifflin Co., 1952.

Lossing, Benson J., ed. *Harper's Encyclopedia of United States History*. 10 vols. Rev. ed. New York: Harper & Brothers, 1912.

Paullin, Charles O. *Atlas of the Historical Geography of the United States*. John K. Wright, Carnegie Institution of Washington, the American Geographical Society of N. Y., eds., 1932.

Shepherd, William R. *Historical Atlas*. 9th ed. With supplement of historical maps for period since 1929 prepared by C. S. Hammond & Company. New York: Barnes & Noble, Inc., 1964.

LITERATURE

Apperson, George L. *English Proverbs and Proverbial Phrases*. New York: E. P. Dutton & Co., Inc., 1929.

Baker, Ernest A. *The History of the English Novel*. 10 vols. London: H. F. & G. Witherby, Ltd., 1924–1939. Reprinted in 1960–1961 by Barnes & Noble, Inc., New York. Vol. XI by Lionel Stevenson, 1967.

Bartlett, John. *Familiar Quotations*. 14th ed. Boston: Little, Brown & Co., 1968.

Baugh, Albert C., and Others. *A Literary History of England*. New York: Appleton-Century-Crofts, Inc., 1948.

Benét, William Rose. *The Reader's Encyclopedia: An Encyclopedia of World Literature and the Arts*. 2nd ed. New York: Thomas Y. Crowell Company, 1965.

Brewer, Ebenezer C. *Dictionary of Phrase and Fable*. 8th rev. ed. New York: Harper and Row, 1963.

———. *Reader's Handbook of Famous Names in Fiction, Allusions, References, Proverbs, Plots, Stories, and Poems*. Philadelphia: J. B. Lippincott Co., 1898.

Bulfinch's Mythology: The Age of Fable, The Age of Chivalry, Legends of Charlemagne. New York: Thomas Y. Crowell Company [1947].

Cary, M., and Others, eds. *Oxford Classical Dictionary*. Oxford: The Clarendon Press, 1949.

Frazer, James G. *The Golden Bough*. 13 vols. 3rd ed. rev. New York: St. Martin's Press, Inc., 1955.

Gayley, Charles M. *Classic Myths in English Literature and in Art*. Rev ed. New York: Blaisdell Publishing Co., 1939.

Gray, Louis H., and MacCulloch, John A., eds. *Mythology of all Races*. 13 vols. New Boston, N. H.: Marshall Jones Co., 1916–1932.

Hart, James D. *Oxford Companion to American Literature*. 4th ed. New York: Oxford University Press, 1965.

Harvey, Paul. *Oxford Companion to English Literature*. 4th ed. Oxford: The Clarendon Press, 1967.

Leach, Maria, ed. *Standard Dictionary of Folklore, Mythology and Legend*. 2 vols. New York: Funk & Wagnalls Co., 1949–1950.

Mencken, H. L. *A New Dictionary of Quotations on Historical Principles from Ancient and Modern Sources*. New York: Alfred A. Knopf, Inc., 1942.

Millett, Fred B. *Contemporary American Authors*. New York: Harcourt, Brace & Co., 1940.

———. *Contemporary British Literature*. 3rd ed. New York: Harcourt, Brace & Co., 1935.

Otis, William B., and Needleman, Morriss H. *Outline-History of English Literature* ("College Outline Series"). 2 vols. 4th ed. New York: Barnes & Noble, Inc., 1960.

Oxford Dictionary of Quotations. 2nd ed. London: Oxford University Press, 1955.

Peck, Harry T. *Harper's Dictionary of Classical Literature and Antiquities*. New York: Harper & Brothers, 1897.

Spiller, Robert E., and Others. *Literary History of the United States*. 3rd ed. New York: The Macmillan Co., 1963. Vol. IV: Bibliography Supplement, 1964.

Steinberg, Sigfrid H., ed. *Cassell's Encyclopedia of World Literature*. 2 vols. New York: Funk & Wagnalls Co., 1954.

Stevenson, Burton E. *The Home Book of Quotations*. Rev. ed. New York: Dodd, Mead & Co., 1967.

Trent, William P., and Others, eds. *Cambridge History of American Literature*. 4 vols. New York: G. P. Putnam's Sons, 1917–1921.

Ward, A. W., and Waller, A. R., eds. *Cambridge History of English Literature*. 14 vols. Cambridge: Cambridge University Press, 1907–1927. (Home Study Edition, 15 vols., 1950.)

MATHEMATICS

James, Glenn, and James, Robert C. *Mathematics Dictionary*. 3rd ed. New York: D. Van Nostrand Co., Inc., 1968.

Newman, James R., ed. *The World of Mathematics*. 4 vols. New York: Simon and Schuster, Inc., 1962.

Sarton, George. *The Study of the History of Mathematics*. Cambridge, Mass.: Harvard University Press, 1936.

MUSIC

Apel, Willi. *Harvard Dictionary of Music*. Cambridge, Mass.: Harvard University Press, 1944.

Grove, George. *Grove's Dictionary of Music and Musicians*. 9 vols. 5th ed. (edited by Eric Blom). London: The Macmillan Company, 1954. Vol. X Supplement, 1961.

Oxford History of Music. 7 vols. and intro. vol. 2nd ed. London: Oxford University Press, 1938.

Scholes, Percy A. *Oxford Companion to Music*. 9th ed. New York: Oxford University Press, 1955.

Thompson, Oscar. *International Cyclopedia of Music and Musicians*. 9th ed. (rev. and enl. by Nicolas Slonimsky). New York: Dodd, Mead & Co., 1964.

PHILOSOPHY AND PSYCHOLOGY

Avey, Albert E. *Handbook in the History of Philosophy* ("Everyday Handbook Series"). 2nd ed. New York: Barnes & Noble, Inc., 1961. A chronological survey of Western thought, 3500 B.C. to the present.

Baldwin, James M. *Dictionary of Philosophy and Psychology*. 3 vols. in 4. Rev. ed. New York: The Macmillan Co., 1928 (reissued in 1949).

English, Horace B., and English, Ava Champney. *A Comprehensive Dictionary of Psychological and Psychoanalytical Terms*. New York: Longmans, Green & Co., Inc., 1958.

Harriman, Philip L. *Encyclopedia of Psychology*. New York: Philosophical Library, Inc., 1947.

Hinsie, Leland E., and Campbell, Robert J. *Psychiatric Dictionary with Encyclopedic Treatment of Modern Terms*. 3rd ed. New York: Oxford University Press, Inc. 1960.

RELIGION

Catholic Encyclopedia. 15 vols. and index and supplement. New York: Catholic Encyclopedia Press, c. 1907–1922. Supplement (2nd), 1955.

The Interpreter's Dictionary of the Bible. 4 vols. Nashville, Tenn.: Abingdon Press, 1962.

———. *Encyclopedia of Religion and Ethics*. 12 vols. and index. New York: Charles Scribner's Sons, 1908–1927. (Reissued, 1951.)

Universal Jewish Encyclopedia. 10 vols. and guide and index. New York: Universal Jewish Encyclopedia, Inc., 1939–1944.

SCIENCE

Clark, G. L., and Hawley, G. G., eds. *The Encyclopedia of Chemistry*. 2nd ed. New York: Reinhold Publishing Corp., 1966.

Michels, W. C., sr. ed. *The International Dictionary of Physics and Electronics*. 2nd ed. Princeton, N. J.: D. Van Nostrand Co., Inc., 1961.

Sarton, George. *Horus: A Guide to the History of Science* ("The Chronica Botanica Series"). New York: The Ronald Press Company, 1952.

Van Nostrand's Scientific Encyclopedia. 4th ed. Princeton, N. J.: D. Van Nostrand, 1968.

SOCIAL SCIENCE

Seligman, E. R. A., ed.-in-chief, and Johnson, Alvin, assoc. ed. *Encyclopedia of the Social Sciences*. 15 vols. New York: The Macmillan Co., 1930–1935. (Reissued in 8 vols. in 1948.)

Zadrozny, John T. *Dictionary of Social Science*. Washington: Public Affairs Press, 1959.

Bibliographies by Subjects. For many subjects there are comprehensive bibliographies—volumes filled with conveniently arranged lists of writings on various topics that constitute the subject concerned. The following are examples:

Bateson, F. W., ed. *Cambridge Bibliography of English Literature*. 4 vols. Cambridge University Press, 1941. Vol. V: Supplement, 1957.

Darrell, Robert Donaldson, comp. *Schirmer's Guide to Books on Music and Musicians: A Practical Bibliography*. New York: G. Schirmer, Inc., 1951.

Handlin, Oscar, and Schlesinger, Arthur M., and Others, eds. *Harvard Guide to American History* [revision of and successor to Channing's *Guide to the Study and Reading of American History*]. Cambridge, Mass.: Belknap Press (of Harvard University Press), 1954.

INDEXES

Libraries have various periodical *indexes*—some general, others specific—for use in locating information in magazines and newspapers. The currently published indexes are very serviceable, for most are cumulative and are kept as up-to-date as possible. In consulting an index the student must always make sure that the time covered by it is the time when articles on the subject being investigated are most likely to have appeared in print. For instance, on the subject of airborne invasions of World War II, the most helpful volume of the *Readers' Guide* is Volume XIV, which lists articles published from July, 1943, to April, 1945.

General Indexes. These are indexes to periodicals of general interest.

International Index to Periodicals, 1907 to date. The *International Index* formerly indexed selected periodicals of various countries but now includes only American and a few British titles. The earlier issues include listings on science, but current issues are restricted to social science and humanities. Listings are by subject and author.

Nineteenth Century Readers' Guide to Periodical Literature, 1880–1889. (Work to include earlier decades has been suspended.)

Poole's Index to Periodical Literature and supplements, 1802–1906. *Poole's Index* lists—mainly by subject, occasionally by title, but never by author —the materials in most of the general periodicals of America and England in the nineteenth century. References are to volume number of bound magazines and to beginning page of article, not to date of issue.

Readers' Guide to Periodical Literature, 1900 to date. The *Readers' Guide* is the most useful index to periodicals in general. Semimonthly issues of the *Readers' Guide* appear shortly after the periodicals themselves. The *Readers' Guide* is cumulative, each of the earlier volumes covering several years. Listings are by subject, title, and author. References are to volume number of bound magazines, inclusive page numbers of article cited, and date of particular issue in which article appears.

New York Times Index, 1913 to date. Issued semimonthly, this newspaper index is made permanent in annual cumulations. Listings are primarily by subject (or by names of persons who are subjects in the news). References are to date, section, page, and column of *The New York Times.* Since articles on important events appear on the same or nearly the same date in most of the leading newspapers throughout the nation, the *New York Times Index* can serve as an index to almost all daily newspapers in the United States.

Times Official Index [London *Times*], 1906 to date. Issued quarterly, this is a comprehensive index to news of the British Isles and the continent of Europe.

Special Indexes. Special indexes like the following, because of the restriction in the subject matter they cover, are often more serviceable than the general indexes. Most of the special indexes listed here refer to periodicals, but some refer to books, pamphlets, and other sources.

Agricultural Index, 1916 to date monthly.
Applied Science and Technology Index, 1958 to date monthly.
Art Index, 1929 to date quarterly.
Bibliographic Index, 1937 to date semiannually.
Biography Index, 1946 to date quarterly.
Biological Abstracts, 1926 to date monthly.
Book Review Digest, 1905 to date monthly.
Business Periodicals Index, 1958 to date monthly.
Chemical Abstracts, 1907 to date semimonthly.
Cumulative Book Index, 1898 to date monthly.
Dramatic Index, 1909 to 1949 annually.

Education Index, 1929 to date monthly.

Engineering Index, 1884 to date annually.

Essay and General Literature Index, 1900 to date semiannually.

Firkins, Ina Ten Eyck. *Index to Plays,* 1800–1926. Supplement, 1927–1934, 1935.

Granger's Index to Poetry and Recitations, 1895–1950. 4th ed. rev. Supplement, 1951–1955. R. J. Dixon, ed., 1957.

Guide to the Performing Arts, 1957 to date annually.

Index Medicus, 1879 to 1926, and *Quarterly Cumulative Index Medicus,* 1927 to date quarterly.

Index to Legal Periodicals, 1908 to date monthly.

Industrial Arts Index, 1913 to 1957 monthly. (Continued since 1958 by two publications: *Applied Science and Technology Index* and *Business Periodicals Index.*)

Logasa, Hannah, and VerNooy, Winifred. *Index to One-Act Plays,* 1924–1950.

Music Index, 1949 to date monthly.

Ottemiller, John H. *Index to Plays in Collections* [1900–1956], 2nd ed., rev. and enl., 1957.

Psychological Abstracts, 1927 to date monthly.

Psychological Index, 1894 to 1935 annually.

Public Affairs Information Service, 1915 to date weekly.

Short Story Index; an Index to 60,000 Stories in 4,320 Collections, 1953. Supplement, 1956.

Social Science Abstracts, 5 vols., 1929–1933.

Song Index, 1926. Supplement, 1934.

Technical Book Review Index, 1917 to 1929 quarterly, 1935 to date monthly.

United States Superintendent of Documents: *Catalog of the Public Documents of the 53d to the 76th Congress,* 1896 to 1945 biennially (1 vol. for each Congress).

————: *United States Government Publications Monthly Catalog,* 1895 to date monthly.

Vertical File Index, 1955 to date monthly. (Formerly *Vertical File Service Catalog,* 1935 to 1954 monthly.)

Solutions to Exercises

Chapter 1

1. a. Exposition   b. Argument   c. Description   d. Narrative   e. Argument
   f. On the surface, description; in its fundamental purpose, argument (to persuade readers to rent or buy real estate in the area)
   g. Narrative   h. Description   i. Argument   j. Exposition
2. a. False   b. False   c. True   d. False   e. True
   f. False   g. True   h. False   i. True   j. False
3. a. Formal
   b. Informal
   c. Informal (In strict formal usage the pronoun *Who*, object of the preposition *to*, would appear in its objective form, *Whom*.)
   d. Informal (The contractions *We're* and *won't* would be inappropriate on the formal level.)
   e. Formal
   f. Informal (The word *fix* in the sense of *predicament* is colloquial.)
   g. Vulgar (The word *hep*, and the word *dope* in the sense of *information*, are slang.)
   h. Informal (The word *snap* in the sense of *vigor* or *life* is colloquial.)
   i. Informal (The word *up* as a verb meaning *cause to rise* is colloquial.)
   j. Formal

Chapter 2

* 1. a. Swiftly she ran down the narrow path to meet them. (The adverb *swiftly* is moved from its normal position to the beginning of the sentence.)
   b. While he was talking with her yesterday, she gave him some wonderful news. (The first clause is subordinated to the second.)
   c. His employer told him to be sure to do the whole job, to get it done on time, and to do it correctly. (The most important phrase, "to do it correctly," is put in the emphatic final position.)
   d. I have been reading some stories by Poe, who is known as the father of the short story. (The second clause is subordinated to the first.)
   e. Even if it rains tomorrow, we will go anyway. (The first clause is subordinated to the second.)
2. a. 3   b. 1   c. 2   d. 3   e. 1
3. a. Sound
   b. Unsound: the major premise is faulty. (It is itself perhaps the result of inadequate sampling.)
   c. Unsound: inadequate sampling
   d. Sound
   e. Sound
   f. Unsound: *non sequitur* (The major premise is not all-inclusive.)
   g. Unsound: faulty analogy

* Here, and at other points below marked with an asterisk, the solutions given are not the only possible ones; they represent acceptable versions.

h. Unsound: irrelevant issue (ignoring the question; the argument *ad hominem*)

i. Sound

j. Unsound: faulty causal relationship (oversimplification)

* 4. a. Public buildings may be classified on the basis of their principal function or use as buildings used chiefly for government offices (e.g., city hall, state house); for cultural activities (state or municipal theaters, auditoriums, concert halls); for the storage and use of books, documents, or objects of art (libraries, archives, museums); for the confinement of offenders (prisons); and for commemorative purposes (the Lincoln Memorial).

b. The latter part of March, April, May, and most of June belong to the spring; the rest of June, July, August, and most of September, to the summer; the rest of September, October, November, and most of December, to the fall; and the rest of December, January, February, and most of March, to the winter.

c. In table silverware, the principal types of implement are the knife, the fork, and the spoon. Knives may be subclassified as luncheon and dinner knives, butter knives, and knives for special purposes (e.g., fish knives). Forks include luncheon and dinner forks, salad forks, serving forks, and special types like oyster forks. Spoons include teaspoons, iced teaspoons, tablespoons, coffee spoons, clear and cream soup spoons, dessert spoons, and special types like ladles and sugar shells.

5. (For sample solutions here, consult your dictionary now.)

6. a. The classification is not complete: quarterly magazines, for instance, are omitted.

b. The classification is neither complete nor consistent: the Air Force and the Coast Guard are omitted; and the Marine Corps, which is actually under the Navy, is listed as though it were an entirely separate unit.

c. A form or derivative (*comic*) of the word to be defined (*comedy*) is contained in the definition.

d. The genus is omitted. (Improved: "Biology is *a science* which deals with living things.")

e. This is an attempt to define with an "is when" construction. (Improved: "A touchdown is a scoring play in which one team gets the ball across the other team's goal line.")

Chapter 3

1. a. True b. False c. False d. True e. False f. True g. False h. False
i. True j. True

2. a. knowledge . . . interest   b. sequence .   c. sentence . . . topic
d. central idea . . . central emotional effect
e. alma mater . . . country . . . God

3. a. Not appropriate: this is a statement about the writer's intention rather than about the subject itself.

b. Appropriate

c. Appropriate

d. Not appropriate: for the same reason as part *a* above

e. Appropriate

4. a. Not logical: each main division has only one subdivision.
   b. Logical

Chapter 4

1. a. The primary purpose of exposition is to explain.

b. The basis of a natural classification is made by nature and observed by man, whereas the basis of an arbitrary classification is chosen at will by man.

c. The writer may use the second person, imperative mood, in explaining a process to an audience of participants (or potential participants).

d. The general rule governing the length of the summary is that the summary should be shorter than the original, how much shorter depending on the purpose of the summary.

e. "Lytton Strachey's biography of Queen Victoria is weak in plot" is an unfair evaluation based on an unfair standard; plot is not an essential component of biography.

2. a. Age b. Color c. Mineral content d. (1) Function (2) Grammatical structure (3) Rhetorical form e. Purpose for attendance.

3. a. Analysis (Here the analysis explains a process.) b. Review c. Extended definition, primarily; and analysis (Here the analysis helps to extend the definition.)

Chapter 5

1. a. (1) N (2) E (3) S (4) E (5) N (6) S (7) E (8) N (9) E (10) S (11) N (12) E (13) S (14) S (15) N

* b. (1) After we had been walking for several minutes in the cave, through an opening in the rocks we saw the crescent moon.

(2) She realized, closing the book and staring out the window, that it was a duty enjoined upon her by her deepest faith.

(3) On our side of the valley, when we stopped talking, we could hear the rattle of rifle fire.

(4) As he reached the top of the staircase and paused to consider, something was dripping on his neck—something cold and wet.

(5) When his ship finally came back to the port after two years on the high seas or abroad, in the crowd of people who were shouting and gesticulating on the pier he could see his wife and children.

* c. (1) When I was deservedly in disgrace, he came to me and offered his help.

(2) Catching sight of her husband talking with the hostess, she stalked over to him and said, "John, it is time for us to leave."

(3) He allowed an innocent woman to be punished for the crime of which he was guilty.

(4) When he entered the room, we all stopped talking and glanced at each other apprehensively.

(5) An hour or more after the dance had started, he noticed that the girl in the yellow dress was still sitting alone. Walking over to her, he smiled and said, "May I have this dance?"

2. *a. (1) By fostering a spirit of brotherhood, fraternities make a unique contribution to the experience of undergraduate men.

(2) In college, attendance at classes should be not compulsory but optional.

(3) Police protection in my community is inadequate.

(4) Colleges caught in the vise of rising costs and relatively fixed income should be granted Federal aid.

(5) Religious denominations ought not to discourage their members from marrying persons of other faiths.

*b. (1) The fraternity system is undemocratic.

(2) If attendance were not required, some irresponsible students would cut classes indiscriminately, and their education would suffer.

(3) The community simply cannot afford to enlarge its police force.

(4) Federal aid inevitably brings with it some measure of Federal control.

(5) Actually, the likelihood of a truly successful marriage is lessened when the persons involved hold differing views on issues so fundamental as religious doctrine.

c. (1) A   (2) D   (3) D   (4) A   (5) D

*3. a. (1) peace   b. (1) a hilltop, overlooking the field
      (2) confusion   (2) that of a student operator at the
                                               cash register
      (3) shrill merriment   (3) an upstairs office (not air-con-
                                               ditioned) across the street
      (4) anticipation   (4) a box seat
      (5) indignation   (5) that of an intern in the ambu-
                                               lance crew

4. a. True   b. False   c. False   d. True   e. False
   f. True   g. False   h. False   i. True   j. True

Chapter 6

1. a. The thesis the research worker uses in his outline and his paper is the answer (in one sentence) to the question he is investigating.

b. The information on the note cards is the authoritative evidence that answers the question and that, when assimilated by the researcher, enables him to formulate the thesis.

2. a. The student should avoid a topic on which materials are not available in his campus library; even if the materials are available in an off-campus library, the necessary trips will probably prove costly in time. He should choose a topic the investigation of which will help him acquire self-reliance in using his campus library.

b. If he finds equally adequate materials available on two (or more) tentative topics approved by his instructor, the student can then base his choice on his interest in and desire for knowledge on the topic. The greater these are, the better motivated he will be through the steps of the research process.

3. a. Primary sources contain first-hand evidence (for example, an original manuscript), evidence that is as close as possible to the topic. Secondary sources contain second-hand information (for example, an interpretation or commentary) based on the original evidence. If primary sources and secondary sources are

available, the writer should use both kinds. Primary sources will allow the writer to make his own evaluations and interpretations of original evidence; secondary sources, if carefully selected, will provide him scholarly judgments by which he can measure his own and with which he may even disagree if he can substantiate his own conclusions with reliable evidence from primary sources.

b. The treaty between the United States and France in 1803 and the letters and other papers written by Thomas Jefferson on the Louisiana Purchase are primary sources of information on that subject. Chapters in American history books and a recent dissertation on the subject are secondary sources.

4. Here are possible ways in which the researcher can work from an author card to extend his bibliography: (1) he can learn from the author card whether or not the book listed contains a bibliography; (2) he can find the subject heading or headings under which the book is also catalogued, and by turning to these and to possible "see also" cards following them he will probably locate useful books by other authors on his subject; and (3) he can check the cards filed before and after the author card to see if the same author has written other books on the same subject.

5. a. Essential information on a bibliography card for a book includes full name of author or editor (followed by *ed.*); title (underlined); name of the magazine; and facts of publication (place, publisher, and date). Essential information on a bibliography card for a magazine article includes full name of author (if available); title (in quotation marks); volume number (if magazine is bound); date of issue; and inclusive page numbers. An optional notation on the content or probable value of the source is often useful on a bibliography card.

b. The preliminary bibliography lists all the sources that the research worker believes will be useful in his investigation of his topic, whereas the final bibliography lists only the works he has referred to in his paper and perhaps a few others that have helped him in a general way to understand his topic.

c. The entries in the bibliography are arranged alphabetically by authors' last names; footnotes are not arranged alphabetically.

6. a. The three basic kinds of notes are isolated facts, summaries, and quotations. An isolated fact is a single piece of factual information extracted from its context and recorded in brief form, possibly in less than a sentence. A summary note is a condensation, in the research worker's words, of the content of an article, chapter, or other unit of source material; the summary note preserves the original author's central idea and main supporting points without borrowing his language. A note recording a quotation shows the original language clearly enclosed within quotation marks.

b. In addition to the note itself, the note card should show the exact source of the note and a label naming the phase of the topic to which the note pertains. The information on the source is necessary for a corresponding citatory footnote; the label is necessary for ease in filing the note card.

7. a. A citatory footnote gives credit to the exact source from which information has been borrowed. An explanatory footnote provides supplementary information that would not be appropriate in the text of the paper.

b. Citatory footnotes are required to give credit to the sources of (1) all but very well-known quotations; (2) all types of borrowed facts and ideas except those commonly known; and (3) borrowed graphic material or borrowed data for graphic material.

8. a. "Industry's New Frontier," *Life,* XXV (October 4, 1948), 93.

b. Ernest Hemingway, "The Killers," *Studies in the Short Story,* eds. Adrian H. Jaffe and Virgil Scott, pp. 199–208.

c. Elswyth Thane, *Dawn's Early Light,* p. 114.

d. James Edward Tobin and Others, eds., *College Book of English Literature,* pp. 302–303.

e. W. Trelease, "Description of the Missouri Botanical Garden," *Popular Science,* LXII (January, 1903), 221.

9. *Sic* is a Latin word meaning "thus"; *sic* enclosed by brackets indicates that what appears to be an error immediately preceding the brackets has been quoted exactly as it stands in the original.

Ibid. is the abbreviation for the Latin word *ibidem,* which means "the same." *Ibid.* in a footnote indicates the source named in the immediately preceding footnote. If the page reference differs from that already cited, the new page reference follows *ibid.*

Op. cit. is the abbreviation for the Latin *opere citato,* which means "in the work cited." In a footnote, *op. cit.* following the last name of an author indicates that author's work which has been cited in an earlier footnote than the immediately preceding one. A new page reference may follow *op. cit.*

P. and *pp.* are abbreviations of *page* and *pages,* respectively. These abbreviations are appropriate in footnotes and other places requiring page references.

Col. and *cols.* are the abbreviations of *column* and *columns* respectively. They are appropriate in documentation referring to newspaper articles.

Ed. and *eds.* are the abbreviations of *editor* and *editors* respectively. They are used to distinguish between editors and authors.

Suspension periods are three spaced periods used to indicate the omission of part of a quotation; the three periods are used in addition to whatever punctuation appears in the quotation before or after the omission.

Brackets in a quotation are used to enclose words supplied by an editor.

10. In writing the paper entitled "Sicily and Holland: A Study of Airborne Tactics in World War II," Russell Linsin used all the methods of organization named in the question. In the first three paragraphs (the "beginning" of the paper), he presented the thesis and supporting evidence in microcosm: after an experimental application in the July, 1943, invasion of Sicily, American airborne tactics became highly effective in the September, 1944, invasion of Holland. In the next thirty-five paragraphs (the "middle" of the paper), he used the chronological and spatial orders in giving detailed, factual accounts of the 82d Airborne Division's action in Sicily and Holland. Here, too, he explained the causes that led to the different results of the two invasions. By using cause-to-effect rather than effect-to-cause arrangement, he also achieved climactic order in the separate analyses of the invasions; climactic order in the paper as a whole was almost automatic because of the historical significance of the Holland invasion. In the last two paragraphs (the "end" of the paper), he reiterated the thesis as an inductive conclusion based on documented facts.

Chapter 7

1. The internal structure of the paragraph is sound. The first sentence states the topic idea, "Man exists to do creatively, as craftsmanlike as may be, all things

that must be done," and suggests applications of the idea in a wide range of specific jobs. The second sentence coheres by reiterating the idea of "joy in creativity"; the third, by reiterating the idea of "tasks to be performed." The last sentence completes the unit of thought with the significant, hence emphatic, idea that of the two ways of doing things—the uncreative way and the creative way—the latter makes life "good."

2. a. The pattern of reasoning is inductive: the paragraph first presents specific facts on a number of accidents and fatalities at a particular place in a highway, then gives the general conclusion that the section of highway was "too hazardous for public safety" and mentions the action resulting from the conclusion. (The name "Suicide Curve" is also an inductive result of the earlier specific happenings.)

b. The pattern of reasoning is deductive: the paragraph first presents a generalization on an existing earnings tax, then applies the general rule to five individuals and shows how it affects each of them.

* 3. a. Enumeration   b. Illustrative instances   c. Sustained analogy
d. Enumeration   e. Chronological incidents   f. Definition
g. Pictorial details   h. Comparison
i. Cause and effect, or illustrative instances
j. Illustrative instances, or enumeration

4. a. Topic sentence stated: first sentence   Method: definition
b. Topic sentence stated: first sentence   Method: illustrative instances
c. Topic sentence stated: first sentence   Method: pictorial details
* d. Topic sentence implied: Jos made a ridiculous exit, his manner provoking scornful comment by Mrs. O'Dowd.   Method: chronological incidents
e. Topic sentence stated: first sentence   Method: sustained analogy
f. Topic sentence stated: first sentence   Method: enumeration
g. Topic sentence stated: first sentence   Method: combination of illustrative instances and multiple reasons.
h. Topic sentence stated: first sentence   Method: illustrative instances
i. Topic sentence stated: first sentence   Method: combination of comparison and definition.
j. Topic sentence stated: first sentence   Method: sustained analogy

Chapter 8

* 1. a. A five-cent newspaper contains much practical information, such as hints on cooking, sewing, gardening, and building.

b. Curiosity motivated me to begin reading articles on nuclear physics.

c. The executioner's job in revolutionary France often went from father to son.

d. From then until I entered high school, I used only one section of the library, the section on airplanes.

e. The driver admitted that he had been exceeding the speed limit by twenty miles an hour.

f. Any person unaware of the role of the bullet in knocking the can from the post might think the man with the rifle had mysterious control over distant objects.

g. I received nine calls in response to my ad, three from business firms and six from individuals.

h. Military glory had been his goal since his early childhood.

2. a. After an airplane has crashed and burned, inspectors can usually tell what the cause was.

b. Almost everyone in the group wanted to discuss his own problems first.

c. Each witness gave a report on what he thought had actually happened.

d. When my uncle was in Boston, he saw the president of the company. (*Or:* When the president of the company was in Boston, my uncle saw him.)

* 3. a. Without advertising, our radio and television stations would not be readily available for announcements of public interest.

b. His encouragement produced good results, for many people took his advice and became more useful citizens.

c. For a good while after he begins painting, the novice may still have trouble with perspective.

d. After graduation, time seemed to pass slowly for me: from June to September, I stayed on the farm and helped my grandfather.

e. The system is still inefficient, for two channels are needed to transmit one program.

f. My uncle is paying for my educational needs, except for tuition; he does not expect to be reimbursed when I have an income of my own. (*Or:* My uncle is paying for my educational needs; except for tuition, he does not expect to be reimbursed when I have an income of my own.)

4. a. The second version is better because parallel ideas are in parallel form.

b. The first version is better because the construction beginning *As far as a solution* . . . is completed with . . . *is concerned.* (Incomplete construction makes the second version incoherent.)

c. The second version is better because the intensive *so* is followed by a clause showing result.

d. The first version is better because the phrase *identifying it with vice* appropriately subordinates a minor idea. (In the second version, the minor idea is inappropriately placed in a series with two other ideas to which it is not coordinate.)

* 5. a. Crossing to the west side of Main Street, a pedestrian can see the bus station. (The noun *pedestrian* has been supplied to name a logical agent of the action asserted by the verb *can see* and referred to by the participle *Crossing.* The verb has been changed from passive to active voice. The entire revision was necessary to provide a word that the participial phrase *Crossing . . . Street* can clearly modify.)

b. Patsy could see the sun shining brightly through the window. (A change in word order has been made so that the participle *shining* follows the word *sun,* which names the agent of the action referred to by the participle.)

c. By purring softly, the kitten showed gratitude to the little girl. (The noun *kitten,* which names the agent of the action referred to by the gerund *purring,* has been placed immediately after the phrase containing the gerund. The main clause has been changed from passive to active. The revision was necessary so that the gerund will not seem to refer to an illogical agent, *girl.*)

d. To do an auditor's job, one needs mathematical skill. (The pronoun *one* names the person the infinitive *To do* refers to and also names the agent of the action affirmed by the verb *needs*. The main clause has been put into active voice so that *one* can appear immediately after the infinitive phrase.)

e. To be an auditor, one needs mathematical skill. (The revision is similar to the preceding one; the only difference is that *To be* refers to the agent as existing.)

f. Walking along the top of the hill, a person can see parts of the distant city. (The word *person* has been supplied for the participial phrase *Walking . . . hill* to modify, and the main clause has been put into active voice so that *person* can be in the logical position immediately following the participial phrase.)

* 6. The art of conversation began to decline in America over a century ago, probably as a result of the industrial revolution. Before the machine age, when a large percentage of the population lived on farms miles apart and neighbors could not see one another very often, they nevertheless did talk over their experiences at the specified times when they did meet. But when job opportunities caused many people to move near the factory and neighbors saw one another at work almost every day, they were no longer eager for the privilege of conversation. Soon mass entertainment, a product of machine-age inventions, became a substitute for conversation. People watching movies or listening to the radio do not say much to one another. And now, when I go to visit a friend, I am greeted with "Shh! *Gunsmoke* is on!"

(The number of independent clauses has been reduced from twelve, half of which were not directly on the topic idea, to six, all of which are directly on the topic idea. The supporting ideas have been placed in subordinate clauses, phrases, and other minor sentence elements. The average length of sentences has been increased from thirteen to twenty-six words; the range, from between ten and fifteen to between thirteen and forty words.)

* 7. a. Jim raced down the track and cleared the hurdle easily. (A subject is necessary to make a complete sentence.)

b. Betsy Trotwood is an interesting character in the novel *David Copperfield;* she has some eccentricities but also many good qualities. (The semicolon separates independent clauses not joined by a conjunction.)

c. Each student should bring his books to class. (The singular *his* agrees with the singular antecedent *each student.*)

d. He wrote his theme and then studied his algebra lesson. (The verbs *wrote* and *studied* show a consistent use of the past tense.)

e. The melodious song of the cardinal cheered me. (A predicate is necessary to make a complete sentence.)

f. The lecturer told several humorous stories; the audience seemed to enjoy them. (The substitution of a semicolon for the comma prevents a comma fault.)

g. Mr. Murray enjoys traveling, whether by land or by sea or by air. (A subject and a predicate are necessary to make a complete sentence.)

h. Every person has opportunities for mental growth, and he should make the most of them. (The pronoun *he* and the antecedent *Every person* show a consistent use of the third person.)

i. The teacher read the poem aloud and made the lesson interesting. (The verb *made* and the verb *read* are consistently active in voice.)

j. He had studied hard all semester; therefore he was prepared for the examination. (The substitution of a semicolon for the comma before the conjunctive adverb prevents a comma fault.)

8. a.
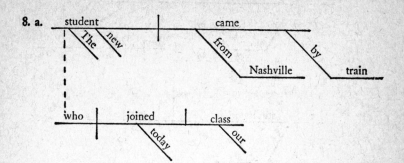

b.
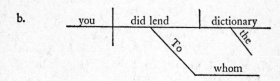

c.
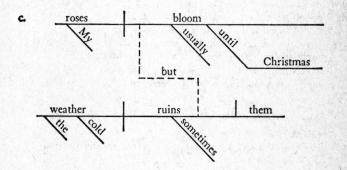

d.
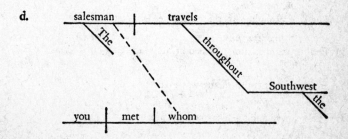

e.

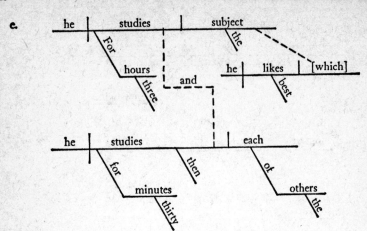

Chapter 9

1. a. (1) its   (2) us   (3) you   (4) she   (5) my, mine
      (6) him   (7) your, yours   (8) they
   b. (1) whom   (2) those
2. a. I am sent.   b. You will know.   c. They have been taught.
   d. We shall have sung.   e. He fixes.   f. Hurry.   g. I were given.
   h. We be dismissed.   i. You shall say.   j. He do.
3. *ger.*—gerund   *inf.*—infinitive   *part.*—participle   *v.*—verb
   s.s—simple subject   *d.o.*—direct object   *i.o.*—indirect object
   s.c.—subject complement   *o.c.*—object complement   *app.*—appositive
   o.p.—object of preposition   *mod.*—modifier   *w.m.*—word modified

              ger. (d.o.)   *ger. (d.o.)*
a. (1) Do you prefer reading a play or seeing the performance?

       inf. (s.s.)   *ger. (o.p.)*
   (2) To master the art of swimming in a year is an achievement.

                   ger. (o.p.)
   (3) He crossed the street without stopping.

     w.m. part. (mod.)   *ger. (d.o.)*
   (4) The chair standing in the corner needs repairing.

    part. (mod.) w.m.   *w.m. part. (mod.)*
   (5) The surprised janitor frowned at the mud lying on the floor.

               s.s.   *v.*   *s.c.*
b. (1) His first impromptu theme was excellent.

               s.s.   *o.p. v. s.c.*
   (2) The most valuable player on the team is ill.

    s.s.   *v. i.o.*   *d.o.*
   (3) Mr. Brown told me a fascinating story.

         o.p. *s.s.* *v.*   *s.c.*

(4) On the track he is an expert.

        s.s.   *app.*   *v.*   *i.o.*   *d.o.*   *o.p.*

(5) Dora's uncle, a painter, gave the school a picture of the sea.

        s.s.   *v.*   *d.o.*   *o.c.*

(6) The class elected Rodney president.

       s.s. *v.*   *s.c.*   *o.p.*   *o.p.*

(7) Julius was the chairman of the committee for a year.

                            d.o.

   v. *s.s.* *v.*   *s.s.*   *v.*   *s.c.*

(8) Did you know that speeding is dangerous?

     s.s.   *v.*   *d.o.*   *o.c.*

(9) He painted the fence white.

       s.s.   *app.*   *v.* *i.o.*   *d.o.*

(10) Miss Jones, the teacher, gave us a long assignment.

4.	*Subordinate Clause*	*Use as a Part of Speech*
	a. that . . . interesting	noun
	b. when . . . rang	adverb
	c. which . . . explained	adjective
	d. If . . . evening	adverb
	e. What . . . now	noun
	f. where . . . study	adjective
	g. because . . . sleepy	adverb
	h. who . . . diligently	adjective
	i. whoever . . . it	noun
	j. about . . . told	adjective

5. a. Neither my uncle nor my aunt *is* free to make the trip. (A subject composed of singular co-ordinates joined by *Neither . . . nor* takes a singular verb.)

b. Is she the girl *whom* I saw yesterday? (The objective case is needed because the relative pronoun *whom* functions as the direct object of the verb *saw* in the subordinate clause.)

c. Correct. (The singular verb *varies* agrees with the singular subject *quality.*)

d. The best part of the game *was* the home runs. (The singular verb *was* agrees with the singular subject *part;* the number of the subject complement has no effect on the verb.)

e. Everyone should prepare *his* own report. (*His* agrees with the singular antecedent *Everyone.*)

f. Correct. (*More* is construed as singular because *entertainment* is singular.)

g. Is he one of the seven men who *have* been selected for training? (The relative pronoun *who* takes a plural verb because the antecedent of *who* is the plural *men.*)

h. Correct. (The plural verb *are* agrees with the nearer co-ordinate *both.*)

i. Neither of them *has* tried to increase *his* reading speed.) (The singular verb *has* agrees with the singular subject *Neither*. The singular *his* agrees with the singular antecedent *Neither*.)

j. There *are* several reviews of the book available. (*Are* agrees with the plural subject *reviews;* the expletive *There* cannot be a subject.)

k. The letter, along with several pamphlets, *has* disappeared. (The singular subject *letter* takes the singular verb *has,* regardless of intervening modifiers.)

l. Each of the children should have *his* own supplies. (The singular *his* agrees with the singular antecedent *Each*.)

m. *Who* do you think will be there? (The nominative case is needed because *Who* is the subject of the verb *will be* in the subordinate clause.)

n. I am certain she is younger than *I* [am]. (The nominative case is needed for the subject of the elliptical clause.)

o. The agreement is strictly between you and *me*. (The objective case is needed for both parts of the compound object of the preposition.)

p. Three friends—Bob, Ted, and *I*—will be leaving at the same time. (The nominative case is needed for all parts of the compound appositive to the subject.)

q. Correct. (*Him* is correct because the subject of an infinitive is in the objective case. *Your* is correct because a pronoun modifying a gerund is in the possessive case.)

r. She has never approved of *his* working at the bakery after school. (A pronoun modifying a gerund is in the possessive case.)

s. Correct. (The singular verb *was* agrees with the singular subject *stack*.)

t. Correct. (The plural verb *are* agrees with the plural subject *books*. *Whoever* is correct because the nominative case is needed for the subject of the subordinate clause.)

Chapter 10

1. a. 3—2—4—1   b. 2—1—3   c. 2—3—1   d. 2—4—1—3   e. 2—3—1
2. a. aroma   b. God   c. water   d. casement   e. cloak   f. children
   g. plume   h. alarm   i. hero   j. mother
3. a. irony   b. synecdoche   c. overstatement   d. simile   e. metonymy
   f. understatement   g. personification   h. irony   i. metaphor   j. simile
* 4. a. the comedy *She Stoops to Conquer,* by Oliver Goldsmith
     b. emerald brooch   c. a portable typewriter   d. baked Alaska
     e. crimson and orange, merging imperceptibly into pale violet above.
* 5. a. There is a great need for more engineers.

   b. Central has defeated Parkhurst, and we have beaten Central; it is logical to believe that we will win the game with Parkhurst.

   c. I think you are wrong; the Parkhurst game will really be the decisive test for our team.

   d. I think I had better see the Dean and get an approval from the Administration.

   e. The coach gave instructions vigorously and unequivocally; when he had finished speaking, there was complete silence.

6. Any five in each of the following lists would be correct:

Suffixes		Prefixes	
–er	(writer)	a–	(aground)
–ful	(scornful)	be–	(bedecked)
–ie	(birdie)	fore–	(forewarn)
–ish	(sheepish)	out–	(outmaneuver)
–less	(reckless)	over–	(overemphasize)
–ship	(partnership)	under–	(undervalue)
–some	(foursome)	up–	(uphill)
–y	(sunny)	with–	(withdraw)

7. a. *astro* (Greek)—star
   b. *temp* (Latin)—time
   c. *clam* (Latin)—shout, cry out
   d. *strict* (Latin)—tie, bind
   e. *fact* (Latin)—make, do

8. *apricot:* French, through Portuguese and Arabic, ultimately from Latin and Greek   *campus:* Latin
   chief: French, ultimately from the Latin *caput,* head
   dollar: German and Dutch
   dun: Anglo-Saxon or old English (i.e., a native word)
   homonym: Greek   *poltergeist:* German   *seraph:* Hebrew
   sky: Old Norse   *theater:* French, ultimately from Latin and Greek

9.

	American College Dictionary	Webster's New Collegiate Dictionary	Webster's New World Dictionary
a.	19	15	16
b.	14	11	11
c.	17	11	13
d.	23	12	14
e.	18	11	15
f.	11	9	11
g.	19	12	15
h.	8	7	7
i.	45	28	32
j.	23	12	15

* 10. a. The intramural athletic program includes competition in tennis, softball, touch football, and similar sports.

   b. A *faux pas* is a breach of some rule of etiquette.

   c. He is rather a poor teacher, but he is a pleasant man.

   d. I cannot help thinking that she is prejudiced against me.

   e. Not having heard him distinctly, I do not really know, but I am reasonably sure the teacher implied that the next assignment would be difficult.

Chapter 11

1. admitted, admitting
   benefited, benefiting
   dined, dining
   dropped, dropping
   guided, guiding

   liked, liking
   located, locating
   maintained, maintaining
   occupied, occupying
   occurred, occurring

   planned, planning
   referred, referring
   treated, treating
   tried, trying
   vacated, vacating

2. achieve   belief   ceiling   chieftain   deceive   field   fierce
   freight   grief   leisure   niece   piece   reign   siege   seize
3. a. capital   b. immigrant   c. prophesy   d. respectfully   e. role
   f. since   g. than   h. stationary   i. threw, their   j. whose, advice,
   effect, your

4. airstrips   alleys   allies   alumnae   alumni
   armies   baseballs   bases   beliefs   boxes
   Cs *or* C's   chairmen   children   Chinese   dishes
   echoes   heroes   hobbies   houses   indexes *or* indices
   Kellys   knives   leaves   libraries   losses
   menservants   mice   oxen   potatoes   problems
   quarterbacks   radios   salesmen   sevens   sheep
   sisters-in-law skies   solos   spoonfuls

Chapter 12

1. a. In which direction were the geese flying? (A question mark closes a direct question.)

b. She explained why she prefers Beethoven to Bach. (A period closes a statement incorporating an indirect question.)

c. How far is it from Paris to Rome? (A question mark closes a direct question.)

d. The question for discussion concerned whether or not a new expressway should be built. (A period closes a statement incorporating an indirect question.)

e. How absurd it is to think that mankind is perfect! (An exclamation point closes an exclamatory sentence.)

f. I wondered why he was running down the street. (A period closes a statement incorporating an indirect question.)

g. Will you please hand me the dictionary. (A period closes an indirect request, that is, a request in interrogative form.)

h. The police questioned the suspects for an hour. (A period closes a declarative sentence.)

2. a. He learned to distinguish the word *allusion* from the word *illusion*.

b. The victim's father, who saw the accident occur, testified in court.

c. The *Skate,* a famous submarine, came to the surface through the ice at the North Pole.

d. Anyone who likes social drama will probably enjoy Ibsen's plays.

e. Ghana, located in West Africa, and Kenya, located in East Africa, are both on his itinerary.

f. Tom lives in the house built of California redwood.

g. He read Joseph Conrad's novel *Victory*.

h. *Victory,* a novel by Joseph Conrad, is a story which concerns an individual's detachment from society.

3. a. The crowd shouted, for the quarterback had just scored a touchdown.

b. High above, the jet plane streaked through the sky.

c. Just when she tried to swallow, the dentist began drilling on her tooth.

d. The class continued to wait patiently, for the professor had explained that he might be detained.

4. a. The store on the corner has been vacant since Monday, October 20. (The comma after *corner* has been omitted because a comma is not needed between a short subject and its verb. The comma after *Monday* is needed to help set off the second item in the date.)

b. He decided that he would enroll in three courses in day school and two courses in night school. (The comma after *decided* has been omitted because a comma is not needed before the subordinating conjunction *that* introducing a noun clause used as the object of a verb. The comma before *and* has been omitted because a comma is not needed before a co-ordinating conjunction joining two words or phrases.)

c. He bought apples, bread, coffee, and cream. (The comma before *apples* has been omitted because a comma is not needed before the first unit of a series. The commas after *apples, bread,* and *coffee* are needed to separate units in a series.)

d. For as long as I can recall, the neighborhood has been a quiet, peaceful one. (The comma after *recall* is needed for clarity. The comma between *quiet* and *peaceful* is needed to separate co-ordinate, consecutive adjectives. The comma after *peaceful* has been omitted because a comma is not needed between an adjective and the word it modifies.)

5. a. Janet plays four instruments: the piano, the harp, the flute, and the violin. (The colon anticipates the series of terms functioning in apposition to *instruments.*)

b. The meanings of some words ameliorate; the meanings of other words pejorate. (The semicolon separates independent clauses not joined by a co-ordinating conjunction.)

c. The chairman presided at every meeting; however, he did not participate in the voting. (The semicolon separates main clauses joined by a conjunctive adverb.)

d. He had three duties when he worked in the library: answering the telephone, shelving books, and operating the microfilm machine. (The colon anticipates the series of phrases functioning in apposition to *duties.*)

e. During the tour they stopped at Grant's Farm, where they saw several Clydesdale horses; Forest Park, where they visited the zoo; and Lambert Field, where they watched the airplanes take off and land. (The semicolons are necessary to separate terms in a series when the terms contain internal commas.)

f. When he entered college last year, Bob had already studied trigonometry, analytic geometry, and calculus; but Harry, who is already a junior in college, is only now studying trigonometry. (The semicolon separates long independent clauses joined by a co-ordinating conjunction when the clauses contain internal commas.)

6. a. "Did you call me?" asked Nora.

b. "If you wish," said the instructor, "you may write two short papers instead of one long one."

c. "The short story entitled 'Brooksmith' is one of my favorite stories," said John.

d. The officer said, "Mrs. Jones, you were speeding"; but Mrs. Jones insisted that she was not.

7. a. Father brought in a tree from the timber; we children decorated it with cranberries, popcorn, and pictures. (The semicolon separates independent clauses not joined by a co-ordinating conjunction. The commas separate terms in a series.)

b. We went fishing on hot, humid days. (The comma separates co-ordinate, consecutive adjectives.)

c. "Miss Brown, how soon will you need my book?" asked Ruth. (The comma sets off a name used in direct address. The question mark follows the direct question quoted within the sentence. The quotation marks enclose the exact words of the speaker.)

d. The children are looking forward to a party, for Judith will celebrate her birthday next week. (The comma prevents the misreading of the conjunction *for* as a preposition.)

e. All night long the snow fell and the wind blew; consequently, many roads were drifted the next morning. (The semicolon separates independent clauses joined by a conjunctive adverb.)

f. The boys carried blue banners; the girls, white balloons. (The semicolon separates independent clauses not joined by a co-ordinating conjunction. The comma indicates the omission of the verb understood from the earlier clause.)

g. She ordered the following supplies: ink, paper, and pencils. (The colon anticipates a series used as an appositive. The commas separate terms in a series.)

h. Goodness, beauty, truth—these qualities continue to influence the development of civilization. (The commas separate terms in a series. The dash indicates the suspension of one kind of construction and the continuation of the sentence in a different form; the dash also anticipates a general term that has already been illustrated by a series of specific terms.)

i. Thomas DeQuincey (1785–1859) was an English author. (The parentheses enclose supplementary information that is structurally unrelated to the sentence.)

j. William Shakespeare, who was an actor as well as a playwright, must have led a busy life. (The commas set off the nonrestrictive clause.)

8. a. A group of tourists guided by Professor Kent Larson sailed from New York on the *Queen Elizabeth* in July.

b. She went to grade school in the South, high school in the Midwest, and college in the East.

c. Chapter 10, "The Technical Report," in the book *English Communication* is part of the assignment.

d. Students of Central High School had a holiday the day before Thanksgiving.

e. Tom's course of study includes English, Latin, algebra, biology, and history.

f. Matthew Arnold's poem "Dover Beach" and John Henry Newman's essay "The Educated Man" are both in the anthology entitled *Adventures in English Literature*.

9. a.

Singular Possessive	*Plural Possessive*
adult's	adults'
albatross's *or* albatross'	albatrosses'
bird's	birds'

Singular Possessive (cont.)	*Plural Possessive (cont.)*
child's	children's
Davis's *or* Davis'	Davises'
deer's	deer's
donkey's	donkeys'
editor-in-chief's	editors-in-chief's
governess's *or* governess'	governesses'
horse's	horses'
Irishman's	Irishmen's
laborer's	laborers'
man's	men's
Negro's	Negroes'
passer-by's	passers-by's
poet's	poets'
son-in-law's	sons-in-law's
student's	students'
Swede's	Swedes'
woman's	women's

b. another's, anyone's, his, its, one's, her *or* hers, someone's, their *or* theirs, whose, your *or* yours

Index